P9-BJA-835

CALGARY PUBLIC LIBRARY

THE NEXT CANADA

THE NEXT CANADA

In Search of Our Future Nation

MYRNA KOSTASH

M&S

Copyright © 2000 by Myrna Kostash

All rights reserved. The use of any part of this publication reproduced, transmitted in any form or by any means, electronic, mechanical, photocopying, recording, or otherwise, or stored in a retrieval system, without the prior written consent of the publisher – or, in case of photocopying or other reprographic copying, a licence from the Canadian Copyright Licensing Agency – is an infringement of the copyright law.

Canadian Cataloguing in Publication Data

Kostash, Myrna
The next Canada : in search of our future nation

ISBN 0-7710-4561-1

1. Canada – Social conditions – Public opinion.   2. Nationalism – Canada – Public opinion.   3. Generation X – Canada – Attitudes. I. Title.

HN103.5.K58 2000   306'.0971   C00-930214-X

We acknowledge the financial support of the Government of Canada through the Book Publishing Industry Development Program for our publishing activities. We further acknowledge the support of the Canada Council for the Arts and the Ontario Arts Council for our publishing program.

Design by Ingrid Paulson
Typeset in Minion by M&S, Toronto
Printed and bound in Canada

McClelland & Stewart Inc.
The Canadian Publishers
481 University Avenue
Toronto, Ontario
M5G 2E9

1 2 3 4 5   04 03 02 01 00

To the memory of Anna Svarich and Fedor Kostashchuk, Paulina Kossovan and Ivan Maksymiuk, who left their homes in Galicia, laboured hard in Alberta, and made me a Canadian.

My sincerest thanks to the Canada Council and the Alberta Foundation for the Arts for financial support in the research and writing of this book; to the Regina Public Library's writer-in-residence program in the course of which, 1996–97, I was able to get this book underway; to the people of *The Prairie Dog* newspaper in Regina who so generously invited me to use their pages to begin my conversations with "the next Canadians"; to Darcia Dahl for heroic transcription labours; and to Duane Burton for unflagging research assistance and invaluable discussion and encouragement through the whole process.

CONTENTS

INTRODUCTION

> "But a nation does not remain a nation only because it has roots in the past. Memory is never enough to guarantee that a nation can articulate itself in the present. There must be a thrust of intention into the future."
>
> — George Grant, *Lament for a Nation*

In the fall of 1996, Peter Gzowski announced he was stepping down as host of the long-running and popular CBC radio program *Morningside*. Immediately, Canadian media were filled with nostalgic appreciations of his tenure and alarmed speculations about Life After Gzowski. And in 1997, masses of Canadians were in the grip of nostalgia for a twenty-five-year-old hockey game in which our players had saved our international reputation in the last seconds of play. About this time, I was standing in front of classes of high school students in Regina, where I was a writer-in-residence at the public library, stymied by the realization that my audiences had only vague knowledge of what I was referring to when I talked about the Plains of Abraham or the War Measures Act or Margaret Laurence – or, more to the point, *why* I was talking about them. By the same token, I had no doubt that had they quizzed me about what they knew, I would likewise have drawn a blank. Here we were, they and I, sharing the same space and time with totally different data clattering about in our brains.

I could choose to react to this generational gap in one of two ways. I could join the chorus of my peers who were widely deploring the social and cultural "deCanadianization" of the post–Free Trade Agreement era, and the apparent loss of historical memory and social cohesiveness that had still characterized the last truly "Canadian" generation, namely, my generation, the architects of cultural nationalism and anti-American imperialism. Or I could make an expedition out into the terrain of the next Canada to see if our pessimism and defeatism were justified.

As a university student in the late 1960s, and as a writer who began publishing in the 1970s, I was a beneficiary of the nationalism that championed made-in-Canada social, political, and cultural policy. I wrote for subsidized magazines and public radio, received arts grants from governments, and reached audiences who themselves were increasingly patriotic. But, as I began the research for this book, that kind of Canada seemed in retreat.

According to the 1996 national census, there were more than four and a half million Canadians between the ages of twenty-five and thirty-five. These were the men and women I decided to investigate, the generation opportunistically referred to in Pepsi ads as Generation Next. Rather than belabour what we sixties people have lost politically and socially over the stretch of our middle age, I wanted to learn what kind of country is taking shape in the imaginations and subcultures and arguments of the generation on my heels.

The first salient observation about them is that the socio-economic and technological context in which they have grown up is radically different in many respects from that which formed the "boomers."

We know that trends in the workplace are altering the culture of work and that huge numbers of young Canadians will know only the downsized enterprise, the "telecommute" from home-based computers, short-term contracted employment, longer work weeks, and McJobs, when they are working at all. It is a society which accepts that "full employment" now means an unemployment rate of 7 per cent, or about a million people without work.

In the Alberta I grew up in, in the fifties and sixties, there was still a collective consensus to invest in institutions servicing the common good. Now even Liberals and Blair-ite social democrats were in retreat from such investment in "public space." With the declining public funding of education and health care, with the devaluation of civility and co-operativeness, and the marginalization of the arts, there was little I recognized of the often exhilarating open-endedness of our youthful possibilities in the public-spirited 1960s and early 1970s. Instead, Canadians were being offered the culture of the marketplace: shareholder "interests" and consumer "preferences."

That the Reform Party – the antithesis of all my own political values formed in the 1960s and 1970s – was attractive to a twenty-something in the late 1990s, says something, I'm afraid, about the failure of left liberalism to sustain its message after the debacle of the struggle against the Free Trade Agreement in 1984 and – double whammy – the fall of the Berlin Wall and, with it, the agenda of international socialism.

Furthermore, that legacy of the 1970s, the ecology movement, spearheaded by the young, has been under severe stress from profoundly compromised federal and provincial environmental management.

And though I'm not exactly shocked, I do wonder how it happened that the agenda of 1970s feminism (I'm thinking of wages for housework, abortion rights, an end to sexist advertising), which was so broadly social and economic, seems almost entirely absent from the young feminists' discussion about sexuality. Now topics like "sex resistance" and bisexuality and "transgressive sexual identity" had become central to the discourse, and it occurred to me that sexuality was the site where many other forms of identity, class and race and ethnicity, had been collapsed, as though socio-economic feminism no longer speaks to the new generation. Only the commodification of sexuality and its pervasiveness through the media do. There was also the minefield of "identity politics" and the backlash of Canadians calling for a return to "core values," a far cry from the hopefulness and even cheerfulness of first-wave official multiculturalism and feminism.

Where would they come from, I was wondering, the "next Canadian" radicals for whom everyday politics has been articulated by Brian Mulroney, Jean Chrétien, Ronald Reagan, and Bill Clinton, and framed by the language of free trade and transnational capitalism?

I assumed, if they existed at all, they would be lying low.

As I surveyed the terrain, I thought I saw what Douglas Coupland, in *Polaroids from the Dead*, called the "denarration" of his generation, the personal "storylessness" of a generation whose narratives of experience had been dissolved in the saturating soup of borderless, denationalized media, and whose continuity with familial, class, and cultural memory had been broken, along with the communities that had transmitted them.

But was this the only salient observation to make?

Mindful of George Grant's remark about how a nation may be able to articulate itself in its present time, I wondered if, among the next Canadians, there might be a "thrust of intention" into their future. Was there a common desire, in their disparate expressions as workers, artists, businesspeople, social activists, and politicians, to extend some meaning of their personal experience forward into a collective purpose? Was there something they wanted, as Canadians in their own geo-historical place?

(It was important to separate their desire out from mine. In an interview early into the project, I was asked point blank by the twenty-seven-year-old I was talking with, "So what are you, politically?" Startled, because I thought it was obvious, I replied that I was a "graduate of the sixties." He snorted: "I was born in 1970.")

The people you will meet in this book – characters and voices woven in and out of the main themes – were not selected by any scientific measurement; they are simply twenty-five- to thirty-five-year-olds I wanted to meet and put questions to, because they seemed, each in her or his way, strategically located in Canadian society, whether as frontline community activist or technological wunderkind or ecologist or sexual dissident or social philosopher or experimental artist or entrepreneur or McJobber or fisher. And others besides. I reasoned that those young people, if not already influential in shaping how Canada goes about its collective business, soon would be.

I met them in a variety of ways. An inveterate newspaper and magazine clipper, I was soon stuffing folders with articles and reports about or by potential interview subjects. (My research assistant cruised the Net and watched a lot of television.) Others I already knew personally or knew someone who knew them. I contacted community newspapers, radio stations, and film production studios for suggestions. I went straight to MPs' offices, food banks, health clinics, and art galleries and asked to meet anyone who would be willing to talk. I interviewed with a cassette recorder so that I could be fully present in the conversation – this project was, after all, a kind of dialogue, not a questionnaire. I read hundreds of books and journals.

The interviews took place right across the country, with the exception of Yukon, the Northwest Territories, and Nunavut. My funds simply ran out before I could go north. Although I did interview some Montrealers, and regularly read the French-language Montreal press, I did not pretend that my project would account for how the Quebecois discuss their own society in any comprehensive way.

Most importantly, I did not try to anticipate what I would hear. I wanted to find out something, not confirm my own fears and prejudices.

And I was rewarded, as I hope my readers will be, with an astonishing series of conversations that have made me a Canadian all over again.

The material is organized into five major topic headings. "The New World Order" includes economic themes, from workplace experiences to the new entrepreneurship to issues of wealth and poverty. "Culture" looks at media, the arts, and the theme of cultural community. "Beyond Identity Politics" encompasses sexualities and ethnicities. "Acts of Resistance" covers the so-called decline of politics, political resistance, eco-activism, and the struggle for the social commons. "Homeplace" ranges over the rethinking of social values, the rebuilding of the idea of the public good, and the notion of Canadian identity in a new century.

The New World Order I

Remember economic nationalism? "Canada is a satellite of the United States," the "51st state," the "branch plant economy." Canada should be "master of its own destiny." Walter Gordon, the Watkins Commission on Foreign Investment, the Waffle, the Committee for an Independent Canada, the Foreign Investment Review Agency, PetroCanada, the Canadianization of the oil industry, which an astonishing 84% of Canadians (including a majority of Albertans) supported.
— "The Return of Economic Nationalism," Gordon Laxer,
Parkland Institute Newsletter, Spring 1997

Anyone less than thirty years old would find Laxer's list of goodies a form of gobbledygook, untranslatable in an era in which the vocabulary of debt crisis, market fundamentalism, government self-mutilation, and the whimpering end of socialism has shaped a whole new generation's point of view.

Yet here they were, a sold-out crowd of mainly university students at the University of Alberta in Edmonton in September, 1998. They had come to watch a great big screen showing a live feed from the University of Calgary (another sold-out crowd), where Noam Chomsky was to deliver the Palmer Lecture. Chomsky, the New World Order's Arch Enemy gnawing at its bowels, who has made it his unflagging business for forty years to document, from his perch at the Massachusetts Institute of Technology, capitalism's and American imperialism's pillaging of the rest of us.

The students jostled each other through the lecture hall doorway, notebooks open and ready for note-taking, and hung on every word of this intellectual granddad. The New World Order? "Deceit, hypocrisy, and outright fraud," Chomsky began, almost laconically. So-called radical nationalism, the bane of business interests everywhere, he went on, is simply the belief that the "primary beneficiaries of a country's resources are the people of that country." A shudder of recognition in the hall. "Therefore, economic nationalism – the regulation and control of capital flow to allow governments to make social policies without fear of capital flight – must be stamped out by investors' agreements like the NAFTA." A groan, a hiss.

The so-called Golden Age of post-war state capitalism ended, Chomsky continued, in the 1980s, when capital controls were abandoned in developed countries. And in its place now reigns the order – we knew he meant in the United States especially – of deteriorating workplaces, eroded social programs, enfeebled infrastructures, soaring profits, "astronomical" increases in short-term capital flow and "dramatic" increases in incarceration of the poor, the "surplus population unnecessary for wealth formation." It was vintage Chomsky, the world as the students had always known it, and his indictment of it, giving no quarter, was a huge hit. The packed hall yelped, clapped, cheered at his outsized, genial, bespectacled face as though to encourage him on in his Sermon from the Screen.

For all his dire prognostications, Chomsky was not giving up. Not for him – or, I began to understand, for his young audience – the belief that the globalized economy is "out of control," that there are no alternatives to the "cult of impotence" and the radical fatalism of individual survival strategies. "Unaccountable economic tyrannies are not self-justifying," he wound up. "At the same time, democracy cannot survive without conditions of socioeconomic equality," as Aristotle reminds us from 2,300 years ago. People *will* try to wrest some control back for themselves and their communities. Believe it or not, society of the 1990s *is* more civilized than the 1960s, "thanks to women's rights, cultural diversity, ecology movements, and Third World resistance, much of it led by young people." Then, with a graceful flourish, just before the feed went dead, he congratulated his audience for Canada's "unique" popular resistance to the MAI (Multilateral Agreement on Investment). Within the miasma of international economic pathologies, Chomsky had noticed *us*, the Canadians, and our gift of political difference.

Surely, I thought, as the students filed out practically radiating bliss, even if Chomsky's argument were utopian, *this* was the catechism my generation would like to pass on, and not the mean and wizened presumption of Tom Courchene, economics professor at Queen's University, that by early in the twenty-first century, "while a political entity called Canada will exist, practically speaking it probably won't matter."[1]

Yet Canada is in the world, unsheltered from the new economic order of transnational corporations, hierarchical and authoritarian, that merge at such a diabolical rate. Of the one hundred largest economies in the world, fifty-one are now corporations, and the top five corporations control 70 per cent of the global market in consumer durables.[2] This market now includes the post-communist societies of ragamuffin Eastern Europe and the 200 million Indonesians saddled with the $80 billion foreign debt racked up by fifty businessmen "rescued" by the International Monetary Fund.[3] Transnational corporations control 33 per cent of the world's assets and employ less than 1 per cent of the world work force.[4] In the game known as Winner Take All, the share of total global wealth that goes to the one in five humans who are poor has *declined* since 1960 to 1.4 per cent.[5] David Korten, visionary American economist, tells us that the "smart money" does not waste itself on something as prodigal as "long-term commitments to productive enterprises engaged in producing real wealth to meet real needs of real people." It prefers short-term returns from speculation: for every dollar circulating in the productive economy, twenty to fifty dollars circulate in the world of pure finance.[6] And this has taken place inside an ideological regime of mass media that justifies such predation with the rhetoric of economic freedom. ("Free" of labour and trade unions, employment policies, social security programs, environmental regulations . . .)

In the lobby of Windsor Park community hall in Edmonton, venue for a talk by Vancouver social activist Murray Dobbin, I recognized Anna, the young woman who had been leafletting against the MAI at the weekend farmers' market, and who was here, ever energetic, with more leaflets from Albertans Against the MAI, announcing a rally at the Legislature with Maude Barlow of the Council of Canadians and local hero Mel Hurtig.

Did I know that the MAI would give corporations the power to regulate governments? That corporations would have all the "rights" and governments all the "obligations"? I knew it very well, but I took a handful of her leaflets out of sheer gratitude that *she* knew it. After all, she was probably no older than Nike Corporation itself (1972) or Microsoft (1975). The hall was already full and the program had begun with announcements of local interest. An upcoming lecture by a visiting professor from Simon Fraser University about the role of journalism in democracy. A visit by an expert in the field of mind control (that's what I wrote down): "I'm sure it will be very interesting to all of you." A man I recognized as a political science professor of mine from the 1960s stood up to introduce Dobbin. "The term 'good corporate citizen,'" he began, "makes as much sense as 'married bachelor.'" Ho ho.

Dobbin has been fighting the good fight of the democratic left for decades. Walking softly on the earth – "I drive a twelve-year-old car, wear old clothes, and have a twenty-year-old stereo," he told us – he wields a big analytical stick with authority. "One of the Right's most powerful weapons is our isolation from each other," he began, and we knew that what had gathered us was some primordial memory of solidarity. "The Right uses vocabulary that obscures what's really going on. 'Globalization,' for example, which sounds like the voice of God. *Resistance is futile.* Transnational corporations see the world as one large market, borderless, and they are trying to make it that way."

None of this was a revelation, but all the same, it was a comfort that someone was on the case.

"Strong domestic economies are not the point anymore. *Global* products are being created with identical marketing and advertising for each. To distribute them you need a global culture. And young people are the target."

Bingo. We all looked around. Where *were* the young people? Here and there in the crowd, the slender and unwrinkled, propped up in puffy, Day-Glo windbreakers, nodded at the rest of us in benign fellowship while we grinned barmily back at them. *See, socialism isn't just for old fogies!*

"Not as many young people as I had hoped," Dobbin acknowledged. "It's a fault of my generation, not to connect."

God, let's hope it's not too late! If Dobbin is preoccupied by the isolation of the young it is because he sees them as trapped in "the most nonconsensual culture in the history of the world," inexorably ground down into consumer hamburger, bereft of the idea of the primacy of their citizenship rights to make things happen according to their own collective will.

"There is a ferocious attack on our [democratic] expectations being waged. What happened in Nicaragua could happen here – the attack of the Contras [counter-revolutionaries] not on soldiers but on workers in co-ops, medical clinics, daycare centres. And what was their message? *You can't make anything better. There is no hope.*"

To gasps of dismay from his audience, Dobbin said he had no doubt that what he thought of as the Contras of Canada – the Business Council on National Issues, with its relentless pressure on government to deregulate and privatize; the Fraser Institute, with its morbid fixation on the "unfreedom" of a Canada still incompletely opened to foreign investment; the National Citizens' Coalition, with its shrill call for lower taxes on business – would be prepared to "drag us out of our beds and shoot us. Absolutely. When we become that effective, that's what will happen to us. But we're going to stop them."

This is where the young Canadians come in. Inspired by the involvement of an impressive number of twenty-somethings in the country-wide grassroots campaign to stop the MAI – "No other country is at the level of opposition that Canada is" – and by the resilience of "Canadian values" – "Even Albertans would rather pay higher taxes than further bleed education" – Dobbin hoped for a cultural revolution. This would be the revolution of the young, the first generation to grow up in a global culture "with ads everywhere" and able to recognize corporate logos from the age of *twenty months.* "Coke drinkers have more connection with each other than with their communities and their own history." To disrupt this global identification with corporate culture, to reconnect the young with their compatriots, who may or may not be Coke drinkers but who are surely sharing the everyday transactions of their immediate neighbourhoods, Dobbin argued for a revolution of "the things that we do together."

The things that we do together. Once upon a time, Canadians assumed a co-responsibility between themselves and government or, at the very least, a mutual attachment to a shared social space and an investment of *public* finances in *public* goods: health, culture, transportation, and so on. At least, Canadian governments used to make that argument. But a simple listing of the retreats and withdrawals from, and outright cancellations of, previously sacrosanct governmental involvement shows a much narrower definition of government responsibility. From 1993, the year the first Chrétien government was elected, to 1998, the year a federal budget surplus was declared, the following initiatives show the pattern: cuts to Via Rail, the CBC, social housing; replacement of the Canada Assistance Plan and cuts to the Canada Health and Social Transfer plan that took its place; cuts to and limitation of employment insurance. Since 1986, when Canada was launched into the Free Trade Agreement era, journalist April Lindgren found that we no longer have the Crow Rate subsidy to farmers, but we do have "super mailboxes" in the suburban back-of-beyond; no more coast-to-coast railway service, but private sponsors for the RCMP musical ride; no more public interest in National Sea Products, de Havilland, Air Canada and Petro Canada; and lots of homeless people and food banks.[7] The point of such stock-taking is to be able to ask, in our urgency to get rid of the deficit and drive down the debt as decreed by the market gurus, *What is a man profited, if he shall gain the whole world, and lose his own soul?*

With governments' "adjustment" to market-driven "realities," and *dis*investment in public welfare, Canadians should squirm at the top ranking of our quality of life, accorded us by the United Nations' Human Development Index in 1999 for the sixth straight year. *Whose* quality of life? In 1997, a record 1.5 million Canadian children – one in five – were living in poverty. In 1999, according to the Human Poverty Index, an addendum to the UN Human Development Index, Canada placed ninth.

We step over the panhandler bundled in her sleeping bag because we have got used to her, although perhaps most of us can still remember the first time we came upon the sight, *in our very own Canadian city*, and were ashamed. She and her fellows never did go away, in fact more and more of them have set up home on the street, and now they seem to have always been there. Writing in the *Guardian Weekly* in 1997, English journalist Martin Woollacott, veteran of two decades of Thatcherite attack on the welfare state, believed that the worst damage it inflicted was to social conscience itself: people have actually come to believe that, just as government and business were "correct" to withdraw from their obligations to us, so are we correct to withdraw from obligations to each other. It is what has been referred to as the "democratic deficit"[8] and we are all the poorer for it, especially the young who have no memory of a social order that once hoped to be egalitarian.

How is it possible to make a film in 1996 with street people as its theme without showing the young people in the streets, the junkies, the syringes, the binges, the scuffles for a piece of territory, for dope, or even for a girl? Indeed, we see no pimp, no hooker except for a girl who agrees to go down a manhole with two municipal employees without even negotiating a price. Even an HIV-positive heroin junkie would not go down a sewer. Not a word about the vulnerability of a growing number of people who have one foot in the system and another in the street. Nothing, furthermore, about the survival tactics in this jungle that is the street: petty larceny, handing out flyers, selling street newspapers. . . . Finally, we have no sense of the gaze of citizens on the people of the street.

– Jean-Marie Tison, Sylvie Gingras, Nathalie Labonté, Serge Lareault, on viewing Denys Arcand's dramatic film *Joyeux Calvaire*, in *L'Itinéraire*, January 1997

In Vancouver, the Portland Hotel on Carroll at Hastings is not at all conspicuous from the street, in this most tormented of Canada's poor neighbourhoods – a "ragged, unfettered market of drugs, drink and despair," in the words of one journalist.[9] The Portland's green residential door is set staunchly into a blank wall down the street from the hotel's bar entrance, and I looked in vain for the buzzer I was meant to ring. I gesticulated hopefully at a bearded face that suddenly popped up behind a mesh grille set into the door, and the affable hotel resident, in windbreaker and jeans, admitted me. Liz Evans, project manager of the hotel (along with her partner, Mark Townsend), was on the phone, and her assistant, Chris, was passing out the morning's "meds" to my affable doorman, noting the dosage in an account book.

As I took in the scene I thought about Jenny Kwan, the young MLA for Vancouver–Mt. Pleasant who had sent me to Evans, Townsend, and the Portland Hotel. Kwan had told me her constituency included six distinct neighbourhoods, ranging from "the poorest of the poor, with its postal code of V6A where advertisers don't even bother sending their junk mail," to affluent avenues of heritage homes near City Hall. As Kwan had listed the issues her poorer constituents were embroiled in – IV drug use, the sex trade, pestiferous housing, suicide of young Natives, an impending HIV epidemic, and "more pawnshops, liquor-licensed lounge seats per capita than any other district in Canada" – and then added that, for all their difficulties, people in the east side are "fighters," I understood that she was in fact describing a *community* of the poor.

Vancouver–Mt. Pleasant does have low-cost housing, an infrastructure of social services the community itself has built up, and, says Kwan, "a level of legitimization – whether you're rich or poor, speak English or not, live on income assistance or otherwise – that other communities haven't got to yet." And perhaps the Portland Hotel – backed by the B.C. Housing Commission and operating since 1991 as a residence for the virtually unhousable of the downtown eastside, envisaged from the beginning as an alternative to care facilities and institutions, a home from which its seventy tenants cannot be evicted – is also part of Kwan's idea of community. "Basically, we're in this together," Evans told me after we had settled into her second-floor office, a quiet sanctuary lit dully by the murky daylight of a rainy December. "Everybody needs housing. We all deserve a place to live." The monthly rent coincided precisely with what British Columbia's welfare system provided for shelter (in 1999), $325.

Seemingly unflappable amid a storm of telephone calls, Evans told me she had once worked with street women in an Ottawa shelter. As a psychiatric nurse, what she liked about her work with the women was the "community aspect." In Vancouver, after the downsizing of Riverview mental hospital and the arrival of former patients on the streets of the eastside, Evans and the Portland found themselves in almost intimate contact with the mentally ill. "So we decided we would take them," Evans related half ruefully, half proudly. "Not the comfy, cozy mentally ill that people immediately feel sympathy for, like the distinction between deserving and undeserving poor. Some of the residents we take are perceived to be 'bad' people, but I don't see them that way."

In the Portland, staff are part of a "community of tolerance," and, as Evans described the principles of the regimen of care at the hotel, I heard the echoes of 1960s "radical psychiatry" as espoused by the heroic, some thought barmy, British doctor, R. D. Laing. Evans and her staff do not force the residents here to take their medication. "I've seen people go through psychosis and not be hospitalized, not go anywhere, just stay here, and a month later not be psychotic. We've been accused of 'benign neglect' because we've told residents it's okay to be where they are and we're not going to force them to do or be anything else, but just try to provide what they need, like food and clothing and supports."

Actually, there's more to it than that, more to the supports in the hotel than the laundry room and the little kitchen where hot food is served: there are conflict-resolution meetings (to deal with the person having a bad week and kicking the doors down), doctors and nurses who drop by to change dressings and provide immunizations, staff therapy sessions, visiting lecturers.

And on this day Evans had spent the morning arranging a funeral service for "Sue," a long-term resident who had died after only two days in hospital: she hated hospitals, and the Portland community "tried to hang on to her as long as possible. Everybody loved Sue." Sue raised hell for years. "She was considered a borderline personality disorder, a multi-service user, IV drug user. She turned tricks to make drug money. She kicked and screamed, totally out of control . . . but she was so endearing and sweet, like a little child."

Sue died of AIDS. In the three years since 1995, *all* the people referred to the Portland were HIV positive, increasingly a condition of the very poor, of the people living in dumpsters or in and out of shelters, cocaine addicts shooting up twenty, thirty times a day, people so chaotic and alienated they just want you to "fuck off, leave me alone, let me die."

By one o'clock it had already been a hectic day, but Liz Evans, suddenly mournful, a woman about to bury a friend, took one more moment to reflect on the deep meaning of what she was trying to do in the Portland Hotel: "I've been dealing with the value of the life of the poor person in the face of so much death from HIV, dealing with grief, futility and hopelessness, and the sadness of their lives – or is it our own hopelessness that we're grieving?"

After I had taken my leave of Evans, I sat a while in the lobby, joining residents seated along one wall as though in a waiting room, smoking, helping themselves to coffee, watching television. A man bandaged under his chin from ear to ear helpfully explained the plot so far and, just as I was becoming engrossed, a woman came down the staircase from the second floor with a great clattering, and ostentatiously deposited a pair of oversized sneakers into a trash can with voluble indignation. I understood that someone had helped himself to *her* shoes, leaving this outlandish pair behind. A skeletal man of indeterminate age shuffled in front of us with grave deliberation while another in a raincoat walked back and forth in the opposite direction, leaning back at a dramatic angle as though blown by a great gale and terrified of losing his footing. In its own way, the Portland Hotel was a neighbourhood, with its private and public spaces, its characters, its scandals and pleasures, its laws, and its sufferings from which our own distractions obscure us. Evans had spoken movingly to me about how the residents had given back to her "far much more than I've given them," meaning, that fellow feeling for those who are alone and sad and in pain is not a question of her *caring* about the poor. Nor thinking, I interjected, that the poor are just empty vessels into whom we pour the contents of our "concern"? No, she said, it's about seeing that their lives are as important as hers.

Noah Weisbord, doing his Social Work internship at Montreal's Foster Pavilion, a provincially run drug-rehabilitation centre serving the anglophone population, would say that *ethics* drive his work with the addict-desperadoes in treatment. When we met, his day had begun with a telephone call from a woman in a panic, fearing her son was dealing drugs. Then the therapy team to which he was attached met with a young man sent over from the Shawbridge detention home for self-mutilating and a suicide attempt, "and these huge binges where he would take every drug, mixing crack, heroin, PCP and mescaline all at once." What Weisbord saw was a youth who was so disordered he would assault the Shawbridge staff, "doing anything he [could] to mess them up," and so was forever being confined to the lock-up units. Their next patient was a "child psychopath," beaten by his stepfather, institutionalized since childhood in group or foster homes. He was what Weisbord called a "system kid," who feels so utterly determined by regulations and powers external to his own being that "he is totally out of control of his actions."

Weisbord approached such people "holistically," he explained to me, "as connected to their environment, to their family, their culture and to politics in society," as opposed to looking at the person as an isolated phenomenon of psychic breakdown. Depression does not just arise spontaneously in the person; depression is a "social construct." Nor is the person just a problem for the law. The law, said Weisbord, is not ethical. The law is about stripping "rights and powers" from whole groups of people, and what he wants to do as a social worker is to see how people are in fact not free but are part of a "complex series of patterns. There is a reason why someone is depressed, a certain set of events has led to this," but at the same time there can be an intervention, from a healer, a community, a lover, "some sort of epiphany that changes the course of their life."

There was a tenderness in his speech that made me fear for his future in the actual world of social-service agencies. For the moment he was teamed up with an exceptional group of "experts" from diverse backgrounds of experience – an Italian woman working with youth, a woman from India working with feminist groups, a Polish-born doctor – who had helped him see that the link between "drug use, depression, and disempowerment" is the experience of oppression. His much loved grandfather, formerly a Communist, had helped him understand that the principle of social justice means "people should be treated with respect no matter who they are or what their situation – drug addict, prostitute, pedophile." When Weisbord is in session with someone – offender, mutilator, would-be suicide, junkie – "I don't offer them my opinion, and I'm not the person to deliver an epiphany; all I do is create an environment where they can stumble upon it themselves."

In spite of a five-year waiting list for social housing, of shelter allowances cut by 21.6 per cent by the Common Sense Revolution of Ontario premier Mike Harris, street people are trying with a kind of desperate defiance to regroup in a community anyway. Liz MacLean works at The Meeting Place in Toronto, right downtown at Queen and Bathurst. It is a sort of community centre where the homeless come to get something to eat, wash their clothes, use the computer and learn work skills, or just have a coffee and shoot some pool. You enter from a pleasant little courtyard, past the community bulletin boards posted with warnings about the batch of bad heroin that's just arrived on the street and about shelter vacancies and job opportunities, into a large, brightly lit, multi-purpose room. The space is full of "buzz," with telephones ringing, people drifting in for appointments with the public-health nurse, the lawyers from the Parkdale Community Legal Services and the Women in Focus group, squeegee kids shooting pool, old men peacefully hunkered down over a jigsaw puzzle. Right outside, at the corner of Queen and Bathurst, MacLean points out the staircase of an old bank building that is a gathering place for panhandlers, drinkers, tokers, and anybody else just wanting some company for a while. Someone, a chronic alcoholic, died from exposure there just the other night, and someone else from a beating, at the hands of the police, according to the talk on the street, and lately a few "younger folks on bad drugs," had overdosed. "We don't know if it was self-inflicted."

Alcoholics, derelicts, the mentally ill – these are the familiar homeless, the ones whose personal catastrophes occurred so long ago in their lives that it is no longer the story they tell about themselves. But MacLean says there are new populations, people who never dreamed their lives would come to this and who obsessively tell the tale of their lost jobs, their exhausted benefits, their disappeared families, their evictions. And there are the kids, the runaways from all kinds of homes and circumstances, who have ended up in the same place together – on the street. MacLean has watched them with fascination, how they have formed their own "subculture," with a shared music and clothing style and work – "there are people who pan and squeegee on a regular basis, it's their job and they have it down quite well" – and how they come to The Meeting Place to cook their meals together and do each other's laundry.

Once upon a time, to hear MacLean tell it, there was a kind of Golden Age for the poor in Ontario, when the social democrats, the NDP, were in power (1991–95) and operated with a "harm reduction" model of care, which aimed not so much at the eradication of people's self-destructive addictions and sexual practices as at how to do drugs and drink and hustle "safely." MacLean called their approach "holistic" in its realistic expectations of how long it could take a person to become healthy enough to look for work, find affordable housing, finish grade ten.

The key element in the story isn't even really The Meeting Place, for all its good efforts in keeping some bodies and souls together that would otherwise have succumbed to the routine violence of hunger, cold, and loneliness. The key element is *work*, or lack of it. The vulnerability of people on the economy's margins – workers precariously hired and so poorly paid that their basic needs cannot be met by wages; people unqualified for employment insurance; part-time and seasonal workers –

is profound. Our indifference to their misery is evidence, to some, of our coarsening as a society.

When I visited Stop 103 food bank in Toronto, its director, Nick Saul, told me that "all job-training programs over-subscribe ten to one; people want to work."

The food bank's location on a traffic-heavy street in a semi-industrial neighbourhood drew in what Saul called the working poor. "You are not panhandled on these streets, but the poverty is deep nevertheless." Since 1990, I knew, the number of low-income families in Canada had increased by 32 per cent in a "booming economy" that delivered to a female cashier an average yearly income of $16,977.[10]

As for the trends since 1995, Saul could see that people were using the food bank because their paycheques were eaten up as soon as they paid their rent: "Broadly defined, homelessness is paying more than fifty per cent of your income toward rent, or doubling up." We were standing in the main food-service area, shafts of afternoon light spotlighting the counters and chairs, racks of used clothing, crates of perishables, in a deep calm before the storm of clients who would soon be lining up at the outside doors.

I asked Saul what sort of emotions people came to the food bank with; after all, most probably couldn't believe this had happened to them – that they were compelled to feed their families from the kindness of strangers. "They will keep their eyes to the floor," he replied. "When their name is called, they will sign the form, pick up their groceries, and then just bolt. Some people will wait outside until they hear their name called. Some are so embarrassed they won't bring their kids. They don't want their kids knowing."

Stop 103 was serving two thousand clients a month, once a month, with three days' worth of food each visit. Food banks are called "emergency" food programs and Stop 103 had to turn away clients who, in genuine emergency, came for seconds. To keep the shelves stocked even for monthly distribution, normally provisioned by Daily Bread central food bank and individual and church donations, the staff had sometimes to buy stock themselves. "If we were to open twice a month, it would just put us further behind the eight ball, and as an agency we are barely hanging on as it is." Stop 103 had run a continuous deficit for the past four years.

Unlike some food banks, however, this one did have the resources to offer clients their choice of tomato or chicken noodle soup, "but we can't trade a soup for a tuna," and if someone should grumble, "what the hell am I supposed to do with a chickpea?", they would be directed to Stop 103's cooking classes in its little kitchen, which were social events too. Every now and then the centre got lucky with donations of "gourmet" food, leftovers from wine and cheese receptions; the week I visited, Saul was still gleeful about the leftovers from a $500-a-plate arts event. "But this all comes down to the issue of lack of choice that low-income communities have. If you are living in the street, you are told when to wake up, when to go to sleep, what to eat, where to walk. So 'quality of life' is built around having choices, and we give them a minimal choice."

> The 1998 *Maclean's*/CBC year-end survey found that fifty per cent of respondents thought the government should more actively intervene to narrow the growing gap between rich and poor Canadians. Only twenty-four per cent of respondents felt that the rich deserve to be rich and the poor deserve to be poor and that there is nothing government can do.
> – "Federal Budget Watch," *Prairie Dog*, February 1999

A couple of governments did decide there were one or two things they could do. In March 1999, a new federal cabinet minister was named as minister on homelessness, albeit with no money attached; and the government of Ontario, perhaps in advance of an election campaign, found some $50 million of its own money (in addition to $50 million in federal funds) to service the homeless, although it would be "months" before the money was to be available as rent supplements to the poor.

I had asked Liz MacLean what the street people did after six o'clock when The Meeting Place closed. Mainly, she said, they went off to find housing for the night. Once upon a time, not so long ago, people lived in rooming houses or in a variety of non-profit accommodations, or at least had the hope of being able to get into them. Now they were going to emergency shelters or taking their chances on the street, avoiding when they could the hostile and unsafe environment of the hostels. "When they leave, it's to go squeegee, or to the squats, or to one of the winter overnight shelters."

In the old days, when MacLean saw people off at the end of the day, they would be waving goodnight to her and going home.

At a labour summit in fall 1997, the chief economist of the Canadian Auto Workers, Jim Stanford, pointed out that Alberta had the highest economic output of any province but had slipped to third in weekly wage rates and had the highest poverty rate west of Quebec. Yes, tax rates are the lowest in the country for those earning $75,000 a year, but fifth-highest for those at $20,000. "The problem with the Alberta economy," said Stanford, "is the failure of the [economic] success to spread through the rest of the economy."[11]

In St. John's, if you're looking for a working Newfoundlander, you're advised to try looking in Alberta. That's where the trades are needed, according to Damon Etheridge, whose brother is in Calgary. His bitterness was as sharp as his beer was flat. "Welders are a dime a dozen here," he went on. "Eighty per cent of the fishermen who went on the TAGS [The Atlantic Groundfish Strategy] program for retraining took up welding." Did that mean that they got all the jobs when they left the program? "They work for nothing. They had the money from TAGS and then went working for nothing. Retraining fishermen is a joke anyhow. You take a man fifty-five years old, got a grade three education, you put him in school with com-puters . . ." You could imagine how it was working out, retraining for jobs that weren't there in the first place, according to Etheridge, and then every-one wondered why young people were leaving. In ten years, as he saw it, the island would be a wildlife preserve, "because there will be no one left here." The federal government listens only to the people of Quebec and Ontario. "Nobody listens to Newfoundland. Nobody." Pause. "Everybody's gone." Pause. "Dead." Of the forty-five students who graduated with Etheridge from high school in 1991, maybe two were still on the island. "Meat-packing company from High River, Alberta, came here to recruit. My brother went in for an interview and a week later he had a call from Alberta. It was a Friday. Told him to be there Monday morning for work. He was already a supervisor on the floor when he later quit for a better job in a power plant. He was only nineteen when he left. It nearly killed him to leave us."

Etheridge was trying his best to stay on in St. John's. He enrolled at the university but ran out of funds after one semester, couldn't get a student loan, and had to quit. His divorced parents had each remarried, so, according to the provincial government, he had four parents and was in no need of a loan. "But I don't have anything to do with either 'father,' and I've been working since I was twelve years old and saving my money for university, and then when I needed to find a job, the federal government was spending millions and millions of dollars keeping the fishermen on TAGS and taking jobs away from young people." And you couldn't get into training programs here. "We're talking about thousands of fishermen that took up all the seats, they took up all the federal money, wasted federal money by training for jobs that weren't there. . . . That's what Newfoundland is for me."

Far from cooling him down, this outburst fed another. For all his grievance with the layers of insensitive government, his biggest disappointment was his father's generation, the middle-aged, uneducated fishermen who were now sucking out the funds from unemployment and retraining programs just as they had sucked up the fish from the ocean floor. He was only twenty-five but he had already seen plenty. Fisheries officers watching their brothers and cousins on their draggers, "supposed to be two miles out but they're three-quarters of a mile out, dragging for cod," who, as soon as they left the wharf, dropped non-regulation mesh nets over the side and caught everything swimming. "When the catch is too small, they'll dump it. I tell you that in the northern peninsula in the Straits of Belle Isle you could walk from Quebec to Newfoundland on top of the dead small cod in the water in the summers of '88 and '89. And they did this for years. Running around in sixty-thousand-, seventy-thousand-dollar trucks, million-and-a-half-dollar boats . . . I'm ashamed. Because that's where I'm from."

"You were eligible for social assistance?"

"At that time, yeah."

"Why?"

"Because I was young and I didn't have anything."

"Unemployable."

"Not really. I was employable, but I wasn't employed and they had to take care of me, because in Canada it's kind of against the law or the constitutional rights to allow anybody to go out and freeze to death in the street."

– From an interview with James van Allen,
grade eleven student

At the age of twenty-five, James van Allen was back in school, which was where I found him, in the offices of the students' council of Alberta Vocational School in Edmonton, an institution of about five thousand students with an average age in 1997 of thirty-one. He responded with disarming candour to my questions, which were aimed at learning how he had found himself back in school as a grown-up. I assumed it had much to do with his employability, and I was right: for four years he had worked, off and on, at minimum-wage, under-the-table jobs with no benefits, washing cars, cleaning and stacking recycled bricks – not only because he had only a grade nine education, but also because, as he claimed, instead of lying on the job application forms about his level of education, he'd tell the truth, "and for telling the truth I ended up getting that five-dollar-an-hour job." You got the impression, from this straight-backed, open-faced, voluble young man, that he wouldn't do it any differently today.

In fact, van Allen grew up on a farm near Edmonton, but when his parents divorced he and his mother moved into the city. He was, he figured, just plain "farm stupid" when he enrolled in Automotives in the "school of last resort," a vocational high school, a program he conceded was better than sitting at home doing nothing. Automotives began at grade nine level and he, predictably, found the going tough, having missed grade eight math.

He dropped out, switching to an inner-city school where he was constantly "fighting for [his] life" because of the school-based gangs. He lasted there two weeks, then moved to another school and enrolled in Welding. He did all right in Welding, but his academic subjects suffered, especially his old nemesis, Math. Halfway through the year, he gave up. At that point, he decided, it was more of a hassle to stay in school than to go work for five dollars an hour. "I mean, what's the point of going to a class you don't understand and the teacher looks at you like you're an idiot? I was nineteen and this sense of hopelessness was looming over me. I just couldn't do anything right. Everything I touched turned to crap." So he quit school, took spending money out of his mother's welfare cheque, and began hanging out at the arcades.

When his mother cut him off, his life went "in the toilet." He moved from one friend's house to another and then to the Youth Emergency Shelter and, in the summer, slept in a picnic shelter in the river valley park.

In the winter he qualified for social assistance, which helped pay the rent in a buddy's home; "the rest of the money we drank."

Social Assistance provided van Allen $470 a month. It was, he said, a sad existence, but when he looks back on it, he is profoundly grateful that the assistance was there. It helped him survive. But it wasn't until Premier Klein's government instituted welfare "reforms" in the early 1990s, cutting his Social Assistance to $393 a month, not even subsistence, that he made a heroic effort to find work. "It took Ralph Klein to kick me in the butt," he said. Meaning, just as the Klein rhetoric had it, that an able-bodied man should be at work, not on welfare, and reforms made the transition easier by allowing welfare recipients to work and keep assistance until they could replace the social-services income. He managed to replace the $393 by doing part-time jobs, and he started to like it: going to work, having his own money.

At the beginning of 1998 he was working on his high-school diploma. He was the father of a four-year-old and was looking to the future. He had plans to pursue post-secondary education with a goal to having his own business, and to finance this by qualifying as a heavy-equipment operator through courses at Keyano College in Fort McMurray. Then the plan called for working on the oil patch for the two or three years it would take to make enough money to pay for further education without having to take out a student loan. He wanted to be able to qualify for a mortgage, "to own something of my own."

To own and to labour: welcome to the class at work.

WORK

> Percentage of jobs that will require computer knowledge after 2000: *90*. That will require a university degree: *15*. Ratio of white-collar to blue-collar jobs in 2000: *4 to 1*. In 1970: *2 to 5*. Percentage of today's high-school students who will be employed in jobs that do not currently exist: *60*. Number of people unemployed worldwide: *1 billion*.
>
> – *Shift* magazine, September 1997

Gone is the worker's expectation that a steady, full-time, unionized, perhaps even unskilled or semi-skilled job would provide a family's living;

gone is the steadily ascending career path of the white-collar professional rewarded for maturing competence and loyalty to the firm. Gone, most shockingly in post-war Canada, is the federal government from job creation and regulation of the labour market, declaring 45,000 public servants "surplus" in 1995 while investing nearly $4 billion in information technology.[12] Gone, in other words, is the workplace culture my generation had assumed would be a constant of civilization as we knew it when we got our first paycheques back in the 1970s. It isn't a generation that is lost, as Kiké Roach cried out in her conversations with fellow activist Judy Rebick, "what's *lost* are the good jobs, the opportunities. We can't all be entrepreneurs, computer programmers, and casino workers."[13]

The same year that *Shift* magazine compiled its statistics about the future of jobs, an economist at the Royal Bank of Canada, Derek Holt, had good news for Canada's under-30s. Thanks to the "turnaround" in public finances with the elimination of government deficit, the next generation of workers would enter a "friendlier" job market than the fiercely competitive one in which Generation X had been forced to support itself during the grim era of downsizing. Never mind that, of the 302,000 new jobs created in the first eleven months of 1997, only 15,000 went to people under 25, Holt expected another 400,000 jobs to materialize by the end of 1998, of which young people would get their fair share. Barring that happy development, they had the long-term prospect of inheriting a "wad of cash" from deceased parents.[14] In the meantime, of course, they would have to work.

> I felt like a genuine Vodun zombie from overwork and no play
> but still it was a pleasant feeling, to know that very very soon
> I could fling these homicidal shoes from my feet and ask
> someone to get me something and not the other way around.
> *Arbeit macht frei*: Joe jobs shall set you free. Service sector über
> Alles. The Nazis knew a thing or two.
>   – Mark Anthony Jarman, "New Orleans Is Sinking,"
>   *subTERRAIN*, Spring 1998

Some of the most hair-raising reading I encountered while researching this book came from the files of newspaper and magazine clippings I had been amassing over a two-year period and the shelfful of books, some dating back ten years, on the subject of the present and future of work. The vast majority of the literature is alarmist, pessimistic, and even apocalyptic in its account of the radical changes working people have had to absorb over the last twenty-five years (since the small computer first appeared on individual office desks).

Even the optimistic literature – or at least the promotional literature – was steeped in premonitory directives about how to get ahead, stay ahead, and be the last to be downsized. This, for example, from a brochure mailed out to Bank of Montreal customers: "When change comes, . . . [m]ake it a personal rule to step forward *automatically* into any *inevitable* change." (My emphasis.) There follows an anecdote about how "opportunity" can often lie directly beyond "difficulty": a secretary, who accidentally spilled coffee on a high-ranking executive, instead of giving into "fear and shame," laughed. "Then he laughed. It became a joke between them. From then on she was noticed, as was her work. Eventually, she was promoted to be the executive's assistant."

It occurred to me that there was no one among my interviewees who had not had his or her consciousness, and hopes for the future, shaped by this culture of white-knuckled anxiety about making a living, in which change can only be adapted to, never challenged or resisted. "Negativity" is all your own fault ("get rid of things that are creating negative energy"); "skill-acquisition" is a neverending process; and CEOs look for "personal flexibility, ingenuity, and leadership over traditional hard or technical skills." Which translates, at the end of the day, to a promotion based on the absolute contingency of a spilled cup of coffee.

Like the depopulated cities with their edifices still standing in the wake of a neutron bomb attack, the new culture of work in a post-industrial, digitized, market-regulated economy – in which women are almost as fully present as men, companies have "restructured," and the full-time, steady job is an oddity – employers, in public and private sectors alike, offer "nonstandard" employment such as part-time work, contract work, and temporary work with all that entails for a worker's social benefits and qualification for employment insurance. By 2001, 900,000 Canadians are expected to be working from home, "teleworking,"[15] sustaining a trend between 1989 and 1997 when eight out of every ten new jobs represented some form of self-employment.[16]

Between 1990 and 1996 the self-employed grew from 14.4 per cent of the workforce to 16.6 per cent, accounting for 377,000 of the 511,000 new jobs created in that period. According to a 1997 report in the *Globe and Mail*, adults over twenty-five filled almost two-thirds of part-time occupations that bore little resemblance to the ones people hoped for.[17] At least half of these people indicated they would rather be employed full-time. A few months later, Canadian Policy Research Networks reported that, while employees would like full-time work, employers, such as supermarkets and private health-care firms, want to hire them for fewer than thirty hours a week for the flexibility and lower wage structures that part-time employment provides.[18] The same year, striking part-time workers at an Edmonton Safeway pleaded for "more hours!" so they could begin to qualify for benefits and to hope that some day they would reach the minimum number of qualifying hours of service – a number which the company had *doubled* in its "final offer" prior to the strike – for the top wage rate.[19]

"Don't blame the workers in the cafeteria for feeling a little confused," reads an advertising feature in the March 21, 1997, *Globe and Mail*, "Their company today has full-time staff who are telecommuting from home or doing telework from the office of clients, and who never have lunch on the premises. The company has flex-time people who show up every Monday, unless it's Wednesday or Thursday instead. Meanwhile, contract workers appear for breakfast every day of the week until they disappear altogether." Kelly Services, the employment agency once known for its staffing of temporary "Kelly girls" or office workers, now also places temporary scientific and technical specialists to companies "reluctant to hire new staff" because they may be stuck with full-time employees (and all those EI premiums and paid vacations, not to mention severance pay) whose job could be done by a new computer program three years hence.[20] A year later, Statistics Canada reported that the temp/contract job market, which was worth $2 billion in 1997, would account for 20 per cent of all jobs by 2008.[21]

The self-employed working out of their own offices pay for their own benefits, the telecommuters stay at home where they pay for their own utilities, the contract workers don't expect a cafeteria or furnished staff room to be provided for them. Writing in *Report on Business* magazine, Richard Bingham, of "Generation X," observed that when the first big wave of downsizing and re-engineering hit his generation in the early 1990s, they were stunned to realize that the old ethic of "reciprocal loyalty" between boss and employee had been broken. The new ethic of loyalty, as Bingham describes it, is to shareholders, period. "This is the world my generation takes for granted. And we're comfortable with it. . . . Fun is a key word for the Gen-X worker. . . . *It's only a job*. We see ourselves as *in* the system, but not *of* it."[22] As I read this, part of me is intensely irritated by this overly defensive justification for accepting a system that treats his generation with careless arbitrariness, and by his exasperating naïveté about just who is using whom, system or worker.

Yet, to judge from my clippings, these "new workers" *are* satisfied – to avoid rush-hour commutes, organize their own day, eat lunch with their kids, dress casually, take stock options in lieu of promotion, and turn hobbies or avocations into businesses. They think of themselves as thriving on unpredictability, challenge, and adventure. But they may be making a virtue of necessity: "downsized" from normal office routines and struc-tures, they burn out as workaholics who labour seven days a week and never take a holiday, just to break even in an enterprise all their own.

As for the "willingness" of the twenty-three-year-old journalism grad-uate who had "volunteered" at a commercial television station: "The job market sucks," she told the *Edmonton Journal*, "and no one wants to give anyone a break. No one's going to put out money when they're cutting their own staff. Everyone wants more for less and it drives me crazy."[23]

Crazy like a fox, in some instances. Nathalie Labonté, salaried writer at *Recto Verso*, a Montreal bi-monthly of labour and socio-political journal-ism, graduated in Anthropology and Journalism in 1995. Wanting to work as a journalist, but without the all-important experience in a competitive job market in which Radio-Canada and the big dailies were laying people off, she decided to do volunteer work and apply for welfare as subsistence income. "I come from a middle-class family and this was a big shock," she told me, "a big shame for me, but in the end it was a good experience. The first time I went to see the social-services agent, she said to me I shouldn't be there, I have a degree, I should work in a restaurant. But I wanted to work in my profession, so I didn't listen to her, and a good thing too. Otherwise I'd still be there, at some coffee shop." Hoping for freelance assignments, she called up *L'Itinéraire*, "a street journal that helps homeless people. They said they were looking for someone like me on welfare. They said they could pay me $516 per month. I wrote and wrote for them for a minimum wage. I stayed ten months and by then had a lot of expertise in the welfare law." She had become interesting to an employer.

> Why plunge into new media alone when you can partner with a company that will show you the way? The WebPool Syndicate is recognized as a leader in interactive media. Established in 1994, this dynamic team serves the new media needs of outstanding private and public companies. The WebPool excels in project management, ensuring that the client is informed and involved in every phase of the production. The company has produced over 40 projects in industries as diverse as entertainment and biotechnology.
>
> – From the WebPool Syndicate's brochure

The impressive adaptability of the so-called "new worker" to the fearsome economic changes of the last twenty years, especially the much-discussed retraction of the promise of full-time, salaried, permanent employment in public and private sectors, has drawn the attention of sociologists-cum-consultants who are intrigued by these adaptive successes in a cruel environment. Who are these people who keep changing jobs or jump from contract to contract or pursue personal dreams, income (often) be damned? Dr. Barbara Moses, president of BBM Human Resource Consultants, has even worked out a typology: they are personal developers ("identification is to their work, not employer"), authenticity seekers ("motto: I gotta be me"), lifestylers ("motto: I work to live, not live to work"), independent thinkers ("want to own or build their own work"), and collegiality seekers ("what's important is working with people they enjoy").[24]

They sound terrific. No boring, stupid corporate norms for them, cancel the endless meetings, down with hierarchies, bring on the team! Money? Okay, if you insist.

In December 1997, I interviewed WebPool's vice-president, Emma Smith, in her office in Vancouver on West Pender over Harry's Diner. WebPool's offices are lit in perpetual twilight, shedding a subdued, bluish glow over the staff at their computers as though they were working in an aquarium. It's to make the images on their screens that much brighter, apparently, but I wondered if it had something to do with "Webheads'" indifference to the transitory worlds of light and dark and climate outside their darkened windows, so absorbed are they by the online world.

Smith did not have a computer in university; she had a little Panasonic word processor where the print came out the back. "I studied Communications at Queen's University, and took a course on mass media. It focussed on the printing press. Not a single mention of the computer and Internet in the courses I took, and we're talking 1992 to '93. It's frightening. But now you simply can't get a job, in ninety per cent of the enterprises out there, unless you're comfortable with at least some level of the technology. It doesn't mean that everyone has to be in multimedia and doing 3-D games, and it doesn't mean that nothing else matters, but it's a big part of it."

For the longest time it didn't matter in her life either, growing up in a small northern Ontario town where for seven years she worked retail, selling Ski-Doo parts to loggers and miners, took her coffee breaks in a small room decorated with porn, and was halfway through university before she met a feminist. With her Communications degree she found work with a media training firm in Ottawa and volunteered for a project to develop a software package, even though she still had no formal computer training. By the time she moved to Vancouver in 1995, she was ready for WebPool, a high-tech producer of new media projects. "Our programming team works to develop industry- and technology-specific software solutions, including groundbreaking virtual reality products, publishing tools, robust databases, search engines and intranets."

"Sheesh," I said, owning up to my ignorance of such things. "I'm a boomer."

"As for the fate of boomers," Smith commiserated, "it's going to be really difficult to manage a company ten years from now if you don't understand the technology. If you're a CEO who doesn't see the value of the Internet and that you can save millions of dollars by letting your staff communicate with Internet technology instead of by 1-800 numbers and faxes, then your business is not going to compete. The Net is free. And it's considerably easier to put something new online than to print new brochures every year. If you're running a company and you don't know who is a good person to hire, you're going to miss the boat. Take a nineteen-year-old designer who you put into a traditional cubicle office space: they're going to hate it and leave anyway, to go start the WebPools of the world."

I hauled out my notes, with a list of the features of the "mindset" of the so-called Next Generation: "Driven to innovate, driven by immediacy requiring fast results, plugged utterly trustingly into the Internet, in love with hard work because work and play are the same thing for them."

"Is this WebPool?" I wanted to know.

While Smith acknowledged that WebPool was in a constant battle with the traditional idea of workplace hierarchy, nevertheless the staff generally accepted a team-oriented, "collaborative" approach to doing work. "Work hard, play hard. The way to get good work out of people is to have them happy and challenged. And it's totally true that they will consider poor digital instruments as 'cruel and unusual punishment.'"

Smith and her five partners started up WebPool by default: they didn't mean to be entrepreneurs, they just couldn't get jobs. So, in a sense, they could design the perfect company, the one they would want to work for, one that employees could "believe in, trust," a company that was ethical, green, community-oriented. There is work WebPool does not take, namely porn, the biggest money-maker on the Net. Not even soft porn, which was pretty tough when they were each making $300 a week.

"We are very, very quality conscious and proud of it. Everything that has gone out the door of this company is as good as we can make it, even if it has meant that four people worked until midnight over the weekend. That's not an option in a bigger, more inflexible company, putting in that 'extra' for no money if you want to. The employees love this company. Just as much as we do."

The goal for Urban Juice & Soda Co. is to be the leader in the beverage industry – in every aspect. We must prove to the industry that consumers will find it more acceptable for beverage companies to invest in causes and changes rather than colored signs. . . . Our products are mainstream, our consumers are young, and they realize that change has to occur. We must accept this responsibility, and we must prove there is, in fact, a better way of doing business.

– From Urban Juice & Soda Co.'s Mission Statement

In 1986, when he was twenty-three years old, Peter van Stolk had a business, Food for Thought, selling fresh juice and fruit and salad greens from a kiosk in downtown Edmonton. "I wrapped them up and made them real pretty." When a fruit supplier suggested he branch out into freshly squeezed, flash-frozen juices, he sold his car, bought a load of orange juice, and tried to sell it in a city going through the protracted blues of a deep slump in world oil prices. "I couldn't even get people to sample it for free." By 1990 he was in Vancouver. He was still there in 1998, as founder, owner, and manager of Urban Juice & Soda, which, compared to chopping fruit, is making him very stressed. "It's the roller-coaster ride from hell, you get so high and so low, *instantly*. But on the positive side, if I can compete against Coke and Pepsi, I think I can get a lot of things done. Unlike earlier generations of business, mine has a responsibility for future generations. The earlier ones used up a billion years' worth of resources to make profits. Now, if you're making money from an environment, a community, you have to think about what you're doing to make it better for the next generation."

Yet van Stolk is enough of a realist to acknowledge that he has no hope of competing with Coke or Pepsi, who control shelf space in supermarkets and will never yield it to "product" they don't own. "What you see on the shelf is only what they want you to see, that's how it works." He was not overly perturbed: "That's capitalist society, those are the rules." Then he added something really very interesting: "But if you try to play by them, you'll lose." And this is where his mission statement about a "better way of doing business" comes in: bending the rules to give his own designer soda a chance.

He researched the market and decided that, whereas the marketing buzzword was "positioning" a new product, as in "putting something in front of somebody and hoping they bump into it," *his* was going to be "grounding," as in "planting something under your feet and watering it and giving it sun and waiting for the groundswell so it comes up from under you." This approach, it seemed to me, was overly bucolic, but van Stolk is a canny marketer under the overalls, so to speak. "The big guys are not that smart or creative. They're followers, not leaders. Fruitopia is a copy of Snapple. Traditionally, that's what will happen: the small, innovative companies like ours come up with something. Remember New York Seltzer? Within two years there were five, six copies. Remember Koala Springs? Same thing. Dead."

Each of the Big Five had sales that rose quickly to a head and then went flat. And the decline of one hit beverage roughly corresponded to the rise of another. From that, van Stolk concluded that New Age beverage success had little to do with product quality. Sure, the product had to be good, but beyond that "it's all fashion," he says, "like yellow power ties or acid-washed jeans."

– Christopher Caggiano, "Brand New," *INC Online* magazine,
April 1997

He checked out high schools to see what kids were wearing and which music they were listening to, watched their television programs, read their magazines, and made the decision to place Jones Soda where the kids were, places soda pop had never been sold before: skateboard shops, ski shops, tattoo parlours, computer shops, navel-piercing establishments, music stores, Chinese restaurants. Soda as environmental accessory, as he put it. (For the record, "soda," he explained, is upscale for "pop," which is just sugared water.) The previous week he was in Hangar 18, a skateboard shop in San Diego, watching how customers behaved with his product. But wait, why did he care whether Americans drank his pop? "I've beat my head against the wall, saying I'm cool in Canada . . . but no, no, no. You're cool in New York, you're cool in L.A., and *then* you're cool in Toronto and Vancouver. If I tell you I'm in West Beach store in Vancouver, well, okay, that's cool. But if I say I'm in Soul Shack in San Diego, that's way cool. Period. End of story. Have a nice day. The kids came in to talk about the latest technology with each other, they walked over to the soda cooler, checked out the label – our labels are always changing – plopped the guy a buck, kept on talking." Cool.

Particularly cool are those labels, designed often from photographs customers send in, which change every three months and which make the company "interactive" with its public and invoke an "emotional connection" between drinker and drink. "People want to send us all kinds of messages. 'Free Tibet!' Sure, why not? It builds brand loyalty."

When I expressed disbelief that kids can be made to care that their soda, that "accessory," comes with a socially responsible message, van Stolk assured me that his young market wants to *believe in* the products they consume as a generational statement. "You're telling the consumer, 'Look, Coke is not the soda of your generation, not something *you've* discovered.' Second, we support anti-cultural icons like skateboarding and raves and extreme sports. You've got to be real, not some advertising agency guy sitting in funky wraparound sunglasses, sitting up there, making things up. Third, we're sending out messages. We believe that industry has been far too concerned with market share." In an interview with *INC.* magazine, he had to have a laugh: Pepsi spent over $30 million on the national launch of Crystal Pepsi. The product lasted six months.[25]

Yet van Stolk truly believes that "the world does not need another soda." Thinking of the cheerless lives of Eastern Europeans and Chinese who've been absorbed willy-nilly into International Cola Inc., he suggested that what they really need is to "laugh a little, smile, to embrace products that have a positive impact on their community and their environment."

The alternative capitalism. The beverage producer who uses only recyclable glass, paper, not plastic, and never Tetra Paks. The alternative employer who hires full-time staff, provides benefits and company stock, and invites employees to "challenge" his management, who holds Friday meetings with beer, for "our goal is not to keep the payroll down but to increase sales."

I sighed. We sat at the window counter of a coffee shop in Marpole, feeling a bit subversive as we talked about his mother, Mary, a "from-the-ground-up" social activist of 1960s Edmonton, and his father, Dr. Jonas van Stolk, who is a member of Physicians for Social Responsibility. Father and son have big arguments about why Peter is not in the peace movement: "I tell my father, 'If you want to move anything in this society, you have to remember what game it is you're playing. This is a capitalist society and it's about who has power.'" No argument there. But I'm left puzzling over a guy with a shaved head and a cell phone, from which he makes his appointments while driving back from California, who believes that selling soda pop with "soul" is a way to post-industrial power.

Some 46% of new small businesses are led by women, making up nearly one-third of all firms in Canada. While 45.6% of businesswomen still operate in the retail trade sector, some 54.4% are evenly distributed throughout all other sectors in Canada.

Overall, businesswomen in these sectors tend to be younger than their male counterparts. Almost 50% of the women are younger than 45 while nearly two-thirds of the men are over 45.
— "Canadian Women – Making an Impact,"
Statistics Canada, 1998

When Colleen Whelan started up Venture Consulting in 1993, a consulting and servicing company for computer systems mainly in small and medium-sized businesses, she had already been working with the technology for thirteen years, since her summer jobs as a high-school student, and knew that by being able to read technology manuals and understand them she had been given a gift. Other than one college-level course on hardware, she is self-taught, and this perhaps explains her low-key approach to what she is doing – which she described as "fifty per cent public relations" – translating the language of the technologies for the mystified "end user" sitting baffled in front of a screen. Her emphasis, in fact, is on having an office of people accept their computer system as another and ideal employee, "because then people don't feel out of control." Her encounters with the human psyche have fine-tuned her approach to public relations, and so she is willing to do one-on-one training with executives afraid of losing face in training sessions with staff, overlook a client's potential misgiving about her gender while coping with the stress of their "panic situation," and always, always be available, at all hours of the day or night, exactly like a doctor on call, because if "somebody's system goes down, they feel absolutely helpless."

"Have you ever failed?" I asked.

"Define 'fail.'"

"Couldn't figure out the problem."

"Maybe two or three times in the last five years I've had to say 'I don't know.' But that's part of my job, which has taught me infinite patience: when you can't find the answer you still cannot get frustrated, you must continue and find the answer because there *is* an answer somewhere."

Whelan's modesty, about everything, is disarming: the almost comically humble beginnings of her business in downtown Toronto, living on $10,000 a year, working out of her bachelor apartment with a single computer that she assembled herself with parts worth twenty-five dollars; her desire to provide "a really good service at a very, very reasonable price"; her focus not on money but on her "responsibility" to clients who have become accustomed to "slimy salespeople" and consultants who disappear just when your system needs servicing; her claim that she never stops learning, that every day on the job is a kind of training; her acute awareness that her business has a short lifespan because, breathing down her neck, is the generation of twenty-somethings already computer literate and presumably not in need of her services. In the meantime, money is a "spinoff" she uses to finance her backpacking travels.

She has had to rely wholly on herself since she was a kid, her family having provided no support whatever. To my jaundiced observation that the new hype about the home-based office work conveniently obscures the boundary between work and leisure time, Whelan responded that "this is what my generation has grown up with." Unionization of the new workplaces? She cannot imagine, simply cannot. Her self-sufficiency seemed almost chilling to me, and I wondered where she found a camaraderie of workers, but then the new "venture capitalism" isn't about solidarity, and Whelan's Venture Consulting isn't about capitalism. It's not money that drives her, she said, she owns no house or car, and has never, not ever, been in debt. She is not, she said, a materialistic person.

By contrast, Erin Clarke, user-services representative at Web Networks in Toronto, was more familiar to me. Perhaps it was her "long march" of social engagement in Toronto through volunteer babysitting at a daycare centre and her eight years working in a shelter for homeless women and children, a relief worker at a shelter for assaulted women, women with children, immigrant and refugee women, street women, and runaway teenagers, and her snail's pace through the Ontario College of Art while she worked full-time and where she became interested in how artists use computers and electronic media creatively. There was little if anything here that resonated of power and profits, but she was no less passionately attached to her work for it. As with van Stolk, though, neither was there a breath of Generation X's indolent indifference to the notion of vocation. "*Occupational Slumming: Taking a job well beneath one's skill or education level as a means of retreat from adult responsibilities and/or avoiding possible failure in one's true occupation*," as Douglas Copeland nailed it back in 1991.[26]

"That's another thing about my generation," Clarke added, having looked back on the zig-zag course of her work life up to Web Networks, "the work ethic doesn't exist any more in the sense of keeping a job for life. We know we have to keep getting re-educated and we're not going to do the same job for a lifetime, because the ones we're doing now are going to disappear anyway. But this is not the same as detached transience. I personally feel, wherever I am, I am one hundred per cent committed in that moment."

Working with Information Technology has not been without its ethical dilemmas for Clarke, who has known a "very deep understanding of humanity from my own experience of living on the street and working in the shelter and living in a shelter." That long and difficult experience, being the child of a single mother in a home with little money, and never a hope of having her own computer as a kid, lends a depth to her sense of humanity, she feels, that she couldn't have got at university or in books. (She mentions her friends who are now doing their Ph.D.s in developing multimedia operating systems and wireless network protocols and thinks, "Wow, they are the ones who had computers when they were growing up.") But it informs her use of technology, and thus the dilemma. "At what point do I acknowledge participating in the oppressive side of the IT industry, acknowledge the wage slaves in Malaysia who put together the circuit boards that are in the computer that I am using?"

The compromise is to work at Web Networks with people who have found a way "that is not industry driven" to use the technology. A network of networks linking activists and supporters in various causes and actions, Web Networks has put together a Labour Network, Faith and Justice Network, women's networks, "facilitating their ability to communicate with each other, coast to coast." This is in fact how Clarke got to know about Web Networks in the first place, taking a fund-raising Net workshop while working at Nellie's women's shelter. Now she works for them, a unionized, community-oriented organization where discussion is free-for-all and management not corporate at all. But she has no illusion that this is some sort of revolution; technology is not a revolution, she agreed, after I had reminisced about how, in the 1960s, with such "technology" as the Gestetner and the long-distance telephone (through the long-distance operator!), activists had nevertheless participated in an extraordinary internationally linked student movement. "But technology is a tool," she went on, and the current technology is one of the means that activists have that can hope to match the worldwide web of corporate expansionist enterprise. "This ties in with how I feel as an artist – that there have to be other voices, there has to be a counterbalance to the industry, a voice that can speak closer to the true voice of humanity with the medium."

In the same building as Web Networks, Jennifer Welsh has her office as consultant and partner in d-Code, a small (four full-time staff) consulting firm that works with companies to recruit and retain young workers – workers who need constantly challenging work and "interesting" colleagues if they're not going to drift off to the competition. I was thinking that Welsh would undoubtedly include Web Networks in the non-profit sector she sees as having a "huge potential" to employ her generation of workers. (Publicized as the "third sector" by Jeremy Rifkin in his massive bestseller *The End of Work*, it groups "communities of self-interest" in which the public, dumped or cold-shouldered by downsizing companies and governments, organize themselves to "secure their own futures.")[27] On one of their contracts, d-Code had asked eighteen- to thirty-five-year-olds to rank occupations and were startled to see that "director of a non-profit" ranked quite high. But if you think about it, as Welsh has, it makes sense: "The non-profits need our skills. We're comfortable with technology, we have an understanding of business, we're very flexible, we know about public/private partnership, we're very well educated."

This generation, her generation, doesn't want to make money, it wants to have a life, she argued, and at the centre of that life is work – meaningful work. A Rhodes scholar in International Relations, she herself had quit an extremely well-paid job with an international management consulting company to work for d-Code, where she is the oldest member with no particular title ("we kind of avoided titles"), with the chance to "be part of something, to build something." Thus the attraction of the small firm with flexible work schedules, no obvious hierarchy, and large enough salaries to satisfy the generation's indulgence in travel, entertainment, and educational sabbaticals. But there is something else at work here. Large numbers of the generation are still unmarried and childless, they are not living with or near parents, they don't go to church, they have never dreamed of joining the Optimists' Club or the Shriners, and so, "for my generation, the workplace is where a lot of that [gathering together] is happening. It's the *workplace* that's seen as the communal space." The home office, telecommuting from your pristine, perfect, Ikea-furnished office? Forget it. "We want to be with our friends at work."

For all the hyped-up business journalism about the attractiveness of such work (for "go-getters" and "self-starters" who revel in their "flexibility" and "freedom of choice"), the large majority of young workers or would-be workers would still rather be hired on long-term for a job they are qualified for and trained for, thank you very much. But if the projections are correct – that within the decade less than 50 per cent of the total Canadian workforce will be engaged in full-time, salaried employment – many of them are just dreaming.

> Through the years, PanCanadian has shaped a committed workforce of skilled individuals who have driven the company forward to its present position as one of Canada's leading oil and gas producers and marketers. This growth could not have occurred without dynamic leadership and motivated people at all levels of the organization; people willing to take on greater decision making in their work and accountability for the results.
> – PanCanadian Corporate Profile

The very long escalator in the PanCanadian Building in downtown Calgary took me up to PanCanadian's main reception and security desk in a pink granite lobby adorned with a lot of greenery and a waterfall. I was there to interview Mark Heard, one of the company's twelve employees in Corporate Communications (in a workforce of 1,600). Good-looking in a black shirt, dramatic geometric-patterned tie and white jeans, the fresh-faced Heard was in rather startling contrast to the sleek atmosphere of the boardroom where we spoke. He was of Irish immigrant, working-class origin in Castlegar, British Columbia, and happy to be where he was for the moment, although his dream had been to be a freelance magazine writer, having graduated from SAIT (Southern Alberta Institute of Technology) in Journalism in 1996. One option then had been to go back to Castlegar and work for the *Castlegar Sun*, but the prospect of making his way up a career ladder "town weekly by town weekly" did not appeal. Another option had been to apply to the *Calgary Sun* and the *Calgary Herald*, but he was not "impressed" with the *Sun's* journalism and the *Herald* rarely had openings.

His third option was to "try for corporate Canada" in one of Canada's most corporate cities, Calgary.

A program known as Career Edge was providing him with job experience at $15,000 a year (he had taken a second job as a waiter). "Financially, it's a bit difficult," he had told a *Globe and Mail* reporter, "but career-wise I'm definitely moving ahead." Or, as he put it to me seven months into the job, it was an excellent foot in the door to a world where he had absolutely no connections – an uncle at Gulf Oil, say – and no university degree. "But with Career Edge you have the chance to show them what you can do." And what he was doing was "basic writing" on computer, the company's internal bulletin delivered by e-mail. He was underwhelmed by the role of technology in his work: "It's still writing, but without getting ink on your hands. I've been computer literate since high school." More impressive was the new social world he was moving in at the office, "the world of husbands and wives and house-buying."

I asked Heard how the corporate "lifestyle" was suiting him. Initially, he had had his misgivings, the country clubs and petroleum clubs and golf clubs, and there was a certain loneliness in the crowd – "I'm never going to join the Reform Party, let's put it that way" – but he had kept his sense of humour.

Heard was as cool as a cucumber: in the end, I reasoned, not that hungry for this job, this corporation. He let slip that he had been interviewed in Edmonton for a WUSC (World University Service of Canada) posting with the Hanoi Tourist Board in Vietnam: "What an experience that would be! To be somewhere so utterly different at the other end of the world . . . and to write about it." He looked dreamy-eyed for a couple of minutes. "But PanCanadian may end this internship and offer me a permanent job. I'll probably take it."

More than a year later I telephoned his parents' home in Castlegar to learn his whereabouts. "Right now?" his father asked, chortling. "You really want to know? In a tiny Vietnamese village on the Chinese border." Far from having been offered a permanent job, Heard had been "downsized" at PanCanadian. In July 1998, he was off to Hanoi with WUSC, to develop a CD-ROM, among other communications aids, for the Hanoi Tourist Board. "He's rather enjoying what he's doing, helping people in the Third World," his father said with understated parental admiration. He'd just received an e-mail from Mark, posted from an Internet café in Hanoi: he had tried to telephone Christmas Day but a rat had chewed through the wire in his room. "His contract will probably be renewed. We're so proud of him."

UNIONS

> In 1971, Starbucks opened its first store in Seattle's Pike Place public market. At a time when canned supermarket coffee was the standard, selling fresh-roasted whole beans in a special store was a revolutionary concept. . . . We were the first of our kind. Today, we still have a unique reputation, because we do things in a very different way than any other coffee company.
>
> – From a Starbucks brochure

In 1996, two Starbucks employees in Vancouver, twenty-somethings, decided they were fed up with being "pushed around" by the Seattle-based coffee company while being paid the hourly equivalent of two grande mocha cappuccinos.[28] They approached the Canadian Auto Workers, and ten months later they and the staff of nine other Starbucks coffee shops had a union, a contract, and a raise.

"Why is Starbucks so interesting to the CAW?" I asked John Fryer, formerly an elected officer of the B.C. Government Employees' Union and now a freelance negotiator who had been involved with the CAW's negotiations with Starbucks.

"Where are the places where, *a*, there are loads of unorganized workers and, *b*, not very effective unions with jurisdiction?" he answered. "As my old boss in the Packinghouse Workers said, 'He who has signed the membership cards has the jurisdiction.' So you go in there and sign them up. If you put workers together who have an economic rationale, who can't live adequately on a day's work – and the service sector is classic: there's no carrot, there's only the job and it's a lousy job – and get them together with a union that believes in the principle of collective action and has talented organizers who know how to put that message across to workers, you've got a powerful combination."

By September 1996, five Vancouver Starbucks outlets had signed up with the CAW, the first successful drive at any Starbucks in North America.

Contract negotiations began a month later on the key issues of shift scheduling, wages, and sick leave. The Canadian Auto Workers also mentioned they objected to the working conditions of Guatemalan coffee workers, who Starbucks had promised in 1995 to treat according to a "code of conduct" by buying only from growers who shared "Starbucks' values of treating workers with dignity and respect."[29] October, November, December: talk, talk, talk.

When there was no progress in negotiations by the spring, 92 per cent of affected Starbucks workers voted to go on strike. In April, Starbucks informed the CAW that it was not interested in resuming collective bargaining, and four days later employees went on "unstrike," reporting for duty wearing their own clothes and a CAW button, and leafletting customers. NO PASTRIES AT STARBUCKS! *The Province* blared on May 18, 1997. STARBUCKS STRIKE HITS LOTUSLAND'S SWEET TOOTH! chimed in the *Globe and Mail*. Later that month the tenth Starbucks unit was certified. At the end of June, negotiations between the CAW and Starbucks resumed. In July, success! Starbucks workers ratified their first contract. They won an immediate wage increase, seniority as a key factor in shift scheduling, and the chance for longer instead of piecemeal shifts.[30]

Five months later I sat down with Paul Tartaglio and Kahmaria Pingue, two Starbucks employees (or *baristas*, as the company chairman and CEO, Howard Schultz, has named them) who had been involved in the negotiations. Pingue poured us scented tea in her apartment on East Broadway. She was a student of early childhood education, and Tartaglio an independent filmmaker who had in development, at the time we spoke, a script about a woman who stages her own death to escape her student loan repayments.

Pingue had been interviewed for retail jobs, but it was Starbucks's promise that she wouldn't be "just a worker" that appealed to her; she had images of herself as an assistant manager, based on her long work experience. But when the company learned she would be going back to school, they decided they didn't want to invest all that time training her, so "I started out a *barista* instead." Soon she felt she might as well be working at McDonald's: no breathing space, go-go-go all the time, advancing at a snail's pace (one assistant manager had worked seven years to get there), stagnation.

In 1992, Tartaglio had needed a part-time job, saw a "Now Hiring" sign in a Starbucks window, thought "Groovy," and was hired on. It was so groovy that Tartaglio saw the vice-president for marketing "practically on a daily basis." The following spring the atmosphere altered considerably: the company introduced the concept of the "partner-member" (providing equity in the company with stock options), and staff-management relations switched from everyone being on a first-name basis to staff being given "partner-numbers." Tartaglio's was 202042.

Nevertheless, on graduating from university in 1994, and with all the hype in the media about the "emerging managerial class," not to mention his own family background in Reform Party politics, Tartaglio reasoned that, if Starbucks would train him as a manager, he could use that as leverage to have a career at, say, IBM. "So I went through the training and shot up the corporate ladder, because I was an affable guy and they liked me." And then one day the management trainees were taken down to Seattle to Starbucks's coffee-roasting plant.

"It was a Dickensian nightmare. It took my breath away. It was all immigrant workers, all making the minimum wage, I think about four dollars an hour, in horrific conditions in the cold, repetitive tasks eight hours a day. One cat we talked to had been there eleven years and hadn't left his little work cubicle. We talked with a couple of others who begged us not to let 'them' see them talking to us. I'm serious. The whole thing came crashing down when I realized, 'We're not fricking partners, man.' We had just been up in Howard Schultz's office, him living the high life, Gucci shoes, etcetera, and I'm down here, looking at these workers, and I say to my district manager, 'You know this is wrong.' He just looked at me. 'But, Paul, if they didn't do it someone else would.' Man oh man, the whole corporation was supposed to be built on something *different*, or so we were told: 'We're all friendly here, we're all partners, and we're here to take care of you.' But they're just as fraudulent as the next asshole out there. I was immediately blackballed. That was it, I was on the skids."

I work for Starbucks Coffee Company. . . . I believe Starbucks is one of the few companies that endeavors to create a comfortable and stress-free work environment for its partners. (That is what we are, partners: we don't just work for the company, we all own it.) . . . It is creating unique cafes that are conducive to the

communities in which they are built. I have never worked for a
company that goes so far out of its way to reduce, reuse and
recycle. . . . Starbucks takes a very active role in the community."
— Vikas Sharma, letter to the editor,
NOW magazine, December 18-24, 1997

The "thing" that had come crashing down on Tartaglio was the structured "hype" that Pingue had endured in her training sessions when she realized with alarm that a lot of her fellow trainees "couldn't separate themselves" from the image of the company as very cool, very West Coast, and a caring, socially sensitive, *alternative* company to boot. Many *baristas* don't feel cynical about Starbucks. At an "open forum" of employees, Pingue observed how energetic and "gung-ho" they were listening to managers lecture about the company's fiscal well-being and its anticipated profits, and how gleefully they accepted awards for "*Barista* of the Third Quarter!" Tartaglio called the phenomenon a "cult."

"That's exactly what it is," agreed Pingue. "These 'open forums' are perhaps the ugliest, most scary thing about Starbucks. At the one I went to, they were talking about 'infiltrating' Europe. They had giant maps with arrows like on 1933 Nazi maps showing columns of tanks moving into Vienna – 'the birthplace of coffee!' – and there's Howard Schultz, rah-rah-rahing about how our shares are up fifty cents. All the people in the audience are making barely enough to live on, including the managers, who are one of the worst-paid management teams in all of corporatedom, but they're all cheering. They've actually got cheerleaders doing back-flips. "GIVE US AN S, GIVE US A T!" I'm dead serious. You look around you for someone who doesn't have glazed eyes."

Pingue thought, "Is this really happening?" One girl had received a special award for having gone beyond the call of duty by taking home with her a big bag of the shop's laundry. There were tears in everybody's eyes at how she had sacrificed for her partners. "They're going to have to set up AA groups for *baristas* who've left Starbucks and can't cope."

In the spring of 1996, Starbucks's head office decided that, because profits in Canada weren't up to snuff, they would roll back the starting wage, by fifty to seventy-five cents, to seven dollars an hour. Then they introduced the Star Labour scheduling system, a computerized program that makes up the *baristas'* scheduled hours: "They give you an arbitrary skill number from one to nine and they plug in when you're available, how long you've been there, and the computer spits out your schedule based on that."[31] This innovation in scheduling, which no longer took into account people's actual needs, proved to be a huge issue in negotiations – perhaps *the* issue.

For the company, all this had the happy effect of driving average earnings down, but within six months of this new regime Tartaglio and his co-workers were steaming. They contacted the CAW, then called a meeting of co-workers in the back room of a local pub, "spun our hearts out," and signed everybody up. Tartaglio was elected to the bargaining committee, where he met Pingue, who had joined on because she was fed up with the fact that, at her shop, it was the managers' favoritism that determined employees' hours, rather than employees' seniority or competence.

Tartaglio and Pingue's account of their experience negotiating a first contract with Starbucks, even so many months after the deed was done, came burdened with heavy traces of the anxiety, frustration, and fury of the process itself. "We had no clue," they said, finding themselves across the table from a labour-relations expert, the man in charge of Starbucks human resources, and a senior district manager. The negotiations had been dragging on for eight months when Pingue joined the team in 1997: "The three company representatives acted like they didn't understand what we were asking for, constantly asking us to explain yet again what the issues were." They felt they were being condescended to as a bunch of kids who had inexplicably betrayed the family of Starbucks by being unhappy. Then the doldrums of mediation. And then you start to realize that it's *ideology*, man. "These two sides, the union and the managers, fricking hate each other. And maybe it was that much harder negotiating with a so-called progressive company whose slogan is 'It fills your soul.' Coffee! They literally have holes in their souls that are filled with coffee," said Tartaglio.

They had felt, said Pingue, that they were up against a Goliath. But they won. So why did I get the impression it was an anti-climax? Although Pingue was becoming more and more involved with the union's human rights committee and saw a role for herself in public education about workplace rights, Tartaglio was positively glum, recalling, perhaps, one of his bad moments when he realized, after the first big victory – the signing up of the employees in the first two stores – that it wasn't going to get much better. After the smoke had cleared, "We had five stores . . . and B.C. is labour friendly! Man oh man, how far have we come? And it gets harder to fight these companies who use television images. They're not goons. They wear blue jeans and say, 'Hi, I'm your friend!'"

Very few of the original *baristas* who were involved in the organizing and negotiating process were still working in the unionized stores. Four were left at Tartaglio's. The rest of the staff were teenagers still living at home, their wages going for beer and a bag of grass. What did you need a union card for? Okay, join the union, but be prepared to have your stock options in coffee beans taken away. "We're not going to be there forever, and if no one is signing union cards with the newly hired, then when it comes time to renew the collective agreement, no one is going to be left who remembers, and the store will be decertified." In the event, his pessimism was premature. By mid-1999, three more Starbucks stores had been certified and none of the original nine had been decertified – a clear indication, according to the CAW's Ryan Krell, of the organizing department in B.C., that the contract had really worked out very well for the employees. There was no grumbling "out there" among the members, for the union had been able to achieve and hold the most important condition of a *barista*'s job – longer shift scheduling.

Signage at Starbucks's Commercial Avenue outlet announced that October was "At Home with Espresso Month" and summer was "Frappucino." I supposed these were the sort of products the *baristas* were meant to "push" when the unsuspecting customer had merely dropped in for a cup of normal brew. Signs behind the counter reminded staff to "upsell," which meant, Pingue explained, to employ catch phrases such as "Would you like a pastry with it?" "Have you had breakfast today?" "Can I make that a grande?" But this staff, being unionized, refused to say any such things and so far had not suffered any repercussions. And that, I thought, was precisely where the difference lay between being a "partner" and being an Auto Worker.

"I think the Canadian Auto Workers is a beautiful thing," said Paul Tartaglio, before I shut off the tape recorder.

Reports from the Members. CAW: Casino Windsor got contract ratified after a one-day strike. UNITE: Unionized Suzy Shier store

is closing at the end of April. Management says they are losing
money but refuses to open the books. Black's main plant has
first contract offer of 0% in the first year and $0.20 in the
second.

— Author's notes from the Ontario Federation
of Labour Youth Caucus, April 4, 1998

There it was in a nutshell, the new unionism: labour organizing where
the next generation of workers increasingly finds itself, in small shops in
the retail and service sector (how many of Windsor's sons and daughters of
auto workers were finding work spinning the roulette wheel?); and the
sector fighting back, closing "unprofitable" locations rather than pay their
workers a living wage. It was all redolent of earlier, nastier struggles of the
working class to carve out a slice of wealth for itself from the prodigious
millions and billions it had created for the owning class. Only this time it
was almost intimate, low-key, taking place ten, fifteen workers at a time:
appearances at labour-relations boards, meetings behind closed doors with
resentful management challenging certifications, big guns from HQ being
sent in to apply the pressure. Turn the screw, degree by degree, on teenagers
threatened with a blacklist, or, as in the case of a Tim Hortons coffee shop
in Halifax in 1995, literally bulldoze the workplace to smithereens shortly
after its five-dollar-an-hour employees are certified by the Bakery,
Confectionary and Tobacco Workers International Union Local 446.

To judge from union representatives at the OFL Youth Caucus's 1998
meeting, which I sat in on, education of exploited working youth was at
least as important as organizing the shops where they laboured. And they
discussed the importance of building social cohesion in "Mike Harris's
Ontario" by bringing older and younger generations of workers together in
the same union movement. But are these high-turnover, low-pay workplaces enough to sustain the unions?

Theoretically, no. It costs just as much money in staff and communications to service a small local of soda jerks as it does to service a factory-full
of machinists, and the dues coming in from the former are a fraction of
the latter. And precisely because it is better educated and more ambitious
than the generation that preceded it, the youthful workforce of the service
sector cannot conceive of committing thirty or forty years to subsistence

employment in the same place; in other words, it is not going to stick around flipping hamburgers long enough to be unionized. More and more it has been finding freelance, contract, and home-based work, all of which is destructive to the idea of belonging to a community or house of labour.

So said conventional wisdom in the mid-nineties. The OFL has had its youth caucus only since November 1997; in Quebec, the labour congress CSN had a "comité jeune" since 1986, but in 1996 the FTQ, the formidable federation of industrial, multinational unions, had still not bothered, arguing instead that youth is but a "stage" in the life of the worker.[32] A 1996 national survey of current attitudes about unions, prepared by Dr. Reginald Bibby, who's been checking our demographic pulse for decades, found that respondents tend to substantially overestimate how many workers they think are in unions. But a slight majority continued to "approve of" unions, down ten percentage points since the 1960s.

The most interesting finding in 1996, however, was that the decline in this approval rating had not occurred among the young: approval levels are actually highest among young adults.[33] This is, of course, the same generation that is "allergic" to arbitrary and unfair management, has an exquisite sense of its own individual entitlements, and finds itself with a diploma or degree and no steady job except at the photo-processing lab or ticket booth, where it is asked to work early and stay late without any mention of overtime. This is the generation that, if faced with harassment or exploitation, picks up the phone and calls an organizer, as Candy Palmater, twenty-six, did at a Halifax Tim Hortons, hoping for a contract that "gives us a break sometime, let's us take a vacation. . . . These are just simple, simple things we are asking for."[34]

The unions were ready for them. After losing 300,000 members in the nineties, when the proportion of workers in the service industries rose to 73 per cent,[35] the "aristocracy of labour" smelled the coffee: the next working class was out there, toiling in the hamburger joints, the call centres, the discount retailers, cinema concession stands, big box electronic retail outlets, coffee boutiques. The unions got down to business, and by 1998 only a third of the CAW's members were auto workers.

Nowadays I work down the line from a gaggle of liberal arts grads, teachers, nurses, engineers and at least one pharmacist.

We are probably the most educated crew of shoprats ever. When the hiring was first announced in the fall of 1993, Chrysler made it clear that the days of having little education inside the plant were over. Those without a high school diploma were told not to apply. . . . According to Chrysler, this was necessary to ensure that the company had a highly skilled workforce to meet the ever-changing manufacturing environment of the 21st century, or words to that effect.

This sounds really good. It would be even better if it were actually true.

– Kevin Wilson, "Auto Body: Educated, in Debt
and Desperate – How I Ended Up Making Vans
for Chrysler," *NOW* magazine, April 23-29, 1998

Wilson *almost* got a university degree, but the money ran out and he could no longer outrun the fate that had nailed his father for thirty years to an assembly line: a steady job with good wages in a Windsor automobile factory. The awful irony is that, far from being the escape route out of the factory, Wilson's education had led him straight back in. As a buddy of his, a one-time freelance reporter, ominously concluded from Chrysler's interest in him, "The longer you spend in the education system, the more conditioned you are to be a 'good' employee."

As Wilson later wrote in *NOW* magazine, the day he told his dad he'd filled out Chrysler's application was the worst day of his father's life. Reading that statement piqued my curiosity about Wilson and his situation, for it reminded me of something I had read years ago about the "injuries of class," about how the working-class family is wounded by its members leaving to join the middle class, disappearing into another culture; at the same time, the heave-ho off the line is also their hope for their children. I wondered if Wilson, for all his education and caustic eloquence in print, had been saved for the working class.

He was in town for a meeting of the Youth Committee of the Ontario Federation of Labour and suggested we meet in a café-bistro on Queen Street West, where hipsters galore clog the sidewalk patios. He showed up in a black leather jacket and nerdy eyeglasses (very nineties, those Buddy Holly hornrims). We settled into an uncomfortable wooden booth away from the din of the street.

"Reading your *NOW* article," I began, "I was struck by the fact that though your family had enough money to consume like a middle-class family, you would never have called yourselves middle class. How does that compute?"

"My father earned his family a decent standard of living, working at Chrysler, but he did it the way working-class people do – selling his labour," Wilson answered bluntly. "If you want to get into the Marxist idiom of it, he was alienated from his labour, he had no kind of association with it. A factory is a very monotonous place. It's Taylorism taken to its limit, in which every task is broken down into the smallest number of components and you have no affinity for what you are creating. It's very standard proletarian.

"There's no other class in the world where a grown man has to ask another grown man to go and take a pee. You can't walk away from the line to take a pee! It'll stop because you skipped your job. You press a little button that turns on a light that summons the supervisor: 'I have to take a piss!'

"The place I work in is relatively clean, because it's had forty years of improvements going into it. But factory work is dehumanizing, it's thoroughly deskilled, requires no mental prowess whatever. One of the things people do to keep themselves sane in there is they bring stimulus into the plant to keep their minds off the fact they have another four hundred and ninety-nine vans to go. You bring in books, newspapers, set them up on your work table, work really, really fast, and have maybe five seconds to glance at your paper. One guy makes jewellery. I write my columns, in between widgets. It makes for a very Hemingwayesque style. Sparse."

October 1993 – The face-to-face interview was . . . surreal. It took all of five minutes with a company guy who knew the procedure for the bullshit that it was. "Where do you see yourself ten years from now?" he asks me. I'm totally unprepared for this question. I begin to talk, just to cover up my speechlessness while I wrack my brains for an answer. "In ten years I see myself . . ." the answer came to me in the nick of time. "Ten years up the seniority list and building quality products for

Chrysler Canada." I still don't know how I said that with a straight face.

– *NOW*, April 23-29, 1998

Nevertheless, it was five years later and he was still on the line. But he can walk away from it any time, unlike his father who, once he scored the coup of signing on at Chrysler ("You got your work boots? Call in and report. One thousand guys just like that, right off the street. It was the mid-sixties"), stayed the full complement of thirty years.

"My parents tried to get as much of the mortgage paid down as possible. There are times when Dad would work twelve hours a day, seven days a week. But, yeah, working at Chrysler was a coup. You had a modicum of protection from arbitrary treatment, you earned a decent wage. You had a benefit plan, which was unheard of. This is pre–Canada Health Act. My dad's mom had thirteen kids. They all lived in a houseboat on the Detroit River and wore big galoshes all the time because water kept sloshing in. That's where my father grew up. They used to have to chase the coal truck to pick up the coal that fell off."

"Hold it," I interrupted. "It was your *grandparents* who were chasing coal trucks, in the Dirty Thirties."

Wilson gave me a look of forbearance. "There was really grinding, ghastly poverty in the west end of Windsor in the sixties, and it still exists in small pockets to this day, mostly Social Assistance recipients who don't fall into any particular demographic. When I moved back to Windsor I plunked myself in the west end. I had an atavistic urge to go there. It was 'home.'"

You get the feeling that it is precisely this identity, and the class struggle as it is waged at Chrysler, that has given Wilson's impressive literacy its content. Far from preparing Wilson to take his place mutely and uncomplainingly in the cogwheels of industry, his education seems to have been the "finishing school" of his labour radicalism.

Take the issue of overtime, for instance. Wilson had fastened onto a vivid metaphor for the issue: overtime is the "crack cocaine" of the workforce. Swift in its effects, dizzyingly addictive, and bad for you.

He told me that, by law, an employer can schedule a *mandatory* eight hours of overtime a week, "no ifs, ands, or buts." At Chrysler, a unionized plant, those eight hours are paid as overtime. "So you're getting an extra twelve hours on your paycheque for working an extra eight," he spelled it out for me, "and you do that for a while and suddenly, instead of a $90,000 house, you've got a $140,000 house that you're paying a mortgage on, you've got a boat and two cars and a vacation you take up in the Muskokas every year. It's much easier to move up to a higher standard of living than to move down to a lower. And then all of a sudden that overtime dries up and, boy, watch those poor bastards scream." But after the initial "screeching" from the workers denied their "fix," "people started to get to know their spouses and kids," Wilson reported. "Bodies that were taxed to the limit got an extra day to mend."[36]

His own back and wrists were pain-free for the first time in years. When the orders flowed in again at the factory, Wilson did not flow back with them to work Saturdays. He had rediscovered weekends. More important, he had realized that "every five overtimes I work translate into a week of employment that I'm taking from someone else." If the entire Saturday shift were eliminated, Chrysler would need to hire on twelve hundred new workers to meet production demands.

Despite his university education, Wilson's most important lessons were learned in the labour movement as an activist with that Galahad of syndicalism, the Canadian Auto Workers. His is a very capacious radicalism, the antithesis of the so-called aristocracy of labour in the industrial plants. He argues passionately against labour's satisfied "segregation" of itself from what he calls its "surroundings," the armies of the homeless, the panhandlers, the squeegee kids who "give the lie to the neo-con utopia," which the unthinking worker, cocooned by health and safety laws, hefty paypackets, and American television, is as capable of believing in as are the drones at the Fraser Institute. How Wilson himself escaped that conditioning is perhaps explained both by his wide-ranging intellectual sojourns away from "home" *and* his principled return to it, on his own terms, as a union militant as concerned to agitate for low-income housing and daycare programs as for job security.

Then he tells me about "the Lecture," the requisite tour of the Chrysler auto plant for Windsor schoolkids and laymen about how a piece of raw metal turns into a functioning automobile at the end of the line. He remembers from his own tour the "filthy dirty, greasy, pornography pasted all over the place" (cleaned up now) and the big, angry-looking men, many of them carrying hammers or power tools, standing at their metal work tables as the kids paraded by. "And they have metal work tables. And they were banging on their work tables, screaming, STAY IN SCHOOL! STAY IN SCHOOL! For God's sake, stay in school! There was something beautiful about it too: we were their brothers' and sisters' children, and they didn't ever want us to suffer the way they were suffering. DON'T END UP LIKE ME IN THE FACTORY! Okay, I'm getting a little dramatic here. But to this day I remember the banging."

It is spine-tingling for his listener too and hangs shimmering between us in the atmosphere of our conversation, a stone's throw from the squeegee kids of Queen and Spadina and the "so hip it hurts" kids down from the suburbs. Wilson has to leave for the Youth Committee meeting in Don Mills. "I think you can try and deny the existence of your roots but you can't escape them. The reality is, I was raised in a working-class household, a fundamental reality." Yes, the big, angry men screaming at their work tables told him to get the hell out. But they didn't mean forever.

MONEY

Paul Ghezzi, consultant with the Investment Planning Council of Canada in Toronto, has a commitment as a chartered accountant, he told me, to work on behalf of ordinary, working Canadians – much like his immigrant parents – who need "someone they can trust, can turn to for objective advice." People who were "tired" of banks, of not getting any service, of being told that the only thing they could do with their money was put it into GICs. Ghezzi was preparing to write the Certified Financial Planner exams so he could advise on estate planning, tax planning, portfolio, and retirement planning.

"You seem to feel passionately about this," I observed.

"Very passionate. Let's take my parents and my immediate family. I've seen them come to this country and work forty years and end up with nothing except a house, which is great, except the house has already appreciated all it's going to, and they have to live in it after retirement. They missed the greatest growth in the world during the last twenty years because they never believed in anything aside from going to their bank and locking in their money, and that to me is a travesty, almost an injustice, and that is why I feel passionate about it."

His parents never worked for companies that had pension plans for their employees, and it was no use looking to the banks – "the way the world works, and it's getting worse, the rich get richer and the poor get poorer, and I honestly believe that banks don't care whether you make money or not, so long as *they* make money." Ghezzi is in this for the long haul: "This is for life," he said, this sense of mission as a financial consultant, hoping to help and protect people preyed upon by what he calls the "hacks out there" who call themselves financial planners, "taking people's money" in a market saturated with competitors all trying to do the same thing, "wannabe millionaires who are going to cash out in five years, and who cares."

> When [Barry] Gordon helped Triax Capital raise $250 million in a deal, the firm figured it'd better hire him – quick. Gordon was working for a Toronto law firm when he came up with an idea for a new investment. He told a friend at Triax – a small, entrepreneurial investment house – and in no time they landed a big-time client. Now Gordon is Triax's chief operating officer, developing still more investment products. "It's a great environment," says the 29-year-old. "We've got a pool table on our trading floor."
>
> – "Barry Gordon, Investment Broker,"
> *Shift* magazine, November 1997

"What's an investment broker?" I asked Barry Gordon, deciding I had best not intimate knowledge I did not have. I had had no idea how to go about finding an interview subject on Toronto's Bay Street and was happy to have come across a reference in *Shift* magazine, which I had been reading religiously for just such a purpose. "That was a misprint," Gordon replied. "They took artistic licence." *Shift*'s editor at the time, Evan Solomon, happened to be Gordon's oldest and best friend, and Gordon felt compelled to straighten him – and now me – out. "A broker is somebody who has individual clients and who sells securities – stocks, bonds, options – to the public. What I do is known as 'structured finance.' I try to find out what's going on in the U.S. and the U.K. – the Canadian financial markets notoriously lag behind the others in terms of innovation – and sift through them for ones that will work in the Canadian marketplace, and then work with tax lawyers and accountants, securities lawyers and investment bankers, to come up with the right [investment] structure, and then go out and raise the money."

We both had the impression that I was following this, and Gordon chatted on, seated casually in a swivelling armchair at the boardroom table, light radiating off the glassy surface of Lake Ontario far below outside; from another angle I could see the pool table. No one was playing. In fact, the entire premises of Triax Capital were as quiet as a funeral home. Gordon carries the title of chief operating officer, but then so does Gordon McMillan, his old university friend with whom he "hooked up" while still practising as a securities lawyer with McMillan Binch, and for whom he did some work, structuring a couple of transactions, before being asked to come over and join Triax. "That piece in *Shift* gave me full credit for the development of this one large, $250 million deal, but it wasn't my brainchild." The real geniuses were the guys at Triax who preceded him and some investment managers at Altamira Management Ltd. who together saw the possibilities of so-called closed-end high-yield funds that operated in the U.S. market, "raising so much money and doing so well, particularly in a low interest environment, that they were just throwing off lots of cash." So why not try to do it in Canada? Even as we spoke, Triax was five days away from filing a preliminary prospectus on a new deal "that has never, ever, been done this way before, nowhere, never."

Would he describe Triax as a "collaborative operation"? I wondered. "Extremely," he readily agreed. "There's nothing that's a solo effort here." There's very little hierarchy – I imagined them all playing pool together – and no managerial fat: eight officers, including two women, of whom the oldest was thirty-two years old. "We have a reputation for being somewhat cutting edge, aggressive and innovative, trying to figure out what the marketplace wants. A lot of people need current income, so how do we generate something for them? We scan around, trying to find what's going on, what people are doing to create higher cash yields, then we try to emulate that structure and adapt it."

"What's cutting edge about that?"

"We're doing stuff that nobody else is doing. Assessing the state of the market and where it's going so we can be first in terms of developing something for the Canadian investor, something they need, or our perception of what they want."

"What would constitute a failure?"

"That we structure something and we don't raise any money. The investors look at it and say, 'I'd rather buy bonds.'"

At this point I could have usefully left, company brochures in my briefcase for further translation, satisfied that I'd had my peek at what my generation in the Prairies called the Bay Street Boys. But I stayed on for another hour.

I had been looking for a stereotypical thirty-something capitalist, and Gordon did not at first disappoint: "I am capitalist-minded," he had said, "I think that human nature is fundamentally capitalist." But before we had even got into that, he had told me he was one of the founders of *Shift*, a backer and pseudonymous contributor, and had worked five months at *Saturday Night* magazine under the editorship of John Fraser, who had been one of his father's high school students in Lakefield, Ontario. He loves books and writing and still ghost-writes the occasional piece for *Shift*. He always knew he'd grow up to be a lawyer, but the writing itch, he feels, will someday also have to be scratched. For the rest of the interview he had my full attention as a capitalist who was violating my stereotyped views.

I had assumed, for instance, that his clients would be the corporate elite – after all, he did seem rather well connected – looking for ways not to pay their income tax, but in fact they are people "like you, my mother, my sister," able to invest a set minimum that can be as low as $2,500. "It's meant to be accessible to people, to give people access to an asset class they didn't otherwise have access to. We have a very grassroots approach to marketing." And he described four of the Triax officers fanning out across the four hundred branch offices of Nesbitt Burns, TD Securities, Wood Gundy, drumming up support for their deals. "We really have to work hard because, when you're getting $2,500, $5,000 increments, it takes a lot of people to make up $100 million."

This seemed an echo of Paul Ghezzi's enthusiasm for opening up what had been only a rich man's game to the financial ambitions of individual Canadians who, as Gordon reminded me, couldn't be sure there would be a social-safety net in their old age and needed to provide their own. As a capitalist, he went on, he was politically centre-of-the-road. "I think there is a responsibility to look after people, and I don't mean that in a patronizing sense. I think you have to provide a safety net for people who fall through the cracks. If I was to design a social system, I would start by putting myself at the bottom of the heap."

Gordon was insistent about this, about the collective responsibility of society, whether through government or a broader range of institutions or even philanthropy, to maintain the safety net. He saw no contradiction between making "tons of money" and being willing to "redistribute it" through taxes, although he did concede that this was probably an anomalous position, the majority of his fellow capitalists objecting to being told *where* the wealth would be redistributed. But the principle was intact: a "definite role for government to moderate the excesses of capitalism."

Had I heard him correctly? I had. Did I not know it was "all the rage" on Wall Street to read *The Communist Manifesto*? I did not; I mean, why would I? In what sense had the financial class of North America, especially the one that had grown up within the culture of bottom-line neo-liberalism, ever betrayed a conscience about the social costs of their global wheeling and dealing? Well, I was wrong. "It's so fascinating to watch the predictive quality of Karl Marx," Gordon mused, "because it's all very true – the expansionism, the trend of mergers and acquisitions, the growth of businesses and the squeezing at the margins of labour. There are lessons to be learned here. Some fundamental truths in Marx."

"So, you read the *Manifesto* to be forewarned about what an unfettered, unregulated capitalism would be like?"

"I think so. I think he's bang on that, left to capitalism's own devices, you're dead. More and more capital concentrated in fewer and fewer hands, we see that. No offense to Bill Gates, but left unchecked, Microsoft would dominate the field – it already does – completely to the exclusion of the people."

The people. There it was again, a whiff of the populist. As we wound up our conversation, I got a better sense of who these "people" are in Gordon's world. They are, to use the example he did, fellow Ontarians in hospitals. Given his spirited willingness to take responsibility for sustaining social services, I had asked him if he agreed, then, that it was all the more important to maintain public investment in public institutions we all collectively derive benefit from? He couldn't have agreed more, once "waste" was cut out from them, but there were other cuts you just didn't make, or didn't make so drastically, particularly when, on the other side, government is talking tax breaks. "I would get an extra fifty bucks a year. Like, *take* my fifty bucks! When the Ontario Tories say to me, 'We're cutting the provincial tax rate by three per cent,' and I go, 'Hey, that's great!' and then I get an extra hundred bucks for the year and they've shut down a half dozen hospitals, then I go, 'It doesn't make sense. Like, *take* my hundred bucks!'"

> Canada, like the U.S. before it, has spawned concentrated pockets of poverty in its major cities, which threaten to become breeding grounds for an urban underclass, a disturbing federal government study warns. The report . . . highlights Edmonton and Calgary as the most striking examples of this trend. "In Calgary, the share of poor families living in very poor neighbourhoods increased from 6.4 per cent to 20.3 between 1980–1990. . . . It's feared the trend, which began in the 1980s, may have accelerated this decade as a result of cuts in government social spending. . . .
> – Eric Beauchesne, "'Pockets of Poverty' Could Lead to Urban Underclass," *Edmonton Journal*, October 27, 1998

I had been lured to my local health-food store in Edmonton, the venue, that night, of a press conference/town-hall meeting on alternative health care, hosted by my MP, Rahim Jaffer of the Reform Party. The subject of discussion was the federal government's threat to regulate the distribution and sale of herbal supplements as pharmaceuticals. I was lured by the prospect of seeing that personable if misguided young man hold his own in an audience of NDP greybeards, which is how I thought of the clientele of that health-food store, myself included. By the time I arrived, it was standing room only, and so I took my place behind the last row of chairs and propped my notebook up against a stack of Annie's Whole Wheat Shells and Cheddar, guaranteed organic. I wondered how many of those present were as surprised as I was to find themselves convened at Reform's invitation. On the other hand, *somebody* had voted for this guy, up there in front of the herbal teas display, resplendent in a red tie bright as new paint, who delivered his remarks like the star of a university debating society. "The government doesn't care if I smoke a pack of cigarettes and eat a cheese-burger for lunch, but they want to stop me from taking Kava Kava. . . . Health is not a motive behind these policies. . . . I'm not opposed to regu-lations as long as they're reasonable and fair. . . . Alternative health care users are often poor and elderly." (*Poor?* Has he any idea how much cold-pressed evening primrose oil costs?) "Gone are the good-old-days when the government only meddled in your bedroom; now they're banging on your bathroom door. . . . We're not here to discuss whether ginseng can protect your immune system; we're here because we're losing our health-care freedom." It went over rather well, even though it was patently clear that Reform's, if not Jaffer's own, motive behind the protest was to unfurl the flag of "freedom of choice" at any opportunity. Ginseng? *Whatever.* (To give credit where it's due, in March 1999 the federal government announced it would spend $7 million over three years to establish a new division within Health Canada to oversee natural health products.)

But in his heart of hearts, what did Jaffer think about that other health-care issue, the spending of public funds – taxpayers' money! yikes! – to ensure the viability of a universal health-care system? I asked for an interview in his constituency office between his stints in Ottawa, and he obliged – graciously, articulately, and volubly.

"What do you think of the fact that, whenever they're asked the question about tax cuts," I began, "an impressive majority of those polled consistently say they don't mind our rate of taxation as long as we keep up the social pro-grams?" I opened up the newsletter he had mailed out to his constituents, *Your Voice in Ottawa*, to the column headlined, "Canadians DO Pay More in Taxes!" I continued: "Don't you think you're flogging a dead horse about over-taxation when people are generally not demanding tax cuts?"

Although Jaffer is a strong believer in the trickle-down effect of "tax relief," he immediately conceded that the Reform Party had "always expressed the fact that governments have a role" in the provision of social services and especially in "prioritizing" social spending in the areas of health and education. And in "taking care of the core social conscience, so to speak, that we have evolved with." I listened in some amazement, never expecting a man of the populist right to acknowledge "social conscience" as the accumulated achievement of Canadians over the course of our shared social experience.

"But [with Reform there is always a 'but'] because government has grown so large in its sphere of influence and is trying to be too many things to too many people, those core things that we all believe we should be taking care of and should be prioritizing are not being done effectively. The government cannot meet its obligations. . . . People are finally starting to realize that [Reform] is not talking about dismantling social programs. We are *not* talking about moving to an American style of society."

> Calgary is the best place to work in Canada, according to a new ranking developed by the Globe and Mail. Once a city that was home to only a few oil companies and the Stampede, Calgary has grown into the West's business centre and the only legitimate challenger (though a distant one) to Toronto's throne as Canada's capital of commerce. . . . Peter Hall, an economist with the Ottawa-based Conference Board of Canada, noted that many of the cities at the top of the list were low-tax jurisdictions.
> – Mark MacKinnon, "Calgary Branded Best Place to Work,"
> *Globe and Mail*, March 15, 1999

Craig Chandler, president of the Progressive Group for Independent Business (PGIB), lives in a Calgary suburb, so far south, said a friend, that it's called Calgary's "Deep South" and may as well be Alabama. It's a numbingly new housing development, sprawling up and down dale, blotting out the gorgeous hills with very large *faux* country cottages crammed together in Mews, Closes, Terraces, Gardens, and Rises, the only sign of human residency being the occasional young woman pushing a baby stroller. "Never been a downtown person," Chandler explained to me with satisfaction. I'd arrived as he was watching the House of Commons channel. A real political junkie, I thought, even though he'd been out of party politics – namely, Reform – for some time. His basement office was chockablock with computers, printers, and fax machines, and electoral maps papered the walls. I admired a photocopy of a particularly goofy-looking Ralph Klein. "He looks drunk," I noted. "That's the point," said Chandler.

Chandler wants to make changes in the political environment in which businesspeople work, whether they support him or not. Together with a partner, since deceased, he began the PGIB in 1992 in Ontario as a lobby for job creation within a "better business atmosphere." More jobs would be created, he believes, by allowing businesses to opt out of the Workers Compensation Board regime with their own private insurance program, by disallowing "racist" employment equity programs that privilege "a black woman in a wheelchair over a white male," and by eliminating official bilingual policies except where numbers warrant, such as in Kapuskasing or Timmins. "Sure, no problem there." With lower taxes on business, too, "more businesses will start up with more employment and more income tax paid."

When Chandler moved to Alberta in 1995, he moved the headquarters of the PGIB with him to Calgary, and by 1997 was "demanding," he told me, that Calgary mayor Al Duerr allow a question to be put on the electoral ballot about privatization of Calgary's utilities. "Our logic is that government doesn't belong in business. It can't compete – or has to lay off civil servants to do so."

Chandler makes a disconcerting argument for someone like me, used to more cleanly separated Right and Left rhetoric. When the PGIB was still in Ontario, the group was widely acknowledged as the "brains" behind soon-to-be-elected Mike Harris and his Common Sense Revolution ("We wrote seventeen policies for it," Chandler claimed). At the same time, his oft-repeated concern about employment, especially for his generation, seemed to come from some political value other than hard Right: "We started the Group as a lobby for small business, because we looked at what Bob Rae [then NDP premier of Ontario] was doing to the province – killing it, just *killing* it. Somebody was losing their job every five minutes. Even an NDPer can look at that and go 'Ho-lee.' . . . That should have taught the NDP their platforms don't work. They're great on paper – Communism would be the ideal state, but it doesn't work in reality." *Communism would be the ideal state?*

But Chandler imagines the Progressive Group of Independent Business as a kind of "self-defence for small business and Generation X against the raiding of our wallets even further" by the socialist wreckers. Yet he is not a sentimentalist about his generation; if anything, he argues, any taxpaying individual of his age is "forced" into right-wing conservatism out of simple fear of a future in which "we're going to be left holding a tremendous amount of debt," whether in the form of student loans or depleting pension plans or government arrears. "God bless the young," he had sloganeered in 1993, when he ran federally as Reform candidate in Hamilton-Mountain, "for we shall inherit the debt."

Like the Right, he is obsessed by the national debt. Like the Left, he is, or purports to be, aroused by the threat to "free" health care. "It isn't social spending that's the problem," he acknowledged. I had expected an argument more along the lines of the Fraser Institute and its wunderkind, the excitable Ezra Levant ("What was once a reliance on charity as a last resort is now a statutory right to demand funding from taxpayers," Levant wrote of Social Assistance.)[37] No, Chandler is not so much ideological as pragmatic: for all of us who value public health care, the biggest threat is *not* posed by the conservative political movements, he said, "it's that forty cents of every dollar go to servicing the debt."

"Most conservatives of my generation," Chandler concluded, "still believe that those who can't take care of themselves should be cared for." Then, without prompting, he added that, compared to American conservatives, "we Canadians are still left-wing. To be right-wing in Canada isn't to be real right-wing."

> Our President Craig B. Chandler seems to have the best attitude and frequently quotes Bertrand Russell: "Be isolated, be ignored, be attacked, be in doubt, be frightened, but do not be silenced."
> – From the *PGIB Informer*, October 30, 1998

Yet the platform created by a "Roots of Change" conference hosted by the PGIB in Toronto in 1998 – namely, end government funding of abortion; seek an alternative to Canada's first-past-the-post electoral system; repeal the Charter of Rights and Freedoms; promote less government; lower taxes; limit law-making to those issues that protect individual rights; end forced unionism, and support right-to-work legislation, and much else besides – smacked of pure Americana.

Meanwhile, over at the left-wing Canadian Centre for Policy Alternatives (CCPA) and their 1997 publication *Help Wanted: Economic Security for Youth*, the agenda is radically opposed to the nostrums of the Right, beginning forthrightly with a call for "a commitment on the part of governments to full employment" and ending with a visionary evocation of "an economy that serves people" when its youth are working not to pay off fiscal deficits but to crush "social deficits."

Calls for a policy of full employment and a people-serving economy, though not *designed* to be radical, resonate with the zeal of the well-intentioned crackpot, so inured has the ear become to the mean-minded and mean-spirited counsellings of the Right-dominated media. But here we are invited to consider a monetary policy targeted at achieving permanently low real interest rates, for instance, or a job guarantee for youth, or the reversal of social program cuts,[38] as though their authors cared nothing for the last two decades of market-driven wisdom, having aligned themselves instead with another traditional political culture, complete with its own economists and inspirational texts and collective memory: social democracy. The CCPA's authors even evoke the Golden Age of the pre-cynical 1970s, when the federal government under Pierre Trudeau implemented job creation programs that gave youthful workers a boost: Opportunities for Youth, Local Initiatives Projects, and Canada Works. I am feeling wistful: such a political regimen must seem breathtakingly exotic to those of my interviewees who hadn't yet been born when my generation was cashing cheques for working as community organizers.

Myrna Kostash: Does it make you nervous being a relatively small player in a small country that is open for business to the rest of the world?

Barry Gordon, CEO, Triax Capital Holdings Ltd.: Not really, but maybe it should.

MK: This is my generation talking: "Now you be careful and don't squander our legacy!"

BG: I'm not much for protectionism. Certain things deserve to be protected, but not when it affects my business – twenty per cent foreign-content restrictions in RRSPs, for instance. Well, the Canadian market doesn't make up eighty per cent of the global capital markets.

MK: So you welcome globalizing.

BG: Yeah, the globalization of capital markets. But I know if you have a mobility of capital to the extent where it doesn't make any difference whether or not I manufacture my product in Tibet, and I can do it a hell of a lot cheaper there than here, then to the extent that there's no incentive to keep my capital here in Canada then [capital mobility] potentially can erode the labour force, which has its own consequences, as we all know. It's a very, very complex interplay of factors that I can't even begin to tell you how I would manage. But I think that it would be a mistake to think we can isolate ourselves from the changes.

The Free Trade Agreement with the U.S. has been characterized as a Bill of Rights for corporate capitalism. By all accounts, friendly and hostile, with its implementation after 1988, Canada entered a revolutionary period marked by an abrupt departure from the historical patterns of national development of and national identification with the welfare state. Political economist Stephen Clarkson has called this reversal of made-in-Canada, government-led economic policies the "neo-conservative scourge."[39] Where once Canadians had anchored their collective identity in the epic achievements of social policy in welfare benefits, trade union rights, the Charter of Rights and Freedoms, public ownership of resources – if only, as some suggest, because other sources of national identification were "unavailable, weaker or divisive"[40] – the term "welfare state" became almost a term of abuse. In its place came the mantra of "harmonization" with American models of laissez-faire governments, corporate freedom (some would say aggression), and the acceptance of an "external constitution" in the rules and regulations of international trade agreements beyond the FTA. Right through the 1990s, decisions about our farms, our health-care system, high-tech production, and even the Auto Pact were disputed at the level of the World Trade Organization, where officials in no way accountable to the Canadian public negotiated largely in secret, and issued rulings that could be overturned only by a unanimous vote of the member countries.

In fact, the sought-after "harmonization" resulted in Canada losing two-and-a-half times more jobs in the 1990s than were lost in the U.S. As for jobs created, 80 per cent of new jobs in Canada have been in self-employment, compared to 10 per cent in the U.S. The rate of part-time employment has remained steady in the U.S. but has doubled in Canada.[41] According to the Council of Canadians, on the tenth anniversary of the FTA, Canadian agricultural exports doubled after 1989 to around $20 billion, while farmers' net incomes increased by only one per cent, showing that free trade was less about the spreading around of new wealth than about highly lucrative trade between multinational corporations.[42] From a low of 26.9 per cent in 1988, foreign-owned companies in 1999 accounted for 31.5 per cent of the nearly $1.3 trillion in corporate revenue generated in Canada – and the Trudeau-era Foreign Investment Review Act, designed to curtail foreign investment, has been replaced by Investment Canada and then Industry Canada in an effort to encourage it. Canadians might have hoped that all this investment would produce jobs and technology, as the free-trade gurus had promised, but according to Industry Canada, of the $50.5 billion spent by foreigners (half of them American) on business ventures in Canada in 1998, 98.5 per cent was used for take-overs. Only 1.5 per cent represented new business investment.[43] In the meantime, Canadian manufacturers – citing NAFTA, cheap labour, and the chance to service southern U.S. markets in a couple of days' time – moved into Mexico's *maquiladora* zone, a region "synonymous with sexual harassment, workplace intimidation and poor working conditions" in a country that does not even enforce its own labour laws.[44]

So, Wal-Mart buys Woolco while Eaton's bled through all its orifices. Nike buys the parent company of Bauer's, synonymous with Canadian hockey skates, and closes down one of two Bauer's manufacturing plants. Wendy's International Inc. of Ohio buys the iconic doughnut chain Tim Hortons, Interbrew SA of Belgium buys Labatts, Borgosesia SpA of Italy buys Henry Birks & Sons.[45] In 1997, shareholders of United Grain Growers, based in Winnipeg, approved a deal in which the giant U.S. food processor Archer-Daniels-Midland acquired a 45 per cent stake in the company after "fending off" hostile takeover bids by the Alberta Wheat Pool and Manitoba Pool Elevators. This prompted fears in some quarters of an end to Canadian sovereignty over Prairie grain handling.[46] In 1999, MacMillan Bloedel, profoundly if contentiously rooted in the social history of British Columbia, agreed to a $3.6 billion takeover by Weyerhaeuser Co. of Federal Way, Washington, already well-established in B.C. as the one to have racked up the most violations in 1998 of the Forest Practices Code.[47] Also in 1999, economists Thomas Courchene and Richard Harris of the neo-conservative C. D. Howe Institute called for Ottawa to negotiate a common currency with Washington, arguing in essence that Canada is not so much a country as a series of overlapping provinces and border states,[48] and demonstrating once more the timelessness of George Grant's observation in 1965 that the economically powerful elites of Canada "lost nothing essential to the principle of their lives in losing their country."[49]

John Fitzgerald, his family eleven generations in Newfoundland, reminded me that there are Canadians who understand colonialism in the very marrow of their bones. With a Ph.D. in Canadian History from the University of Ottawa (his thesis topic was the politics and culture of nineteenth-century Irish Newfoundland Catholicism), he returned to Newfoundland to do more research on the Irish of Newfoundland, which is to say, his own roots. "Newfoundland is a fishery," he told me. "An educated Irish middle class was being produced here with nothing for them to do, so there was a net out-migration in the 1840s to 1860s, 1880s to 1920s, mainly to Boston, which joined the Irish stream from Ireland during the famine and produced our Yankee cousins, the persistent American strain."

In narrating certain anomalies of Newfoundland history, Fitzgerald seemed both bemused and aggrieved. For example, the desperate measure taken by the Newfoundland Parliament in 1933 in the face of national bankruptcy has given Newfoundlanders the certain distinction that, "among all the dominions, we are the only one to have voluntarily voted our Parliament out of existence; Britain took over our debts and ran us with a Commission. These were my bedtime stories." His father was a hotel doorman, his mother worked in a haberdashery. "So you realize there is the official history and then there are the stories."

For all the folklore and mythology about the fish and fishery, Fitzgerald's view of the true nature of the soul of modern Newfoundland – that is, post-Confederation Newfoundland – is that it lies in its mineral wealth, or rather in the mining of it. "It was during the 1940s our world changed forever. We had the largest military bases in the world [during the Second World War] and the largest iron-ore mines in North America. Our world wasn't about fish any more; Confederation was about resources. That's what colonies are for. Take the iron ore out of Newfoundland, ship it down the St. Lawrence, and the Iron Ore Company of Canada in their towers in Montreal decide Newfoundland will get five per cent of whatever 'the company' decides the profits are. The economic lifelines of the past fifty years have been the iron-ore minerals, and the plethora of commissions studying everything about Newfoundland and the alphabet soup of government projects and programs are trying to make up for the fundamental inequities built into the structure of the Confederation. When you use your hinterlands for resources and people to the benefit of the centre, that's what you get: a colony. That will continue as long as people are willing to tolerate it."

In January 1999 a new national survey showed that 43 per cent of Canadians in every region felt that the NAFTA was doing the country more harm than good, with only 28 per cent agreeing it was helpful and 29 per cent unsure. For good measure, Canadians also complained about the secretiveness surrounding the negotiations for a Multilateral Agreement on Investment (popularly known as "NAFTA on steroids") and the government's willingness to put the country's sovereignty over health, education, culture, and the environment on the table.[50] When the idea of a union with the American dollar was bruited about, the young new president of the Canadian Labour Congress, Ken Georgetti, speaking for many thousands of workers, made the obvious point that, even in a free-trade age, there were still radical differences between Canadian and American *societies*, for all the harmonization of their economies. Our wealth remains more equitably distributed, thanks to stronger social benefits and a much stronger trade-union movement (one in three workers are in unions, double the American rate), with wages rising exactly in line with increased productivity. "The key point is," Georgetti wrote, "that having our own dollar has given Canadian workers, and Canadian society as a whole, some protection from free-trade-driven integration with the harsh U.S. social model."[51]

Was it in defiance or despair that a Canadian fisherman, during the Canada–U.S. "salmon wars" of 1997, set the Stars and Stripes on fire on the docks of Prince Rupert? Unlike Georgetti, many talk of the "inevitability" of Canada's social and cultural convergence with the United States, given the ineluctable integration of our economies and the increasing invisibility of the border between us. Some talk of the "forces" of assimilation now beyond our governments' control, so that, even if we were blessed with a political class that stood on guard as the very embodiment of our collective desire to live together with integrity, we would still not be able to resist the magnetic pull of the United States and its money. But that is just it: we learned from George Grant that "dominant classes get the kind of government they want,"[52] and so we see our politicians stand apart from the public will, servicing instead corporate need for borderless enterprise in the client states of empire.

THE DIGNITY OF LABOUR

Predicting short-term developments in the employment market is a mug's game, as anyone who has made a point of clipping daily newspapers for labour reports over a period of time can tell you: one month it's a "golden future," the next it's all about "precariousness," and always from the same official databases. For their part, my interviewees reported an entire range of expectations: both the bitterness of the unemployed in the diminishing fishery, and the optimism of the brand new high-school graduate, rescued from the dole; both the canniness of the volunteer who is plotting a strategic resumé, and the downsized corporate employee who sees his chance in the non-governmental sector; the disappointed management trainee who turns in hope, if not belief, to the unionized service sector, and the industrial worker who saves himself from terminal boredom by dreaming of a life as a writer. None believed there was no good work to be done, none was bereft of imagination in seeing him- or herself doing it, but not all had the greater courage of their convictions to commit themselves to it no matter what it paid them. On the other hand, even those who were making a comfortable living had no illusions that this would be their job for life. Yet they almost all seemed remarkably hopeful, in spite of the gloomy prognosticators, as though the long stretch of time ahead of them might still toss up the possibility of getting everything they wanted.

Unfortunately, there is much to be alarmed about in the long-term developments in employment, both in Canada and internationally. Inexorably, irreversibly, Canadian society may be evolving into two new solitudes, the employed and the unemployed, or what writer Richard Gwyn identified back in 1996 as two "economic nations" within the bosom of the Canadian state.[53] Blame this first on technology: far from being the creative source of countless new, as-yet-unheard-of job categories, the digitized technology of the post-industrial era has in fact eliminated jobs by the hundreds – especially the repetitive, drudge tasks of the factory assembly line and the secretarial pool. In such a contracting environment, labour becomes *downwardly* mobile and deskilled as more and more of the jobs remaining are part-time and contractual with workers providing for their own training and professional development. In Quebec alone it is predicted that by 2017 the "atypical" job will have superseded full-time work.[54] This raises the question, around the much-touted solution of job-retraining for the economically redundant worker, "retraining for what?" In the vivid phrase of the *Guardian* journalist Victor Keegan, work is being transformed from the central, dependable fact of our lives in the community to a series of fitfully available jobs "we will have to scavenge after."[55]

More ominous still, these employment patterns have emerged in a time of economic *growth*. For the first time since the Industrial Revolution, new technologies and their attendant productivity have failed to replace the jobs lost to their innovations. In the first six years of the 1990s, the Canadian economy produced fewer than half a million jobs, some of them for the new aristocracy of the well-educated and adaptable high-techies, some for the toilers at the telephones and computer screens of the information industry, but not nearly enough to clear the backlog of the unemployed and those who had even stopped looking for work.[56] It is as though, with the arrival of the workerless factory and the virtual online enterprise, late capitalism will have arrived at a state of perfection in which autonomous human labour, often fractious and dissatisfied, has disappeared altogether from the act of production.

Not everyone is sanguine about such a future. Given a good scare by the much-quoted, everywhere-interrogated American futurist Jeremy Rifkin – who has warned us that, for example, by the middle of the next century, hundreds of millions of workers in the Western industrialized nations will be left permanently unemployed[57] – British Columbia's premier Glen Clark, for one, envisioned in 1996 a kind of barter system with corporate Canada in which access to the province's natural resources is exchanged for companies' expanded payrolls. Less visionary and increasingly popular ideas for the redistribution of existing work include shorter work weeks, spread-around overtime, and work-sharing, although unionized workers may take a dim view of "sharing" hard-won workplace privilege. Richard Gwyn offered the invention of new forms of "public employment (such as a national service agency for the young)" – or is that the *re*invention of the Pearsonian and Trudeauvian Company of Young Canadians and Opportunities for Youth of the sixties and seventies? And many commentators, inspired as well as terrified by Rifkin's theses, muse about the generative possibilities of the "voluntary sector," in which it is no longer a question of redistributing jobs as it is of income, and goods, and services. Shocked into altruism, the managers of our economy would find means to pay us for socially useful, if not profitable, contributions to our communal well-being, such as we perform free at the moment. "There is no limit to potential growth of employment," argues the Canadian Labour Congress's (CLC's) senior economist, Andrew Jackson, "in education, health care, elder care, publicly financed recreation, publicly funded artistic endeavours and so on."[58]

More concretely, Sally Lerner of the University of Waterloo's Faculty of Environmental Studies calls for specific programs to make the post-employed person's self-sufficiency realizable, "actually helping people . . . do more with less, build co-op housing, cut back on consumerism, consider import substitution, start co-operative businesses, or barter goods and services in an informal economy," as well as to realize the potential of new jobs in alternative-transportation and energy-conservation schemes.[59]

At the heart of all such alternatives to unemployment lies the conviction that work is not just an economic activity, it is also social, emotional, and creative activity that shapes our identity and self-esteem, and the esteem and recognition we extend to others, as mutually dependent members of a community. We have believed, in industrial society, that this esteem is guaranteed by the security of the waged job, but in fact it is not the wage but the activity itself – the *self-realization* through work, as socialists have always appreciated – that is most in need of our collective defense. To be without work is not just to be without income, it is to be outside human community, for it is through actual relationships in everyday proximity that we receive the gift of social identity.

Culture   II

MEDIA

> Nexus remembers a time before the hand-held calculator, the
> 100-channel universe and e-mail, but is extremely comfortable
> with the technologies driving change today.
>
> – d-Code prospectus, *Building Bridges:*
> *New Perspectives on the Nexus Generation*

In coining the term "Nexus Generation," Jennifer Welsh and her colleagues
at d-Code have identified a generation born between the early 1960s and
the late 1970s, some seven million Canadians who, they claim, bridge the
two ages of technology popularly known as the Industrial and Information. This means, interestingly, that while the older members of the generation accept and live under today's fiscal realities, they can still remember
the "heyday" of Canada's social programs, and have their own generational
experience of the new norms of environmentalism, multiculturalism, and
sexual equality, not to mention their own media.

The Nexus Generation may be reading *Georgia Straight* as their newspaper of choice, watching reruns of *X-Files* and never missing *This Hour
Has 22 Minutes*, repeatedly renting the videotape of *Trainspotting* or *Star
Wars* and getting a kick out of the television ads of Nike and Volkswagen,
but, like Curtis, the lead character in Don McKellar's CBC television drama
Twitch City, they may also be watching too much television while waiting
for their lives to happen.

Television is the language of the generation and their fluency is a kind
of skill. "It's a bit of a curse," McKellar admitted. "It's this thing stuck in our
heads. I was playing this eighties trivia game recently, and we all knew all

the answers, but we hated the fact that we knew. At the same time, people use that as ammunition against our generation and I don't think it's fair. We have perspective, we are critical. It doesn't make us morons, just because we know that stuff. I think there's a smart side to being media savvy that previous generations don't understand."[1] He might have been thinking of the rant raised on Nexus's behalf by the American media critic Jon Katz, who, when visiting Toronto in 1997, told a *Toronto Star* reporter that his message was simple: "The older generations and their old media have declared cultural war on youth and new media." The elders still gather around the big network newscasts and read the national newspapers as authoritative while their kids subscribe to Internet magazines, set up their own home pages on the World Wide Web, and chatter for hours on self-generated Internet chat groups with correspondents flung around the planet. Katz conceded that much of this communication is intellectually substandard, but that shouldn't obscure the fact that "there's lots of good stuff too: museums, community conferences for older people, book Web sites, online magazines. The culture is filled with indications that this stuff isn't decivilizing us but is enhancing civilization in many ways."[2]

There is a stringent irony in the simultaneous phenomena of, on the one hand, the seemingly infinite subdividing of media audiences among the young – each "downloading" their own digitized programs onto personal computers – and the global concentration of media ownership, on the other. While Nexus zaps onto hotlinks between, say, an artist-run gallery's Web site posted in Winnipeg and an art critic's essay scanned in Amsterdam, Time Warner, Disney, and Bertelsmann, supported by forty or fifty "second-tier conglomerates," including Conrad Black's newspaper empire, have asserted control over most of the emerging global media economy.[3] In Canada, concentration threatens to shut down the wondrous polyphony of opinionated voices spread out among the layers of private and public media at the local, regional, and national levels – from neighbourhood weeklies, gobbled up by newspaper chains, to the CBC, its budget chopped by a third. At the end of 1998, seven corporations were in control of Canada's 106 daily newspapers; three of them, Hollinger Inc., Sun Media, and Thomson, accounted for 72 per cent of daily circulation. When such concentration involves the maximization of profits through the brutal layoff of staff, the aggrandizement of the Business section and erasure of the

Labour beat, and the power to decide not so much what readers will think but what they will think *about*, then we can say that the *public* interest is imperilled.[4]

In the breach between public and private sectoral interest has emerged and flourished a range of alternative news and entertainment weeklies across Canada, some distributed nationally, like the Toronto-published *Exclaim*, some only with local distribution, such as *See*, "Edmonton's alternative urban newsweekly," which has done a market survey and knows that the median age of its readers is thirty-three, evenly divided between men and women, overwhelmingly college educated, and likely to have bought a compact disc in the last year. Targeted at users of restaurants, music stores, cafés, libraries, and banks, *See* bets that its readers are not just consumers of urban goodies but also citizens looking for "commentary not normally found in the dailies." Examples have been coverage of city by-laws affecting the working conditions of prostitutes, a billboard project criticizing consumer culture, and class-action suits against the government of Alberta.[5] In Regina, the *Prairie Dog*, with its roots in community-based social activism and with an avowed agenda to pummel Conrad Black's interests in the *other* Regina newspaper, the *Leader-Post*, performs a tricky balancing act between political journalism to the left of the NDP establishment and service journalism that keeps its readers up to date with the club scene and accepts beer and cigarette ads, to the consternation of the social activists. The point, as its self-composed, workaholic editor, Mitch Diamantopoulos, keeps saying, is to survive. A dead virtuous paper is still a dead paper.

Montreal's *Vice*, a monthly with an attitude of severe censure of the "boomer" generation, which it characterizes as the "corny, backward, knee-jerk, holier-than-thou intelligentsia," was founded by three well-educated young men who could find neither jobs nor a bank loan, but who found more than enough off-the-wall advertisers to carry a publication that specializes in "spectacularly risqué" streetwear ads and outrageously incorrect editorial content.[6] The April 1998 issue, for example, featured a "*Vice* guide to French Canadians," which breezily discussed "frogs" and "sex": "Wow, can these people bang a gong."

The oft-told anecdote of Halifax's *The Coast* – that its founding editors, Kyle Shaw and Christine Oreskovich, wanted it to be the east coast's *Village Voice* – belies its more modest achievement as the purveyor of the news that

Hollinger Inc. no longer sees fit to print. Tucked into the masthead in tiny type is a wealth of information about its procedures. "*The Coast* is a newsweekly reporting on Halifax's cultural, artistic, and political life. *The Coast*'s goal is to be provocative, entertaining and truthful. . . . Coast Publishing takes absolutely no responsibility for the Hamilton, Ontario, girl who was suspended from St. Agnes school because she didn't do her homework. . . . And if you ask to be put on a cover, you won't be. The staff and management of *The Coast* neither advocate nor encourage the use of any product or service advertised herein for illegal purposes."

When I interviewed Shaw in *The Coast*'s "snazzy new" offices (according to *Maclean's* magazine), I asked straight off what it was about the *Village Voice* that he wanted *The Coast* to be. "The first," he replied. "The first alternative – in our case weekly – newspaper here." But I was puzzled how a New York paper, the creature of journalists in the 1950s, could be an inspiration. "The *Voice*," Shaw explained, in the first of repeated evocations of that hallowed journal, "was the first to say 'let's disregard the mainstream media and let's be a weekly newspaper that speaks to a community.'"

Like all "alternatives" ever since, the *Village Voice* runs pages and pages of entertainment and community-service listings, and such listings are the heart of *The Coast*, "the reason why people pick it up week after week after week," said Shaw. "We had one club call recently to say that whenever the manager doesn't have his act together enough to get their listing to us in time for deadline, they have people calling, wondering if they've gone out of business."

As for the large community of Haligonians, Shaw is proud to point out that the weekly *Coast*, for all its budgetary limitations, still covers stories before the *Chronicle Herald* and *The Daily News* get to them, and provides reporting that is more in-depth. Stories about citizens' hostility to the proposed amalgamation of Halifax, Dartmouth, Bedford, and Sackville into a so-called SuperCity, about the glib business boosterism of the "Halifax: Positively Magnetic" campaign, about Mi'kmaq Heritage Month, about a Cuban agricultural co-op. One of *The Coast*'s writers, a young woman active in a "socially minded NGO," was the only journalist in Nova Scotia to have travelled to the monastery of Nova Nada during the monks' dispute with JD Irving Ltd.'s logging operations. "That's just what the *Herald* should have been doing."

As with so many other full-time journalists of the alternative press, Shaw, his co-editor, Oreskovich, and their four partners met while working on King's College's student newspaper when they were all journalism students. There is a simple continuity between student and community-service journalism, in Shaw's mind: working at *The Coast*, "you keep up a studenty sense of activism or unrealistic expectation about what a paper can do and what the market can bear. You can take risks. You don't come from a background of having to appease advertisers or even imagining doing it. People have fit it in around their school schedules, there are all-nighters, and a radical bonding thing." If you want just to get a job and have a career and financial stability, go write for the big dailies. If you want to change the world, welcome to *The Coast*. But you shouldn't have any illusions about Halifax. While still a student, Shaw noticed that the noisiest people at student rallies were "from away" and that there is a "Maritime stoicism" about the possibility of change. "But there is only so much you can do to 'make the revolution' as a mere newspaper," I offered. "What people hope their newspaper is doing is paying attention, not letting the wool be pulled over our eyes, being one step ahead of City Hall." Shaw looked a bit doleful: "We don't have enough of a reputation for doing that, and maybe it's the budget or still being small, but the *Village Voice* . . . they're dangerous."

Nevertheless, Shaw has high hopes for the future of his paper. ("His" in a more limited sense, now that he and his partners have entered a partnership with Catherine Salisbury, publisher of the alternative Montreal *Mirror*, thanks to which they now have a sales manager and a payroll for their burned-out volunteers, and themselves.) Halifax is becoming a younger city, attracting professionals "from away" who are working in the entertainment, film, and high-tech industries. He hopes *The Coast* will be their paper, as they integrate into their new city and tune in on the voice that best represents their new citizenship.

Andrea Curtis, editor of Toronto-based *This Magazine* the summer of 1998, has no quarrel with boomers, or at least not that group of them that raised the flag of cultural nationalism in the 1970s and, in independent journalism, normalized Canadian content. "And now," I put it to her in an interview in the scrubbed-brick offices of the magazine, which was in its thirty-second year of continuous publication, "since the point has been won, you can just get on with being journalists covering the here-and-now, which happens to be Canada?" She agreed: "We do have that to thank you for, there's no question."

"That" is an entire political culture which incubates a publication like *This Magazine*. It may no longer be the radical education movement that inspired *This Magazine Is About Schools*, as it was originally called, at the end of the 1960s, or the broader New Left, culturally nationalist movement of the 1970s that segued into the neo-con 1980s and sustained the publication as simply *This Magazine*. But, as a read of the magazine's end-of-year newsletter in 1998 makes plain, the 1990s version, under the invigorated management of a generation of leftist journalists who have graduated from the university newspaper struggles of the late 1980s, the magazine is still solidly implanted in a milieu of diverse activism. Among its board members are Sam Gindin, assistant to the president of the Canadian Auto Workers Union; Rachel Giese, features editor at *Xtra!*, a lesbian and gay biweekly; Mark Kingwell, associate professor of philosophy at the University of Toronto; and Jesse Hirsh, a "network analyst." *This* presented a dramatic reading of a Depression-era play, *Eight Men Speak*, shut down on its opening night in 1933 for its agitprop treatment of the story of the embattled Communist Party of Canada. *This* held a benefit party timed with its cover story about the legal campaign of the Friends of the Lubicon against paper giant Daishowa. *This* published stories ahead of the mainstream media: the national emergency of homelessness, the "bust" that is Ontario's Workfare, the "outrage" of the so-called APEC inquiry into police brutality against student protestors at UBC. *This* is also a notable publisher of short fiction and poems, and was proud to announce its three National Magazine Awards, a Journey Prize nomination, and two *Utne Reader* Alternative Press Award nominations. Not at all bad for a little magazine (circulation 4,000) that was cut off from Ontario Arts Council funding in 1999 because its brand of cultural journalism fell outside arts funding criteria.

Like other alternative publications, *This Magazine* has attracted readers and writers who not only care about the craft of writing, about fairness and accuracy, but also hope these "make a dent in the monolith of information fed to people every day, thinking it might actually contribute to making life better for people," as Curtis wrote in a disarmingly optimistic editorial at the beginning of 1999. Unmoved by socialism's putative collapse in the rubble of the Berlin Wall in 1989, Curtis remains steadfast in her hope for alternatives to the "hegemony of capital": social and political "free zones" in Canada as well as internationally that contest the Brave New World of Filipino women gluing on the soles of big white sneakers in the sweatshops of Nike Inc.

Curtis would soon be stepping down as editor to write full-time and there was a whiff of nostalgic retrospective in her remarks about "vision." I had been pursuing the subject of community and said I was doubtful that the plugged-in generation, surfing the Internet, was acting out a form of "global citizenship," as has been claimed. "Far from being involved in a fantastic range of interests," I continued, "we can see that they go only to those places where they feel 'comfortable,' join chat groups of shared interest where they never have to hear views or receive news from another mentality, never have to feel a sense of allegiance to something other than a group that sounds just like themselves."

"Yeah, it's frightening," agreed Curtis. "What *This* is doing about it is telling the story of an era – telling the stories, looking beneath the rhetoric, questioning it, but also *prescribing* . . . and this is the hardest part. I worry about it all the time. The vision."

An earlier editor (1993–95) of *This Magazine*, Naomi Klein took "the vision" to her columns in the *Toronto Star*, where she wrote in high dudgeon and with a mordant humour, like a globe-trotting conscience of the Left. Klein started out as editor of the University of Toronto's student newspaper, the *Varsity*. She had entered student journalism already radicalized by the mass murder in 1989 of women students at Montreal's École Polytechnique, but by the time she left she felt that a lot of her colleagues were crazy. "We had gone from having almost no awareness to being terrified of saying the wrong thing," she remembered. "There was this enormous rage on campus and we [journalists] tried to stay one step ahead of it by out-radicalizing the next person and calling somebody else a sexist or a racist or a homophobe or whatever. . . . If I wrote a memoir of my university years it would just be called *Grievance*."

But eventually Klein had had enough of the campus radicals. "You know what?" she said to herself. "I am not going to let the world be run by moronic idiots," and she and her *Varsity* colleagues decided to "stand up to" some of the hard-core bullies of political correctness, and say to them, "Look, read our paper. We live our politics. It's about what you write, it's not about how perfect you are and it's not about trashing somebody across the room."

In retrospect, however, Klein is now embarrassed by what they, as journalists, did *not* deal with at the time. There they were, present at a portentous moment of history, the "key years" of globalization and economic disparities between developed and developing worlds, and the targets of the university papers were getting smaller and smaller. Elsewhere, in other contexts, this kind of holier-than-thou political rage has been called the politics of despair, I intervened, thinking of the sloughs of despond into which my generation of feminists had sunk in the 1980s, when it became clear that our program to smash the capitalist patriarchy had failed to bring down Thatcher, Mulroney, and Reagan, and some activists took despairing aim at pornography instead. Klein remembered that when she got to *This Magazine*, the Left political community was in "incredible depression," and feeling defeated ("How did David Frum get so powerful?"). When somebody suggested that *This* have a re-launch party, Klein counter-proposed a wake.

When Klein was hired as editor of *This Magazine* by a board that still represented the old guard of the sixties Left, she saw that "they were keeping the magazine alive on life support," and, when they ran four covers in a row about the Meech Lake constitutional amendment controversy, that "they were bored even with themselves." But waiting in the wings was virtually an entire cadre of keen young journalists – from the *Varsity*, *Excaliber, McGill Daily* – seasoned by their time in the trenches of Canadian University Press (CUP), out in a lean job market (there was a hiring freeze at the dailies), and looking for a forum for their issues. They were grateful for the tradition and continuity of a magazine like *This*, but it felt like their parents' magazine and they wanted journalism "in real time," their time. They wanted to drop the "boring" politics of economic nationalism and introduce what Klein called "poppy" issues around pop culture. The Left needed to understand there *was* politics in the everyday concerns of identity, sexuality, music, clothes. Except for the ever-energetic Mel Watkins, professor of political economy, the old board resigned to make room for the new. Some subscribers cancelled in protest, but a large number of young readers sent in their cheques. A subscriber since the early 1970s, I have a vivid recollection of those first issues produced under the new regime: sassy-looking, confidently assertive in stance, and almost aggressively cheeky in the "spin" put on issues from lipstick lesbianism to fast-food wage slavery to New Right financial webs. I remember feeling immensely cheered.

Klein left *This Magazine* to write for the huge readership of the *Toronto Star*, where, when I interviewed her, she was carrying on her journalism-in-real-time. No longer intimidated by the overwhelming topic of global economics but in fact repoliticized by it, she was letting fly at the sweatshops of the developing world, the kow-towing to the repressive governments in APEC (Asia Pacific Economic Co-operation), and the Multilateral Agreement on Investment, and looking for signs of resistance, whether in the East Timor Action Network (notorious for its protests during the Canadian visit of Indonesia's then-president Suharto in 1997), a global teach-in at Berkeley, California, about the impact of a single world marketplace, or, closer to home, University of Toronto Students for a Corporate-Free Campus. It seemed that even the professors were now aroused. Shortly before we met she had spoken at a conference on the topic of her new book, *No Logo*, about the youthful politics of culture jamming and ad busting. "After my speech, three professors, including some famous ones, told me they had headed to the bathrooms and defaced the ads."

> There is one voice that has belonged to us for generations. There is one voice that belongs to us all. That voice is CBC.
> – CBC Radio ad, spoken breathily by gritty male voice, 1998

While some adventurous, techno-literate young Canadians go cruising around cyberspace in search of "community," others have found it while listening to the old-fashioned radio, mainly to its alternative programming from university and community stations, but also to the CBC. They take seriously the difference between public and commercial radio, which may be defined as "an example of how the concept of 'communication' has evolved into the concept of 'media' and through this, communities are defined as types of consumers."[7] The CBC, *the* public broadcaster across Canada since its creation in 1932, has from its inception been symbolically charged with the responsibility of "cultural uplift."[8] In 1997, a group of former CBC presidents, protesting the federal government's unrelenting attack on the broadcaster's parliamentary allocation, vehemently reminded the Canadian public that this "most important" of our cultural institutions had been launched on a mission, "essential to the existence of a distinct country on the northern half of the continent," all those generations ago: "All of us have a need to be part of a web of community roots, drawing on our heritage and feeding our common aspirations and dreams."[9] More to the point, all of us have a need to not be Americans. One of the CBC's earliest lobbyists for public funding, Graham Spry, famously challenged parliamentarians to choose between the "State or the United States," while one of its most recent presidents, Perrin Beatty, girding his loins for the legal battle with American media interests in an era of free trade, reminded the public that "every second of American commercial programming [on CBC television] takes us further from the reason we exist."[10]

As an avid listener to CBC Radio, I was an immediate fan of the Saturday afternoon AM pop culture show *Definitely Not the Opera* (DNTO), and sought out a producer while in Winnipeg, where the program originates. Producer/technician Chris Boyce and I talked in the basement cafeteria of the CBC building, having made a tour of the production facilities upstairs, where it was impressed upon me that the shape of the show is an outcome of its production process. Boyce called it "breaking down the boundaries," technically and conceptually.

Cross-skilling is the order of the day: the "segregated universe" of the technician who just rolls tape, the host who just talks, the managers who just manage, has been demolished – and, in the same way that the offices of DNTO's staff are open to the to-and-fro of traffic, so the production process, which Boyce calls "co-operative," is open to the sharing and exchange of tasks and inputs. The results of such a process are impressive – a staff of five or six is able to produce a high-production four-hour show every week – but it also calls upon the team to trust each other enough as collaborators not to feel anxious about losing "ownership" of individual ideas.

Over its block of prime time Saturday-afternoon programming, DNTO throws enough variety of material and approach at the listener that grandparents are known to listen with their grandchildren and, if you don't like the segment of in-your-face opinionated movie reviews, just wait a minute and you can have a special documentary about the lonely, frantic Canuck in Los Angeles trying to break into the "biz," or a feature by Ross Porter, "borrowed" from his late-night FM jazz gig, on Canadian songwriters. I told Boyce that I will stop driving my car, or switch over from the Metropolitan Opera's *Rigoletto*, or suddenly decide to do stretching exercises just to hear Cathy Bond's video column, but Boyce guaranteed me that "there are an equal number of people who can't stand her and would die for her to be off the show as soon as possible. Same with Rex Murphy. [That geezer! What's he doing here?] Half the country thinks he's amazing, the other half think he is full of crap. To me that's what makes interesting radio."

For all the gee-whiz factor of the new broadcasting technology, Canadian *content* is at the heart of DNTO's procedures. Boyce, like the rest of his twenty-something cohorts, is fully at ease with the relaxed boundary between American and Canadian pop culture. Anti-Americanism is not on, but neither is making a fetish of all things American. "That was one of the first things we wanted to do," Boyce explained about the show's concept, "for it to be Canadian, because so much of the pop culture we consume in Canada is American, and so much of what is reflected back is American, but there is so much great Canadian stuff out there that is just not getting exposed. So right off the bat we decided we weren't going to spend all of our time analyzing American pop culture. Not to say we don't pay attention to it, but first and foremost we are a Canadian show." This is not a strain, Boyce emphasized. The producers surround themselves with Canadian pop culture, "soaking it in," not even necessarily noticing it is Canadian, just that it's entertaining, intriguing, well-done, but speaking to them and to their audience in a manner that American culture does not, with specific Canadian references, points of view, tones. Boyce called it "people's culture," Canadians looking at their pop world – independent music production, DJ subcultures, new television programs, trends in food and fashion, comedy, hot new "alternative" bestsellers – as though it were the most natural thing in the world to be Canadian and cool.

Boyce is a true believer, not just in CanCon but in the CBC. He once worked as a producer of a wrestling show on commercial television, but cannot be lured back to the private sector, at least not in radio production. "I just don't think there is any – or very little – interesting radio being made beyond the CBC. It's a fascinating, exciting medium to be working in, especially in a city like Winnipeg that has no community or college radio. Especially where someone will *pay* me to make ideas."

While Boyce keeps his faith with the public broadcaster, will it keep faith with him? Since the most recent cutbacks, the television schedule has dropped U.S. imports, and new Canadian drama and comedy have been added, but three foreign bureaus have been threatened with closure, and new labour contracts leave open the ominous possibility of further staff lay-offs in order to finance upgraded pay scales. The next generation of radio heads may well tune into Internet broadcasting such as the Virtually Canadian Broadcast Network Inc., which delivered its first online audio feed in 1997 and, a year and a half later, had 40,000 listeners who needed nothing more than a PC, a 28.8-kilobytes-per-second modem, and free Real Audio software.[11]

AT HOME IN CYBERSPACE

http://www.spankmag.com/taggings/tagwall.html
If you have just added a tagging, please reload to view your addition.

Why are all you people so incredibaly lame. Young people like you justify teenage suicide. I don't want you worthless little shits running the world. angry old man

DEATH TO THE WHITE RACE!!!! BLACK YOUTH RISE UP AND KILL YOUR OPPRESSOR!!!!

Hey all you fellow christians! What's up. I love the Lord and all of you! Have a good summer. P.S. Class of '99 is the closed you'll ever get to 100! Heather, Illinois

What's up? I'm new to this, so I don't know what I'm doing. All you guys out there . . . I'm a brunett and athletic and a cheerleadeer! Peace out! A.k.a. Melissa

– Random Taggings, *Spank!* e-zine, n.d.

In Calgary, Stephen Cassady and his business partner, Robin Thompson, co-edit and co-publish an e-zine (electronic magazine) on the Internet called *Spank!* When my research assistant looked for it, using Yahoo search engine and typing in "Spank, Calgary," up popped an impressive list of pornographic magazines. "Yep," nodded Thompson and Cassady together when I told them this over clanking cutlery in a diner below *Spank!*'s offices. "We've had parents worry that 'spank' has a certain sexual connotation, and they offered alternatives, like 'spunk.' Huh." The anecdote is a tidy instance of the generation gap that drives the editors' ambitions. "The usage of the word 'spank' has changed dramatically for each group," Thompson elucidated. "For our demographic, 'spank' is fresh, in motion, exciting." As in "spanking new."

In the actual world, Thompson and Cassady live and work out of one of the vintage brick blocks that punctuate the urban Prairie landscape like grim survivors of a redevelopment furore. It has been much repainted, and the long staircase to the second floor creaks hideously; inside Thompson's flat a hedgehog shares cozy living space with the paraphernalia of electronic publishing. We retreated to the diner, where the onion soup proved inedible. Thompson, a no-nonsense former American, sent it back, with the complaint it was the "worst onion soup I've ever had." Waitress: "Can you be a little more specific?"

At home, like their readers, with the ubiquity of the new media, with interactivity, instant data processing, and electronic formats, Cassady and Thompson were clearly excited by the innovative possibilities of the new publishing technologies. The boundary between reader and writer is blurred in an interesting way when *Spank!*'s readers send in their own editorial copy for a "Write for *Spank!*" page, are invited to add their own "reviews" of movies and music, to "spout off" about gun control, and to fill out the Writer's Guidelines and "tell us what is interesting about your neck of the woods." The fact that *Spank!* pays them a cent a word also blurs the distinction between professional and amateur writer. This does not bother Cassady and Thompson. Quite the contrary. They were thinking not just in terms of finding readers on the Net, but also assisting them in "building community." Cassady meant the Net surfers who visit *Spank!* on a daily basis, sending in material from Alaska, Ireland, and Singapore, as well as from Calgary, spilling out their fears and hopes in chat groups.

Thompson expressed a high regard for these under-28s: "I think this is the most literate and thinking generation in history." When I objected to such a bold statement about a generation that can't always find itself on a map, she countered that this was a red herring. "The kids can tell you more about what's happening in the world, not because they're paying attention, but because they are processing information." I wondered then how a generation that isn't "paying attention" can also be lured into "community," a word that used to mean taking responsibility for interaction with the daily lives of people who lived next door or in the neighbourhood, actual, not virtual. According to Cassady, this is still true: "Everybody's looking for community – in gangs, schools, churches, clubs. The new media create a new sense of community." And Thompson explained that there is a "computer community" in just this sense – a "caring" about who you're communicating with, a "worrying" about their troubles, an agreement that "jerks and racists can be forced out."

But Cassady and Thompson also mean community as a generational experience, as though social bonding takes place among the under-28s by sheer dint of being able to process and react to information more quickly than any previous generation in human history, a kind of shared "ethnicity," if you will, with its own language, codes of behaviour, and collective memory – not to mention spelling.

> I HATE MALLS!!!! dammit! Why the hell do those idiotic stores they have only cator to the sickenly thin?!!! i tried to get a freaking bathing suit today and couldnt fit my ass into any of them. . . . only my little buhlimic (and I'm being literal, she is buhlimic) friend was able to find anything . . . hrm . . . really really healthy standards nyah? . . . id shop somewhere else but since i live in the middle of no where there aren't any cool goth/punk shops to get duds in!! Dammit! Girl Named Sandoz, Homepage: http://www.angelfire.com/oh/squirll
> –Posted on *Spank!*'s "Random Taggings" guestbook
> by a reader who could, of course, be anywhere.

Thompson, in her thirties, is part of a generation that goes back as far as the first generation of Macintosh computers in the schools, while Cassady, still in his twenties, is nevertheless an adept of the print world, having managed and edited a creative-writing magazine and freelanced as a typesetter and layout designer. He surprised me when he claimed that the Internet is "still a print medium, concerned with legibility and comprehension" and the Web "just another way of communicating," for I had blithely assumed that anyone who conceived of the computer screen as an "interface" with people would have long foregone the more leisurely communing with the printed page. (Just as editor Kyle Shaw and the staff of Halifax's *The Coast* alternative weekly neither read online publications nor have any interest in posting the paper on the Web.) Cassady is in fact a ferocious reader of magazines such as *Wired*, *Forbes*, and *Mondo 2000*, none Canadian, and is a *Globe and Mail* junkie ("I'll go without other papers in order to read it"), while Thompson, who hates the *Globe and Mail* and stopped reading *Maclean's* a long time ago, is a fan of the *Sunday New York Times*, *Miami Herald*, *People*, and *Time*. Cassady had stopped watching television and was getting all he needed in life from the *Globe* and CBC Radio, which he claimed to listen to non-stop. "TV sucks," he said, making a sucking sound through his lips. "Oh, look, there goes my brain!" Thompson demurred; the night before, she said, she had watched a fascinating show about caterpillars.

If Cassady's and Thompson's enthusiasm about their readers is not misplaced, then coming on-stream is a "highly motivated, excited group of young people that sees change happening, whether it's new political parties or changes in the social fabric or in technology," who have overcome the miasma of hopelessness that has reputedly dogged Generation X just ahead of them. Media guerrilla theorist Douglas Rushkoff seems to agree. Writing of the pre-electronic phenomenon of the "zine," the low-circulation, do-it-yourself, ephemeral print publications spawned by the advent of the inexpensive photocopier (and which have "morphed" into the computer-produced variant), Rushkoff claimed that the zines "present alternative realities to the ones that mainstream media foist on [readers] the rest of the day. Zine readers do not see themselves as ostriches hiding from reality; they are independent thinkers, disconnecting from the particularly mind-numbing mainstream media deluge that has replaced reality."[12]

Broken Pencil, edited by Hal Niedzviecki in Toronto, is a journal that regularly reviews current Canadian zines and can be picked up in hard copy at the newsstand or online on the Net. The zines may be fly-by-night, photocopied at midnight at the corner copy shop, smudged and curled, fat or thin, and aimed at denizens of urban micro-cultures that will have transmuted into yet another variant of neighbourhood sleaze by the time you've heard of them, but Niedzviecki takes zines very seriously indeed. Individually, he says, they may not amount to much, but collectively "they are amazingly pervasive documents that insist on the sanctity of a life where independent creation is still possible in a society, a country, a world that might have it otherwise."[13] He finds something admirable in them all: the way the writers of *Radio Free Elvis*, for example, "subvert nostalgia and narrative" simply by telling the truth about the familiar (a break-up, a sleep-over); or the very cool *Brink*, which "validates every citizen's right to their own pet theories" (about the Spice Girls, say); or the forum provided by *Let It Be Known: Experiences of Women Activists*, "truncheon by truncheon" paragraphs that tell political stories – students arrested in Guelph! – sure to be ignored or misconstructed by the mainstream press. There are comics and collages, scribbles, sketches, and photos, and spare, or rambling, or even dubious or offensive prose. It doesn't matter that the particular one you're reading stinks – it's enough for Niedzviecki that he knows that out there is someone else whose life is going to be saved when it falls into her or his hands.

> Seeking 12 slightly warped souls, ready to cast off the shackles of the 20th century and chart a course together into the next millennium. . . . We promise four months of sheer exhilaration, punctuated by dark moments of intense self-doubt, even terror. We will issue no maps or guide posts, just state of the art tools for survival . . . to crack the code of the digital frontier. . . . (Misfits and adventurers only, please.)
> – From a promotional postcard of the MediaLinx H@bitat program, Canadian Film Centre

For someone of my generation, Canadian animation meant the artistes at the National Film Board like Norman McLaren who won international awards for painstaking cartoon artistry on film. The NFB was still the mother of all non-commercial animation when, in 1974, it released the world's first fully computer-animated short. Since those halcyon days of artistic licence, the NFB has been grievously wounded by unrelenting government cuts to its budget. Not that the twenty-somethings graduating in waves out of the computer-animation schools of Canada, notably Sheridan College in Toronto, called the most famous in the world,[14] would notice. They are snapped up by animation studios around the world, where they vanish into the half-lit world of digital imaging and 3-D graphics, there to toil on the latest versions of software, developed, as it happens, by Canadians. The ghost of Norman McLaren must be hovering in the vicinity, for "Alias, Softimage and Side Effects – today's big three high-end computer animation packages – built their temples on the foundations laid by the National Film Board."[15] But by 1997, Canada's two top companies in the 3-D software market were American owned; Microsoft had bought out Softimage, and Silicon Graphics had bought out Alias. Side Effects was still hanging out the maple leaf, however, and Vancouver-based Main Frame was still the only company in the world successfully producing long-form 3-D animated shows for television.[16] Later in 1997, Montreal was successful in bagging the Reichmann family's billion-dollar Technodome project, which will comprise two million square feet and include an enormous entertainment centre, movie studios, 3-D cinemas, and, improbably, a rain forest. Clearly, the big business of animation has surpassed to an astonishing degree what one journalist called the "genial" filmmakers of the National Film Board[17] and effectively marginalized it and the CBC and Radio-Canada in the rush to develop a purely commercial industry. As a result, "films have improved on the purely technical plane but at the cost of content," lamented Marco de Blois, of the Cinémathèque Québécoise. "We are in the midst of a new generation of animators which idolizes hardware but which has nothing to say."[18]

The troops at MediaLinx H@bitat don't see themselves that way. It is in the hurly-burly of commerce, techno-entertainment, and digitized razzle-dazzle that director Ana Serrano bets her generation of Canadian computer artists and technicians will find their opportunity. Before joining H@bitat – a media training facility with the Canadian Film Centre – in 1997, Serrano had done research at the consulting firm of media specialist Dan Tapscott on the impact of emerging technologies on business and enterprise, and had developed a "digital knowledge management tool-kit" CD-ROM. While at McGill University she had studied English and hung with the anglophone literary crowd in Montreal. So she is multiply literate, and seemingly at complete ease in the warrenlike facilities chockablock with digital gadgetry that are housed in suburban Toronto, with the Film Centre, on what had once been the rural estate of Timothy Eaton.

Where the Film Centre, founded by film director Norman Jewison, has been training directors, producers, and writers for film and television, H@bitat, with major funding from Bell Canada, is the training ground for digital technologies in the new media, developing writers, programmers, designers, artists, and filmmakers for the new content of a "digital network infrastructure," whether CD-ROM servers, Internet, or private networks. Participants – who've been between twenty-three and forty-five years old and have included the president of the Ontario Architects' Association, HarperCollins' creative director, and a musician or two – make their way through four training "modules": Leadership Development ("looking at ways of solving a particular problem in a non-traditional way"), Business and Financial Management, Technology ("we try to demystify the computer"), and Storytelling ("we have to start figuring out what are the potential story models for this medium"). "How did you find teachers for this?" I wondered. "Begged, borrowed and stole," said Serrano. "Our teaching methodology is that H@bitat is not a teaching but a learning space. So it's more of an iterative process." "Iterative?" "Meaning, that we go over the same things over and over again, and so our points of view may change. We believe in creative tension." This is not training people for *jobs*; the H@bitat graduates are going to be what headhunters call "smart people," smart because they can solve design problems, not because they know how to use thirteen software applications.

Was I in the presence of a techno-evangelist (a term, along with "digerati," "cyberist," and "computerjungen," I had come across in literature cross-examining the hyperboles of the new technicians)? Was Serrano a representative of that cyberspace community that American culture critic Mark Slouka says is convinced that "there's nothing 'real' out there. Reality is just a habit. A way of thinking. It's all just information"?[19] Yes and no. Serrano is a true believer in the "democratizing character" of the new media, in its "accessibility," compared to the old media of television networks and film studios, which have control over the programming that the public consumes. "With a $1,500 computer, $2,000 worth of software and maybe $30 a month for Internet access, you can produce your own Web site and showcase your ideas. There's a potential for hundreds of thousands of people to see it."

On the other hand, Serrano is a techno-*realist*, who rejects the "extremely libertarian" views of the trans-national elite of thinkers interested only in the simulating genius of the technology – the way it erodes boundaries between the real and virtual, the animate and inanimate, the unitary and multiple self.[20] Serrano is more taken with its communicating capacity. The technology is a mere tool, she argued, through which a communications medium is made possible. "I think there are certain narratives that are important and that we have to tell each other; I just don't buy the idea of hypertext linking here and there on the screen as being somehow good enough or even more interesting than the story of jealousy or love or whatever." Sven Birkerts's *The Gutenberg Elegies* is one of her favourite books,—— and it was Birkerts who wrote that, after immersing himself in the hypertextual world of infinite choice (click *here* if you want another ending!), he had retreated to the enclosure of his books, more than happy to be "dominated" by an author and taken "in unsuspected directions under the guidance of some singular sensibility."[21] Empowerment by linearity! Turn the page to find the ending.

The actual world, or what Serrano calls physical community, is where the communication she is so enlivened by takes place. She remembers a younger, less corporatized environment of the new media when "we shared ideas with each other, we had an association that was incredibly active, and I felt like I was part of an artists' commune as opposed to a corporate entity. Then very quickly after that the multinational corporations got interested, the first Web browser came out, and it seemed that with a click of your mouse you were on the Web and the quality of community changed." The digerati are aroused by this, convinced that public institutions and the life that went on in them (main street, union hall, artists' commune) are so emptied of collectivity that we will have no choice, writes Sherry Turkle of MIT, but to "retribalize" at the computer interface, "liv[ing] in each other's brains, as voices, images, words on screens. We are multiple personalities and we include each other."[22]

Serrano, too, is impressed by the way in which people in Internet communication try to recreate relatedness, "that same sense of wanting to help each other out even if just sharing information," and wasn't half so concerned as I about the quality of that translation from the physical world, which I worried like a dog with a bone: "How do you take responsibility for and accountability to each other in these virtual communities?" Even the redoubtable Sherry Turkle, who can write fearlessly of a "zeitgeist of decentered and emergent mind, of multiple subjectivities and postmodern selves" in the computer culture, asks, "Is it really sensible to suggest that the way to revitalize community is to sit alone in our rooms, typing at our networked computers and filling our lives with virtual friends?"[23]

Serrano would angle the question differently: Can we see the virtual community as the incubator of a new social organization in which people attempt the reconstruction of their deteriorating actual community? "Because relationships in physical space have become strained and even severed, because we haven't shared a common physical ground since the impacts of industrialization [which broke up the old communal life], people are turning to cyberspace to find them," she claimed, although somewhat tentatively. With the help of databases, videotext, audio pictures, and linkages, computer software can help fulfill a need for social organization that will mature in cyberspace and then move back into the physical. Something like that. And then Serrano told me the story of the online book club called Guess This Book which, after a period of conferencing with each other electronically, decided to meet in a pub. "A real pub?" I asked, suspecting a trap. "Yeah, in the San Francisco area," she confirmed. "I think that's what is going to happen once these virtual communities start to mature." I still don't get it: her generation needs to go through cyberspace in order to meet for a beer?

> If we see ourselves as victims of our culture, then every extension of technology will be seen as further victimization of us by this "other," by this dominator. If we first see ourselves as creative beings doing something, and that our lives are connected to some personal or even global purpose of moving towards greater states of awareness and creativity, then every piece of technology is an opportunity to extend our consciousness outward.
>
> – Douglas Rushkoff, interviewed for
> the television documentary *Cyber Space*

Ironically enough, it was precisely a variety of "victimizations" that drove a number of my interviewees straight into cyberspace from real space. At different stages of her life, Erin Clarke, whose Web-based art project is called *Queer Nerd*, had felt an outcast from the communities around her. It was "real life" that she was alienated from, she says, so fragmented are current social structures, so disconnected are most people from the deep integrity of their inner selves. Ever hopeful of politics, I asked her whether these fragmented parts of the self can meet together in a cohesive social project? She replied, "I think that the only place all our parts can be at home is within the self." But to get back "home" she trusts only the safe anonymity of the Internet: "There is no pre-judgement on who your online correspondent is, there is only toneless text." In chat groups for survivors of sexual abuse or for parents of children with cancer or for recovering alcoholics, the Internet functions as a virtual shelter for people who want ongoing support and healing that is beyond real shelters to provide.

Emma Smith, vice-president of WebPool, told me that women her age, about thirty, have a historical memory through their mothers of the time when "women didn't used to be people" and will readily call themselves feminists, unlike younger women, who "assume it's their right to be equal and they won't run into any problem, everything's just going to be fine." Smith knows very well everything is not just fine: from her first co-ed experience with the computer she watched how men sought to control the mouse all the time. It was, she remembers, a computer-age version of the old battle for the TV remote. When she was hired in 1996 to teach the multimedia production course at the Vancouver Film School, there were no women on staff. Those who were there were producing "very, very cool stuff" on CD-ROMs and exciting Web sites with thought-provoking content, while the guys were focussed obsessively on bandwidth, Bill Gates and Microsoft, browser battles, and telephone companies – that completely male-dominated realm of the *relay* of content, she said. "In ten years' time everything we see is going to be coming at us from computers, so if women aren't out there, working on the things we're going to see, the content, it's just going to be a re-run of what happened to television, created and run by men."

Convinced that women really would write software differently – once broadcasting was interactive and "not just one guy talking to a whole bunch of people, that male authority thing" – and that in the future we're just as likely to be wanting a war report from a little girl who is living it as from a CNN reporter, Smith decided to do something to help it happen. It began with the "total blast" of a first meeting of women at a local café.

"These were women and students who worked at high-tech companies who I knew vaguely. We just had the best time! Pulled a bunch of tables together and drank coffee for five hours, telling stories and venting about women working in IT, about getting hold of the mouse and keeping it, about doing a magazine together and, yes, for sure we should keep meeting, and what about guest speakers, and blah blah blah. Even if nothing had come of it I would still look back on that afternoon as one of the finest lunches I've had."

But much did come of it. They founded Wired Woman Society, a technology group by and for women dedicated to help women's entry into new media work, not to be confused with what Smith calls "traditional" women's groups, "all giving and nurturing. You should get something back: volunteer for Wired Woman, learn to build a Web site, do a training session. This goes straight onto your resumé."

They still have a hoot when they get together. It's so very different from the typical technology workshop, where men are present, are dominant, up at the front of the room asking all the questions, women at the back afraid to open their mouths in case theirs is a stupid question. "We had a woman at one of our workshops who put up her hand to ask what a modem is, and she got an answer. The next day someone gave her her old modem. Women have begged for a course on how to buy a computer, because they just can't stand going into the computer shops staffed with eighteen-year-old men. It's like buying a car all over again."

Wired Woman is a hybrid community, doing its work both on the Internet through its Web pages and magazine, but also getting together in real life. The purely virtual community – whatever that would be – is a rather scary idea for Smith. "Are we going to have people all in their little pods, who never actually learn to communicate?" She doesn't think so. But we will have people with computers *and* a social life, people who have walked away from the television set to go to their computer to log on to e-mail or chat groups, who use it to read, research their school projects, check information. The Internet allows for "different discourses," Smith said. It is neither apocalyptically the flight from community nor the only postmodern organization of it. It's more like a switchboard (if I understand her), coordinating and relaying a multiplicity of speech. You could also just go down the street to the neighbourhood café.

Canada's own techno-evangelist, Don Tapscott, believes the so-called N-Geners (Net Generation), from babies to those in their early twenties who have grown up with the sheer ordinariness of computers, are "wired" for social and working relationships that depend on collaboration not hierarchy, innovation not obedience, economic justice – the view that "I should share in the wealth that I create" – for themselves at least, and skepticism about corporate interest.[24] This was the audience, sixteen- to twenty-five-year-olds, for the television magazine *Utopia Cafe*, an "imaginary place" where political and social conditions are "perfect," perfection is defined as "diversity," and the "emerging global society" is an invitation to be curious if not critical about how everything fits into everything else. It was also explicitly a Canadian place. As its producer, Stephen Hall, put it on the *Utopia Cafe*'s Web pages, "We provide our audience with a valuable perspective. They see themselves reflected in a global context. That's today's reality. Canada is where we live – it's our home – but our international neighbours are closer than ever, brought into our homes through the Internet and instant television."[25] Among viewers' feedback came a fan's notes from Mexico where "the TV company only plays comic shows like *Home Improvement*, the *Fresh Prince* and *Beverly Hills 90210*," a sociology professor's request to use segments of *Utopia Cafe* in her course on the sociology of the body, and the relief of a guy called Alex that finally there was Canadian television product that "doesn't look like *Anne of Green Gables* or *The Fifth Estate*."

So now that the generation is wired for cyberspace, what do they do when they get there? Some try to make money, like the three young doctors in Edmonton, all self-taught programmers, who develop computer games, turning a hobby – an addiction – into a forty-three-person company, BioWare Corp. In 1998 they won a six-figure advance from Interplay Productions of Irvine, California, for a game called *Shattered Steel* – in which the player battles insectlike aggressors – that was subsequently translated into six languages and had more than half its units sold outside

Canada.²⁶ In Calgary, three companies under youthful management produce security encryption software, Internet filtering and rating systems, and CD-ROMs. Twenty-seven-year-old Jim Morrison of Jaws Technologies became fascinated with coding and encryption at the age of seven, when, assigned the task of completing all his homework on the computer (his Banff elementary school was part of a testing ground for computer-based pedagogy), he became severely annoyed when "access denied" popped up on his screen. He figured out how to get around it.²⁷

Others want to be electronic artists. In Winnipeg, art history student Kevin Matthews, an aficionado of the Internet, where he belongs to "communities" of e-mail mailing lists of Tom Waits fans, anticipates a system of artists' networks, artists who are influenced by each other not because they live nearby to each other and drop in on each other's studios but who are connected by the Net. "You can make videos and send them over the Internet. Real paintings and drawings don't move around fast enough, they hang around in the same place for weeks at a time, but you can photograph and digitize them and send them down the Net."

Since 1982, InterAccess, the electronic media arts centre in Toronto, has been acting as a community network and resource base for artists who want to work at the intersection of culture and technology. The centre provides equipment and training (they emphasize the importance of "sharing" of knowledge and expertise) for digital works in the areas of audio, photography, the Web, virtual reality, and robotics. It offers hands-on production facilities – a computer studio with all kinds of software, a scanner, digitizing tablet, and a CD-ROM burner – and a "dynamic and globally accessible Web site" that supports online conferencing and discussion forums, interactive artworks, electronic art catalogues and a "knowledge resources section." It seems all too good to be true (for a writer who drudges at word processing and e-mail), but it *is* true.

Nothing could be further from the alarmed view that the next generation is condemned to geekdom in the basements of the nation or to slick cybercapitalism, morphing into cyborgs with computer chips where their root and heart chakras should be. Witness Web Networks, "Canada's online home for over 3,000 non-profits, charities, unions and activists" (as it says on the bottom of an e-mail from Web Networks), who jockey for space in direct competition with commercial interests equally interested in "community" (the Microsoft community, the telco community, the Future Shop community . . .). "You – like us – are deeply committed to the principles of social responsibility, ecology and economic justice embedded in our mission. Many support us because we are non-profit. Others support us because we are one of the only unionized services in this area." So read their 1999 New Year's message to their subscribers, that constituency of people wanting a cost-effective way to build a dynamic Web site, wanting to get their message across onto the Internet for public use, wanting to be a self-reliant community-based enterprise or action "serving change," and believing that the Internet could hook them up with fellow travellers around the world.

The explicitly politically engaged also roam the Net, like the environmental justice protesters who occupied Shell UK's London headquarters and, despite the electricity and phone lines having been cut off, connected a small digital camera to a palm-top computer and a mobile phone and within minutes were broadcasting their protest live on the Internet and e-mailing it to the press. Thanks to the Internet (and earlier the fax machine: remember the students of Tiananmen Square?), activists have been internationalizing right alongside the corporations. In the 1980s, Cree opponents of the Great Whale power project in northern Quebec used the Web to network with New York environmentalists. The Zapatista National Liberation Army in Mexico, right after the promulgation of the NAFTA in 1994, combined low-intensity armed conflict with high-intensity media activism, mainly a rapid production of press releases on the Internet (which, unlike the fax machine, allows for instant response), bypassing media conglomerates to broadcast the voices of the rebels of Chiapas who might otherwise have been "managed" right off the screen. *I am Alvaro. I am indigenous, I am a soldier, I took up arms against being forgotten. Look. Listen. Something is happening in the closing of the 20th century that is forcing us to die in order to have a voice, to be seen, to live.*[28] Anti-APEC protesters in Vancouver, site of APEC's summit in 1997, told me that the Net "was an unfiltered means for us to get our message out." Foreign Affairs minister Lloyd Axworthy reportedly found himself apologizing to Indonesia's foreign minister for the "Wanted" posters – for crimes against humanity committed by Indonesian president Suharto – posted on the East Timor Alert Network Web site, a site that also regularly received messages of support and encouragement from around the world. Preparing for the 1999 protests in Seattle against the World Trade Organization, activists had networked internationally for months by e-mail and zine.

None of the young people I talked with about the Internet approached the utopian intoxication of a Frances Cairncross, author of *The Death of Distance*, for whom the new technologies are revolutionary in their potential for, among other things, "profitless prosperity." We will buy and sell on the Net, but without fat profit margins, Cairncross predicts; we will become ever more literate as we hone our communication skills; knowledge will be diffused horizontally; electorates will become better informed; and so on, right through to mutual understanding, tolerance, and world-wide peace. "In all these ways, the communications revolution is profoundly democratic and liberating, levelling the imbalance between large and small, rich and poor."[29] This is an inspiring, if bloated, vision, but it suffers from the mechanistic assumption that the riggings of technology can be the agent of our salvation.

As long as both e-commerce buccaneers and anti-imperialist guerrilla media warriors find the Internet useful for their purposes, then one must suppose that the technology is neutral, neither more nor less democratically programmed than the user is democratically motivated. Many webs of power, corporate and institutional and political, enmesh the user at her screen, however strong and true may be her desire for tolerance and peace and justice, and she cannot even begin to disengage herself from them if she is not first a *citizen* implicated in a web of living, breathing social relations. As Rushkoff claimed above, everything proceeds from how we see ourselves and what we see ourselves doing, long before we log onto the Net.

THE ARTS

Is not precisely some impulse to move . . . the primordial intent of everything that really belongs to culture? After all, that is precisely the mark of every work of culture: it sets our drowsy souls and our lazy hearts moving! And can we separate the awakening human soul from what it always is – an awakening human community?

– Vaclav Havel, cited in "Awakening the Creative and Imaginative Spirit: A Brief to the World Commission on Culture and Development," Canadian Conference of the Arts, 1995

In Russell Smith's 1998 novel, *Noise*, the much beleaguered protagonist, James, making a sort of living in the slim pickings of freelance arts journalism in Toronto, is on his way to Burlington to interview Ludwig Boben, iconic author of such classic Canadiana as *Cold Season*. To his travelling mate, the bodacious but unlettered photographer Nicola, James explains Boben's importance. It has little to do with literary excellence any more and everything to do with the fact that, as a younger writer, Boben and others of his generation became famous, right here in Canada, for writing about . . . Canada! "As long as," James hastens to add, "it was about small towns and nature." He then summarizes the production of that golden era of consciously Canadian art in the late 1960s and 1970s in a hilariously half-bewildered, half-deferential resumé ("I had to study them in school") of Marian Engel's *Bear* and Margaret Atwood's *Surfacing*. But Nicola still wants to know if James thinks Boben is "any good." Suddenly shrilly derisive, James replies that "good" is not the point. Boben is now part of "our history" and it doesn't matter if James or anyone else admires his work:

There's one Boben book . . . which ends with the line, 'a story which Canadians must never tire of telling.' What do you think of that line? A story which Canadians must never tire of telling."

She shrugged. "I have no idea."

"I'll tell you what you think of it. You don't give a shit. I'll tell you what I think of it. I don't give a shit either. But I also think it's the worst bullshit I've ever heard. I think," he said, accelerating, "that Ludwig Boben is a fucking asshole."[30]

It's an odd moment, for later, in an editorial session with the American magazine editor who is buying his piece about Boben, James learns that, to spare the easily bored American reader of *Glitter*, "we cut all the stuff about Canada." James is *hurt*. That's his *country* that New York wants to edit out. He protests feebly.

> "Frankly," said Maya with a slight briskness, "our readers aren't interested in Canada. And we are most concerned with pleasing our readers. Right, James?"
> James whistled.
> "Right, James?" This time the sharp edge was in the open.
> He sighed. "Right, Maya. . . ." [31]

I suppose we should not be surprised that, for a generation that has come to political consciousness during the international regime of the free-marketeers and government downsizers, the notion of the particular preciousness of made-in-Canada art, sustained impressively by publicly funded subsidy, has been vulnerable to the scoffers, nay-sayers and enemies of culture's argument for the public good. Yet, as with the fictional James, so with many contemporary young artists: the troubling double-mindedness of the lure of a global audience and the foundational appeal to their loyalty as Canadian citizens. To whom do they belong? Some would immediately say, to no one but themselves. But most others I talked with and read about were deeply engaged by this challenge to their relationship as artists to the lives of the people around them. That these are specifically *Canadian* lives also mattered.

That there are artists who, even in their mere twenties, are conscious of their Canadian specificity in a McLuhanesque world of dissolving national identities (at least at the political level) is a kind of miracle, given the unprecedented penetration by American cultural influence of the very environment in which they have chosen to work: Canadian head space. In 1997, 70 per cent of the music on Canadian radio stations was foreign, 60 per cent of English-language television programming was foreign, 70 per cent of the Canadian book market consisted of imported books, and 95 per cent of feature films in Canadian cinemas was foreign, I assume including Quebec's screens, of which 85 per cent are given over to American films.

"So the notion of a level playing field in culture," writes *Globe and Mail* columnist Jeffrey Simpson, "is almost completely bogus." [32] And there is this other miracle: that within that risible space left relatively unmolested by the transnationals, Canadian artists have actually made an impression.

When the *Globe and Mail* surveyed the terrain of "cultural nationalism," its policies and goals and achievements, in late 1998, arguably the most impressive scorecard had been registered in the field of music and radio. Thanks to thirty years' worth of quotas of Canadian recordings imposed on airtime, "nobody but a small group of free-market policy wonks . . . is agitating to get rid of CanCon," so positive have been the results: a strong domestic music industry and a mob of fans coast to coast.[33] In 1996, when the Tragically Hip, with their opening band the Rheostatics, hit the road on "the biggest tour by a Canadian band in the history of music in Canada," no one was more acutely aware than the Rheostatics' rhythm guitarist and vocalist, David Bidini, that his generation of pop musicians had coasted to fame and fortune compared to the grim progress of the pre-quota generation across the near-oblivious landscape of the Canadian consciousness. "In those days," Bidini wrote, in a memoir of the 1996 tour, "it was much harder to communicate with your own country than with the States."[34]

These days, the fan at a sold-out concert of the Tragically Hip sports a T-shirt that reads: Canada Kicks Ass. When a 1999 tour brought the Hip to Edmonton, a local journalist took fashion notes of the audience, who were as casually dressed as the band: "Several guys were spotted in hockey jerseys – a fashion *faux pas* at many concerts where people feel they have to wear their hockey duds just because they're in an arena. But hockey is Canadian and so are the Hip." An excited seventeen-year-old girl is interviewed: "I've been counting down the days for a month now. When someone asks you what is Canadian, you say hockey and the Tragically Hip. The Hip are just so Canadian."[35] The overt patriotism of the youthful Hip fans took the *Edmonton Journal* reporter by surprise: they "roared with madness" in a kind of mystical transport of recognition as lead singer Gord Downie "warbled through" the Hip's paeans to hockey.

While there continues to be a "tension," as the Canadian Conference of the Arts noted in 1995, between the economics of scarcity and public support of the arts, the *basis* of such support, laid down by the 1951 Report of the Royal Commission on National Development in the Arts, Letters and Sciences, remains the bedrock of the collective decision taken by the

Canadian people's governments to defend the right of Canadians to choose their own culture. This choice has since been expanded to include production by cultural and social minorities such as First Nations and women, so that Catherine Crowston, for example, senior curator at the Edmonton Art Gallery, acknowledges that, when she first came through the "system" as a young curator in the late 1980s, "that wave [of cultural inclusion] was cresting" and she "rode it out," right to the EAG. "I know we shouldn't say that the feminist struggle is over or that racism is over, but I think we've made such remarkable strides within a short period of time and, for me, the cultural institutions have been at the forefront of that."

Like Catherine Crowston, Toronto multimedia artist Camille Turner was a beneficiary of the "diversity struggles" that had overtaken the art schools and galleries at the time she was a student at the Ontario College of Art in the early 1990s. The "hubbub" had originated with five young female faculty members whose contracts had not been renewed, and from that "everything got tossed into the mix," including curriculum content. For Turner, the important discovery was "women's mythology."

At the time we talked, in the summer of 1998, she was mulling over an installation, featuring interactive video, under the working title "Suit of Armour." The idea had emerged from considering the absence of an "iconic" representation of black Canadian female identity, so Turner was going to create one. "The Canadian part is important to define," she said, curled up among the artist's paraphernalia that cluttered her small living room. "My parents always talked about 'going back home.' We had left Jamaica when I was nine, and it was weird to travel there and realize I wasn't a Jamaican. But I'd grown up believing I wasn't Canadian either, because of the way I had been treated as 'other.'"

When she came to work on "Suit of Armour," Turner's idea began with using representations of her sixteen-year-old niece, Andrea, as "an identity, an innocence, being formed" as a black Canadian woman without, however, "racializing" her. "What defines 'Canadian'?" Turner asked rhetorically. "The moose!" And she thought of photographing Andrea wearing different Canadian outfits such as the moose, the Mountie, and "Aunt Jemima with Canadian flags all over her." So far, she's videotaped a series of moving mouths and was planning a photo shoot with Andrea after which the photo lab would produce not prints but a photo CD, digital information direct to compact disc, and then to computer, where she will animate them. She was thinking of images from teen magazines – "almost every single image in them is of a white woman" – and of sequences of Andrea in fairy-tale costumes suggested by her own favourite girlhood reading, inhabiting the identities of Snow White, Cinderella, Sleeping Beauty, and the girl who kissed the Frog Prince. "Snow White will stand in front of a mirror. 'Mirror, mirror, on the wall, who's the fairest of all?' And Andrea, this young black girl, answers, 'I am.'"

REBUILDING CULTURAL COMMUNITY

> The question as to whether it is good that Canada should dis-appear must be left unsettled. If the best social order is the uni-versal and homogeneous state, then the disappearance of Canada can be understood as a step toward that order. If the universal and homogeneous state would be a tyranny, then the disappearance of even this indigenous culture can be seen as the removal of a minor barrier on the road to that tyranny. As the central issue is left undecided, the propriety of lamenting must also be left unsettled.
>
> – George Grant, *Lament for a Nation: The Defeat of Canadian Nationalism*

Substitute "market" for "state," and the central issue is still left undecided: whether the universal and homogeneous market is the best possible social order for the twenty-first century, and whether we should lament, or celebrate, Canada's continued existence as an "indigenous culture" in spite of it.

Among the welter of descriptions of the current global cultural transformation, the French writer and former diplomat Jean-Marie Guehenno's succinct summation is one of the starkest. No less than the future of democracy is at stake, he warns us, "for the transition from the former institutional age [when policies were framed within the competence of the nation state] to the coming imperial age dominated by large supranational organizations and loyalties, involves a massive shift from public to private purposes and the disintegration of the common good and to irreconcilable selfish interests."[36]

In 1998 and '99, Canadians had their own bitter experience of this sub-version of what they supposed to be their cultural sovereignty and, with it, their pursuit of the common Canadian good. In a series of disputes, counter-disputes, legislations, and settlements over, of all things, the fate of separate editions of American magazines printed for the Canadian market and containing Canadian advertising, known as split-run, citizens wrung their hands and tore their hair in an agony of impotence. While the regulatory arm of international trade agreements, the World Trade Organization (WTO), struck down made-in-Canada policies and compelled revisions of legislation generated by Ottawa to comply with the rules of the open market between the United States and Canada, the Americans for their part threatened retaliation for non-compliance. The United States is only one of 134 member nations of the WTO, but its displeasure – whether over European protection for small-scale banana producers in the Caribbean, which Washington argued was "damaging" to its economy, or for Canadian protection of Canadian-owned and Canadian-produced magazines – is awesome to behold. Aggressively pursued, American grievances tabled at the international level have the effect of shoving WTO discipline right into the heart of countries' internal affairs. Or what *used* to be understood as the affairs of a nation's interest under the custody of national governments.

In a retrospectively poignant last hurrah as a Canadian sovereignist, international trade minister Sergio Marchi (before he was shuffled to the WTO as Canada's ambassador) wondered out loud whether, even in the global marketplace, there was not the chance or means to demarcate "no-go zones" where the rules of the marketplace could be suspended in the name of a higher good: a unique Canadian culture. The context was the embattled progress of Bill C-55, which sought to protect the market for Canadian magazines by penalizing advertisers in American split-run magazines and keeping the $350-million advertising pie in Canadian hands. "Are you telling me," he addressed the United States through the hapless interviewer from the *Ottawa Citizen*, his indignation steaming off the page, "that the great United States of America . . . even if you are absolutely indifferent to our national interest and everyone else is supposed to genuflect to yours, are you telling me that you also need this little piece [controlling magazines in Canada] as well? . . . And we'll say tough, because you ain't getting it."[37]

But they did get it. In spite of culture and heritage minister Sheila Copps' passionate oration before the Canadian Association of Business Economics that "carving out room for Canadian voices . . . requires the exercise of national will,"[38] and her steely assurances in the House of Commons that "we retain the sovereign right to pass laws to support our culture," in the end the Americans won their point. Without even going to the WTO for final adjudication, without challenging the legally dubious American position, the Canadian government buckled under the U.S. threat of a trade war (to compensate their losses in magazine advertising revenue in Canada) and amended Bill C-55 to grant concessions to American magazines and the Canadian advertisers who buy advertising space in them. The concessions had wiped out the line-in-the-sand drawn with such impressive bellicosity by Marchi and Copps. "It's not about culture any more," Maclean Hunter Publishing CEO, Brian Segal, mused. "This deal says we're now in an environment based on pure business principles."[39]

Pure business always did have its hands on our cultural goods, of course, especially American hands, for, as Canadian culture critics have pointed out, Americans notoriously cannot tell the difference between marketing a widget and nurturing a work of art. Even the then-editor of the pro-free-trade *Globe and Mail*, William Thorsell, noted the "odd provincialism" of wealthy and powerful interests (read: American) that chafe at impositions on their market wheeling-and-dealing by cultural protectionists and so completely miss the point that Canadians, as a "national community," are protecting something of value, culture, from corporate commerce.[40] The Americans see only that they are being thwarted from maximizing the profits of their media and entertainment *industries*.

> The arts of a community reflect their common civil and historical experience and the community's desire to live with intelligence and harmony. The specific processes and artifacts of artistic creation give expression to our multiplicity and individuality, our flexibility and courage, and to our solidarity with fundamental human rights and the quest for social and political justice.
>
> – Charter 94, The Writers' Union of Canada

The Charter, adopted at the 1994 annual general meeting of the Writers' Union, may have claimed too much for the arts but, on the other hand, much was at stake. As writers saw it, having survived the perils of sovereignty referenda in Quebec and identity politics in English Canada, Canadians pulled back, preferring to live together in a federation cobbled together by the broadly shared habits of a public culture rather than drift apart on separate ice floes of tiny, perfect unanimities. But governments were retreating from their commitments to that public culture, and citizens wanted to know where was "home," that encompassing frame of belonging in which they could express themselves in language that did not (yet) belong to the marketplace. Well, there were the arts – from impassioned amateur to *haute* – in their splendid diversity the ever-ready metaphor for free civic consciousness. American political scientist Benjamin Barber told an Edmonton audience in 1997 that it is precisely art as a *unifier* of distinctive multicultural peoples that "allows Canada to exist as a nation."[41]

This is not an obvious truth. More pessimistic critics of our neo-capitalist moment have argued that, while ordinary people have been deprived of their unifying myths (think: Workers of the world, unite! Sisterhood is powerful! Beauty is truth, truth beauty!), big business is unified as never before. The myth of the inevitable and irresistible discipline of global capitalism is *the* universalizing myth of our time, driving the rest of us to huddle for sanctuary in a variety of fractured and localized identities.

But, as Barber suggested, identity politics is not the only strategy of minority cultures. Granted, they want in the first place to live free of discrimination and racism *in their difference*, then want to be recognized as part of the multi-stranded diversity of Canadian society, then want to participate, without erasing their difference, in public life. The Canadian debate about identity politics, not always civil, did ascribe renewed value to the authority of the personal, an important stance for many artists facing death by homogenization. But neither did artists want to remain fixed in the personal, as though, having looked into the face of the Medusa of assimilation, they remained frozen by the trauma. *Communicability* has remained the first obligation of the arts, or, as defined by critic Michel Theriault, "the capacity to effectively move personal experience into the arena of the collective. . . . How can one experience penetrate another? How can it remain ours while being significant to others?" The re-valorized personal, he suggests, has revealed new and unsuspected abilities "to exchange experience" along the continuum from us to others.[42]

This democratic task has had also to embrace new and dissident minority cultures, which risk being neutralized by an indifferent marketplace (or, worse, absorbed by it as *outré* flavour-of-the-month) or killed in mutual suicide pacts. Jowi Taylor, host of CBC Radio's *Global Village*, joined techno fans at a Toronto club one night in 1997 and shared warm and fuzzy feelings about the anarchist *A* tattooed on a shaved head, the Cocoa Puffs logo on a T-shirt, and the silver stud pierced through a tongue. But he also experienced some serious nausea from the *Zeitgeist*: "In the current postmodern climate of the global economy, the corporate mega-merger and the government-as-business ideology, our ideas about community have become seriously unhinged from local realities."[43]

Regionally based cultural production with its deep sense of geographic placement is sited precisely at the crux of the Canadian identity crisis – in Northrop Frye's famous dictum, not as "Who are we?" but as "Where is here?" And Frye wasn't even dreaming of the radical displacement from "here" that globally transmitted media represent. "This is the key question in our time," wrote Saskatchewan filmmaker Robin Schlaht. "Do we, the people of Saskatchewan, value possessing a culture which is a reflection of our social character, or are we content to have our cultural identity superseded by pre-fab movie and TV product from Toronto and Los Angeles?" The question is rhetorical: Schlaht assumes that he, and they, do want "a dialogue about who we are and what our place is in the world."[44]

But we speak not of our sense of place but of our *dislocation*, not of communities' stability but of their *fluidity*, not of blood ties and inherited identity but of our *migrancy*. Assaulted by a contingency aided and abetted by the amoral machinery of transnational capital,[45] what are the cultural fundamentals we could all agree on? Is there a solidarity that can be unmasked nevertheless? A common language of the arts that binds us together in a shared cultural space?

Jowi Taylor thought he had seen just such a thing in action that night in the club in the neo-tribalism of the fans of "hip-hop culture, techno culture, urban-primitive culture, drum-and-bass, jazz-house, ambient, hard-step, bhangramuffin or jungle culture," which, for all its taxonomical mania, was an unconscious strategy to stay one step ahead of the whiz kids in the ad agencies.

> Dave Foley [of the *Kids in the Hall* TV series] once spoke proudly of the program's utter disregard for anything outside its own obsessive sphere of inspiration: "Some of the greatest events of the past several decades have taken place recently and we're proud to say they have had absolutely no bearing on the show.
> – Cited in *Mondo Canuck: A Canadian Pop Culture Odyssey,*
> Geoff Pevere and Grieg Dymond

Wes Borg, thirty-two-year-old writer, actor and funny man, member of Edmonton's Three Dead Trolls in a Baggie comedy troupe, ecstatic Canadian patriot, was twenty-four years old before he listened to CBC Radio, and he has *never* watched *Hockey Night in Canada*: "I hate hockey. I really hate it. I never had a pair of skates that didn't hurt."

Borg grew up in the Edmonton suburb of Sherwood Park (originally built in the 1950s as a "let's pretend" country acres for the working classes), where he spent his time watching the three television channels, in black and white, that kept him entertained off the hockey rink and out of trouble with the "hard right-wing politics" of his parents. Then one day he flipped to *Monty Python and the Holy Grail* and his life changed forever.

"And I had *never* in my life . . . it was like nothing I had ever experienced in comedy, Bill Cosby, Cheech and Chong. I never saw *Saturday Night Live* when it was good, and when I finally got cable, it sucked, and continues to suck. But *Python*: they all had university degrees, they were extremely literate – philosophers playing soccer – with layers of book-learning. I memorized everything." He was twelve. At fifteen he played for the first time in local Theatre Sports and was hooked on improvisation. It fit his worldview, once he had abandoned Christianity. He works mainly in live theatre and cabaret now and knows enough about the so-called Prairie Gothic tradition in Canadian theatre to be able to make fun of it – "Don't leave me," he bursts out on my cassette tape, "Don't leave me in the prairie wheat, son! . . . But, Poppa, I gotta go to Toronto!" But it was the zany Brits on television who "formed" him.

Borg is precisely the sort of young Canadian I would never have expected to grow up sprouting maple leaves from his considerable thatch of corkscrewed red hair, but there we were in his basement workroom, listening to Rheostatics CDs while he rhapsodized about why the band are his heroes. As a high-school student, none of the music he cared about was Canadian; now he's not really interested if it *isn't*. "It looked to me like everything just got good all of a sudden, stuff worth listening to." The Rheostatics, for example, are Canadian "without looking like a dork; being proudly Canadian, singing about playing hockey and the bush party and the two-four, without being an idiot. When I was growing up all the culture I got was on TV and movies, and the Americans just looked cooler. You'd turn on the CBC and there'd be the *Tommy Hunter Show* and it didn't look very cool.

"Same with Canadian movies. Growing up, my experience was that a Canadian movie was probably crappy. Now, thank God, there's David Cronenburg and Bruce McDonald. . . . I don't think the Americans would get it, nor should they have to. I'm more proud of stuff that doesn't work in the U.S., like Stompin' Tom. You don't want to be popular in the States by being like one of them." I wondered if this was a dissonant note of anti-Americanism that had crept in, a kind of penance Borg was paying for all those youthful years of uncritical consumption of American television, but no, it was, if anything, a back-handed compliment to the Americans. *They* are the giants of pop culture, triumphantly astride the global neighbourhoods, with Cap'n Crunch for brains. *We* are the skinny, runty guys in thick eyeglasses, keeping our mouths shut and plotting a zig-zag getaway from behind the television set.

"What's so funny about being a Canadian?" I asked Borg. "Is it funnier than being an American?" There was a very long pause. "I think Canadian comedy comes out the only way we know how to channel rage: angry but polite. That's what causes comedy. For me, for sure, it's a way to channel anger, a way to funnel and twist the things that piss me off. Americans have so many other avenues of rage." No, you don't want to be like one of them.

Toronto artist Sally McKay plays with the shared language of consumption. She loves toys, the mass-produced kind that line shelves of the big-box toy stores in their awesome multiples: plastic embodiments of cartoon characters, such as Ernie and Bert dolls from *Sesame Street*; or replicas of grown-ups' tools, like Fisher-Price plastic Chatter Telephones with rotary dials on their "forehead." She collected the toys, long after they've been discarded, from garbage cans, friends' children, and second-hand shops. I saw them in meticulous, almost martial, arrangement in the Art Gallery of Ontario and wondered, not only at the unexpectedness of seeing recycled toys in a Temple of Art, but also at my own smiling amusement in looking at them. Eventually, the horde of bushy-browed Ernies and Berts, each with his own almost imperceptible variation of expression, here a button-eye missing, there a tear in the trousers, began to spook me, but I had to admit there was some kind of enchantment at work, even in this parodic field of low-brow entertainment. McKay had anticipated the response: "Obviously, some of the things we get pleasure from are actually not doing us any good," she wrote in a brochure accompanying the exhibit. "And yet the pleasure is real and good and the sharing between people is real and good and communication is always better than nothing." Fair enough. But the art critics had serious language for her goings-on: *intervention* cropped up repeatedly, as in McKay's use of humour, novelty and parody to "intervene in the normal cycle of mass-production, consumption and disuse."[46] *Commodification* was also at issue, as in her "potent demonstration" of the way her generation of artists address "the communality of a commodity culture."[47] And *desire* on top of that, as in the way she reveals "how we function in a culture driven by commodity desire."[48]

When I commented that her installation didn't seem to make any reference to the "natural world" (all those *commodities*, those creatures from television!), she disagreed vigorously. She's an "urban environmental activist," and her motivation, if not her content, comes from incessant thinking about the "screwed-up" state of the planet. "I try to work to change that, but I believe in cities and culture and people." She once used two canine figures, Skippy and Butch, one the so-called real Walt Disney dog with a huge corporation behind it, and the other, a cheap, made-in-China plastic dog, in a snout-to-snout moment of doggy-bonding. "Two kinds of dogness with nothing to do with a real dog. I don't concentrate on the wilderness but on how we create the concept of nature for ourselves within our culture," she said.

This may be the source of the new generation's identity crisis as Canadians – having an almost too-sophisticated relationship with American culture: flexible, strategic, canny, evasive, and above all – a favourite observation by culture analysts – *ironic*, a stance succinctly described by Winnipeg's klezmer musician, Myron Schultz, as "we all want to be something else, Canadians, say, so long as we can still be American." Sometimes it's expressed in the soulful self-examination of artists who wonder if they shouldn't just be done with it and move to the United States, as 67 per cent of the Writers' Guild of Canada membership has done, as *Hard Core Logo*'s screenwriter, Noel Baker, confessed to "plotting" in his diary and which he dramatized in the tragic betrayal of friendship between that film's two main characters: Joe Dick, who wants to keep the punk band *Hard Core Logo* intact in Canada, independent and marginal, and Billy Tallant, charismatic lead guitarist, who wants to take his chances in Seattle's grunge rock scene.[49] Tallant at least had paid his dues on the Canadian road, rain or shine, playing to beery yahoos and driving to the next gig fuelled on bennies, but others have been, in Dave Bidini's words, "kids from North York [who] affected Birmingham accents to be cool, who spoke of achieving glory in the U.S.A. without ever seeing Saskatchewan."[50]

But there are artists who position themselves in relation to a regionally based community, which, in big-city Canada, has typically been interpreted as living "at the margins," out of sight and mind of the metropolises. It was precisely at the grassland "margins" of Saskatchewan that a team of independent filmmakers grouped themselves in the late 1970s as the Saskatchewan Filmpool (their name a deliberate echo of that mainstay of Prairie self-reliance, the wheat pools); a generation later, Filmpool was still committed to making film "which reflects the individual and collective cultural expression of Saskatchewan people," to quote from their 1997 Mandate. When Mark Wihak joined up in 1989, he had a "surreal" vision of the landscape and isolation of his Saskatchewan. In his award-winning *Stories from the Land of Cain*, he speaks of a winter back alley in west-end Regina where he stood as a child and stared into the late-afternoon sunlight and dreamed of walking northward, through Jack pine and birch, out onto the tundra and into the caribou. "That was Canada, wild and wide, and waiting for me, at the end of the alley, in Regina, Saskatchewan." This is the Saskatchewan that grew a socialist movement out of the farms and small towns, the so-called hinterland to the metropolises of Canada that is still a stronghold, said Wihak, of a "community's desire to take care of itself as a whole." Even to evoke the nostalgia for a more perfect collectivist past still has a function, according to Wihak: to remind the rest of us of what we once imperfectly believed, even if the route to the caribou is now blocked by a Wal-Mart store.

Sometimes local, regional, and ethnic or racial communities overlap, as when klezmer musician Myron Schultz could not meaningfully separate out his Jewishness from his boyhood neighbourhood. We had been chatting about multiculturalism and who had benefitted from it, when he mentioned his "gratitude," as a Jew, for an official multiculturalism that had given Winnipeg's Jewish community "a stage for awareness," meaning "a little bit more pride walking down the street into a different neighbourhood and not being afraid that they are going to be laughed at."

His neighbourhood – and that of his father and grandfather over a fifty-year period of running the family business, W. Schultz Furs – is Selkirk Avenue. Myron is in the business himself, sitting at the vice-president's desk, taking orders for sheepskin coats. The neighbourhood is also the wellspring of his art on the klezmer clarinet. "Selkirk Avenue was the heart of Winnipeg's North End. It was a bustling avenue in this city-within-a-city, where Eastern European immigrants, Ukrainians, Poles, and Jews bargained, discussed, bought and sold," to quote the liner notes from the CD, *Crossing Selkirk Avenue*, put together by his klezmer group, Finjan. "Families shopped at Oretzki's Department Store and Henya's Grocery, where one could buy anything from Chanuka menorahs to snow shovels." So, now that the Avenue is a shadow of its former self, the CD is a homage to Schultz's own youth, to the cafés he hung out in and the dry-goods stores he shopped in – if Eaton's didn't have it – and the public school where, he thinks, far from being picked on, he was actually given "extra respect." Even now a walk along the Avenue, keeping smart step with the flamboyant and orotund phrasings of Finjan's shtetl-inspired tunes that pour in from the Walkman, can bring a whiff of garlic and screech of a streetcar back to life. *Finjan*, I learn, is Hebrew for "the *haimish* feeling one gets while sitting around a campfire," or maybe at the delicatessen counter, elbow propped up against the dill-pickle jars.

Schultz was raised in a home that valued classical music, and he studied classical music for years. When the Jewish community got together at a wedding, they danced to rock 'n' roll and David Clayton-Thomas singing "Spinning Wheel"; and then, together with the rest of Middle North

America experimentally swinging its ethnic hips, danced a circle dance to the beat of *Hava Nagila*. In the background he could hear the phantom strains of Broadway musicals and big-band music and a whiff of something Jewish in Gershwin's *Rhapsody in Blue*. Unlike the folk revivalists of the 1960s who were able to go down to the southern United States and find gnarled, gritty blues musicians playing away in the back of beyond in the Mississippi Delta, Schultz had to make do with second-generation Jewish musicians still making a living in New York, and with records and tapes, trusting his own musical instincts to find the treasure amid the dross. And when it finally came time to go before an audience at the 1982 Winnipeg Folk Festival, he was terrified that his family and relatives would feel he was "lowering the standards," playing "devil music," slumming, in other words. But they were thrilled and remain his biggest fans. Schultz had brought them along with him on his route back to the ancestral community of music.

When Pamela Edmonds, thirty-five-year-old curator at Halifax's Multicultural Arts Resource Centre, moved to Halifax from Montreal when she was eleven, she discovered that her parents' black Haligonian roots did not help her much in her own integration. In Montreal, in a French-speaking neighbourhood, she had felt much more part of the life around her than in the white, suburban area of Halifax into which the family now settled, a large distance, socially as well as geographically, from the historically based black communities of East Preston and North Preston in Dartmouth. "There are certain [black] families that have a long history here, and, being from Montreal, I didn't feel like I was part of that community. It's not as simple as 'You're black! Hey, come on in.' It's, 'What is your last name and where are you from?'" To part of black Halifax she was a true "exotic," and this was intensified by her light-coloured skin, which generated a certain amount of skepticism when Edmonds would insist nevertheless that she was black, because that's the way she was raised.

"Both my parents are black, they experienced racism growing up in the 1950s, and that is the way I consider myself."

"You are black," I repeated.

"Plain and simple to me."

"Are you a Nova Scotian black?"

"No. I don't consider myself African Nova Scotian or African Canadian. I consider myself Canadian."

She returned to Montreal to study Fine Arts, and it was while she was studying contemporary Canadian art that she befriended an artist from the West Indies who, like her, was querying the place of non-Europeans in Canadian art production. "So we dug. We looked in Concordia University. Nothing documented. I spent a summer in Halifax, looking in the Nova Scotia College of Art and Design. If you want American, you're laughing, but Canadian? We were hard-pressed to find something. So what we did was start our own association, the Canadian League of Black Artists." They were twelve, mostly in Montreal, a starting point toward a discipline. "People question why we are doing this, why are we separating black artists out from Canadian art, but no one has trouble talking about German and Flemish schools, and that's what we're going after, to see if there are particular issues and styles shared by artists of a similar cultural experience." That shared experience is Canadian as well as black, for it is equally interesting to Edmonds that the blacks of Nova Scotia are not Americans and their artists have a right to the validation of their enquiry as people of this particular place.

Or an artist will think linguistically, like Daniel Cournoyer, artistic director of Edmonton's francophone L'Unithéâtre, for whom the community is the whole of *la francophonie* in western Canada – a perspective with interesting artistic consequences. A predecessor theatre in Edmonton, Popicos, had a long tradition of importing artistic directors from Quebec, but as an Alberta-bred francophone, Cournoyer had another "philosophy": "As long as we keep importing talent and pushing local francophones aside and intimidating them because they haven't mastered the language like a Quebecois, we're holding back our own development."

Having staked their claim within Canadian communities, another problem confronts artists: the *limits* of community within which they work. For Regina visual artist Gary Varro, "community" is both the city itself and the gay culture within it, neither of which has been sufficiently "urban" for him to have had the dialogue and feedback he has craved as a queer artist. In a larger city, he feels, he would have been seen for what he really is, a "soft activist," not particularly "overt," instead of as a community activist (he has programmed a festival of gay film). "Gary!" people say to him. "This is so great, what you're doing for the community!" He's not that comfortable with this "necessary fiction," as he calls it, of a cohesive, like-minded subculture, a "solidarity, unity with a cause" when in fact not all gay people of Regina agree that they are helplessly stripped of rights and marginalized with all the other social minorities.

Sometimes the confining solidarity is regional, as in novelist Lynn Coady's bleak retrospective on growing up in Cape Breton, and her fearsome revision of the misty-eyed, tourist-brochure version of the island. Of her novel, *Strange Heaven*, she told an interviewer, she wanted to "write about the mental landscape of a community where any sense of self-esteem or confidence, particularly that of a young woman, is quickly crushed," which is exactly what happens to the teenaged character of Bridget, undone by her own apathy and the suffocating narrow-mindedness of "home."[51]

"We're American anyway," Tobi Lampard of Saskatchewan Filmpool concluded, with a twenty-five-year-old's matter-of-factness. "If we weren't, we wouldn't be going to their movies, wearing their clothes. I battle this at the same time I soak it up. My concern is to do my art. And whatever it is that I will make, driven by what *I* want to do, will reflect my culture."[52] Spoken as a true postmodernist – her culture will be as she constructs it through a camera lens and not as she finds it at the end of an alleyway.

COPING

> The incapacity of our elites to govern as if the society had a culture is one of the root causes of our divisions and of our often unspoken despair as citizens.
> – John Ralston Saul, *Reflections of a Siamese Twin: Canada at the End of the Twentieth Century*

Wes Borg, jack-of-all-theatre-trades in Edmonton, has paid his dues in front of high-school audiences, doing the skit that made him and his buddies, Three Dead Trolls in a Baggie, famous at the Fringe Festivals – a witty, sometimes twisted, version of the War of 1812, with a pretend Pierre Berton as guide – and the only reason he's doing this is to pay a couple of months' rent, because the school kids are awful, "they were terrible, just fucking sat there with their arms crossed, so into being 'cool' that you have to get the social leaders to laugh. If only the teachers are laughing, you're dead. We cut the Laura Secord scene, we were so pissed off at them."

Between Fringe Festivals, Borg plays in a "post-industrial polkabilly-counterpunk" band, designs Web pages and album covers, and stays up-to-date with the technology by scouting out pawn shops. He once spent an entire winter going barefoot and living in a postal van, so that he could tell a reporter some years later that "poor people have more freedom . . . and poor fathers have way more time with their kids."[53] When he gets a paying gig, such as acting in somebody else's play, he swoons from the very idea of a paycheque, and carries lunch to work in a brown paper bag.

In Regina, artist Gary Varro, having blown all his money in Mexico one winter, took a job at the Mackenzie Art Gallery putting up exhibits and hanging paintings, and lived at home to be able to save something from his paycheques. But he was disappointed in himself: he had ended up where he had started, not a curator or full-time artist at all, but with his "face pressed against the window," broke, and with nothing to show for it. Even so, the day he learned his job at the gallery was going to be made permanent, he quit, "jumping off the cliff" to try to live as an artist. He took freelance curating and graphic design, catered for openings, performed in friends' performance pieces, sat on granting juries, and applied for grants himself. He cashed in his RRSPs. "My credit card is 'maxed out,' and I'm into debt up to here." He was looking for a job.

In August 1998, the organizers of the enormously popular Journées de la culture du Québec held a press conference to announce proudly that, for the second year in a row, very important and prestigious sponsors had been found for the festival: Bell, Hydro-Québec, and the ministry of culture and communications. Everyone took a turn to vent their view that culture is very important in Quebec and how gratifying it was that money had been found to invest in the nine hundred cultural activities that would be unfolding all over the province. "Gosh, nine hundred activities, that's really something," wrote Pierre Salducci, a director of one of the funding recipients, "Des livres et des hommes," imagining that, at a minimum of five people involved in each activity, that would be 4,500 people who "gave of their time, their talent, their energy, to put on shows, organize visits, hold meetings, open studios, dream up exhibits, conduct literary soirées, propose ideas, take up the challenge, etc." Fabulous. There was only one problem: no one at the self-congratulatory press conference bothered to mention that all this activity was "purely voluntary and not one dollar was being dedicated to the artists." The audacity was breathtaking. "Under the pretext of promoting culture in Quebec, the Journées de la culture du Québec amounted to a huge swindle and absolutely shameful human exploitation. . . . In acting this way, the directors . . . reinforce the idea that culture isn't worth spending a cent on, that artists and artisans don't deserve even the smallest piece of the pie, that their work is easy . . . as if one were saying to them: 'Your product isn't worth much, it's not marketable, it doesn't bring in money, so you're not worth much either.'"[54]

Some culture workers self-exploit, as did artistic director Ken Gass of Toronto's Factory Theatre when he decided to work nine months without salary to help his company recover from the beating they and the rest of Toronto's arts community took between 1991 and 1996, when $41.3 million worth of grants was withdrawn by all levels of government.[55] As the mother of invention, impecunity in the theatre has produced shorter seasons, smaller casts, the production values of a fringe festival, and staff who double and triple their tasks. Filmmaker Lynne Stopkewich self-financed her Cannes Festival hit *Kissed* with her credit cards. With province after province, not to mention the federal government, boasting of balanced and even surplus budgets, there has not however been a concomitant move to open the purses to the arts. In the much-vaunted 1999 "Health" budget of finance minister Paul Martin, no new measures were included for culture.

The inspired and diligent building of an earlier generation of cultural activists has been deconstructed in a shockingly short period of time, stripped by funding cutbacks and the accompanying public belief that the arts are a luxury only the social elite and their court jesters, starving artists, can afford.

This is a generation of artists that will be making aesthetic decisions under pressure to be more "mainstream" (that is, profitable) and less dependent on the cultural subsidy, supported by the occasional subsistence grant as a gesture of public recognition that it is better to have artists in Canada than not have them. "It's not enough to just be giving out money," contended Michael Herman, president of the Motion Picture Associations of Canada in an interview, talking about the film sector. "Those who show they have the capacity [to succeed] are the ones who should continue to be able to draw on the money."[56]

Jeff Hirschfield, when I interviewed him in 1998, was a screenwriter for the television series *Lexx*, produced by Salter Street Films of Halifax, legendary creators of *This Hour Has 22 Minutes*. "Successful television shows generate funds for film features without their having to go to government agencies, who become the dramaturges and arbiters of taste, with you dancing like a monkey to make a bureaucrat happy."

He's no fan of prescribed CanCon. "I don't subscribe to that notion at all and never did. I have stories to tell; they're Canadian by virtue that *I* am. I don't have to set them at the grain elevator or at the cabin or struggling in Toronto. I totally reject the notion that my stuff isn't Canadian because I don't 'reference' Canada. If a Canadian writes in it and Canadians act in it and it's born in Canada, it is Canadian."

Hirschfield and Salter Street Films were "putting out" *Lexx: The Series*, which had already earned the sobriquet "*Star Trek*'s evil twin." Eschewing traditional good-and-evil heroics of mainstream science fiction, soaked in sexual innuendo and one hundred to two hundred computerized special-effects shots per show, infected with a loopy humour, in short, "raunchy, racy and outrageous," according to Hirschfield, *Lexx* was initially produced for and partly funded by the American Showtime Network.

Hirschfield's experience of writing *Lexx* for the Americans was quintessentially Canadian, however. It was "answering to the masters, and this gave me a lot more sympathy for bad television," he confessed. "Because you're not the master of your own destiny. We wanted to go more with the nihilism of the nineties and not with the utopianism of the sixties, which tells the story of spreading 'enlightenment' around the galaxies. . . . We wanted 'selfish and chaotic.' The Americans said 'Great, great, we don't want another *Star Trek* – now here's your notes.' And it was all Joseph Campbell and Buddha and . . . please! We wanted to do something different. But they don't do anything 'different' until it's been done and been successful. . . . In the end they had script approval; we'd give them the script weeks in advance and it would come back with ten pages of notes four days before shooting. Twenty-four hours before going to camera: 'We don't like your guest star role, expand it or change it.' "

Salter Street Films found co-producers in Germany, kissed the Americans goodbye, and Hirschfield was a happier and wiser man.

When Coach House Press closed shop in 1996, broad were the lamentations across Canada that a brave adventure in alternative publishing, deliberately disengaged from the imperatives of the globalizing, lean-and-mean market, had been defeated. But in fact it soldiers on in the brave new world of electronic publishing. Founder and poet Victor Coleman wrote a poem about the House's demise – *greed had crept under the skin of the interlopers. . . . these turkeys in suits sold the farm to maintain the system* – that fans could read on the press's new Web site. Welcome to the future of literary publishing in Canada. Readers were invited to order books by paying for the privilege of reading them on their computer screen.

Sam Hiyate, publisher of Gutter Press, has a few tricks of his own up his sleeve. His 1998 catalogue, on newsprint, advertises work by the familiar and unfamiliar in the democracy of small, do-it-yourself publishing. In his Publisher's Note, Hiyate tells us that publishing had become his "calling" (after leaving his work at the literary magazine *Blood + Aphorisms*, still going strong), though at first he "had no idea what I was doing." This charming naïveté is probably an essential job qualification for such a risky enterprise. He did not realize he should have a distributor, but he did find "cool" bookstores who would stock his eclectic production, willing to bet, along with Hiyate, that the public would sooner or later clamour at their doors, "in mad anticipation of our new books and everyone says, 'The canon itself speaks through those crazy Gutter fuckers.'"

If they're lucky, Canadian-authored and published books seeking "young, hip, urban" readers may be marketed at home-entertainment megastores that have had the wit to hire young, hip, and urban buyers, such as Jordan Stewart at Tower Records in Toronto (part of a multinational chain), who, at twenty-four, was given an inventory of ten thousand titles, and customers buying music CDs, to play with, and opened it to small press publishers and distributors. Stewart built sections labelled "Beat Poets" and "Outpost Literature," tracked hard-to-find titles on the Internet, and kept every Canadian title he could. His customers "know some of the most interesting music has been produced by the independents, and they look at books in the same way."[57]

Other publishers are not so lucky with the so-called big-box retail stores. In 1997, eighteen independent bookstores closed their doors in

Quebec, under pressure, according to analysts, of the mega-bookstores, which push bestsellers and how-to books, often at discounted prices. As well as restricting the reading choice of the public, this "bestsellerization" imperils the survival of all literature that is not "popular,"[58] a literature already under pressure from the systematic withdrawal of financial supports for so-called cultural publishing. "Economists call this 'market rationalization,'" says literary publisher Pierre Filion. "Creators call it the assisted suicide of culture."[59]

Other forms of alternative culture face their own difficulties. In spite of the fact that hip-hop music is a worldwide phenomenon – perhaps *the* most popular international genre – its Canadian exponents complain routinely of being ignored by mainstream radio, shunned by major labels, misrepresented by the media as being of interest only to black Canadians, and deserted by fickle audiences who rush after the latest American sensation rather than cultivate their own. Record producer Ivan Berry uses the example of American rapper MC Hammer who "made the ultimate commercial rap, sells eight million records, and the record companies go looking for the next MC Hammer who sounds just like him. And the real hip-hop will never get signed." Yet Canadian hip-hop artists insist on their distinct Canadianness. According to veteran artist Michie Mee, it was precisely her Canadian hip-hop experience that was the basis of her music's "flavour" and distinguished it from the American; and now this unAmericanness was starting to pay off, as "all eyes internationally are focussed on what's going on in Canadian hip-hop,"[60] a claim backed by Toronto alternative-radio DJ Denise Benson. "The cultural influences are different, there is way more of the Islands' [West Indies] influence here – the owner of a record store in Bristol, England, home of a musically influential black community doing reggae, dub, down-tempo stuff, says straight up that Canadian hip-hop is amongst the most requested. So there is clearly an international buzz, way more than there is a Canadian music-industry buzz. The industry is so stupid here."

But the Canadian hip-hop scene is not without its resources. Beat Factory's Ivan Berry told me "there are hundreds of labels, all of them selling about two thousand records. They sell on consignment and keep the pocket money. They get on college radio. These will be the new commercial records, because the commercial is built on this foundation. Lots of import/export vinyl in little shops. A reggae record released in Jamaica can be in Toronto the next day." Beat Factory, the only "urban" label to be distributed by a major, EMI Canada, has had considerable commercial success. "We have excellent relations with MuchMusic, fashion magazines, the newspapers. Urban music is outselling all other forms of music, including country. Our part is to seek, conquer, develop, package, help to sell. We have a staff that markets to the urban culture throughout Canada. We develop it. We record it. We keep it real and spread it to people who understand it. We have two talent scouts who are out at the clubs, and we receive ten to twenty demos a week. When I send out a rap group to tour Canada, we do about thirty-two dates – Yellowknife, Kamloops, Kingston. Talk about stereotypes: when we pulled up to a coffee shop in Kamloops, we saw all these pickup trucks, rifle in the back window, moose on the roof. 'I ain't going in there! *You* go in there!' There were a thousand white kids lined up at the club for the show. I don't know where they come from."

In a strip mall of copy shops and computer firms in the semi-industrial buffer zone of Downsview, Toronto, three ambitious entrepreneurs in their thirties have formed Krescent Records to market local urban music, ahead, far ahead, of the major distributors. The established record companies "don't know where to go into the ghetto, in the grungy areas. They're scared, basically. There is tons of talent," artist-manager Leroy Williams told the *Toronto Star* of their do-it-yourself operation in which, bankrolled by supportive parents, they handpick the artists, write the music, keep the assembly line small, record, mix and master the material in a tiny studio, get it into the hands of sympathetic DJs in the clubs and from there to MuchMusic.[61]

Carly Stasko, who I interviewed hard on the heels of an exuberant free-the-streets festival in Toronto, came to her politics – "I was ready for a community" – through a zine, *Quit Gawking*, with other high-school girls as a self-defense tactic against commercial magazines for teenage girls; and then on her own put out *Uncool*, featuring humorous critiques of media.

"I'd sneak out and use the photocopy machine at Kinko's wherever I could. Copy culture is a big thing now. You should go look at it at twelve at night – it's open twenty-four hours a day – it's all artists, activists, people who are working on issues of poverty, racism, child-care, composing their letters to government, people throwing events. What was once an office tool is now a mass communications tool at the lowest end. You don't need a printing press. It's cheap and simple."

Cheap and simple, cheap and fast, a cultural artifact that can be copied and passed around and tampered with so many times that its authorship becomes erased – such production offers a kind of leverage on the excess of consumption promoted by the franchised output of the Wal-Marts and McDonald's and Sonys that Kevin Matthews, art-history graduate student, associates with the "boring aesthetics" of the modernist suburbia to which so much of his generation was consigned at birth.

One response is video art, reproducible in endless multiples. "Within weeks Madonna ripped off images from underground queer films in L.A. to make her *Justify My Love* video," Matthews said excitedly. "It's seductive, isn't it?" I thought it was theft, but wait. "In one day you can make a video based on something you've seen the day before. The *rapidity* of it. You can make leaflets at the copy shop and distribute them anonymously. You don't know who sees them, they don't know who made them, there's no feedback or critique but it's just so exciting that the work is out there, all over the place." Here today, gone tomorrow: so much for the singular, well-made, built-to-last cultural artifact.

Polaroids; you can even use Polaroids. "Friends of mine," Matthews concluded, "have left Polaroids around as some kind of statement: 'I was here.'"

I was here. The idea of those three words, metaphorically scratched onto fading Kodachrome and abandoned to the urban drift, as though stuffed into a bottle and tossed out to sea, haunted me for a long time – the pathos of the unnamed *I*, of the no-fixed-address of *here*. In fact, I did not believe that this *I* wanted to be unknown to us so much as to drop clues along the public pathway as to where he/she could be found.

Forty Tiny Performances On Your Labour: May 11, Theatre Centre, 1032 Queen St. W. P.W.Y.C. [pay what you can] Forty tiny performers employ forty tiny modes of production to propagate forty tiny opinions about what it is to produce, to labour, to ply, to task, to moil, to toil, to drudge, to slog, to achieve, to hustle, to stint, to strive, to sweat, to scam, to accomplish, to exert,

to struggle, to plug away, to punch-the-clock, to poke the
poodle: to work.
– From the program for *Mayworks Festival of Working People
and the Arts: The Spirit of Resistance*, May 1 – May 15, 1998

There was a sprinkling of grey-haired left-wing stalwarts in the audience, which was to be expected, at an event of Toronto's venerable festival
of the arts on the Left known as Mayworks. In fact, I had expected them to
form the largest part of such an audience: what could be further from the
allures of the wired circuit of the downtown dance clubs than this grungy
"theatre centre" on an insalubrious block of Queen Street West? Inside,
surrounded by black-painted walls and floors, some tables had been set
up café-style with candles, a festive if nostalgic touch of decor in the
Universal Progressive Youth style. For this was indeed their night, the
youthful performers and their claques of family and fans of numerous
ethnicities, acting, miming, parodying, narrating tales of work from their
own lives or those of their friends, and illuminating an astonishing variety
of experiences of exploitation. Waitressing, panhandling, math tutoring,
flamenco dancing, fruit picking, film directing in Karachi, making cappuccinos in the Eaton Centre, singing labour ballads at the union hall,
child-birthing to the accompaniment of a song sung in Anishinabe in a
hair-raising vocalization – and one vicious skit of a young man postering
the likeness of Charlie Manson with a Pepsi logo smack in the middle of
his forehead like a prurient Third Eye. (Even the youngest members of the
audience reacted to Manson's image with recognition. Has their generation recycled his notoriety as celebrity, as Andy Warhol did for mine with
dizzying multiples of Mao?)

This is a way of making or doing politics – of *coping*, if you will, or, to
give the young artists-at-the-barricades of the end of the century their due,
of *resistance* – that is deeply familiar to me, as it comes from a very long tradition of the arts of social engagement in European and New World cultures
and, closer to home, from my own generation's construction of it in politically committed collective theatre and film, underground journalism, and
artist-run spaces. At Mayworks there was still a whiff of the zeal of artists
bent more to social action than aesthetic practice, to an interventionism

from the margins chosen in deliberate defiance of making a living in the corporate markets. Montreal journalist Nathalie Labonté has observed the same will and desire in the "théâtre d'intervention" of groups like Théâtre Parminou, a pioneer of a genre that was once very avant-gardist in its desertion of theatrical space for agitation on picket lines and other public spaces in the everyday life of working people. Now, in a struggle for survival, it searches for a new public in the "workplaces" of commerce with material about health and safety: it may not be revolutionary, one of the actors told Labonté, and it is difficult performing for an unpoliticized public, but it's still "interesting."[62] For Vancouver novelist Larissa Lai, who began as an arts journalist for small, politically-fervent journals and who still wants to make a difference in the world, the chance to write "overtly and baldly" is still enormously attractive: she called that kind of writing "clean."

Perhaps she was referring to agitprop's unambiguous relationship with its public, compared to the complex territory of subconsciousness and artifice shared between fiction writer and reader. The desire for an expression that is not merely intimate and suggestive drives artists at exhibits like *Epilogue*, which I saw at Toronto's A Space Gallery in 1998, whose curators claimed that the emotionally charged, multifaceted installations were testimony to "individual/collective survival in the face of cultural and/or religious oppression and attempted annihilation. The art in this exhibit is not only personal expression; it also belongs to the public realm, where we may examine political issues; the art acts as a catalyst for discussion and education." That sort of language, privileging the socio-historical resonance of a piece of art, I assumed had blown away with the dust of failed political programs of the last twenty years. But here were four women artists – Lillian Allen, Jillian Mcdonald, Stella Meades, and Mia Weinberg – who had succeeded in finding an aesthetically produced equivalent to issues of police violence against the black community, gendered abuse, cruelty to children, and the fragmentary nature of ancestral memory, reminding viewers that there is more than one way to receive political enlightenment.

But I remain perplexed why it is necessary always to claim such work is a "challenge" to the public who are, of course, assumed to be indifferent, or even hostile, to what it has to say. Why assume that these – often banal – "challenges" have not occurred to us already, in our lives as citizens?

Bronwen Trim, who, with her friend Jaffa, had organized a benefit concert in 1995 for an ephemeral movement in Halifax known as Eastcoast Against Racism (EAR), found herself exhausted by the experience and ready to get on with her life and her "own stuff." After the concert, which had attracted mainly white youth, there was one more big meeting, then Jaffa left to work as a cook in a soup kitchen for street youth, "and then the meetings kept getting smaller and smaller, and there was a group of hardcore kids who were about fifteen years old and supportive, but I had to start everything. I just gave up." A black student interviewed in Dartmouth for the film about EAR, *Bronwen and Jaffa*, had presciently observed that "I think black people realize it's going to take more than an anti-racism *show*." When I caught up with Trim in Halifax in late 1998, she was working as a shop assistant and finishing her studies in commercial photography, with a plan to support herself as a commercial photographer with her own project on the side. She knew what that project was going to be: using her camera with high-risk kids "falling through the cracks everywhere, imitating what they see on TV and living crappy home lives."

She has a powerful belief in the power of the still image, inspired by the work of a camera club that went into a school in the North End, saying, "Give us your most difficult kids," then worked with them for ten weeks, handed them disposable cameras, and sent them out to take photographs. "What the kids came back with," Bronwen marvelled, "was pictures mostly full of love and hope, from the so-called bad area of the city."

Denise Benson, DJ, is a self-confessed obsessive. To keep abreast of the music she plays on her two-hour show, "Mental Chatter," on Toronto's CKLN community-based radio station (housed at Ryerson University and where she has been a volunteer programmer since 1987), she reads a huge number of magazines, European and North American, listens to other people's shows, goes browsing on the Internet, hits the clubs, does some music journalism, and deejays once a week at Gypsy Co-op bar and club in Toronto. She is embedded in a music scene where she has a reputation for "finding the good stuff and wanting to share the information with people." Her parents had told the teenaged Benson that, by the time she was twenty-one, she would be a grown-up and ready to leave the music behind. When we talked in 1998, she was thirty-one and still going full-tilt through techno-music, or musics, that have never let her down. "Everytime I get to a place where I am bored by the music, I start to check out, and then something new breaks, something that excites me. That's why I stay in it. There is always something that just makes me go 'Wow.'"

It was four in the afternoon and she was having her lunch, as cool in person as she sounded on air, with that smooth, even-keeled, low-pitched voice and its undertones of excitement in her hyperboles of appreciation: "*Wow wow wow wow wow!*" Short hair, googly glasses, a sliver of a silver ring in her right nostril, sensible clothes. She was patient and unpatronizing of my total ignorance of her favourite music: drum 'n' bass? funkadelic? trip-hop? jazz house? "In the musical world," she explained, "everything has subdivided and categories are free-floating." And I was thinking, how could all this music have happened without my being the least aware of it? Her pleasure is in surprising her listeners with the "connections and paths" she makes among the musics.

When Benson began to work professionally as a club DJ in 1987, there were one or two other women doing the same. "I still get referred to as a female DJ, but it's like, get over it. I still get asked all the time what it's like to be a woman DJ, but every time I turn around there are more and more young women out there. I can't even keep up with how many women DJs there are anymore. I am a feminist, I am an out lesbian, and I'm interested in connecting with people who understand that politic, even if they're straight or a man or whatever."

The politic? "It's about people telling their own stories, bringing people together." So, there it is again, even in the end-of-century tribe of global-techno-urban music fans, as though huddled around some digitized version of the campfire in the Canadian woods: telling our stories to each other, keeping the plot going.

CONCLUSION

What, then, of Canada's place in the new world cultural order? Even the strongest political will in Ottawa (which has been enfeebled by dwindling public investment in culture) seems inadequate to confound the combined power of international trade regimes, new technologies, and the American assumption of their own corporate infallibility. In addition to the stand-down on Bill C-55, which legislated against magazine split-run editions, in 1999 Ottawa allowed the foreign takeover of a Canadian publishing house;

progress on its film-policy review stalled; and the Canadian Radio-television and Telecommunications Commission (CRTC), having already facilitated deregulation of the so-called telcos (corporate telephone companies) even as telcos and cablecos merged and integrated, decided not to regulate the Internet for Canadian content. Canada's celebrated openness to the rest of the world, through cable television overloaded with specialty channels, means that companies like the Discovery Channel and Home and Gardening Channel go for the cheapest way of doing business: unhindered *re*broadcasting of U.S. programming rather than creating more expensive Canadian content. All received their licences from the CRTC, and it is this expansion of the cable system, "with the state's regulatory complicity," that is tipping the fine balance between Canadian and American programming in favour of the American.[63]

So have we done it to ourselves? According to Gordon Ritchie, a former senior trade negotiator, the Americans see us as "a bunch of wimps and cowards" who, confronted by bullies, are always the first to blink.[64] A vehement Paul Gross, star of the television series *Due South*, unable to decide what made him madder – unstoppable American cultural imperialism in an age of free markets or inevitable Canadian faint-heartedness among the freetraders – burst out, "We just rolled over and exposed our testicles almost instantly. Take them!" He didn't want less regulation of Canadian content in our cultural production, he said, he wanted more. It helps to level the playing field in an industry where the average Canadian movie is distributed on a budget of $250,000, versus the U.S. average of $10 million. "We don't own our distribution chains. We don't control the airwaves. We're the only nation that gets slammed by the behemoth to the south."[65] He might have added that we are also alone among nations in harbouring in our bosom a self-loathing Fifth Column of editorial writers, columnists, and pundits who, one jump ahead of the American trade negotiators, decry the subsidies, content rules, commissions, tax and monetary policies – the whole tool box of policy – that have made it possible for Canadian cultural producers to dream of finding an audience among their own people.

Or is the problem more subtle? More to do with certain kinds of media production than with the American "nationality" of films and television and magazines? It isn't true that all of *our* culture is lined up against all of *theirs* in a form of trench warfare, but rather that huge

audiovisual conglomerates, Sony and Time Warner and Disney, purvey-
ors of mega-entertainment wherever they can sell it, from Quebec City to
Bombay to Melbourne, drive independent production, *including American*,
out of the marketplace. This kind of "culture," writes Richard Martineau,
editor of Montreal's *Voir*, "has no flag to wave except the buck. . . . *Titanic* –
American? Come on. It is the product of the fusion of two multinationals,
Paramount and 20th Century Fox."[66] In 1998 the U.S. President's
Committee on the Arts and the Humanities raised the alarm on the slow
death-by-budget-strangulation of the National Endowment for the Arts,
one of the few sources of public funding for non-commercial art, and with
it the possibility of protecting some small cultural lairs and dens in the U.S.
from the snapping jaws of commerce.

Once upon a time the world did dream of a utopian international order
of global collaboration and the free flow of information among its
members, with UNESCO (United Nations Education, Social and Cultural
Organization) as the referee. But it did not anticipate the obscene prepon-
derance of U.S. corporate media products in this "free flow," which, as media analyst
Ted Magder points out, made the world safe not for democracy but for
Mickey Mouse.[67] Alarmed at this imbalance, UNESCO resolved in the 1970s
to correct it with various proposals bolstering "cultural diversity" and "cultural pluralism" among the nations, all of which the U.S. interpreted to
mean sinister threats to freedom of expression, or more to the point,
freedom of commerce. In 1984, the Americans withdrew from UNESCO,
citing political bias against Western countries.

These developments did not bode well for Canada's own cultural strategy, which between 1968 and 1980 included instruments such as the
Canadian Film Development Corporation (now Telefilm Canada),
Canadian content quotas, regulation of cable companies, and subsidization
of book publishing. Along with UNESCO, Canadian governments still
understood culture to be a form of human expression that thrived within
ecologies of public support. But American governments, and those who
lobbied them on behalf of the media conglomerates – the second largest
exporter of goods in the United States – narrowed culture down to a trade-
able good or service. "Culture is money. . . . The free-flow doctrine would
be replaced by the doctrine of free trade," Ted Magder reminds us, and the

Canada–U.S. Free Trade Agreement was the first concerted effort by U.S. trade negotiators to put this strategy into play.

One evening in November, 1988, I sat in a university cafeteria festooned with the brave balloons and spunky posters that were meant to have celebrated the victory of our NDP candidate. By eight o'clock, however, the mood had grown subdued; it was obvious she was losing to her Tory opponent. As I watched the big television screen with its shocking, unexpected news that Brian Mulroney's Tory government had been returned to power, as I faced the awful reality of four or five more years of a Tory-managed state and the appalling prospect of a free-trade agreement with the U.S., I felt that my country had been kidnapped by alien forces hostile to my desires as a Canadian citizen. And I didn't mean the Americans. My despair reflected the unutterable loneliness of the citizen whose citizenship has been betrayed by her own people – Mulroney and those who voted for him – who had devised free trade and parlayed it with unseemly haste into legislation, spurred on by that old continentalist wet dream in which we Canadians merge with Americans and do away with the travail involved in the construction of our own collective. The place I could still call home was no longer nation-wide but only as wide as my work, my neighbourhood, and my friends. That seems a very constricted space, but perhaps in retrospect I shall see this period as the beginning of a new politics of coherence at a time when the centre did not hold.[68]

A decade later there were signs of something hardening in the Canadian solar plexus. In 1998 we took to the international stage where we had first stood as post-war Canadians, the United Nations, with a meeting in Ottawa of twenty-two international ministers of culture and the executive of UNESCO, hosted by our own Sheila Copps, who proposed an international cultural network. Its mission: for governments to sustain national cultures in the face of globalization and to promote co-operation on common cultural objectives. The U.S. was not invited; it does not have a minister of culture. In 1999 it was announced that federal officials were at work with other countries to develop "a cultural distinctiveness" pact that would protect culture under trade regimes such as the NAFTA and the World Trade Organization.[69] An International Advisory Committee of the Canadian Conference of the Arts drafted principles for an international network of non-governmental cultural organizations to be known as the World Coalition for Cultural Diversity, with the goal of developing an international cultural instrument parallel to international trade and investment agreements. Whenever and wherever economic and monetary globalists convene, there too should convene artists in defense of *their* global rights to cultural diversity.

It was the French publisher Jean Daniel who noted that "globalization" is the language of economics, not society, and that it privileges values of competition, not solidarity.[70] If the political will to defend Canadian sovereignty wanes in Ottawa, then we can expect the imaginative young to take their struggle for creative survival to the international forums where the globalists meet, as they did in their tens of thousands in the protests known as the "Battle of Seattle," December, 1999, to assert civil society's interests as WTO delegates met to set the agenda for a new round of trade liberalization negotiations. Their desire to live and work somehow inside a commons, with a social as well as aesthetic imagination, is urgent.

Beyond Identity Politics III

SEXUALITIES

Grrls

Perched stiffly onstage at a forum at Toronto's Harbourfront, writer Donna Laframboise, young "dissident" feminist and author of the recently published *The Princess at the Window: A New Gender Morality*, declared that the feminist movement was in a mess. Feminism was supposed to be about equality and fairness, she gravely reminded us, but by the 1990s had become imbued with "anti-male bigotry" and "male-bashing." For example, she said, feminists routinely violated elementary logic: "Although most rapists are men, it doesn't follow that most men are rapists." Fair enough, I thought, stifling a yawn, but is anti-male bigotry the sum total of feminism's discontents some thirty years after it was launched on its so-called "second wave"? And hiding behind that accusation of bigotry is another, more devastating one: that mainstream feminists, including heterosexuals, hate sex with men.

Was I overstating the case? Take Kate Fillion, for example, author of 1996's *Lip Service: The Truth About Women's Darker Side in Love, Sex and Friendship.* Her reductionist charges against current feminism offered a pretty interesting bulletin from her generation to mine, the second-wave feminists of the 1960s and 1970s; namely, that we older feminists had forgotten our own sexual history. In those formative years of feminism, Fillion reminded us, "sexual equality and freedom were major feminist goals; women's rights to sexual pleasure and to control of their own bodies were symbolic of their right to social equality."

In a curious twist, the dissident feminists of the 1990s were witnesses to the sexual revolution of their mothers' generation, for in their catalogue of grievances against us was the account of what we used to believe. They told us that we fought for sexual equality with men, not, as now, for moral and emotional superiority. That our love-making with men promised pleasure with sympathetic sensualists, not victimization at the hands of sexual brutes. That our bodies lay within our own control and were not alienated "sites" of male sexual terror. That sexual disappointment signalled a fraudulent relationship rather than a traumatizing violence. That pornography, such as we knew it then, was an instance of sexual free speech, not the "theorizing" of rape. And so far were men from being the enemy that we even fantasized an ideal androgynous self that would be male and female at once.

But this does not seem to be the message women are carrying forward. For all that young women may feel themselves "empowered" by their triumph in the universities, professions, and legislative acts, in pop culture and on the street, strutting their stuff, my generation is there to remind them that they are being selfish, that, outside the nightclubs, women are still unrepresented politically, are paid less than men, are coming apart at the seams as single mothers or double-duty wives, are crowding the battered women's shelters. Feminism is not about getting what you want, contrary to the magazine articles, or about the right to every self-gratification or to "self-expression" as an end in itself. Weighing in from her sociology professorship at the University of Laval, Nicole Gagnon, a socialist since adolescence, scorns a contemporary feminism that, far from inspiring women to "transcend their sexual difference in order to take their place within a universal humanity," locks them inside a "differentialism" which, were it inverted, would be pure sexism.[1]

> "Would you be willing to alter your lifestyle to reduce your impact on the environment?" 94% of women 18-34, 88% of women 35-54 said yes. "Do you favor making users of government services pay the true cost of the service?" 51% of women 18-34 and 35% of women 35-54 said yes.
> – *Vancouver Sun*, December 23, 1997

The generations do overlap: feminists who were "on the barricades" in their twenties didn't altogether disappear into the privacy of their own domestic lives or professional ambitions. They are often cohabiting classrooms, editorial offices, conference auditoriums, picket lines, with young women who could be their daughters. And, as Keith Louise Fulton, co-ordinator of Women's Studies at the University of Winnipeg, reminded me with the example of her own life, some boomer women didn't come to feminism until they had had children and got their Ph.D. and a job.

All those years before feminism, she said in an interview in her office in downtown Winnipeg, "I heard about things almost as if I were under-water." What kind of "things"? The "things" of Virginia Woolf's writings, for instance, "things that I wish had already been accomplished, a kind of hope for the androgyny of the artist and the idea that human beings could get past a power differential" – there it is again, that sixties social hopeful-ness! – "to a place where there is a woman-man and man-woman." Instead, Fulton tuned to feminism with *its* promise that she could be a "woman-woman and still get on with things. I didn't want it to be true that, because women had different histories than men, we would have different futures." It is exactly that same desire to be getting on with it, without the weight of the past on their shoulders, that she sees in her young female students, and she sympathizes.

"Their past includes us," I interjected. "And they don't want us on their backs," she continued, "and I don't blame them a bit. But they're going to have to, just as I did. It's an illusion that you get to start from where you are."

Third-wave feminism has, admirably, become a politic of inclu-sion and representation, with a broad, sweeping range. Its rhet-oric, however, has been co-opted by the same exploitative brain-dead players who were vilified (with good reason) during the second wave. Male Hollywood producers and directors espe-cially have seized on the language of power-feminism, often force-feeding it to the press and to many of the hapless female stars. Lately, every time I see a woman being challenged for her role in the power/money elite (or for her role in *I Like Giving Blow Jobs – I'm Not Lying*), she invariably responds in robotic terms: "I am a feminist because I'm powerful, and I am in charge of my life."

– Lynn Crosbie, "Some Things That Make Me Puke," *This Magazine*, August 1995

When Andrea Curtis (editor of the alternative political-cultural *This Magazine* at the time I spoke with her in Toronto) began her work as a journalist at the *McGill Tribune* in the late eighties, she was full of feminist fire. She wanted nothing more than to write about women in the language of feminism, "a language for my dislocation and anger," and then found herself defending second-wave feminists against the backlash of young "post-feminist" women who perceived themselves as fully emancipated and happily in bed with men. (Yikes!) Yet even Curtis felt that "every generation has to reject to some degree their predecessors in order to forge ahead. You don't reject them, you go beyond them. You have to ask new questions."

And they have new questions by the hundreds. How are the giant gains made in women's legal equality to be assimilated into an economic globalization that drives women into precarious employment? When young women see their boomer mothers exhausted and overburdened by stress at work and in the family, will they always sacrifice a family of their own to a career? And what of that feminism of the elders that divides "good" feminists – who struggle for old-growth forests and against poverty, and "bad" feminists, who shave their legs, wear make-up and sexy clothes, and want to "reappropriate the assets of seduction"? This is the question raised by Isabelle Rivest in *Le Devoir*, who went to interview Pascale Navarro, books editor for the alternative Montreal weekly *Voir*. Navarro, the co-author of *Interdit aux femmes*, a polemic against the censorship of pornography, adopts a decidedly more laissez-faire attitude than do older feminists who denounce the negative effects of the porn industry on women. "Women filmmakers are making intelligent, innovative films that have nothing to do with hard-core porn," she told Rivest. "Everything gets thrown into the same basket these days. Do we have to be scandalized every time we see a nude woman?"[2]

In Montreal I dropped in on radical sex researcher Katherine Setzer at her apartment three floors up above the din on St. Denis, and noted the large, bold paintings left over from her art studies and the remarkable line-up of black boots in the entry, all of them versions of *building site moderne*.

"Why is so much feminist discourse now about sex?" I asked without pussyfooting around. "How did the rhetoric of social revolution that was going to smash capitalism *and* patriarchy end up at leather fetish parties?" Setzer shot right back: "My challenge to what you're saying is, why were s&m practices considered to be about representing the patriarchy, about being submissive and not 'real' lesbians? Real lesbians do want to talk about equal wages for equal work! But why was feminism so void about talking about sexuality?"

Hello? I was there and she wasn't, when we were at the threshold of our adult sexual lives. Our passionate and wildly contradictory convictions about our sexual values were as fascinating and urgent to us as our political values. If anything, sex was the lubricant of our community of action and kept us human in the crush of political work. It was not always good sex – and the grievances around that fact fuelled endless debate – but, as sixties veteran Judy Rebick told me in an interview, bad sex isn't necessarily damaging, and if she truly believed men were the enemy, she wouldn't have slept with them.[3]

In the early 1970s I had been a teacher in the thoroughly experimental Women's Studies program at the University of Toronto. (For one thing, you didn't have to be a professor to teach. And you didn't give grades. This was a *sisterhood*.) Since I had not visited Women's Studies since, I now sought out Dr. Lise Gotell, a professor of political science and women's studies whose research area is sexuality and in whose classes, she explained to me in her office at the University of Alberta in Edmonton, high above the swath of the North Saskatchewan River, she spent "a lot of time on bodies and sexuality, because this is a way for the students really to connect with feminism and its ideas and theories. We spend a huge amount of time on the debate 'Can a feminist be a heterosexual?'" Gotell encourages the students to distinguish between heterosexuality as an *institution* and as a *practice*: "If lesbianism can be a choice [of sexual practice] for feminists, why can't heterosexuality?"

Feminism risks losing young heterosexual women if it refuses to "complicate" the discourse around sexual pleasure, if it fails to take notice that young women have already spent most of a lifetime absorbing the lessons and statistics about sexual violence and date rape and abuse within intimate relationships, and that they have grown up in a society in which it is now normal, and expected, that governments will respond to such issues. While it is "rhetorically very powerful" to speak women's narratives from the stance of victims – of women as men's victims – it also acts to insulate that speech from outside critique, because "if you critique that standpoint," Gotell argued, "you appear to be silencing the victims."

The sexual pessimism of such a view of women's vulnerability is, I had heard repeatedly, a complete turn-off for young women, who reject the anti-porn feminists' view that "the more powerless you are, the more truthful you are." When pro-feminist women produce explicit pornography for each other, when they talk dirty in public, "perform" varieties of gender identity and revel assertively in their physical beauty, do we wonder why they also treat older feminists' sexual self-disappearing (Those overalls! The geeky haircuts! The decorous fucking! The pursed lips at the magazine racks!) with scorn? Do we wonder when they flee such self-loathing femaleness for the carnivalesque of queer? Inside "queer" there is no *essential* woman whose sexual self is being dictated by some script of Nature, and no *helpless* woman jerked around by brutish male lust with no sexual agency of her own.

Although Gotell does not teach any distinction between pornography and erotica, the subject invariably comes up with each new challenge to the Charter of Rights and Freedoms, on the one hand, and to the Butler ruling on the social harm of pornography, on the other. The discussion is important, because "anti-pornography feminism never talks about erotica, but there is always the danger, when you're making the distinction, that you are reinforcing that feminist ideal of gentle, nurturing sex as *feminist* sex."

The "grrls" will have none of it.

Gotell mentioned such other discussion topics as sex resistance, bisexuality, and transgressive sexual identity. I was not exactly shocked, but I did wonder how the agenda of 1970s feminism – I was thinking of wages for housework, abortion rights, campaigns against sexist advertising, *socioeconomic* feminism, if you like – seemed almost entirely absent from young feminists' concern (not to say obsession) with sexuality. Unlike other observers of the intergenerational debate among feminists, Gotell does not think we are out of the "second wave" experience yet, rather that the grand theories of the second wave have been eroded. There is nothing "wrong" with older feminists' commitment to equality, solidarity, and justice, but, from the perspective of the next generation, "grand theories miss a lot. The value of postmodernism is to draw our attention to what has been lost and to how power circulates in our society in many different ways, and our struggles have to be *complicated* in response to the complicated nature of power."

And who better than women (and gay men) to respond, like heliotropic plants to the light, to the subtlest flexings of sexual power in our environments, because our lives and well-being depend on getting it right? Latterly, sexual identities and practices have multiplied, completely throwing the old feminist sexual polarities of heterosexuality and lesbianism off their axis, and the young women (and men) of Gotell's classes jump enthusiastically into the debates around what is the sexually "authentic" way to be.

> Zoe Whittal is a former rural Québecer and Montréal enthusiast. New to Toronto, she writes a 'zine called *Mudball*, promotes a chick performance event called Girlspit, and plays in the Bitchin Camaroes, a slick lady revolution punk rock unit.
>
> Thirzla Cuthand was born in 1978 in Saskatchewan. Being a biracial dyke, her outlook was skewed at an early age by oppression. She currently resides in Vancouver, BC, where she is attending Emily Carr College of Art. Besides ranting and cartooning, she also makes queer grrl videos.
>
> – Two contributors to "Revolution Girl Style,"
> *Fireweed* magazine, Fall/Winter 1997

Zoë Newman and Kelly O'Brien, co-teaching gender studies in an alternative high school in Toronto in 1996, were so exhilarated and excited by their students that they wanted to keep on working with them after the course was finished. Powerfully written student diary excerpts gave them the idea of developing a bigger writing project, and so it came to pass, a special issue of the venerable feminist journal *Fireweed*, written and collectively edited by young women, or, as they prefer to call themselves, girls. Or chicks or babes or broads or dames or grrls (as in the Riot Grrl movement of some years back, after the girl band who used their bodies as billboards for the words "slut" and "bitch" slashed in red lipstick and Magic Marker).

Titled "Revolution Girl Style," the issue uses every font known to revolutionaries, edgy layouts, comix-style illustration, obviously inspired by a television-literate generation that is both media and street savvy. But it had never crossed O'Brien's and Newman's minds to produce anything other than a "real" magazine, which they feel is a "grounded" medium that allows real people to meet in real space – in O'Brien's living room, for instance, for almost a year, as the Revolution Girl Style Collective.

As they recalled in the introduction, "Before we knew it, we had more than 500 submissions. . . . We photocopied every submission a dozen times. We read. And we read. And we read. We split up into groups, we did go-arounds, we made notes, we compared notes, we made rules, we contra-dicted ourselves, we made decisions. We argued, passionately. Consensus was sometimes agonizing." (O'Brien and Newman had no voting power in the collective but were allowed to fight for a piece.) And when the maga-zine was finally delivered from the printer, and the girls of the collective filed into the living room with some of the writers whose work had kept them at an anguished pitch for months, they all sat down, each with her copy, totally silent, reading.

The launch for the finished magazine at Ted's Wrecking Yard club at College and Bathurst had the public winding in queues around the block to hear the writers themselves. "Your generation of feminists," Newman told me, "was blown away by it. They said it was history in the making." People had been brought together by the sense that "something was brewing." That here in living colour were all the strands of feminism, the old interwoven with the innovations and shifts of the new. A whole new generation running around from demo to demo, womanning community radio, volunteering at alternative presses, studying at alternative high schools and art schools, riding motorcycles to New Mexico, falling in love and breaking hearts. . . .

So what had they wrought? My first impression of their *Fireweed* issue, I told Newman and O'Brien, after the exhilaration of the sheer, proud voicing of such diverse young femaleness, was that it was overwhelmingly dyke in attitude and tone if not in substance, meaning that its cultural/ political tone was "we like girls and men are jerks." (Though I confessed that I was a bit lost in the new sexual self-labelling: What's a "bi-lezzie chicklet dykester"?) It's not so much that there is anti-male sentiment in the collection, said Newman, as that "guys just don't get talked about," which isn't necessarily exclusively a dyke stance, come to think of it, nor is the disastrous love affair exclusive to heterosexual couples. O'Brien gently suggested I was perhaps "marginalizing" the girls' discourse as dyke when the fact is that "a lot of women in the issue who don't identify as dyke are still incredibly self-confident and writing their own work" and that's what's interesting.

I wondered whether the collective had any discussions about the *status* of the heterosexual experience. As a heterosexual woman I was more than curious to see how this privileged identity fared in the new sexual market-place of DIY genderbending. Not well, in fact. To judge from the pieces about the shame and guilt of abortion, the transformation of "menstrua-tion" into "femmestruation," the "slamming and grunting" of the hetero-sexual embrace, the rapes that send a young woman to prostitute herself ("When men harass me on the street, I dare like I never did before to yell back, 'Don't fuck with me I'm a hardcore baby whore'"),[4] heterosexuality is a catastrophe for women. Had no one in the collective caught the almost hilarious juxtaposition, in one piece, of a reference to "the safety of hetero-sexuality" to its very next line: "get raped, get pregnant, miscarry, prostitute yourself"?[5] Apparently not.

Yet perhaps these young women were merely reiterating the profound ambiguity that lies at the heart of feminist heterosexuality that my genera-tion had anguished over for years: that as a heterosexual woman you are somehow complicit with male power because it is your desire as well as his to be erotically bonded to the sexual Other. Dr. Lise Gotell, from her vantage point in her women's studies classroom, agreed in this essential, that the dominant view of sexuality in feminist discourse has become that "sex is danger . . . pleasure is erased," and that feminism will lose its capac-ity to speak to young women if it does not present a more complicated picture of sexuality, men's and women's.

In a sense, it's the other way around: the young women are speaking to feminism. In a very funny piece in an anthology about how some women have come to feminism, the Toronto writer, actor, and playwright Sonja Mills describes her utter failure to get laid while hanging around a univer-sity women's group. Her "inner feminist" had begun to emerge, gloriously, and now she wanted to fuck. But as she looked around the group, her desire wilted: the woman in the Nicaraguan sweater-vest who had never slept with another woman though she announced herself a lesbian-feminist, the woman who was drinking her own menstrual blood as an offering to Mother Earth, the woman with the "really, really, bad haircut" who testified that pornography exists only to perpetuate the global oppression of women . . . "blah blah blah." The last straw came at a screening of the anti-pornography film *Not a Love Story*, which *aroused* Ms. Mills: "A little hostility, a little humiliation, some dirty talk, and a lot of penetration – it sounded like a recipe for a pretty hot evening to me."[6]

Even Kelly O'Brien and Zoë Newman, not exactly long in the tooth, feel there is already another sexual generation of women after them, women who are "amazingly more clear about the fact they're allowed to have a sexuality and that there's not just one way for them to express it," as Newman said of the younger members of the *Fireweed* collective. "But what's kind of funny is there really is a kind of feminism represented here that's like the bra-burning from your generation, it's out there demonstrating an angry type of rebellion but with a different kind of aesthetic, a certain kind of hipness." But it isn't so much hip rebelliousness as a kind of chilled-out shrug of the shoulders I sense in the irritable apoliticism of a twenty-seven-year-old personal trainer interviewed in the *Globe and Mail* for a story about the "girls" who just want to have fun: "I sleep with women . . . and I sleep with men . . . and I don't stay up at night thinking about whether I'm bisexual or anything else. I'm healthy. I have sex. I have relationships. And I think we're past the politics of all that. I don't march."[7]

> Girl culture has rummaged through the freedom trash can and is reclaiming and recycling all the stuff we've found there. . . . This is not a rejection of earlier feminism. It's just that, along with postmodernism and cultural studies and irony that have emerged in the '80s and '90s, feminist ideas have also evolved. . . . Today, taking our cue from the "queer" movement, girl culture has reclaimed the word "girl." . . . The silly, innocent vision of girlhood that we have been fed is wrong. As girls we were angry, bratty, selfish beasts and the furthest thing from sugar and spice and everything nice. . . . Why should drag queens have all the fun?
>
> – Debbie Stoller, "Girl Culture's Pleasure Principle," *Shift* magazine, March 1998

"Does that sound like your girls?" I asked Newman and O'Brien. "Definitely," said Newman. "What may have brought us from that alternative high school class to this *Fireweed* issue was the realization these were not apathetic kids living their lives out in front of televisions, who have no opinions and are coasting along a corporate wave. They had their own ideas, they were smart, they were feisty."

So, at the end of the day, is there still some way to theorize the idea of "sisterhood" or is that an idea whose time has been and gone? An idea completely deconstructed by the new generation's critique of the second wave?

Newman: "This may be too pat, but it seems there are undeniably moments when the sisterhood exists, works. I think we felt those moments. We all had a common project and we all wanted variations on the same thing."

Transgressions

> BC: Was there a time when you had to hold back on your articulation of desire?
>
> LM: I don't think we do as artists. Where it's necessary we use explicitly sexual language. And sometimes we have a political idea that we're working towards and we know that we want to include explicit material because we're not just sexless revolutionary fighters. We're sexual cultural workers.
>
> – Interview with Shawna Dempsey and
> Lorri Millan, *BorderCrossings*, Spring 1998

Dempsey and Millan were presenting their work in an alternative theatre in Edmonton, as a kind of cabaret-style piece of performance art. Dempsey's wardrobe could have hung in an art gallery – vinyl see-through wedding dress, a forty-pound pink-and-white Formica dress that resembled a kitchen counter, a Saran Wrap sheath dress bristling with four-inch roofing nails. It was called *Under the Skirt* and it was very funny. It also packed a one-two punch at what Millan told *BorderCrossings* is the "systemic culture that is putting females in a place where we cannot be fully what we want to be," and which Shawna Dempsey said they must face as artists "as brave as we can be."

Being brave means presenting a resistant public with their work, which is first of all a performance of visual puns and pop-culture references. They've parodied *Life* magazine profiles with one of their own, "A Day in the Life of a Modern Sex Deviant," which features Millan as Sal the butcher and "bull-dagger"; produced a kind of rap video, "What Do Lesbians Look Like," for MuchMusic's *Word Up* series; and created a brochure, complete with official logo, e-mail address, and corporate history, that is a hilarious send-up of the earnestly cheerful literature that gets handed out at the entrance gates of Canada's national parks, "Lesbian National Parks and Services Wants You!" They use ordinary materials in startling ways. To don her Formica dress, for instance, Dempsey requires the assistance of Millan, who flourishes a high-speed drill and literally rivets her in.

"Two thousand years of patriarchy haven't dampened my sense of style," says Dempsey in the role of the porcupine woman in Saran Wrap and roofing nails.

They'll perform anywhere, at a United Church conference, straight and lesbian bars, community halls, the street, because it's as important to put their work out to people who will resist them as it is to please their fans. Sometimes the public strikes back, once even threatening to blow up the Winnipeg bus shelters and boycott the buses while their *Winnipeg: One Gay City* posters flapped decoratively on the shelter walls.

In conversation with me, they talked about their deliberate embrace of the female "monster" archetype-figure – like the Medusa, the bull dyke, the housewife in her Formica dress, whose fantasies travel from the sparkling cleanliness of the kitchen sink to "wanting to 'off' her husband and children in order to cut down her work load" – because the monster is always about the "perverse" idea of female power.

Earlier, Dempsey had referred to the embittered, polarizing debate in lesbian culture between "good" lesbians and "bad" lesbians. Ah, it's the grrls again, the libidinous, pleasuring, hot, hungry nymphomaniacs licking at the nightmares of "good" girls everywhere, femmes fatales looking out for themselves, more than a bit out of control, "as sex tends to make us."[8] Bad girls. Bad bad grrls.

> BC: In the MuchMusic piece, don't you use the phrase "pushy cocky in your face"? You have to be aware of the phallic impli-cations of that language. So none of that's accidental?
> SD: Not at all, no.

LM: What does Sal say in *A Day in the Life*? She says, "Suck my lesbian dick, buck-o." That's not just a throw-away. We examined every syllable quite extensively.

That sort of talk seems to be particularly liberating of young lesbian speech and, beyond speech, of utopian desirings of stepping over limits and boundaries and violating patriarchal commandments, although to unpractised ears it merely sounds like talking "dirty," without the sniggering. In an article about finally finding her feminist home with a bunch of downtown Toronto lesbians who "talked trash and fucked like dogs," playwright Sonja Mills wrote that they were all "proud" to call themselves bitches, sluts, and whores, even wore these names like "merit badges," as signifying the virtues of "outrageous – even so-called obscene – sexual behavior."9

"Is transgressiveness possible inside female heterosexuality?" I wanted to know from Demsey and Millan, who admit their woman in the Formica housedress is straight. Millan thought so, "totally," because women's social roles are so narrow that, even inside the cultural ideal of heterosexual marriage, a woman can't help but "transgress" in any move to sidestep them. "In some ways," said Dempsey, "there is nothing more angry than a pissed-off straight woman!" I thought about that afterwards, about how for a straight woman it is very difficult to carve out any "male-free" zones in her life where she isn't under even friendly scrutiny and the limitations drawn by intimacy, about how your anger has already been scripted in the eons-old theatre of the sex wars.

But Sonja Mills's agenda is more complicated than simply transgressing "patriarchal institutions" like heterosexuality and monogamy; the "institution" that really gets her going, that makes her seethe with venomous resentment and contempt, is the citadel held by what she calls the "self-appointed women's rights despots." For them she reserves a particularly virulent speech that is perilously close, it seems to me, to the classic anti-woman language my generation was all too familiar with when we first started speaking out loud about our sexuality (outside the safe confines of the "sexual revolution," that is). Listen to Mills: while she concedes that *not* wanting to be fist-fucked is fine, what is definitely not fine, in fact is stupid, is "not wanting to even hear about it – because it offended some prudish

sense of political propriety." Or her references to "whining, anti-porn harridans," or "hummus-sucking, under-sexed feminists," or "strident
women's rights devotees . . . inflexible, repressed, and humorless."[10]
Prudish, under-sexed, strident, repressed: for second-wave feminists such
"transgressive" speech seems to have turned its guns away from the Man
and onto – what could be more predictable? – Mother. "Not surprisingly,"
wrote feminist critic Jennifer Henderson about the theme of matricide in
the film *Heavenly Creatures* and intergenerational stand-offs between nurturing and aggressive values, "matricide has come to enjoy a symbolic value
as the privileged gesture of a sexual avant-garde."[11] Journalist Naomi Klein,
whose real-life mother made the anti-porn film classic *Not a Love Story*,
remembers that, as a nine-year-old in her mother's editing room at the
National Film Board, the "good feminists" in the film seemed to her an
"abomination," revolting in their bad clothes and bad hair, the "gatekeepers
protecting me from the world of strippers, pornos, peep shows, and naked
people – the world of sex." In revenge, as soon as she got the chance, she
became a Girl, delighted with herself in tight jeans, peroxided curls and
electric eyeshadow.[12]

Perhaps I'm taking it too personally. Certainly there is nothing in Mills's
caricatures that suggests her contempt is reserved for "harridans" of my
generation. Nor does Jaime Kirzner-Roberts, in *Fireweed*'s "Revolution Girl
Style," hold second-wave feminists solely responsible for making her want
to "puk[e] up all the crap I've been made to ingest by this rotten and
thoughtless [women's studies] class."[13] It's the class's "over-ideologization"
of women as martyrs and victims that drives her crazy, the feminism represented by the girls who say, "I was sexually abused, my boyfriend beats me
up, I live in poverty, I think I'm ugly, I'm a recovering anorexic, I hate
myself and sometimes I wish I were dead," and would never think of saying,
"I'm just fine, thank you very much. . . . How about great? wonderful?
terrific? We're actually doing what we want to be doing and we're not
afraid. Seems pretty radical, huh?"[14]

Julie Kubanek *is* doing fine, and she's not frightened of her own shadow.
But from her vantage point as a worker at Vancouver Rape Relief, where,
she told me, she sees visible signs of porn's "connection with" rape and
battery on the bodies of women, she is not about to support glibly the

notion that porn is "freedom of speech" or anything else but a "hate litera-ture" intended to control a whole class of people.

"I was a child during the initial wave of the anti-porn movement," she told me. "When I came of age, I had a strong instinct against porn. And where I settled was not a censorship position, but where I asked men to reject porn as an expression of their sexuality and therefore of control-ling mine.

"I would certainly reject porn as an expression of my sexuality. So-called women's 'erotica' seems just to be the same-old-same-old. In one col-lection, there was a story about a woman having sex with a horse, another about a woman having sex with another woman, who turned out to have a penis anyway, who was also black. . . . It reminded me of those student parties where we were drinking cheap white wine upstairs and making out, with porn videos as background, in the dark in the basement."

> Queer City Cinema, then, makes the case for identities which are fluid, multiple, contradictory, shifting and inconsistent. . . . We need a new way of thinking about identity, or at least a new appellation, one that preserves the promise of sexual liberation.
> – Gary Varro, "Introduction,"
> Queer City Cinema festival catalogue, 1996

I had Shawna Dempsey and Lorri Millan all to myself for a couple of hours in an Edmonton kitchen the morning after their show. In their thir-ties, perhaps they were post-avant-garde, post-matricidal. "Do you see there is already another generation of feminists after you?" I wanted to know. Definitely, said Dempsey. "We are 'lesbian feminists' while younger women consider themselves 'queer' and are part of the larger queer culture which is also bisexual, transgendered, gay male." Millan called them "sex radicals" who have a certain assurance about who and what they can be – "and who is going to stop them? Nobody." She looked enormously pleased. But went on to alert me to the danger in "queer politics" of forgetting how hard it still is to be a "homo," how hard it is to be a feminist, to be a female. "And I think that all too often it's just too easy for straight white guys to feel that they are part of something radical because they get to call themselves queer too."

"How can a straight guy be queer?"

"It's an inclusive identity."

I suppose inclusivity is at play among the Toronto lesbians that journalist Rachel Giese reported on in 1994 – from "elegant lipstick lesbians to the post-punk baby dykes" – who very happily boogied on the dance floor to music about lover-men, with not a squeak of protest about the patriarchy or phallocentrism or hetero privilege: "These are Lesbians Who Sleep With Men."[15] A 1995 short film, *Suspicions*, made by Kiki Thorne and Kelly O'Brien of Toronto's queer arts community, announced that an era had come to an end, simple identity politics was too limiting, and the polarity of straight-gay, or even of bisexual, was being subverted by multiple sexual identities that did not have their source in *biological* difference (or what one radical lesbian referred to in an interview with me as *equipment*) but in ambivalence, obsession, doubt, flexibility, shifts. It had all been predicted in the antiquity of the 1980s by the pioneering Canadian sex historian Gary Kinsman, who argued that even such rudimentary erotically defined identities as S&M gays and lesbians "challenge unitary notions of homosexuality and lesbianism."[16]

A decade later, the theatrical diversity of sexual identity was breathtaking. Suddenly, or so it seemed to me, the very *essential* differences between straight feminists and lesbian feminists, between straight and gay men (bisexuality being frowned on as cowardly straddling of the gender fence) on which we had depended to make important political points – lesbianism was "about" rage, being straight was "about" privilege, homosexuality was "about" smashing sexual regulation, feminism was "about" taking down the patriarchy – had disintegrated into a repertoire of self-constructed sexual identity that was as fluid as it was idiosyncratic. And what had distinguished gay from straight from lesbian in the old days – the difference in their sexual practice – was blurring at the boundaries, in order to "transgress" not the hetero codes so much as the categories and behaviours of institutionalized homosexuality. (This would explain in part at least the remarkable hostility of transgressive "speech" toward the older generation of cocooning queers and Birkenstock lesbians, and the bashing that "theory" takes from disgruntled women's studies drop-outs.)

And if it is self-constructed and improvisatory, then in what sense is anyone a "real" lesbian or gay man anymore? Giese's article alone refers to transsexuals, bisexuals, lesbian-identified bisexuals, girl's girls, homo-friendly straights, boy-crazy dykes who still dig chicks, lesbians wearing dildoes and fake moustaches who talk about ejaculation and watch banned lesbian porn. Next come the "glam" dykes in miniskirts, fake eyelashes, and underwire bras, who not only find it fun to dress up, but at the same time enjoy disturbing people's preconceptions of what a "lesbian" looks like. Talking with me in 1998, Clarissa Lagartera, a Winnipeg anti-racist activist who calls herself lesbian, "the name I grew up with," lost friends when she dated a pre-operative transsexual, someone who felt like a "she" but looked like a "he," so that Clarissa was accused of being a hypocrite lesbian. Katherine Setzer calls herself a dyke "because it allows for a lot of stuff," including sleeping with men, "but that doesn't make me not a dyke; I still don't target men for serious relationships," and told me of dykes at testos-terone-shooting parties in London, "now the most radical and transgres-sive act against mainstream lesbogay: turning into men."

Clarissa Lagartera is merely a male impersonator, or, rather, a drag king, layering male personae over an unaltered female body. Hair slicked back, collar turned up, s/he is Carlos Las Vegas, "a dark, Hispanic character who is a sleazeball who gets all the women." S/he does fundraisers for AIDS research, lip-synching to songs, impersonating Kid Cole, a jazz artist, dancing around fully suited while people stick money down her/his pants.

And there are men who turn into women, not surgically but theatri-cally, as when drag queen Darrin Hagen shaves his face, chest, armpits, and stomach, puts on his dance belt (or, in an emergency, duct tape and a rubber band) to flatten "the bulge," pulls on four pairs of Shoppers Drug Mart pantyhose (to smooth out the calf muscles), stuffs two balloons into the bodice of his Value Village evening dress, and slathers on copious make-up, to become, or rather release, the woman inside himself, Gloria Hole. Bert Archer, researching his book *The End of Gay: And the Death of Heterosexuality*, suggested that there may be a "third gender, or a fourth gender, or intergendered or non-gendered people," performing their gender as a kind of self-expression.[17] These identities all come under the rubric "gender outlaws," as though some serious insubordination were afoot, and not just campy cheekiness.

Certainly Hagen, a fixture on the Edmonton theatre scene as a sound artist and drag queen in the group Guys in Disguise, takes Gloria Hole very seriously indeed. In black pumps that hike up this she-male well over three metres, elbow-high gloves, a slinky, black, off-the-shoulder, thigh-high black dress, thrift-store jewellery, and a blonde wig like a hay stack, Gloria Hole exudes an undeniable allure that has nothing to do with fashion, the fashion industry being one of Hagen's *bêtes noires*: "The fashion industry is about controlling people – more for women than men, but it's getting more like that for men too; a beauty myth that can't be achieved unless you're nineteen and hairless."[18] No spring chicken, he's aware of the wrinkles crimping his face as he applies his make-up – one more instance of his solidarity with real women, with whom he is in sisterly conspiracy against the world of male control. "Every time a red-blooded hetero boy is attracted, even for a split second, to that strange Amazon on the dance floor, what is he responding to? Femaleness? Hardly. More like the trappings. His blood stirs in response to the stuff we put on: the big tits, the impossible curves, the come-fuck-me attitude, the unnatural padding, the tortuous shoes. He responds to a woman created completely by another man, using all the repressive techniques men have wished upon women to turn them into fantasy objects, most of which were invented by men."[19]

A group of readers and gender-bending fans gathered in a salon of Chapter's bookstore on McLeod Trail in Calgary in March 1998, surrounded by dark wood furnishings as though in a gentlemen's club, to hear Hagen read from his book *The Edmonton Queen: Not a Riverboat Story.* Hagen was perched on a table, legs crossed, looking very fetching in a silk shirt, baggy pants, and his signature long blonde tresses. I sat in the front row between two queens to whom Hagen addressed his reading, as though they were characters from his story and on-stage with him. The women in his audience (the biologically and socially constructed kind) listened raptly, all smiles, while their men looked steadfastly interested, but not too. Though what about that blonde with the scissoring pink fingernails, was that a man in drag or the real thing?

Earlier this year [1998] the CFS [Canadian Federation of Students] formed the TBLG* Constituency Group . . . wherein the * stands for all those not included in the Transgendered, Bisexual, Lesbian and Gay denominations. Furthermore, these

letters are arranged in descending order of oppression. . . . I'm
not saying that issues of gender are not important. I am wondering how it was decided they were more important than issues
of sexuality. . . . It would be quite possible for the Gay, Lesbian,
Bisexual, Transgendered (GLBT) Centre at Ottawa's Carleton
University to be run by a completely heterosexual man who likes
to wear dresses and a bisexual woman who only dates men. . . .
Apparently, in the brave new world of TBLG*, being sensitive to
and inclusive of straight men in dresses is essential but having
knowledge and experience of man-on-man sex is not.
    – Andrew Griffin, "Alphabet Soup," *Xtra!*, November 5, 1998

Interestingly, many of the same people who see themselves as performing their gender within increasingly broad latitudes of identity are not necessarily happy with all of the trends. It "bugs the heck" out of Clarissa
Lagartera that some lesbians sleep with men, and then boast about it as
though their dykeness has nothing to do with who they were sleeping with.
Radical sex researcher Katherine Setzer is disturbed by the increasingly
generous inclusivity of "queer," which, like "gay" before it, "has got rid of
the lesbians. 'Queer' is the little rave boy who grew up in a middle-class
home, buys really expensive clothes to go out to raves so he can buy his
Ecstasy and say, 'I'm a queer boy.'" She's even getting fed up with men in
drag, and coming to believe that, in spite of their protestations, they do
present caricatures of "blonde bombshells that real women have never
looked like," just as gay fashion designers strip women of their breasts and
hips. "So I do see it in some ways as woman-hating."

Which also brought up the touchy subject of transsexuals. For
Katherine Setzer, being a woman "is not just about what your body is like
but about your position in society, and about how we live differently from
men. So I've stopped calling drag queens 'she.' They've got to earn it. Suffer
PMS." By some other token, she has no problem calling a dyke dressed up
as a man "he" and her girlfriend, her "boyfriend," leaving me to wonder that
masculinity, just as we understood it thirty years ago, is still the "standard"
or "human" gender that can be performed as convincingly by women as
men, while femininity, as always, is the deviant gender that can only be performed tragicomically by both sexes.

"In some ways, the muscle queen is our most feminine creation," wrote Brent Ledger in an essay about the falling away of an earlier defensive masculinity of gay men. "Lush and voluptuous, the muscle queen evokes desire not dread; lust not fear. All those muscles create curves not angles; a pin-up, not a predator. . . . Smooth and silky, the male chest has become almost as sexualized as female breasts. Nipples peek out everywhere. And the light, tight fashions favoured by the muscle-bound only emphasize the delicacy of their creation. This year's trendy tank tops sport straps as thin and flat as those on a woman's camisole."[20] Yummy, peachy bum thrust backwards towards the cameraman's light like the rear end of a horse. Pectorals swollen like mammaries, complete with serviceable teats. But does he get paid a woman's wage?

> your short/small/strong/wiry/thin/little frame/pale u say yellow skin/eyes narrow without fold/bone-straight blk hair/ little fleshy tucked under butt/pussy with fine hairs/fistin-sized hands/angular fingers/small thin lips MET my tall/large/ strong/muscle/marbled with fat/dair i say blk skin/sad eyes/ kinky blk-silver naps/high/generous/rounded stuck-out butt/ poonani with wild thick hairs/big hands/long thin fingers/ shapely lips
>
> – T. J. Bryan, "Of Chocolate Queens
> & Rice Queens," *Fuse,* Special Issue, 1998

When I asked Clarissa Lagartera, Filipina lesbian of Winnipeg, which was the first identity she came to in terms of her political consciousness, her ethnicity or her sexuality, she answered her sexuality, for she had "come out" at age twelve. In the familiar ah-ha "click" of self-consciousness first popularized by the women's liberation movement of the 1970s, her awareness arrived all at once.

"I didn't have male friends," she told me, "I thought they were stupid and jerks. My female friends were more intriguing and turned into crushes, but I didn't understand it. I had a crush on a girl in grade one and she found this annoying, so I knew there was something different about me. In grade six we had our first sex education class, spoke of heterosexuality and homosexuality, about men having sex with other men. And everybody giggled.

Except me. 'What's wrong with that?' I thought. A light bulb went on: 'Maybe I'm one of those people?'

"I wanted to hang out with other young gay people.There was a trans-gendered person in school, a woman who wanted to be a man. I questioned myself: 'Do I want to be a man? Nah, I don't want to be a man.' I didn't have any other identity [apart from lesbian] – a clean slate absorbing everything."

But she *did* have another identity, one that had preceded her sexuality: she was born to Filipino parents, and that particular "otherness" dogged her then and dogs her still, as though in competition for her body, if not her soul. To whom does she belong? Growing up in Altona, Manitoba, in the only family of colour in a population of 20,000, it wasn't until she moved to Winnipeg that she encountered non-white people, whom she immediately labelled "nigger." She admits she was "very racist." In turn she had a hard time fitting in with the Tagalog-speaking Filipino community, and once she was "out," she was rejected utterly.

"And that's when I decided to take the gay issue into the Filipino cliques in the school. But they didn't want to deal with me; they didn't want to talk to me. I had grown my hair really long and tried to be as feminine as possible so they couldn't call me dyke. I said I was a socialist, and that was cool. I said I was Greenpeace, and that was cool. But they didn't think gay was cool; they thought it was gross.

"As a Filipina, I was all by myself, and so I gave up. After five years I'm slowly starting to touch it again and get involved with the Filipino Students' Association on campus. It's taken twenty-two years, but another Filipino actually said he supported me when I said I was active in the gay and lesbian students' group . . . but I think he's a closeted gay man. Well, whatever it takes!"

"How do you say 'queer' in 'South Asian'?" asked Ian Iqbal Rashid, guest editor of a special issue of *Rungh* magazine, where he examined the question of ethnicity and modernity as a gay man. "Can we be queer on 'our' own terms?"[21] For Native playwright and poet Daniel David Moses, speaking in 1997 at a Writers' Union of Canada workshop, the gay spirit may be as old as aboriginal culture itself – as old as the figure of the shaman, the mediator between worlds – for the gay person "is gifted with two spirits, male and female . . . more whole, more centred, more balanced" than the rest of the community, a harmony of femininity and masculinity that was shattered by European colonization.

Now stir in the issue of interracial love-making and the self-consciousness of colour becomes acute. Not only did whites literally colonize a continent, they may now be seen to colonize intimate relationships, as gay writer Daniel Gawthrop in Vancouver acknowledged over dinner in a Chinese restaurant. He told me he is "overwhelmingly attracted" to Asian men – Chinese, Filipinos, Thais, Indonesians, "all coming out of the Orient."

"That looks very bad, of course," I responded, slurping my wonton soup. "I've read Edward Said. *Orientalism*. Wayward sons of the European bourgeoisie in quest of licentious sex in the exotic East and all that."

Gawthrop had read it too. "The part in me that is attracted to the Oriental is irrational, is coming from within me, and I can't feel bad about it, but I'm trying to understand where it comes from. I don't think of the attraction as racist. The term that is used for a male like me is Rice Queen, which is a racist term in itself. The 'bad' Rice Queens don't have the slightest sense of irony about the situation and objectify their lovers to the point where they expect certain cultural traits from them; they want them to be submissive geishas."

But when I glibly compared this to the straight *World of Susie Wong*, Gawthrop said he had a more serious purpose in wanting to write about his "attraction." He wanted to locate it in the reality of the Pacific Rim, "and the political necessity of the goals and objectives of multiculturalism. We have to live together. I want to look at and explore how we actually get along. The entry point is the attraction, how we express it as opposed to the discourse from the ministers of multiculturalism about how we have to all get along."

It's an old recognition in him, this "instant communication" between himself and Asian men and what he calls the "mutual comfort" of their intimacy. The "obvious differences" between straight Asian men and gay Asian men – the gay men are extremely conscious of their appearance, they dress in finer, silkier clothing and pay more attention to their hairstyle – are signals that the gay ones are more "open" to him. "Some are westernized and some are not, some are closeted and others are raging queens – in that sense there's no pattern. It may just be coincidence or it may be karmic retribution but I've learned that my grandfather, who died forty years ago in a car accident, was detailed by the federal government, after Pearl Harbor, to arrange for the deportation of the Japanese into camps in the B.C. interior. And here I am forty years later making love to them."

> Rice Queen: Non-Asian person with racial guilt, internalized racism or racist assumptions who seeks out only/mostly Asian people as lovers & friends. Am I? Chocolate Queen: Non-Blk person with racial guilt, internalized racism or racist assumptions who seeks out only/mostly Blk people as lovers &* friends. R U?
>
> – T. J. Bryan, "Of Chocolate Queens & Rice Queens," *Fuse,* Special Issue, 1998

Like Gawthrop, Bryan lies disquieted in the arms of her Asian lover, wondering what exactly is the object of her passion: the woman herself or the myth of the soft-voiced, exotic Asian chick? Unlike Gawthrop, she is also tormented by Asian prejudice toward blacks – that Asian shopkeeper who followed her around in his store, certain she was shoplifting – and the ineluctable fact that her lover is in the same community of origin as the shopkeeper. "How can I be so pissed at them & still love U?" Then the worm turns. "Chink," she says in her soul. "C-h-i-n-k. No matter how I try, I can't get it outta my head or pretend it ain't mine." Not to mention the family jokes about pet dogs and cats disappearing into the cooking pots of the Chinese restaurant. Finally, the *cri de coeur*: "I want a girlfriend, not a political coalition."[22]

Solution: hang with your own black sisters.

> Wha'ppen? U're listenin' to RADIO BKLD. bringing only tha best vibes from north of the 49th. our stories are many & our voices are fierce! i'm here with DE POONANI POSSE (D.P.P.), a black dyke cultural production house. . . .
>
> D.P.P.: when will we stop lettin' others define us? so much radical sex politic work is bein' done by white queers. they're doin' work on butch/femme roles, gender-play, SM, dyke porn etc. but they've got kindergarten analysis of race & white supremacy . . . we see the word poonani as powerful – sexually,

culturally, linguistically. we gotta laugh when we see non-black people strugglin' with it or when we see bourgie black/brown folks & our tight-assed feminist sistren forced to use such "vulgar sexual vernacular."

SHANIKWA: thanx wimmin. stay tuned 4 the dyewanda jones show. tonite her guests are 5 confused closeted, male, chocolate queens, who masquerade as anti-racist dyke-daddies & get all up in stable, healthy, wholesome woman-lovin-woman unions. Listen in as the gyals who loved them, fell 4 them & fucked them, confront them & beg them to get help.

– Sapphire Shanikawa and DePoonani Posse, "Undoing Diasporic Dyke(otomies)," *Fuse*, Special Issue, 1998

Gender Identity Disorder: 1. A strong and persistent cross-gender identification. 2. Persistent discomfort with his or her sex or sense of inappropriateness of gender role of that sex.

– American Psychiatric Association, *Diagnostic and Statistic Manual IV*

I asked a friend of mine, a therapist, to look up in her copy of the *Diagnostic and Statistic Manual* the most recent references to homosexuality by the professional order of psychiatrists, just to make sure that it was true that homosexuality as such is no longer pathologized – and it is not, although it would be interesting to know when a disorder becomes a pathology from a medical professional's point of view. But my friend stressed that it is *comfort* with one's sexuality that is the point; it is "persistent and marked *distress* with sexual orientation," she read with emphasis from the *Manual*, that is classed a sexual disorder. Fair enough; psychiatrists are visited voluntarily by the unhappy and are not themselves homophobically in pursuit of the sexually "inverted."

Slowly but steadily since the 1970s, *The Bibby Report* on social trends in Canada shows us, attitudes toward homosexuality have become liberalized, so that by 1990 some 80 per cent of those polled agreed that "homosexuals are entitled to the same rights as other Canadians," with the 18-to-34-year-old age group the most accepting of all.[23]

However, the "right" to same-sex marriage is still very much contested.

At the same time that heterosexual marriage has become increasingly unpopular and unsuccessful among young Canadians (since 1971 there has been a 190 per cent drop in marriages among the 24-to-30-year-olds and a 29 per cent increase in the number of children living with a single parent),[24] the reverse seems to be true of same-sex couples. When I asked Clarissa Lagartera, the University of Winnipeg activist with the Gay, Lesbian, Transgender, Transsexual, and Bisexual Support Group, what was that ring she was wearing, she said it was a gift from her "fiancée," who had even made the "traditional" phone call to Clarissa's parents to announce "I love your daughter and want to marry her and spend the rest of my life with her."

Gay weddings and commitment ceremonies, the so-called lesbian baby-boom, and gay social approval of monogamy and nesting, make lesbian writer Nikki Gershbain a little crazy, wondering "if this is yet another tenet of seventies lesbianism abandoned by modern, post-politically-correct dykes. . . . Can we continue to argue that same-sex marriage is so subversive that the very act of registering for china patterns ('no, we're *both* the groom') can eradicate the root causes of our displacement?"[25] Gay Regina artist Gary Varro half-joked with me that, considering the appropriation by advertising of gay iconography and queeresque badness, "the most transgressive thing I could do now is get married to a woman." When Linda Melnychuk was on an assignment from *Hour* weekly in Montreal for a story about gay marriages, she described herself as a "writer who is anxious to get married so her family can see her in her finest leather." No wonder, then, Gershbain's lament that queer just isn't what it used to be – a *social* revolution of sexual liberation that insisted not on queer's similarity with the cultural mainstream but precisely with its *difference*, even its offensiveness.

Much of straight society is still offended. In Toronto the number of reported incidents of violent attacks on gays in 1998, typically perpetrated by young, educated, middle-class white men in a pack, increased by 20 per cent over 1997.[26] Thirty-one-year-old film director Thom Fitzgerald's much-acclaimed 1997 first feature, *The Hanging Garden*, tells the disquieting story of a gay teenager in Nova Scotia who, overwhelmed by the loneliness of his sexual secretiveness, hangs himself in the family garden (an ending that is not an ending, in fact). "I'm queer," Fitzgerald told a *Maclean's* reporter, "I was a teenager. I considered suicide."[27] Artist Lorri Millan was "beat up" in high school, even though she was not yet overtly lesbian. "I just tried to sneak through the halls and get by. They probably sensed I was a lesbian. In my mind I knew I was and I was really aware of what a bum rap it was to be female." These are painful reminders that sexuality, however performative it may be, is still lived in the real world of social relations once we walk out of the bedroom.

So, just how transgressive is queer? Lise Gotell thinks the question is not whether queer represents some ultimately transgressive sexuality or range of sexualities with the potential to completely disrupt the sexual order of society, but whether it represents the ability "to recognize that identities are not stable but are constructed. So what is the value of all this? We exist in a time which is very anti-sex in many ways, and I think that the kind of stuff that's going on in queer politics or gender or performance as strategies are an important challenge. Because, if we're going to have politics or build politics that challenge structures, we have to be pro-sex and reclaim it from earlier generations of feminists."

Three times I sat through the eight minutes of Noam Gonick's film *1919* while hunkered down with headphones on the sagging couch of Video Pool's offices in Winnipeg. I was delighted by Gonick's cinematic evocation of that mythologized event carried around in the brain stem of Prairie lefties, the Winnipeg General Strike of 1919, a battle lost by the plucky proletariat of a more heroic era. The Television Age had come along to wipe it from the screens of subsequent generations, or so I had feared. But Gonick remembers.

Conceived in 1970, during the Manitoba provincial election campaign of his very left-wing father, Cy Gonick, publisher and labour historian (he won), Gonick was practically born in red diapers. I suppose to him, his father's generation, which is also mine, is rather Old Left, but I point out to him that we were in fact the New Left, sexy and anarchist, in contradistinction to the hoary Old Left of Stalinist malpractice. "So what the heck are you?" I ask him. "New, improved Left," he replies. Good answer.

In *1919*, Gonick has revisited the Winnipeg General Strike and given it a new ending. It is not an arbitrary ending but one that opens up suggestively, once you ask certain questions of history; for instance, whether there was anything *funny* or *sexy* or *absurd* about the strike? In the film, a fictional group of gay men are hanging out at Sammy Wong's Steam Bath and Barber Shop, which has become a meeting place for the strikers and their supporters (including lesbian suffragettes) as well as continuing its function as site of erotic transactions. In this overlapping of meanings lies Gonick's meaning: "queering the General Strike," as he told me in conversation, but not just for the sake of being naughty. "I was trying to link sexual liberation and political liberation together and harness them to the same engine, to show that, in doing so, something good can come out of it all, and that you can reverse the outcome of history. That's why my version of 1919 ends in favour of the workers, but in reality we all know the workers lost the strike and that many of them were killed, and in the end the ruling elite regained control. If you ask any left-winger, the city has been spiralling downhill ever since, but I was trying to show what could happen if we introduced homoeroticism as an irritant into the mixture, and how it can be productive. It can help reverse the negative tide of history. Add better ingredients, and everything will turn out differently. So I'm not really trying to lampoon the general strike, I'm just trying to improve the odds."

Given the iconic status of the strike, for Right and Left, Gonick was taking a bit of a risk with his "improvements," and even having a bit of fun with his own ideals, which he described as believing "very heavily" that left-wing people are trying to make the world a better place. If this sounds awfully sombre, his film is anything but, with its slapstick sight gags, sped-up Keystone Kops sequences, and early film sound-effects that interrupt the political commentary, not to mention its eroticized sequences in the bathhouse and the hurlyburly of the closing sequence, in which the anti-strike mayor, taken hostage by strike organizers in the bathhouse, is forced to sign a statement meeting all the strikers' demands, and everyone, including the half-naked bathers in their towels, dances in celebration of their victory.

I told Gonick I did not think his film a "message" so much as an erotic fantasy, not just in its overt narrative of sexual liberation in a time of political and social upheaval but also in its sensual visuals – of the naked man in eyeglasses reading Trotsky and swooning like a maiden, of the two Bolshie labourers kissing amid the macho hissing steam and revolving gears of a factory – that make the beautiful point that eros works its magic in the simultaneity of political and sexual arousal. He agreed that this was what he was trying to tap into, that "you have all this social upheaval, and then you are having public sex, and you are crossing those boundaries," but also saying that the Left had always been "sexy," and that he has a copy of the *Communist Manifesto* beside his bed.

ETHNICITIES

Hyphenations

> How are we presenting ourselves to one another and to the communities that are Canada? I don't think the average Ukrainian woman walking through the village or town is carrying bread and salt, or dancing to the kolomeyka, but for some reason there she is, 3 generations and a continent away, kicking up her heels on stages across the prairies. . . . Far from the urban reality of the aboriginal, multi-racial and multiethnic populations of Canadian cities where most of us live and work, the festival community is a temporary space . . . it is a suspended reality where we indulge in the fantasy of a coherent Ukrainian-Canadian place.
>
> – Mary Anne Charney, "Making Sense of Pysanka: Is This What Ukrainian Culture Is All About?" *Zdorov*, Summer 1998

In 1995, 68 per cent of Canadians agreed with the observation that "on the whole, immigration is a good thing for Canada."[28] The 1998 Annual Poll published by *Maclean's* magazine did not even include a question about attitudes to multiculturalism and immigration. The reason may be that we seem to be *living* multiculturalism as though it were a normal if not a defining characteristic of our collective identity. This is certainly the conclusion I was heading to in conversations with young people whose public self-expression as members of cultural minorities in no way contradicted their hope that freedom and dignity of persons was expanding in society as a whole. On the contrary, they expressed repeatedly their conviction that a broadly shared Canadian identity now includes, *as its own content*, their own ethnocultural distinctiveness, much as philosopher Ian Angus suggests happens when all Canadians apprehend that "multicultural understanding is an us/we relation, not an us/them," in which the "us" is the ethnocultural group and the "we" is the multicultural civic society of Canada.[29]

As a third-generation Prairie Canadian of Ukrainian descent, I began my conversations among Ukrainian-Canadians, the ones right across the street, in fact. Orysia Boychuk and her husband, Volodymyr, had met while selling perogies at the Ukrainian Students' Club at the University of Alberta. Who are the Ukrainian-Canadians who come after me, I wondered, after the so-called golden days of official multiculturalism, after deficit slashing and program extermination, after Ukrainian independence and *Koka-Kola* in the sidewalk cafés of Kyiv? How does one go on being Ukrainian-Canadian in *their* world?

Is it still the case, in the so-called global village, that that hyphen is a kind of hinge between two equally compelling identities? To answer No, it no longer matters, would mean a radical excavation of the self, for both Orysia and Volodymyr were deeply imprinted by a politicization that took hold in childhood: Orysia in the Ukrainian-Canadian organizations in Oshawa, Ontario, and Volodymyr in the Soviet Ukrainian institutions of the U.S.S.R.

For Orysia, this meant *sadochok* (kindergarten), Saturday School for language and history and dance, Sunday School in St. George's Ukrainian Catholic church, youth groups and summer camps, not to mention speaking Ukrainian at home. Meanwhile, Volodymyr made the long march through Young October, Young Pioneers, and Komsomol groups. In the late 1980s, he launched into the most unforgettable years of his young life: the Gorbachevian experiment, the political and social opening up of the Soviet collective.

To hear the list of their community activities – some twenty hours a week – is to wish them both a sabbatical: Ukrainian Professional and Business Club, Ukrainian Media Initiative (concerning representation of Ukrainian-Canadians in mainstream media), Verkhovyna Choir, Ukrainian Soccer Club, and Ukrainian Canadian Congress, most of which are products of the multicultural golden age of the 1970s and early 1980s. "Everything I'm involved in is Ukrainian," Orysia observed, "but as I get older I think about being involved in something that is not Ukrainian. There are times when I've felt over-Ukrainianized, when I've wanted friends who are non-Ukrainians."

She had grown up when Ukraine was still a "captured" nation within the U.S.S.R. Crucial to the Ukrainian-Canadian community in which she was raised was that the Canadian-born generations should not be lost, that the struggle for independence not be betrayed by the fecklessness of westernized youth whose sense of purpose no longer bent to the needs of the groaning motherland. The overriding mission of the diaspora Ukrainians was to *remember*, to be the rememberers of a people whose own texts were systematically erased by terror, violence, and sheer, grinding Russification. Take Volodymyr, growing up in western Ukraine with no connection to Canada. When he finally visited Canada in 1991 and discovered the Ukrainian community in Edmonton, it brought tears to his eyes to hear kids with first names like Kevin and Tracy and Grant recite Taras Shevchenko.

Since Ukraine's independence in 1991, Volodko has realized that "the question now is what we're going to make of ourselves here, as Ukrainian-Canadians." Their duality is important, that residual "otherness" that every Canadian carries as baggage from ancestral cultures. This is the comfort of Canadian society, the multiculturalism that "allows" for this complexity of identity.

But now that their *Canadian* sensitivities have become sharpened, there are issues of their Canadian history they want acknowledged by their neighbours. Orysia emphasized this theme: "A lot of issues relating to Ukrainian-Canadians get put on the back burner." Invisibility. Marginality. A note of grievance entered the discussion. Ukrainians denied equal opportunities . . . their historical experience denied . . . internment of "enemy aliens" in World War One . . . the language suppressed.

Are they overly sensitive? After all, performances of Ukrainian dancing are very popular with general audiences; the giant *pysanka* (Easter egg) in Vegreville, Alberta, is a tourist attraction; and Sunshine Records of Winnipeg distributes over fifty titles in the category "Baba's Records." But this sort of representation of Ukrainian-Canadian ethnicity (Kiss Me! I'm Ukrainian!) increasingly disconcerts those born several generations down the line from the Galician pioneers of western Canada.

Taking up the challenge in Toronto is Nestor Gula, editor of *Zdorov* ("Greetings!"), an English-language magazine for Ukrainian-Canadians, who, having studied magazine journalism, having worked at a newspaper in Ukraine in 1993, having turned down the "opportunity" to work in Ukraine again in 1994 ("been there, done that – all you do is sit around and drink"), decided that the audience he wanted to address was himself: the young Ukrainian-Canadian trapped in a love-hate relationship with the Old Country, one minute bashing away at its "financial crisis, sick people, poor people, government in crisis, law on privatization passed on Monday, cancelled on Tuesday, re-passed on Wednesday . . . yadda, yadda, yadda," the next minute cheering on the Ukrainian athletes at the Olympics, "Let's go, Ukraine!"

Gula cheerfully admitted in an interview with me that he also plays on the "guilt" of the forty- and fifty-somethings who know they *should* be speaking more Ukrainian and buying their own subscription to *Ukrainian Weekly* and sending more money over to Ukraine, but who are really mainly interested in the doings of their own community, mainly in Toronto – the arts, celebrities, travel, food lore, opinion. "Normal," Gula answered, when I asked him how he wanted to represent Ukrainians in his magazine. "Even cool. You can be a Ukrainian and doing something cool as opposed to being a doctor, dentist, lawyer." This was not altogether an ethnic joke.

The model for this kind of journalism was the very cool *Eyetalian* magazine, also published in Toronto, with *Globe and Mail* columnists and a Governor General's Award–winning novelist as contributors, a very snazzy layout, sumptuous ads for trattorias on College Street and holidays in Tuscany. "Right there you have a problem," I challenged Gula. "Italians think it's really cool being Italian and going to Italy and listening to opera, and the rest of the world thinks so too. For Canadians, Italy is the Roman Empire, the Renaissance, the source of civilization, while Ukraine . . ." Gula nodded in agreement. "They think of us as dancers."

But when I interviewed John Montesano, the editor of *Eyetalian* (since folded), I stood corrected about Italian "cool." Montesano reminded me that thirty years ago Italians, especially those from the south, were the "black" immigrants of 1950s Canada. "You come in, do the crappy jobs, then they shit on you for taking away the jobs. In their heart of hearts, what do the Anglos think of us?" Montesano argued that Italian chic is limited to the "white" part of Italy, the north. Tourists don't go to *his* part of Italy, Calabria: "It's too dark." When we say we love Italian culture we're not talking about *his* culture. We wouldn't last two hours in Calabria. "Calabrians are strange, they look at you really mean. Anglos' sense of Italianness is very narrowly defined. You have to get past hanging out on

College Street and ordering arugula salad." But Paul Ghezzi, financial consultant in North York, was not at all mystified by non-Italians' fondness for Italian culture and lifestyle. "It is a romantic and idealistic culture, as you know if you've travelled there. Who the hell takes two-hour breaks for lunch except the Italians and French? They have a view of life that is not money-driven. The quality of life is in happiness and having fun, and we don't always remember that in Toronto."

But Montesano admitted that *everybody's* view of Italianness, including his own, is shaped by the mass media, and told a funny story on himself. It was about how he grew up in Downsview, a Toronto suburb, and never spent time on College, the original main street of the Italian immigrant community, until his non-Italian friends from the York University paper began hanging out there. That's how he learned what bruschetta was. Pronounced: *bru-sketa*. "They'd ask me if I wanted to order some *brusheta*. I'd correct their pronunciation with pride: Hey, get the language right. But I didn't know what the heck it was. You know what it is? Bread with tomatoes spread on it. Well, we ate that at home but we never called it that. Never put it on a plate with little parsley flakes. What the hell is that? We got a piece of bread, put some olive oil and chopped some tomatoes on it and ate it."

Montesano is the only one in an expanded family of fourteen who went to university. Everyone else, siblings and cousins and second cousins, quit school to work, mainly at well-paid construction jobs. He must have been an idiot to study. He told his parents he wanted to be a doctor to get them off his case. And it was in university that he discovered that the whole world wasn't Italian. In fact, in all his chemistry classes there were only two other Italians. Where were all the others? More invisibility, to themselves as well as to outsiders. "There are eight hundred thousand Italians in Ontario. One-tenth of this province. We're a ghetto? But our struggles are invisible. It says a lot about the community, that it's immigrant with a lot of money, and what do they do with it?" Oh sure, he told me, people were proud of Nino Ricci's Governor General's Award, but no one he knew had read the book.

Paul Ghezzi didn't know who he felt more alienated from: the Italian-Canadians he grew up with but who dropped out of grade twelve and in his estimation never really did anything with their lives but stuck to the neighbourhood; or the "WASPY world." He considers his roots to be sunk deep in

North York, not in the *molto* trendy bars and trattorias of Little Italy. "I don't identify with that part of town," he confessed. "I probably never go there. With the Anglos, it's not overt, it's subtle. It's in things like a statement, 'When I was a kid we vacationed in Aspen . . .' The closest I came to skiing was pulling some groceries for my parents on a pair of skis."

When *Zdorov*'s editor Nestor Gula told me he had been inspired by the example of *Eyetalian* magazine in Toronto to create an equivalent glossy trade magazine for and about Ukrainian-Canadians, I bought copies of both and made a comparison of their contents. Letters to the Editor carried the usual complaints from readers that the respective magazine's writers had gravely misrepresented the correspondent's community, whether in "making fun of our [Ukrainian-Canadian] incompetencies" or making "hackneyed criticisms" of the Italian Catholic church. Older generations have generally disapproved of exposing dirty laundry to the "English," preferring what John Montesano called the "we're Italian, rah, rah, rah" syndrome, even when the community's shortcomings are well known. Nestor Gula at *Zdorov* ran a piece about wife abuse among Ukrainian-Canadians and got "zero reaction" from a community presumably in deep denial.

Both magazines ran first-person exposés of the language policing among generations. A reader of *Eyetalian* wrote a letter to the editor: "Now, speaking Italian seems to have contained in it a form of unspoken competition between us first- and second-generation Italian-Canadians for membership into something, as though whoever can speak it best, has the right accent, knows the right words, uses the correct grammar, is the most authentic among us, truer to that which is Italian in us, an outward marker of knowing one's own self."[30] In a similar vein, a *Zdorov* journalist complained of an annual meeting that was conducted almost entirely in Ukrainian: "One woman stood up and sneered [at an English-speaking speaker], 'I didn't understand a word you said. Speak Ukrainian.' Excuse me? You've been in this country forty-plus years and you can't understand a few, simple words in English? . . . No, better some *yolop* [imbecile] who speaks perfect Ukrainian than an English-speaking person who can actually contribute valuable knowledge and experience."[31]

Typical of the ethnic press are the short news stories usually overlooked by the non-ethnic media: the fundraiser; the folk musician; the small human interest stories; a celebrity's act of charity; a documentary film. Also typical are the recipes and culinary features, including restaurants in the case of *Eyetalian*, and humour in the case of *Zdorov* ("Ten reasons why *varenyky* [perogies] are better than sex").

But the publications are only superficially alike. Subtext is all. Take the advertising, for example, signifying hyper-urban design sensibility and *nuovo* Tuscan chic in the one magazine, ethnic ghettoization and unvarnished folksiness in the other. Montesano admitted he was trying to communicate with a certain "demographic, to connect readers back to the city." There are "tens of thousands" like him, "we don't speak [standard Italian], don't identify with Italian institutions like the Columbus Centre or Giovanni Caboto and all that crap, don't go to church. I live downtown." Psychologically secure as urban Canadians, his generation is in a position to "take control over how our identity is being represented," and for the moment, at least, this sophisticated identity of the Italian-Canadian at ease in the upscale trattorias and furniture shops of the metropolis coincides with non-Italian views of the community.

By contrast, Ukrainian-Canadians still generally go along with the popular view of themselves as colourful, dancing, vodka-tippling *hunkies* recently arrived from a wheat farm in Saskatchewan. There is an uneasy relationship between this genial jokiness and the intention of *Zdorov* to air serious issues of Ukrainian-Canadian connection to the wider Canadian community, usually by highlighting the "good news" of Ukrainian-Canadian achievement in the arts, science and business and walking softly around more provocative issues such as the under-representation of Ukrainian-Canadians in the Canadian political, business and cultural elites, and the pursuit of alleged war criminals by Canadian courts. Although Gula had targeted the "yuppies" of Toronto as his "demographic," with their expensive cars, golf-club memberships and monster houses in the suburbs, he knows he treads a fine line between what's "interesting" about Ukrainian-Canadians and what's "negative," and what his potential readership is ready to accept as its representation. There's no getting around the psychological insecurity of a community that has periodically lived under a cloud in Canada as "enemy aliens" in the Great War, "Reds" in the 1930s, anti-Communist extremists in the 1950s, and aging, alleged pro-Nazi collaborators in the 1980s and 1990s. Compared to these stigmatizations, the fun-loving bumpkin is almost lovable.

In the west beyond the Great Lakes the English working out of Hudson Bay and the French moving on from their prairie post at Lake Winnipeg parried each other's thrusts for control of the far western fur trade. In the 1730s La Vérendrye, leaving behind him a trail of fortified posts, reached the Saskatchewan River. . . .

– Kenneth McNaught, *The Penguin History of Canada*

My grandparents homesteaded on a quarter-section near the town of Vegreville, which is how I knew the French had preceded the Ukrainians to that part of Alberta. Later, the more I studied Canadian history and the history of the fur trade and the Catholic missions in particular, the more I understood how *indigenous* the French presence is on the Prairies. When I learned of the annual Festival du Voyageur in St. Boniface, Manitoba, I decided to visit it and its program director, Danielle Sturk.

After six years in the fast-paced dance world of Montreal, Sturk had scooped up her two-year-old daughter and gone home. And home is where I found her a year and a half later, in February 1998, in a hotel café, cell phone in her shoulder bag, directing the thousand details of the cultural program of the twenty-ninth edition of the Festival, which was raging somewhere out there among the sooty and slushy snowbanks, on the grounds of a reconstructed fort.

It takes a village to raise a child, Sturk would tell me later, and in St. Boniface she had a whole village of relatives, all her siblings still there, and all their kids. As a child she had gone every year to the Festival, awed by the big floats in the parade and the beauty contests (both since dropped from the program), and by something else, now that she had thought about it, a "pride thing," the sense of connectedness to all that was *here*: how it felt to be a francophone of Manitoba and to have gone to *that* church and *that* school, to have spent summers at the grandparents' cottage at the lake, the smells of *Maman*'s cooking, the language. "What we're celebrating here," she said in the café, "is our francophone attachment along with the whole development of the area after the *voyageurs* – the people who came here from New France, then moved west and stayed west."

A mish-mash, I suggested, meaning the festival mixture of tuques and red sashes and Hudson's Bay coats, the Indians and the Francos and Anglos and Métis, the *cabane à sucre* and old time fiddling and jigging and the annual beard contest, the whole thing a kind of cabaret played in the shadow of the Selkirk settlers of the Red River in Rupert's Land, the stuff of western Canadian myth-making.

And, yes, Sturk does feel that "Prairie patriotism" I had asked her about, that thing she surely shares with the aboriginals. "You, like they," I wondered, "have no other home country than this one?" Yes, absolutely, that's the way it is for these Franco-Manitobans. A founding nation, even, of "this air, this space, this weather." Quebec was once upon a time the mother country, but no more, maybe not since the first *voyageur* packed out of Montreal for the rivers of the bush country and the plains and settled down with Indian women: "It was the French the North West Company hired, not the Scottish," said Danielle, "and so we have this very direct connection with the natives, who were essential. We sank roots. That's my strongest pride," she said, as we walked together to the Festival site, "the crossing over."

In the factor's house the interpreters divided themselves into three groups – the women of the Selkirk settlement in bonnets and carding wool; Marie Gabourey, the first French woman in the settlement, explaining herself; and the Métis women in cotton frocks, sewing deerskin. But it was in the blacksmith's shop, where I joined a "multicultural" group of schoolchildren, that I saw that Danielle Sturk had got her wish of the "crossing over": this fete of sugaring-off and dog-sled races and bannock on the fire, this display of fur hats and snowshoes and *ceintures fléchées*, this nostalgia of the palisades on the Rivière Rouge, had become the patrimony of us all, including the Vietnamese and Latin American and mixed-race children staring fixedly at the smithy's anvil as he hammered away at a red-hot nail. "This is not so much *our* festival now," Sturk told me, "it is Winnipeg's. It is a celebration of a culture that lies at the base of the city. If you live here, it's your culture."

In Edmonton, in what has become known as the French Quarter, near the Faculté St-Jean on the historic south side of the North Saskatchewan River, the "immigrants from Quebec" have built themselves La Cité. The architect was inspired by the buttresses and crenellated ramparts of a medieval *cité*, the place of last refuge in times of trouble, and so Franco-Albertans have built a glass and concrete four-storey community-centre-cum-cultural-refuge that houses Librairie Carrefour, the offices of *Le Franco* newspaper, Café Amandine, and a state-of-the-art theatre, L'UniThéâtre. The theatre's artistic director, Daniel Cournoyer, is pure home-grown Franco-Albertan, which is why I called him up. Traditionally, francophone theatre in Edmonton imported its artistic directors from Quebec, so what did Cournoyer think he was doing?

"My grandparents came to this province from Quebec at the turn of the century; my parents are now in their seventies, both born and raised here. I was born and raised here and work in the French language; we're not going to disappear." Translation: "Whatever happens to Quebec, *we're* not going anywhere."

Cournoyer's family has been in Alberta as long as mine has – close to a hundred years – and his *here* is right under his feet, or a little to the north, in St. Albert, now a suburb of Edmonton. In my childhood, St. Albert was a destination for a Sunday afternoon drive, a place in the country, the historic site of Father Albert Lacombe's 1861 Oblate mission for the Métis and, built two years later, a convent, school and orphanage run by the Grey Nuns. We were all mixed up together, his people and mine and the Métis, in "my" New Kiev, Myrnam, and Smoky Lake, "his" St. Paul, Duvernay, and Lac La Biche, in the boreal parkland north of prairie, tillers of the virgin soil and of the hopeful new towns along the railway tracks, who begat the generation who went to school who begat us, the third generation, artists rooted in Edmonton, where *he* speaks French, much to the amazement of Montrealers.

"My father has wonderful stories about growing up in Morinville. Why aren't we writing them, why aren't we seeing them? The pool room, the barber shop, the farmers, the foreclosures, the new teacher. We want to keep the language alive and developing and still creating our sense of who we are and what we're doing *here*. Ten years ago I had a staunch loyalty to Quebec, but now I see that was wrong. When my grandparents came out west, there were simply the *maudits anglais* and the French-Canadians. And they were part of developing the west along with everybody else, including the Métis, with whom there were strong bonds of mutual respect. And I'm a Franco-Albertan."

The point is that the grandparents *left* Quebec; the grandchildren have a whole new territorial patriotism; and Cournoyer has a big problem with *cabane à sucre*, the inevitable recreation of the traditional maple-sugaring shack at multicultural festivals. "It has nothing to do with my identity other than that as a kid we always went. Even then, I wondered what we were doing when we don't have sugar maples here. We should be having a harvest festival, an agricultural fete – that's a huge part of our history here. *Cabane à sucre* is an imported idea from the east we associate with as being a 'good French activity.'"

By this time in the conversation we were into third cups of café au lait at Café Amandine, and the waitress, Mireille, was hovering nearby, listening in. I was satisfied I understood Cournoyer's deep and contented sense of rootedness in this particular prairie place. But what of the rest of Canada, anglophone, hyphenated, cross-bred and blended, immigrant, polyphone, all of whom were pleased to identify with an enterprise called Canada. "Is *your* Franco-Albertan identity subsumed within one called Canadian?" I wanted to know. "Yes, yes, definitely!" he responded enthusiastically. "We feel we are participating in a common project with the rest of Canada." Mireille, now standing right by our table, elaborated. "Co-operation," she said. "I can't just be Canadian because I'm also French, and I can't just be French, because I'm also Canadian."

I thought about Cournoyer's earlier observation that, in Edmonton, at L'UniThéâtre, he can work as a francophone "without complexes." He doesn't live in a ghetto; he lives in Alberta. *L'Alberta.*

Sensory Organs

"The ability to 'eat bitterness' – to bear hardships without complaint, to bend to authority without breaking, to internalize grief while presenting a calm and dignified face to the world, to suffer, endure and to survive – is regarded by the Chinese as a special talent of the Chinese soul."

– From the Introduction, *Many-Mouthed Birds: Contemporary Writing by Chinese Canadians*, eds. Lee Bennett and Wong-Chu Jim, 1992

As the chair of the Writers' Union of Canada from 1993–94, I found myself lucklessly having to mediate several competing interests around multiculturalism and Canadian literature when the Union's Racial Minority Writers' Committee proposed to host a conference, "Writing Thru Race," from which white writers would be excluded except for public evening events. In spite of more level-headed interventions into the debate, the Writing Thru Race conference has now entered the official Canadian mythology of "multiculturalism's excesses" in which writers with their own agendas periodically drag it out of the files and have another kick at it, apparently still scandalized after all these years. The excesses are, arguably, their own.

I had become acquainted with writer Larissa Lai when she joined the organizing committee of the Writing Thru Race conference. Then I read the book *Bringing It Home*, to which she contributed a chapter called "The Sixth Sensory Organ," a first-person account of how she had come to feminism and race consciousness and how they had changed her. In it she writes of the Taoist universe and the memory of the reptilian woman Nu Wa, with the head of a woman and the body of a snake, and how she created the human race for her own delight. "Newspaper headline," Lai continues, "Chinese woman tells Chinese story. All is right with the world." There was, in this tossed-off line, something that seemed world-weary if not cynical, or impatient.

Having learned that Lai was writer-in-residence at the University of Calgary, I drove down to talk with her. I had also read her new novel, *When Fox Is a Thousand*, with enormous pleasure. What new experiences had she had of "writing through race" in the time between doing politics and writing fiction? We sat in her rented digs, drank a few pots of green tea, and talked.

Her journey through the minefields of identity politics has been more public than many. It began with a miserable childhood in St. John's, "outside the Catholic-Protestant thing, way outside the loop," then, with a move to Victoria came the revelation that Chinese-Canadians had been there "for generations," and finally, a meeting with the artist Paul Wong in Vancouver and the chance to work, after graduating from university in 1990, on the exhibition "Yellow Peril Reconsidered." It gave her what she saw then as a life project, anti-racist politics through the medium of the arts. "It was to begin to think about the world as though people who look like me and have my experience were at the *centre* of it rather those nice blond-haired and blue-eyed white boys who used to throw things at me at school in St. John's."

Lai had become fed up with living "on the margins" of cultural positioning. A decade ago, the realization that cultural production from the ethnic communities of Canada was relegated to the margins of mainstream concern seemed a progressive insight, an acknowledgement that, up to then, it had been simply invisible. Dragging minority expression into the light and peering at its performance of "otherness" was considered a kind of consciousness-raising for citizens of the dominant culture, but herein was precisely the problem for Lai. "Didn't you argue somewhere," I asked, "that the trouble with margins is that they always imply that there is a centre – and you're not in it?" Indeed. In fact her "project" has become a kind of self-imposed discipline in which she sets herself the task of "thinking what the world would look like, how I would tell stories, how I would organize conferences, how I would treat my family – *if I thought about myself as being at the centre.*"

To understand such audacity, we went back to "Yellow Peril Reconsidered," one of the first exhibits to bring together exclusively Chinese-Canadian artists and then send the show across Canada through the network of artist-run galleries. It changed Lai's life. It was about how people who look like her have been "racialized" (constructed socially as non-white) and about how she had a right to be "mad" without being considered "nuts." But more important was her discovery that there was the basis for solidarity, a community of resistance even, among others who identified as Asians. "We had avoided the issue with each other," she said, "because we knew we weren't supposed to talk about it. If you were going to make anything of yourself in this country, you must not refer to racism or to being racialized. And there was real pleasure – twisted maybe – in the recognition that we had shared experience and that we could get together and talk about it and make Whitey feel bad."

When the Writing Thru Race conference was being planned, Lai was one of those who spearheaded the idea it be a gathering of writers of colour and First Nations only. Making Whitey feel bad was no longer the point; in fact, for the sensitive workshops, Whitey wasn't even invited. That's what happens when you start to imagine yourself at the centre: the Writers' Unions and *Globe and Mails* and Canadian Legions and their concerns disappear from it, and you create a space where *you* decide what the agenda is.

The damage was done by the "hijacking" of the conference's aims by the public frenzy outside its doors: "Our terror of repression, and our forced focus on white folks, after all did really alter the shape and tenor of the conference." There was no room here for ambivalence or public questioning of what the group was doing; if you were to say you didn't entirely "believe in" the premise of the conference, for instance, you had "given conservatives the green light to take you apart before you've got where you were going." Exhaustion took its toll as well on the ten volunteers, only two of them from the Writers' Union of Canada, who had worked ten months to bring it together while being sniped at from several directions at once, including from other artists of colour who accused the organizing committee of being too "apologetic" and said "we should just take the [Writers' Union] money and tell the Union to bug off." But the conference was nevertheless an important "historical moment" in which a varied group of writers did manage to come together with nothing in common except experience of racism, and talk it out.

But this was a far cry from the exhilaration of the "Yellow Peril" exhibit, which in retrospect can be seen also as the collaboration of two generations of multicultural activists. Lai wrote an article for the catalogue assessing what she called the "oldtimers of the 1970s" – my generation in other words, the first beneficiaries of official multiculturalism – including "the guys" at Co-op Radio in Vancouver with their program "Pender Guy" (*guy* meaning "man" in Cantonese), for whom organizing *as* Asian Canadians was very natural, rooted perhaps in a decade's worth of political experience in community and student organizing. Lai did feel a solidarity with them but otherwise the official multiculturalism she experienced in the classrooms in St. John's was "just the shits. I remember the posters, pictures of cute children, one of every colour, with a message about equality. I resented it like mad."

Q: Are you a member of a visible minority?
TONY SINGH: In Toronto, no.
Q: How about in the middle of Saskatchewan?
SINGH: In the middle of Saskatchewan, maybe. I never think about that.
Q: Is Punjabi By Nature reflective of Canada?
SINGH: Definitely! Last summer, we played in New York's Central Park. The band was announced: "From Toronto, Punjabi

By Nature." We are from India, Jamaica, Malta and South Africa.
Our music is Canadian.
— Tony Singh, lead singer and principal songwriter for the
bhangra band Punjabi By Nature, interviewed for "Person,
Place, Thing," *Globe and Mail*, September 26, 1998

On a visit to Vancouver I called at the office of Larson Suleman Sohn &
Boulton, immigration lawyers on West Hastings Street, to see Zool
Suleman, who was known to me as the one-time editor of *Rungh* magazine
of Asian arts and culture and who is now, according to the short biography
supplied by his office, a "consultant to municipal, provincial and federal
governments regarding arts policy," one of the more dismal duties of the
arts activist.

Of Ismaili Indian origin, Suleman and his parents emigrated to Canada
from eastern Africa in the 1970s. Now that Suleman in his thirties is "getting
a little bit older" and overtaken by the demands of a profession and family
life, he is happy to pass on the "good fight" of race politics to the next generation at *Rungh* magazine. Taking the issue to the street with placards
requires a certain kind of energy; raising kids and passing on traditions,
language, and spirituality requires another. It's not a question of "selling
out" but of doing political work where your life finds it – in Suleman's case
in immigration law and adoption cases and the very real possibility of
immigrant communities bestirring themselves against what he calls the
"hardening of the cultural arteries in Canada" around immigration rules
governing extended family members.

Over lunch and a great deal of background dish-clattering, Suleman
seemed to speak from some calmed centre of himself as he reflected on his
life as a cultural activist. His recollections of the "racist manner" in which he
was first treated in Canada as a schoolboy – "spit at, kicked in the hallway,
called Paki in skirmishes at the bus stop" – or of the very Eurocentric curriculum at school and university – "your Elizabethan, your Shakespeare"
– are not embittered ones. He did not feel marginalized, he said, not at all.
His education was an opportunity to learn the things that were "being
spouted all the time" in the world he lived in. He read the African-American
theorist, bell hooks, on his own. And as a university student he discovered

the folk music scene, was politicized by it, by the mix of art and leftist labour views, and hooked up with the Vancouver Folk Festival.

His editorial and community experience with *Rungh* magazine took him to the Writing Thru Race conference, where, he was relieved to discover, the agenda wasn't half so "contested" as participants feared, given the furore raised by the media. Instead, Suleman found that "defiance" in the act of attending the conference at all and then the chance for "insider dialogue" made the event worthwhile. But it must be said that the reaction of the media in Toronto was a very much delayed one: "The reality is that we'd already had protests here about access to the Vancouver Art Gallery, we had meetings all through the 1990s. It was a very active time for a whole host of race-based issues, especially in the mixed-media and arts area. By the time the conference came around, we thought 'so what?'" It was his imperturbability around the "multicultural" flashpoints that persuaded me that perhaps *balance* was the point in these matters.

Thinking of some Alberta politicians, I wondered if the political right wing, the Reform Party in particular, with its number of mid-profile South Asian success stories, saw an opportunity for itself in a younger Asian-Canadian generation's insistence on its own individual "abilities" and its amnesia about its parents' and grandparents' experience of racism. And it wasn't just a denial of ethnicity that lured them into Reform, I speculated, it was also that a certain tradition we've been pleased to call "Canadian" hadn't taken hold of them, so that they were blind to institutions as well as to history. I was thinking of the "Canadianness" inherent in the support of social projects, the collectivity evoked by mutual help, the public benefit that accrues from investment in the arts and public broadcasting. I saw yet another kind of threat to the *publicization* of multiculturalism – that is, its situation not in private or individual but in public discourses – from the globalization of culture and the crushing dominance of American entertainment, which is also out there, in public. Why did politically conscious minorities seem not to identify with the Left as they did a generation ago, with the politics of multiculturalism and immigration and civil rights? Or was I being alarmist?

Suleman's answer lay in people's sense of economic realism: "Who is the NDP really speaking to any more? I don't have a quick answer to that, but I think people experience their economic realities as a daily event, and if some politician makes the promise that they are going to see their daily living improve, they'll go for that. And if you say to them that the very same people they are investing their hope in are the ones who are destabilizing economies and creating massive inequities in our working environment, they don't want to do that analysis. They'd rather feel powerful at the expense of other people. Ask Rahim Jaffer [Alberta Reform MP] what a Reform government would have done for his immigrant parents? Or how he would have become bilingual in a Reform environment?"

It is also Suleman's sense that the twenty-somethings, especially those born or raised in Canada, are dealing with "larger agenda items" such as male violence, poverty, the environment, homophobia. "Is there a danger, then," I pursued, "of erasing *again* the difference in specific ethnic and racial experience and consciousness by focussing on these global issues?"

"I think that's a very real fear – a de-racifying or de-colouring of those issues," Suleman agreed. "Here's where the Reform Party may be correct: if there are a lot of people of colour in the populace, then the concept of pre-serving identity as a minority function starts to lose weight."

Over to Vancouver's east side and the offices of Jenny Kwan, NDP MLA for Mount Pleasant (ex-premier Michael Harcourt's old riding), who works in the very thick of everyday economic realities and ethnic advocacy. But she is no "bloc" candidate of the 250,000-strong Chinese-Canadian community in British Columbia. She is a passionate advocate of her *constituents*, a social democrat whose own life experiences, or "struggles," as she put it, as the working-class daughter of Chinese immigrants from Hong Kong shaped her political mission. So when she takes pride in the elderly Chinese who came out to vote in the last provincial election, it is not in their *Chineseness* that she exults but in the fact of their political participation, "fully legitimate in the democratic system." For a full appreciation of those scenes at the polling booths, it helps to have grown up, as she did from nine years of age, in Vancouver's east side, eight people in a two-bedroom basement apart-ment, your father a tailor, your mother working on the farms of the Fraser Valley for ten dollars a day, every day dreading school, the white children trapping you in a washroom cubicle, chanting, "Chink! Chink! Chink!" and you thinking, "Oh, if I could just not be Chinese."

After the anguish of high school, Kwan drifted in and out of a Business

Administration program, took a secretarial job, and saved enough to buy a ticket to Hong Kong and mainland China in 1987. There, she had two revelations: one, Chinese culture is ancient and venerable, and hers to claim as heritage; two, the staggering social and economic injustices and inequities of Hong Kong and China made her "realize what democracy means and how important it is, and that even within our democratic society we're not all treated fairly and equitably all the time," as she is quoted, in understatement, on her Web site. Back in Canada she knew exactly what she wanted to do: by 1990, a degree in Criminology, and a three-year stint advocating for the poor in the legendary Downtown Eastside Residents' Association. It was among the homeless and badly housed and the evicted, the immigrant, the unemployed, the street kids, the junkies. "On the first day, I knew I had found my calling."

In a four-page flyer prepared for her campaign for the provincial legislature, she listed instances of her community activism: she fought to preserve and build affordable housing and fought for improved services for small businesses on Commercial Drive; she worked with the Strathcona Community Centre youth program; she worked with the Chinatown Merchants Association. This is a bilingual flyer – half of it is in Chinese – and it is liberally illustrated with photos of Kwan: here she is, bright-eyed and smiling radiantly, in a proud family group with mother Po Kwun Tse Kwan and father Wing Yim Kwan; in a Chinatown market; in front of Harry's Café on Commercial; on a residential street talking with a constituent; with Glen Clark; with Mike Harcourt. Message received: Jenny Kwan is a tribune of the people. *Jenny Wai Ching Kwan wants to win this election to become B.C.'s first Chinese-Canadian* MLA. And so she did, in April 1996 (along with Liberal Ida Chong).

And when she rose in the legislature to move the Throne Speech, she spoke for thirty minutes in English, four minutes and ten seconds in a Cantonese summary, five minutes in an English-language wrap-up. There was heckling from the Liberal benches and an outcry in the press, and more than a year later, Kwan still smarted from the suggestion that she somehow had given offense, by speaking Cantonese, in what she considered a celebration and demonstration "in a symbolic way, of multiculturalism and [of] the different faces around the Legislature that reflect the faces of British Columbia."

At the time, she cried openly, and was tagged a weeper playing the ethnic card; if you can't stand the heat, implied some of her colleagues, including those on the Left, get out of the kitchen. "The people who supported me were the young people, and the old ones who had experienced how bad it used to be." That left the middle-aged, the relatively comfortable, who cautioned her that things are going "not too badly" for the community right now, so please, Jenny, don't stir the pot. "This was very hurtful. I got into politics because I didn't want to be silent. I'm sure that when the men and women and children fought for the rights which I now enjoy, there were people then who said, 'Why do you have to do this? There is always going to be discrimination. Leave it alone!'" That's not Jenny Kwan's way, and by this point she was speaking with stirring vehemence. "I wouldn't be a community advocate if I didn't believe that. How otherwise could I go up to people and say, 'Look, if you face injustices, you *must* speak up.' How can I say this to people if, when I'm faced with [an injustice], I'd just say, 'Hey, I don't want to deal with this'?" The multicultural point: not privatization or sublimation or even balance, but *social activism*.

Who did she consider her allies when push came to shove? Her constituents. So we ended as we began the conversation, with connectedness. "It's my job to make sure that the trust they show in me is matched by my actions. I get my inspiration from the people here who are survivors. They have fought the fight."

In her essay "The Sixth Sensory Organ," Larissa Lai had startled me with her degree of self-exposure, critical of the conventional Chinese-Canadian construction of femininity with her evocation of the Snake Woman's lesbian desire to "make family" with other women and of the silk workers in the Pearl River Delta who "resisted marriage" and who she likes to think of as her foremothers. But she goes further even than this, and reveals to her readers that she is frightened by how "thin" the Chinese-Canadian activists have become, those who have agitated against structural inequities and hostile social climates, asserted identities of race and gender and sexual orientation, insisted on their visibility in our collective history.

Now she writes that "real people" cannot be contained within such exclusive rhetorical categories of identity. In fact Lai has had these thoughts, she told me, since 1990. "But I didn't dare say it. I couldn't have afforded to say it. Writing it was a way of coming to my own power." Not that she has stopped believing that racial minorities in this country have been "held back, put down and shut up." Even while writing fiction, she didn't want to stifle her "polemical voice" raised against racism, classism, and homophobia. "But I will not be cornered as a racialized subject." She wants to go far beyond the point where "progressives" find themselves stuck now, after all the conferencing and protesting and lobbying, unable to talk with each other "about the whole extent of what we are as human beings."

Lai is a Chinese-Canadian artist and citizen who, no matter what racist society has thrown at her, still imagines herself entire.

Dream Warriors

The living room of Edmonton schoolteacher Malcolm Azania was one of the most crowded I'd ever sat in. And he was still unpacking boxes – mainly of books arranged by subject to add to the already heavily laden shelves: History of Nations of Islam, History of the Black Panther Party, Spiritual Instruction, World Religions, Noam Chomsky's oeuvre, Kenyan literature. Already on the walls were posters, including one for a Spike Lee film, pictures of the beautiful and the doomed – Bob Marley, Che Guevara, Malcolm X, Marcus Garvey – and inscriptions of ancient Egyptian prayer.

"This is an awful lot lying on your frail shoulders," I commented. To which Azania responded with some earnestness, "I'm just one guy who's trying to live and earn a living and have some fun with my friends and hopefully trying to do the right thing to the greatest degree possible while doing it."

The next time I saw him he was acting in a play under the name Minister Faust, a moniker he also uses as a *nom de plume* when he publishes poetry and short fiction. He is a DJ at the University of Alberta's alternative FM station; and I already knew that he was a dedicated teacher-activist, on the Political Involvement Committee of the Alberta Teachers' Association. Some years ago he had been Minister of Defence of the Militant Rap Party, a hip-hop group loosely based on some of the nobler features of the Black Panther Party.

Azania was named, by his white mother, for Malcolm X, and from an early age he believed it was his responsibility to learn everything he could about Malcolm X and live up to that fearsome legacy. He was self-taught in this regard, learning "not a word" in public school about black history in Canada and coming only as close as *Cry, the Beloved Country* to black literature. He had been in grade seven when a classmate of his leaned out the schoolbus window and spat on a South Asian kid, and Azania knew that if the South Asians weren't around he'd have been the target.

On his father's side, he is Kenyan, on his mother's, Welsh and Pennsylvania Dutch. Acknowledging his hybridity, he prays for all his ancestors, he told me, and intellectually acknowledges European ancestry. But "culturally," he added, "*who* you are is more than just who *you* see yourself as, but also who accepts you as one of *them*." Case closed, then. He's a black man. And to those well-meaning white liberals who, in an effort to be compassionate let him know they are colour-blind, he responds with "more contempt than your text will convey" that they could not be more insulting. Think about it: "Are they so terrified of my colour that they would rather pretend it doesn't exist?"

But he wouldn't go so far as to say colour was a primary identification, privileged above "all the things that we were and are." How could he divide himself up? And how do you separate the African man out of the teacher of English, the English-language writer, the lover of the language of the people who conquered and enslaved Africans? How is the hip-hop artist to be extracted from the pedagogue?

For that matter, as an avowed Afrocentric and anti-racist and a life-long admirer of African-American revolutionaries, to what extent was Malcolm Azania an American? Although highly influenced by the African-American tradition of political activism, he certainly wouldn't call himself an African American. "Canadians in general are overwhelmed by the American influence, including African-American influence. As a Kenyan Canadian it's important for me to be involved in the creation of political consciousness and literature and art that are uniquely our own."

In 1995, the black Canadian writer André Alexis wrote, in an article that still raises hackles, that just because he didn't live in the "version" of Canada that the revered literary matriarch Margaret Laurence imagined in her novels, it did not mean that nothing in her world was recognizable to him. Quite the contrary. Evoking their common "homeland," Alexis wrote that he recognized certain "essential" things in the Manewaka saga: "the earth, the sky, certain people, the way they talk." The fact that he went to Laurence to feel this Canadian camaraderie led him to conclude, "There's an absence I feel at the heart of much black Canadian art. I miss black Canadian writing that is conscious of Canada."[32]

A year earlier, Ayanna Black had edited an anthology of Canadian writers of African descent, the essence of whose writing was not so much its Canadian lineage as its retrieval and borrowing of elements "from the painful and complex history of experiences born of slavery and colonization, cultural genocide, famine and civil war, and tyrannical dislocation."[33] Thinking of Alexis's argument, I wondered what these elements had to do with the inscription of black experience in Canada: Slavery? Cultural genocide? Civil war?

In the introduction to an anthology of African-Canadian literature, editor George Elliott Clarke writes that his bloodlines in Nova Scotia run deep, "to 1813 on my African-American/Mi'kmaq mother's side and to 1898 on my African-American/Caribbean father's side." Then, in a characteristically lyrical volley, he adds, "My heart surges with the North Atlantic and leaps at the North Star."[34] This is lovely; but Clarke also tells us that black slaves were born in the eighteenth-century fortress of Louisbourg and that he himself was the target of child rock throwers in the sixties.

For black Canadians, or Africadians (his neologism), there *is* a "here" here, and he refutes the "misreadings" of other writers who feel only the absence of blackness in Canadianness. Clarke has rediscovered, for instance, the novelist William Stowers, born in Canada West in 1861. But the identification with and within Canada goes much deeper for Clarke than cultural archaeology. *It is one with the land.* In his 1997 article in *Borderlines* magazine, "Honouring African-Canadian Geography: Mapping Black Presence in Atlantic Canada," he writes of the woodlot woodcutters, dirt-poor gypsum miners, hardscrabble farmers: "We have mined nickel in the freezing cold of Sudbury; we have fished on the frigid North Atlantic . . . Canadian nature, climate and weather are second nature to us."

He is profoundly, if complicatedly, at home. And from this position takes shots at "academics" in Toronto who imagine that Africadian culture begins and ends with hip-hop: "[They] need to spend some time in the countrified Black spaces of this nation." Cameron Bailey, a cultural critic in Toronto, told me in an interview, being as "brutally honest" as he could be, that "George is out in a field here on this one" and that, for all the theorizing one does of one's own experience, "the rural African-Canadian cultural tradition is kind of dying."

Rural Canada is where Bailey sticks out like a sore thumb, and he invites Clarke to travel an hour outside of Toronto to see if he isn't accosted by white folks there who want to know where he "comes from." Which isn't to say there isn't "enormous ethnic hostility" in Toronto. "In terms of actually making culture," however, Bailey says, "most of that is coming from the Caribbean immigrants." And it is this *migrancy* of the not-quite-in-Canada, not-quite-in-Jamaica Torontonian that another one of Clarke's "academics," Rinaldo Walcott, finds so interesting about the black experience in Canada, the living "in the in-between," and so uninteresting about André Alexis's "colour-blindness" in the "common homeland" of Canada.[35]

> Bathurst Subway. I say it like home. . . . So we're not going any place, and we're not melting or keeping quiet in Bathurst Subway. . . .
> – Dionne Brand, "Bathurst," *Bread Out of Stone*

This was Spadina Avenue, actually, in the office of Ivan Berry, president of Beat Factory Music, producer and promoter of urban music. The man was so charged with energy that I feared he would simply propel his wiry frame right out of his presidential chair and through the door.

"Urban music has nothing to do with being *music* but everything to do with being a *culture*. It's the strongest culture. When you see a bunch of fourteen-year-old kids – white, black, Asian, whatever – with the baggy jeans falling off their ass and a baseball hat, walking down the street going 'yo, yo, yo,' what do you think? Skateboarders? Rappers? Thieves and vandals? Tommy Hilfiger is making a fortune off that look, which came from the kids in the ghetto who can't afford a belt. Now the suburban kids are eating it up."

I said I was a latecomer to the realization that urban music is the "number-one form of music worldwide today," the rock 'n' roll of the nineties. I told him I could relate to rock 'n' roll. "Urban music is the only music that has come out of rock 'n' roll," he replied. "People say disco, which is commercialized R&B, did too. Excuse *me*. That was urban music, but John Travolta stole it."

But if rap is poetry – a kind of spoken verse – then Berry would want as many people as possible around the world to hear it. Internationally, rap music is blending many cultures and religions together. That's why Beat Factory pitches urban music to the suburbs; white kids *do* get it. They had no problem understanding Public Enemy's hit song "Fight the Power." Kids in general, black or white, understand discrimination: try being a kid sitting down in the Eaton's Centre.

But the kids' music does not go both ways, I argued. "I went to the Rheostatics concert last week and there wasn't a single non-white face there."

"Ha, ha, ha, that's what I'm getting at! If you were to ask five people about rock 'n' roll, I guarantee you four would say black people didn't start rock 'n' roll. Are you crazy? I've been to rock 'n' roll concerts, from Pink Floyd to Nirvana, and it's the most uncomfortable feeling. It isn't that anybody picked a fight with me, I just felt I shouldn't be there."

While Berry changed his tune and saw the righteousness of getting all the people together to listen to the music, it is vitally important that *creative* control of the production of urban music in Canada stay in the hands of people who understand whose music it is.

> The chances that anyone who bought this CD, cracked it open and is reading these words doesn't know The Dream Warriors or what they represent in the cosmos of hip-hop culture are slim to none. Just in case, though, welcome to the world of the originals: King Lu and Capital Q, who first laid claim to fame as the nation's most durable and consistent rap crew in 1988 when they mustered forces with manager Ivan Berry and partner Rupert Gayle to launch themselves as part of Beat Factory Productions. Damn, that's a whole decade right there! Ten large years. And they're still at it!
>
> – Daniel Caudeiron, sleeve notes,
> The Dream Warriors' *Anthology* CD

If hip-hop has become synonymous with urban music, it's because Puff Daddy can sell five- to ten-million records, spreading through suburban markets like wildfire. "Urban reality is suburban entertainment," said

Barry, pithily. And the suburbs is where Beat Factory has to sell The Dream Warriors, which it does under the democratizing notion that anybody is a warrior as long as they are warriors of a dream. Besides, "you sell moonshine not to the people who invent it but to the people who want to experience it." Translation: urban music has to move outside the limited market of urban black consumers if it's going to sustain itself financially.

And if Berry's calculations are right, *Canadian* urban music will leave its own imprint on the international hip-hop scene. Certainly his excitement about it was palpable, now that even the Americans acknowledge that "our" music is slightly different from theirs – the phrasing, the accent – which opens up a market niche. The source of the music is Toronto's Jane-Finch corridor, whose culture Berry calls "ghetto, for lack of a better word," meaning "the people are so poor and saddened that they write great poetry about it." In hip-hop culture, the ghetto is a low-income housing area with no parks, no jobs, but lots of liquor stores and violence and theft. So far this sounded very American to me, and I didn't understand how a particularly Canadian brand of urban music could have emerged from it. According to Berry, there was an enormous difference. Toronto's blacks may live in a neighbourhood called, after the American fashion, the ghetto, but they are not to be confused with their American brothers and sisters: "American blacks are American, and their last stop before America was Africa. Canadian blacks are ninety-nine per cent West Indian. We had a pit stop in the Islands after Africa and we're still coming from the Islands."

Cameron Bailey, who's been following Canadian hip-hop since 1986, said that American hip-hop, like Canadian, has its origins in Jamaican clubs in New York's Bronx area in the 1970s. More to the point, he observed that Canadian artists have always referred to American artists as a kind of touchstone, not to imitate but to "bounce off of" in that perennial dynamic of anxiety: "Are we as good as Americans? How do we make ourselves different from Americans?" More black Canadian artists are signed to American labels than to Canadian, and any Canadian artist who will sign to a major label, in the familiar "curse that all minorities have put on them," will be expected to represent the entire race in their grab for the brass ring.

The way Bailey "reads" the images of blackness in the popular press is as a steady parade of stereotypes – the illegal immigrant, the criminal about to be deported, the rapist, the burglar, occasionally the welfare mother –

young, threatening black men on the loose. Partly, the images come from the "onslaught" of American television, but a lot of them are produced right here in the "Great White North," which sees those images "of a threatening black character, a black person, as not belonging to Canada, someone who needs to be deported, someone who is an immigrant, someone who is a stranger," and so we are back there where we started, with the vertiginous possibility that, even after three hundred years in Canada, black Canadians have no land to light on.

In his award-winning play *Riot*, Andrew Moodie imagined a household of young urban blacks in the summer of 1992, when a riot tore up downtown Toronto after the police assailants of Rodney King in Los Angeles were acquitted. There is a range of blackness among the characters, including the very frustrated and explosive Wendle, a student from Halifax, who has this to say about one of the Great White North's enduring myths about itself: "This country is racist from top to bottom. From the police force, to the military, to the business sector, to the CBC . . . I mean the fuck is it with this *Road to Avonlea* shit? There's not a single black person in sight! My ancestors fought and died to help found this country. They settled right next door to that part of the world [P.E.I.]. I've never seen a black face on that show!"³⁶ If Africadians truly see themselves reflected in American or Jamaican popular culture or in agendas of black nationalism or in African consciousness, it may be because, as George Elliott Clarke suggests, such reflections are a "*necessary* counter-influence to the mainstream dream of Canada as a 'white' country, a fantasy which stigmatizes blackness."³⁷

Imagine just how Canadian an Africadian fan of the Toronto Raptors feels, a basketball freak in the land of King Hockey. How is he to see himself in the fond recollections of father-and-son games on the backyard rinks in Prairie towns when now on offer is a sport played, right in Toronto, by African American supermen and tagged with expensive, desirable brand-names like Nike and Reebok? Here is a "narration" of nation-building, a new black, *American* nation projected onto the "discourse emerging around basketball and Black public masculinities," which Gamel Abdel-Shehid calls Raptor Morality.³⁸ In other words, in a process all too familiar to Canadian culture consumers, the construction of black male American identity around the prowess of African American athletes, which is then circulated in the marketplace as elements of black style, is being appropriated holus bolus by young black Canadian males as "theirs," while the indigenous, Canadian representations of their masculinity are either racist or hidden. Where is the "official narrative" of Canada that shows a black face?

Kristine Maitland went looking for a different kind of narrative, in the Art Gallery of Ontario's European gallery, and found it in a seventeenth-century Italian painting, *The Toilet of Bathsheba*, by Luca Giordana. This was admittedly not a Canadian work but, hey, this was Culture, part of the western patrimony in which Canadians are visually schooled, and in the artist's lush assembly of women, "I can see me."[39] What she sees is a black woman slave attending the white plushiness of Bathsheba.

There is a counter-strategy to this kind of representation, and Toronto multimedia artist Camille Turner is involved in plotting it by creating installations with black women as subjects. "When we last talked," I reminded her, "you said that you don't want to racialize this female figure, and yet her blackness, it seems to me, is the point."

"Well, it's not," said Turner. "It's part of identity, just a part of her identity."

"Okay, so it's the encounter with herself that's important. In this case the subject happens to be black."

"Exactly."

For some years now, Turner has been engaged by experiences of black femininity, especially those in the Jamaican stories she grew up with. She showed me parts of a film she's making with a young sixteen-year-old friend, Andrea, as subject, showing her reading and talking about what she wants to do and be when she grows up, what she thinks is important, what she likes, what she doesn't like. Andrea was born in Canada and has had the benefit of black heritage lessons in school, but still she "is getting those same things that I got, and I wasn't born here." Turner was referring to the inevitable question posed of Africadians: "Where you from, dear?" and was thinking of shooting Andrea as an alien from Ork, just to make her point.

Turner grew up in Hamilton, went with her family to an all-white Baptist church, and was "saved" by the Afro-Caribbean Association, "an excuse for black people to come together in Hamilton," but which provoked in her a burgeoning identity as a black person, especially once she had prepared a black history of Hamilton for the Association. That was a "real eye-opener." In the course of learning, she told me, that "black people have been in Canada as long as whites" (she believes an African accompanied the first Europeans as a translator of aboriginal languages), she went on to discover a whole set of stories of very early contact between peoples of Africa and of Central America that preceded the arrival of Europeans. Turner mentioned that "interesting artifacts that are definitely West African" had been found in digs on the eastern coast of Mexico. Her excitement and pleasure at this discovery were acute. "Like wow, it opened up all kinds of interesting avenues to me. After doing that paper I felt so much more of an entitlement being here."

I felt so much more of an entitlement being here. By this point of my field trip I received such an open admission with a sorry heart. How many times now had I heard this almost melancholic expression of a scarcely imagined belongingness – to a country and homeland, a native soil, a "here" that, to my blithesome way of thinking, could be appropriated by the simple (!) act of desiring it? There were Canadians around me who felt only provisionally attached to Canada as homeplace, not necessarily because they were enraged by its smug white liberalism or gravely injured by its systemic violence to the "othered," but because they were absent from its self-regard. For every inroad they made into our consciousness they had to guard the tracks behind them for fear of their erasure. In such insecurity, it is difficult to see how it will come about that "recent arrivals to a democratic society want to be a part of a process whose real history is in the future, not the past," as philosopher Charles Taylor proposes.[40] This is too comforting by half: Canadian society still has to ask itself whether official multiculturalism isn't still just a mask of reassurance behind which hides the real power to decide what Canadian culture *is* and who belongs to it – issues very much rooted in our past, while decisive for the future. No wonder, then, that Camille Turner investigates all her possible selves as a black woman – the goddess of ecstasy inhabiting the sensual self, the Arubian goddess of the sea, the Luo love songs of the women of Uganda, traces of the goddesses who have come to Africa from India, traces of the Ghanian trade with the Olmecs, as well as the little girl in Jamaica who read the fairy tale of Sleeping Beauty and dreamed of ballet slippers – and takes no consolation in theories of hybridity, nomadism, displacement. People always tell her, she says, that "as a black woman I am poised to be at the forefront of the post-post-modern, but what the hell does that mean as a person who has to live and breathe and belong?"

> *Migmaeio otjosog,* the Mi'kmaq people say, "roots so deep they can't be pulled."
>
> – From the film *Mi'kmaq Family*

In 1997 Winnipeg art teacher Tom Roberts and his Native students at R. B. Russell Vocational High School won an award for excellence and innovation in art education for thirty murals they executed around the city. They called it the Mural Project, an expansion of their classroom walls, and Roberts agreed to take me on a tour of some of them to show me what that meant. We met at the school during lunch break, and the tour began right there in the school hallways, past the ping-pong players and the various informal "groups" of students, which include, said Roberts, gang members, gang posers, non-gang, Special Education, Vietnamese, Indo-Canadian, and traditional Native, all in all "pretty tolerant kids," many of them young adults, in a school that enforces a dress code and institutes three-day suspensions for drug and alcohol abuse.

The school is at the heart of a neighbourhood of community activity: Neechi Foods Co-op, Kekinan Centre for Seniors, the Indian-Métis Friendship Centre, new Habitat for Humanity houses and a women's shelter, and community police on the beat. We had a good look at the Weidman Food Building, a kosher food warehouse at the corner of Flora and Aikens, site of the drive-by shooting death of young Joseph Beaver Spencer in 1994. It was when a thoughtful cop suggested Roberts could help create "positive images" for the rough-and-tumble neighbourhood that he got going on the Mural Project. With Weidman's consent, Roberts and his students painted panels on the boarded-up windows, working late into the fall until the paint started freezing up – and there they were, the warrior with the muscled chest and his eagle companion, the dove of peace in multiples, vying for space on this gritty "canvas" with the declarative graffiti of the Indian Posse gang. *Indian Land! Red power!*

We drove to the Forks, that urban junction of the Red and Assiniboine rivers, to view the murals on the CN railroad mainline bridge on Pioneer Avenue: a huge female face, hair entwined with eagle feathers, a spooky raven flying against a full moon, rusty water sliding like a toxic spill over the entire surface. Around the corner, one of Roberts's best students, Blair Martin, had painted a hand gripping a ceremonial pipe and a noble eagle's head in the wacky purple and orange colours of paint-store rejects. Further on down the overpass, trains shuttled back and forth to the CN station while cars, diving under the bridge, sent muddy slush flying onto bold images of Native women, tipis, skeletal spruce on northern lakes.

Everywhere, the mural images were jostling for space with the ubiquitous graffiti that the Mural Project was designed precisely to contest. According to Roberts, who was seething on this subject, graffiti flourishes in this fading Prairie metropolis because the place is so forgetful of its own richly layered past that its head can be turned around by cable television from Detroit. This was the crucial event in Roberts's account, the images on Detroit's evening news of spectacularly burning cars and barrels of trash in flames in the humbled streets of an American ghetto one Hallowe'en Eve. "Then it started here, with garbage cans thrown through people's windows. Then the hats worn backward. Then Aboriginal kids talking 'black' talk: 'Bitch!' Indians without their own culture." The gang graffiti followed. Roberts figured there must have been exactly three people involved in their production: he keeps seeing the same symbols and slogans over and over again, the equivalent, he said, of dogs peeing on trees.

At that time of year especially, in March, with the unploughed streets clogged by winter's filthy slush, the denuded elm trees, the rubbishy vacant lots and the general air of post-industrial obsolescence, the boldly drawn and coloured murals were a visual exclamation. The artists had, in Roberts's words, all realized "a sense of pride in the community, pride in their craft and admiration from the public at large." I interpreted this to mean also *Native* pride among artists like Blair Martin, who finished grade twelve as an adult and supports a young daughter as a full-time shipper-receiver, a Treaty Indian living in the city with only the most tenuous connections with his heritage. Or like Richard Manoakeesick of Ste. Therese First Nation, adopted in infancy, a school drop-out until he returned at age nineteen to study music and paint murals. It was telling, I thought, that he acknowledged he often found ideas for his murals from "other art," for there had been something dispiriting in the repetitive repertoire of the murals – eagles and eagle feathers, the wolf, warriors built like Tarzan – as though all the diversity of the First Nations had been reduced to a generic representation of *Indianness* as circulated by North American pop culture. But it's a place to start from and can yield rich results.

Mi'kmaq writer and filmmaker Catherine Martin, whose people were among the very first to come into contact with Europeans, took child-rearing practices in her own huge family network as a subject for a film exploring the vestiges of a social-support system that could help heal the fractured white Canadian family while also feeding the deep hunger of the Mi'kmaq youth for restorative knowledge of the "old ways" – ways that now lie entangled in a profusion of borrowings and adaptations from elsewhere. In her film *Mi'kmaq Family*, written by playwright Wendy Lill, Martin joins a family gathering in Cape Breton on St. Anne's Day, a day and a saint hallowed for generations by Mi'kmaq praying for guidance through the desert of their losses, as they pray still, in the words of the Grand Chief, "so the people don't have to go through what we went through in residential school, weeping in bed, parents and children robbed of each other." Martin's film ends on a scene of drummers hammering out the people's heartbeat on the sinewy skin of a big drum that looks exactly like the ones beaten at prairie Native powwows – and so it is. By the time young Mi'kmaq, conscious and alert to the job of picking up where their grandparents had left off, went looking for drumming, it was their relations among the Plains Cree who taught them how.

In New Brunswick, dancer Rocky Paul-Wiseman, a Maliseet, began his dance career under the feathered war bonnet and paint of the traditional Plains Indian dance. Meanwhile, on the plains, young Cree dancers dress up as Hopi eagle dancers.

Sometimes the crossings-over are funny. At least the group of artists whose work toured in 1997 as "Native Love" thought so. Photographer Bradlee LaRocque took a picture of a Native woman in voluptuous décolleté, giving a big smooch for the camera, for the lampoonish cover of *Cosmosquaw* magazine and added the teasing headline "Easy make-up tips for a killer bingo face," managing a critique of both Native and non-Native consumers at once.

Raised in the Cree-Métis colony of Grouard in northern Alberta, in a family that traces its roots to the mission established there six generations ago, Ahasiw Maskegon-Iskwew, a Regina-based video and computer artist, lived inside three languages in childhood: French with his Métis father; Cree with his *kookum* (grandmother); and English with his mother who would speak Cree only when forced to. Thank God for his *kookum*. Ahasiw's mother was a product of residential schooling and simply refused to put her own children through the "torture" of trying to hang on to the mother tongue in a hostile, not to say violent, linguistic environment. "All our lives," he told me, speaking for his siblings too, "we always asked her to teach us Cree, and she wouldn't. We would ask her how to say certain things and she would pretend she'd forgotten." It certainly never occurred to her that someday her son would be able to speak Cree *and* MS-DOS. I found Ahasiw at the computers of Neutral Ground artist-run gallery, banging away at *Isi-Pikiskwewin-Ayapihkesisak* (translation: "Speaking the Language of Spiders"), a First Nations contemporary art Web.

Ahasiw is obsessed by the idea of bilingualism among non-Indians – by the challenge from First Nations cultures to the rest of us to "teach [our] children the Indian words for creation," so that the ancestors' stories will get recited along with all the others and help shape our *collective* world view. "I look forward, perhaps with foolish optimism," he told me, "to a time when it will be a requirement of high-school graduation that you have a certain understanding and knowledge of First Nations' languages and cultures. That to me would be a kind of social justice."

By the same token, First Nations artists are taking up the new tools of technology in order to incorporate their power "into the living skins of our cultures." But the process doesn't stop there, within the regenerated Aboriginal culture. Ahasiw believes it radiates outward, "awakening" the rest of us to the complexity of Aboriginal vision and to the possibility of alliances, sharing "with honour" our respective achievements, "preparing the Renaissance when you will talk Indian to me."

In April 1997 Ahasiw Maskegon-Iskwew and his collaborators on the "Speaking the Language of Spiders" project launched the Web site at a public forum in Regina. For me the sheer wonderment of how these things are done technically – hypertext links, HTML, iconic interfacing, URLs – initially overwhelmed what turned out to be, in fact, an important subtext of the five-hour presentation: testimonials to the ravages of urban life, and the hoped-for recovery. In introducing the Web site, Ahasiw spoke of the Native "diaspora" in the cities, the desperate situation of people trapped in prostitution, drug abuse, and the moralizing assessments of a society that doesn't see the human costs being paid, over and over again, by a people stripped of their sense of continuity with the ancestors that had kept them culturally intelligible, at least to themselves. "This is about the line between spiritual presences which follow us," he said, even into street culture, even into the computer. The Web site's links mean information branches "sideways," utterly deconstructing "linearity." Just like Saulteaux cosmology with its *cycle* of recurrent times.

In that radical shift from traditionalism to post-modernity, was there an Aboriginal alternative to "whitestream" culture being proposed? I pressed Ahasiw about Natives' ease or lack of it with postmodern notions of the break-up of coherent psychological selves into "hybrid" and "performative" selves. He told me he found it "frightening," this notion that meaning is "provisional and contingent" and that essentialism is "suspect." He believed, to the contrary, that "Aboriginal people come from some very essential points of view that don't just depend on 'subject position.' I believe that we are beings of the past and the future, we are manifestations of these linkages, we work around a centre that doesn't shift – and this is incredibly meaningful."

That reminded me of Daniel Paul Bork's tipi at the Féstival du Voyageur in St. Boniface. Danielle Sturk had escorted me outside the palisade and into a large canvas tipi where I waited to be introduced to Bork, interpreter of an 1815 Native hunter-trapper. Splendid in red leggings, white breeches, and antler necklace, he was speaking, back and forth between English and French, to visitors about the cosmology of the tipi.

What was this role he was interpreting, I wanted to know, and who was *he* as he was doing it? Over a bowl of soup in the volunteers' cabin, with my tape recorder in his face, he spoke of the year 1815 and the five thousand Indians in the area, the hundred or so Europeans, of the hardships of the "lifestyle," hunger and toil, of the dependence of the Europeans on the Indians for firewood, pemmican, furs, snowshoes, toboggans – and women, with whom they can be said to have officially started the Métis nation here in 1816. "We were what could be considered a Stone Age development, in harmony with the elements of the buffalo and the fur-trapping." He himself is Cree, with Sioux on the paternal side, with a business as consultant in Native management practice.

This was his second year as interpreter in the symbology of the tipi. "The reason I'm back here is that last year a little six-year-old kid walked up at the end of my presentation – the kids and I had talked about the traditional teachings of the cycles of life, the circle of the tipi, east, west, south, and north, life and death cycles – and he looked up at me, tapped me on the knee, with a big smile on his face, and said, 'Mister, I'm Indian too.'"

Aboriginal kids were always coming into the tipi, kids caught up in a web of Winnipeg's "social ills," who didn't know their history, didn't know that the Forks of the Red and Assiniboine, right here in the city, was a traditional meeting place for the Cree, Assiniboines, and Ojibwa, had no idea of the work involved in hunting and trapping and fishing, in showing the Europeans how to survive, in bringing the furs to trade. Tell them all this, and these kids, who were slouched over a minute ago in a posture of sluggish apathy, suddenly stand up, an almost literal representation of the process that Bork sees the whole Indian people going through, "the transition out of the colonization process."

This is where the tipi comes in and Bork's interpretation of its cosmology of the circle – the physical, emotional, mental, and spiritual elements of a human life through its stages of beginning, mastery, contribution, and guidance. In the circle of the tipi, the fire is at the centre, surrounded by family, extended family, and community. "You see it, and it's real. The tipi shows it so well. It was so simple. You look at it and you ask, 'Why destroy this? Why completely assimilate Aboriginal kids to a completely different way of thinking?' It doesn't make any sense."

Did Bork think that Euro-Canadians could be "of this place" along with Aboriginals? He did, but non-Indians' ignorance of Native history and values, given the destructiveness of colonization, is a major obstacle to mutual understanding. This is a period of reconstruction, he suggested, when "white Canadians are looking at those values again, because they realize there *was* something there."

But for Taiaiake Alfred, identity is a function of citizenship in an Indian nation and in that nation's capacity to control its own territory. Taiaiake had studied International Relations as a university student, anticipating international (Canada and First Nations) negotiations for the "national sovereignty" of his nation. His own biography is proof enough that a man who was schooled after grade seven almost entirely in white institutions, spoke little Mohawk, and joined the United States Marines in 1981 may have his Indianness shaped nevertheless – in Taiaiake's case, in the political conflicts and turmoil on the reserve in the 1970s. This experience was so decisive that you can speak of the pre- and post-1970s Mohawks, the latter, like himself, being self-assured, demanding, and damn the consequences. And blessedly unburdened by the assumption that "white people know better and have a God-given right to govern Indian people. We believe the opposite: white people are corrupt and unjust in any assumption of authority over Native people." In the events at Oka in 1990, the "twenty-somethings witnessed events that empowered them, an Indian nation standing up and telling the government to go to hell . . . that's role-modelling in the best sense of the word." Perhaps it was that early radicalization I was hearing in his solemn reminder to me that "Mohawks have never given their consent to Canada. We're not Canadians. We are internal colonies of Canada."

But many Aboriginals take up their community work where they find it, in the cities, in the interstices of white Canada's institutions. Brenda Fowler led me through the several rooms of the Bent Arrow Society's facility in Edmonton. Brightly lit and muffled by comfortable carpeting, the place was home to a remarkable variety of programs: Coyote Kids, an after-school program; Soup and Bannock, which served meals to the community; Soaring Spirits, providing learning through computers. Fowler and I stood in the Parents' Room for the Inside Out program. At first, she explained, parents, almost always mothers, don't talk; they are obliged to come, on referrals from social workers and child-welfare officers. It takes a while to draw them out, but when that happens they find themselves part of a group, dealing with "self-esteem and past issues, and know they aren't alone any more."

It's their children that Fowler was working with, from newborns to twelve-year-olds. These were children with more than the usual mental and emotional issues, children who had to learn "anger management" in lives already marked by alcoholism, domestic violence, racism, violent neighbourhoods. Every Friday the parents joined their children and literally learned how to play with them.

There is a kind of inevitability to Fowler's work with children: time and again, in the course of our conversation, she invoked her own childhood as a kind of touchstone of her journey to this work in this place. Raised by her white grandmother, Fowler had been a "proud" child, condemned to a kind of aloneness among white children who mocked her Aboriginal pride. She recalled her giddy excitement at viewing, in a travelling museum show, a mannequin of an Indian warrior in full regalia. She had instantly identified him as an ancestor, but when she told her schoolmates of this revelation – "That's me!" – they called her a liar. Then, for the next three years, they called her a squaw. The aloneness was hard to bear.

Then came the decisive meeting with her own great-grandmother, an elderly woman, "defiant, a powerhouse," who lived by herself in the woods, without running water or electricity, chopping her own wood, speaking Cree, with this message for Fowler: "Don't let anyone tell you you can't do anything. If you want something bad enough, you'll get it."

From the elders who visit the Bent Arrow Society she has deepened her ideas of *how* to be Native. She's like the kids themselves, who "know they are Indian but don't know what that means." Does it mean they're like those pictures of warriors with eagle feathers in their hair? It's a representation that exasperates Fowler, who wants to see Indians shown as modern people.

Fowler's "main concern" for her charges is that they learn how to say what they are feeling, and for that to happen they must first have sufficient self-esteem to believe that they will be heard, that what they have to say is important to another person, and that they will be believed.

This emphasis on healing and restoration rather than on confrontation and anger impressed me mightily, used as I had become to the more aggressive rhetoric of classic "identity politics." But there was no rancour in Fowler, only the belief in the "honesty and trust" that lie at the heart of her work. She calls it "passing it on," this task of stitching the children into the weave of First Nations' being and doing. She has been angry and she has been bereaved, but resentment and bitterness are not the point. Love is the point. Children are the point.

UNSETTLING THE LAND

> Sometimes it appears that we Africans in the New World have been weaned forever on the milk of otherness; we have been too long "othered" by those whose societies thought nothing of

enriching themselves on our labour. . . . We need, now, however, to be m/othered by those very societies and culture which have destroyed our cultures. . . . But more important, Canada needs to m/other us.

— Marlene Nourbese Philip, *Frontier:*
Essays on Racism and Culture

Some years ago, in an interview in *Books in Canada*, writer Barry Callaghan, after describing his father Morley Callaghan's literary effort to "set down the language of the place [Toronto in the twenties and thirties]," to "clear" it the same way Canadian homesteaders cleared the land, confessed that he just didn't know "what's going on here any more." Don't get him wrong, he hastened to add, this wasn't about being mean-spirited, but "it does not fill me with a sense of exhilaration and alertness about my own place, and the language of my own place, that Rohinton Mistry is here in Canada, writing about India in the language that is appropriate to India." He felt estranged from a lot of current literature: "It seems awfully strange that we should find ourselves . . . beaming under the umbrella of multiculturalism, embracing colonial voices as if they were our own."[41]

At the time I read this, I was both cheered and discomforted by Callaghan's argument. Cheered, because I remembered with nostalgic fondness the excited discussions that took place in Alberta in the late seventies and early eighties among artists and writers of my generation about the burgeoning production of "our" stories – by which we meant the literature of Margaret Laurence and Robert Kroetsch, Rudy Wiebe and Sharon Pollock, and all the others who had broken the colonial bonds with Britain, New York, and Toronto to write about who and where we were right now, deeply rooted historically, sociologically, and psychically in the Canadian prairie. We were continuing the effort to "set down the language of the place" – an enterprise that has since been overtaken by history, not to say theory.

Discomforted, because there was something unattractive about Callaghan's querulous remarks, something unimaginative, out of date, quaint, not to the point any more. Everything has been problematized, as the theorists say, opened up and exposed to the gaze of Canadians whose view of things wasn't canvassed when we first circulated such comfortable notions as "place" and "here," not to mention "our own." Whose place is it exactly? Is it more my Ukrainian grandmother's than yours from Punjab? Do we all agree what "here" looks like? Is it old or new, empty or full, wild or urban? What on earth is a language "appropriate to India" that's been composed in Mississauga? Are some English languages more Canadian than others? Did Callaghan really mean that, if you're ethnic ("umbrella of multiculturalism"), you live here as some kind of Displaced Person, the flotsam or jetsam of offshore imperial holdings? . . . And even "clearing the land" has a funny ring to it these days.

Now I set the Callaghan interview alongside an essay in an art catalogue by Henry Tsang. Tsang's essay was an introduction to the artists in a 1991 exhibit called *Self Not Whole: Cultural Identity and Chinese-Canadian Artists*, which explored being Chinese in race, ethnicity and gender, and relations with mainstream cultures. Chineseness, it turns out, is not easy to pin down; what the exhibition artists have in common, writes Tsang, is that "this term *Chinese* is vague, floating, and perhaps undefinable." Certainly, there are annual festivities and rituals that bring the community together, but artist Heesok Chang, for instance, isn't even sure there is such a thing as a single Chinese "community." So what do Chinese-Canadians mean when they say "we"? What do they mean when they say "white culture" as though they were completely outside it? Karin Lee wants to deconstruct the idea of the "ethnic," that undifferentiated person who lives in some vague place called the "margin," but also to challenge the alternative – the conservative Chinese-Canadian retreat into traditional culture. "It is this act of redefinition, of continually re-evaluating one's relationship to a cultural background," writes Tsang, "which provides the impetus for this show."

Pace Callaghan. The language of the above-mentioned artists *is* the language of "here," in all its hyphenation, its ambivalence, its confrontation, and its restless exploration of the possibility of belonging to a place they themselves are in the process of redefining.

At a conference on multiculturalism, held at York University in 1997, the writer Dionne Brand said this (I cite from my notes): "Official culture thinks immigrants should be emptied of their past. This is undesirable. [What is desirable is that] stories join other stories to become part of the collectivity. I resist the idea that the collectivity is a done deal that cannot be added to or changed." When immigrants and other hybrids decide to open up their communities to a *sharing* of stories and histories, and to participation in civil society, then the popular charge that hyphenated Canadians are "about" ghettoization and exoticism, and separatism is simply hysterical. There is not a shred of evidence for it.[42] "Identity politics," said Judy Rebick in conversation with Kiké Roach, "is also about belonging."[43]

In just such a way has "Canada" always known itself, by the constant encounter and engagement with just-arrived "otherness" that inevitably undermines old certainties about who we "really" are, what the meaning of our collective experience "objectively" is, and how our constituent cultural diversity is to be integrated into something called the "national" life. This is never resolved by any particular generation once and for all. As is so clear from my interviewees, each new generation of Canadians has to think through its own relationship to the past and to its own civic desires. Even the sober-sided Jeffrey Simpson, columnist in the *Globe and Mail*, has conjectured that, except for isolated outbreaks, Canada has been refreshingly free of the furious backlash visited on American "cultural politics" and cultural diversity, because "Canadians do not insist as fiercely as Americans on a defined national vision and a common sense of historical understanding."[44] It is almost as though we instinctively are aware that to insist on them is precisely to invite disintegration.

> Q: How difficult is it to avoid the potential danger of stereotyping a racial group in order to show cultural differences?
>
> A: . . . I am not trying to "show cultural differences" in my writing; I am not even trying to portray a "racial group." What you read into the text so far as that is concerned depends on your stance, your location. The question presumes a reader who is located somewhere else. The white reader may perceive cultural difference, but I am merely writing myself.
>
> – Dionne Brand, interviewed in *Other Solitudes: Canadian Multicultural Fictions*, eds. Linda Hutcheon and Marion Richmond

In Brand we can read that the theoretical ground has shifted from under the discussion of racism and difference. "Theory" now asks questions about the usefulness of seeing only fixed either/or oppositions (centre vs. margin) and rigid social categories (the dominant, the oppressed) when identities are actually "in movement, in flux and changing," are "multiple and con-tradictory."[45] Activists even chafe at the ideal of entering and therefore changing the "mainstream," because even this way of seeing things "pre-sumes the opposition between these concepts" – grassroots and main-stream – "an opposition that we want to put into question."[46]

"Theory" reminds us not to confuse the ideal of commonality with the assumption that we therefore live in community, blissfully ignorant of the multiplicity and instability that complicate any given group's identity. Artist Heesok Chang, for instance, wants to know if it is possible to live in the same community as those who fear that cultural pluralism means the "silent destruction of English Canada"; or who dream of filling the "public sphere" of newly liberated marketplaces with the goods of Western capital-ism's running-shoe factories.[47]

We are all being challenged to come up with a language that may be employed persuasively in the public sphere where our *collective*, if not common, interests coincide – a collective interest in cultural diversity, for instance,[48] or in social justice.

Certain solutions already present themselves, at least as possibilities. In her exuberant review of identity politics, inclusivity, and the future of democracy, broadcaster and journalist Irshad Manji is skeptical that iden-tity politics can present a sufficient foundation on which to form a com-munity when it so readily "obliterates" personal uniqueness in the name of collective coherence. *I am more than my colour!* With typical bravura Manji escalates from here in one sentence to "ethnic cleansing" and the bloody terrain of ethnic nationalism, which decrees that "individuals can have only one defining identity."[49] But the point is well taken: the health of civil society is measured by the multiple points of entry the citizen has to a con-dition of "belonging" with diverse others. In anthropologist Peter Kulchyski's notion of a "bush culture for a bush country," we are invited to see as at the very centre of our cosmology what has been most marginal – Aboriginal culture – and to "redraw" our internal borders around "bush culture" so that it is not a separate nation but a return of the historically repressed to our collective consciousness.[50]

Others are impressed by the increasing incidence of inter-racial mar-riage in immigrant societies such as Canada[51] and by the racially uncatego-rizable identities of the children produced by them. But perhaps that makes it sound too easy. As writer Malcolm Gladwell puts it: "If you mix black and white, you don't obliterate those categories; you merely create a third category."[52]

How this new identity will have a "race" is a question for the theorists and poets of cyberspace who enjoy speculating about the endlessly re-created self, the multiple, performative self, or rather, Self. Summarizing them, critic Cameron Bailey says race has no biological basis but is socially, politically, and "psychically" constructed. After all, how much can race "matter" when identity is a series of choices the Internet surfer makes, completely disembodied? When, in faceless communication on-screen, the person of colour can "be" white, or the other way around? (Bailey calls this "virtual transvestism.")[53] Is this liberating? Poet Chris Dewdney thinks so, with his vision of voice-activated, ultra-fast home processors that will "enact our desires so quickly that in the long run changing our personal identity will become a primary entertainment."[54] But Bailey is not con-vinced that such sophisticated technology puts us beyond the pull of the social and political. Cyberspaceniks may think their involvement in a con-tactless "community" is forward-looking, but Bailey argues it is another version of white suburban safety inside the gated community of a middle class terrified of difference.

The political theorist Leslie Pol, at the 1997 York University conference on multiculturalism, rhapsodized about the "vertigo of limitless connec-tions" for minority communities, made possible by access to networks and databases. With the new digital technologies, they can create "personal microcultures," and participate in "virtual cultures" with allies and fellow travellers, without the social encumbrances of race and ethnicity. The implications of this for historical memory seem to me staggering. If racial and ethnic identity as historically grounded in collective shared experience is declared obsolescent, then we are only here now and nothing has hap-pened to us.

Perhaps I exaggerate. There are more hopeful perspectives on our post-modern moment, as for example writer Samir Gandesha's bracing account of the benefits of the post-colonial shift. "What is 'post' about the 'post-colonial' world is that what once was strange and had subsequently been familiarized" – the "Chinamen" in their Chinatown, women in the kitchen, "homos" in the closet – returns as something strange. "It returns to haunt and unsettle the familiar."[55] But this is our great opportunity, to be unsettled by the "strange" migrants among us, and familiarize ourselves anew.

> And did you get my message on the people's radio? I wrote it in
> Alberta, across the prairie's spine. . . . And we don't need math-
> ematics, we don't need submarines, to tell how far the land goes
> until it hits the shore.
> – Rheostatics, "Music Inspired by the Group of Seven," 1995

This is the first place we know, the land underfoot, whether we have walked it since our childhood, treading behind our forbears, or have just touched down, pressing a tentative step onto Canada, looking for a toehold. It is young Cory Ollikka, fourth generation on the homestead quarter near Waskatenau, Alberta, raising his cattle in the narrow interstice of family owned cropland spared for now from the roving transnationals who see money, not food, seeded in the loam; it is filmmaker Mark Wihak who walks in his mind, angling northward on the Regina plain until he hits tundra and the howling wolves under aurora borealis, the wide and wild place at the far end of the highway; it is Michel Samson, who grew up around the wharves of Isle Madame in Cape Breton, scudding in his grandfather's boat through the fierce Atlantic to get to the fishing grounds, dreaming of being a fisherman even while the cod are dying below him; it is Maura Hanrahan in St. John's, just staying on as an act of defiance to those who would say her place is not worth saving, this oldest non-Aboriginal culture in the Americas; it is George Elliott Clarke's heart "leaping" at the North Star.

John Curkan, Calgary oil executive, sat in his office suite, the dun autumnal beauty of the foothills at his back, and a weather system hurtling in from the northwest, blowing torrents of dust through the canyon streets and then east, out from the city and over the eastern plain and Curkan's oil wells. He grew up not far from here, in Olds, the son of a field engineer thirty years in the oil patch, and he has always known that his destiny lay in the great western Canadian sedimentary basin. He *believed* in it. His company, Renaissance Energy, a grassroots operation from its beginnings with "a couple of local country boys" who moved in on the "tired old basin" deserted by the oil majors, was drilling wells from Taber in the southern desert to Lac La Biche in the northern parkland. As he spoke of the science of it, the geology and the seismic drilling and pulling samples out of the earth, "working with materials that are hundreds and thousands of feet below you, working with a hole that is about four inches in diameter and two thousand feet down from the surface of the earth, and you are trying to know what's down there," I heard a kind of rapture of the geological deep.

St. John's is called the City of Legends. "Legends are what you tell yourself when you don't know your own history," said historian John Fitzgerald. "It's cozy and cuddly, politically inoffensive, and reinforces the hegemony of the ruling class." He laughed. "We've been here for five hundred years, goes the legend. My arse! Newfoundland was a migratory fishery until the middle of the eighteenth century," with a thin cord of blood trailing back to the British motherland.

He's the first to admit that Newfoundland is an "imagined community" of people of oral genius who thank God they are surrounded by water and who have elaborated a nation as each other's kith and kin, even though the Labradorians will be the first to say Newfoundland is not *their* identity. Not to mention the people of the Acadian west coast, the Mi'kmaq, and the intermarried descendants of the last Beothuks. But the Newfoundlanders know they are a people all of their own, even as they go about reconstructing it with every generation's experience – "We are the only discrete culture in Canada: our restaurants in Ottawa are listed as 'ethnic,' we have our own dictionary, and when we are away we exhibit all the classic symptoms of 'immigrantitis' by going to the Newfoundland store to buy Newfoundland food, we wear T-shirts with Newfoundland on them and people call us Newfie" – even as out-migration from the homeland has tripled since 1993. Fitzgerald thinks the 1637 coat of arms, with the two Beothuks and the Biblical motto *Quaerite Prime Regnum Dei*, "Seek ye first the Kingdom of God," should be changed to show two cans of Carnation milk implanted on a field of baloney, with the heraldic motto *Perdida, perdida.* "She's gone, b'ye, she's gone."

We live in "imagined" communities, writes American historian Benedict Anderson, when we never know or meet most of our fellow members or even hear about them, "yet in the minds of each lives the image of their communion."[56] In Canadians' communion with the land, we have each imagined, in our own versions, its rock and water and soil, its storm fronts and treelines and ice floes, its loons and wolves and maples, and imagined that we live there with the millions of Canadian strangers who, like us, go out onto their back porches and stare, face up, to the North Star. We imaginatively embrace them as co-communicants of this essential Canadian reverie.

But Rinaldo Walcott, who teaches cultural studies at York University, wandered disquietedly among the iconical paintings and their fond public at the Group of Seven retrospective at the Art Gallery of Ontario in 1996. Born and raised in the West Indies, unfettered by Euro-Canadian memory, Walcott was free to consider the meaning of the exhibition from a particular vantage. The atmosphere in the gallery rooms, he wrote, was like a "wake, with folks mourning the passing of Canada." What he could perceive and "folks" couldn't was that the experience of viewers' remembering the Canada represented in the paintings was not just an experience of their loss – of the Canada they had "all" grown up in and "all" recognized via the Group of Seven – but was simultaneously accompanied by an act of great forgetting. And what these Euro-Canadians were forgetting, Walcott writes, is that Canada is not "white." The Group of Seven remain "un-*ethnicized*": their pictures contain no people, not even canoeists or painters, let alone First Nations; the lands are barren, the rocks dehumanized, there are no immigrants. This is an imagined collective history, inscribed on Nature, the aloof Mother, from which the mourners have now been dispossessed, knowing better: "Folks spoke with deep regrets of a time long gone, no longer possible to recapture."[57]

The past is irretrievable because, like it or not, history has intervened and the Others are here.

In a fascinating exchange among four artists of colour on the role of the imagination in forming "imagined communities," Marlene Nourbese Philip, Hiren Mistry, Geoffrey Chan, and Kevin Modeste tossed around the relationship each of them has to that "significant metaphor" of Canada as wilderness. "Yeah," said Mistry, "how come I didn't go to camp?"[58]

Camp, we are pleased to think, is one of the formative adventures of the Canadian child during summer holidays: *everybody* has a lake in her or his memory bank, a shoreline where they learned to swim and build campfires and tie knots, essential wisdom of the "wild." Director Tim Gray characterized the membership and board of Wildlands League as "tending" to be dominated by WASP culture, which did not preclude the second-generation children of immigrants also having an experience of the wilderness. Send a kid, any kid, to Muskoka lakes and cottages for two weeks for two years in a row and you've got them for life. "It's such an inherent part of being a human to be able to relate to wilderness," he told me, "that you have to really work at depriving people of the experience to get them to hate it."

But although Nourbese has rented a cottage outside of Toronto, her family is among the very few people of colour to have done so, and she wondered about the "something that prevents immigrants of colour from thinking about what you might call nature-based activities for ourselves or for our children." Mistry wondered why a South Asian family in Mississauga didn't "get excited" about the idea of wilderness. Could it have something to do with the fact that the land already carries a meaning based on an experience from which they are excluded? Nourbese thought so: the "language of the wilderness" has been influenced by the experience of European settlement, which has already mythologized itself as the line beyond which there is nothing but unintelligible blankness. "It's almost like an unknown language for us which we can't penetrate unless we own a cottage or a boat."

And what are immigrants to make of the relationship between the "heroic" lone voyageur testing himself in the back of beyond and the "scary" Native lurking in the shadows? Where can they interpolate themselves, asked Mistry, in such a dialectic of stereotypes?

They don't. They gather in the safety of numbers in the cities and do not even attempt control of the discourse between "civilization" and "wilderness." But poet Dionne Brand attempted it. She left Toronto, moved to the country, and wrote about it.

Brand wrote a poem in 1992 called "Out There," about the terror of a highway drive in a snowstorm, straight into Canada's heart of darkness: "these white roads, snow at our throats, and at the windshield a thick white cop in a blue steel windbreaker peering into our car suspiciously . . . Three Blacks in a car on a road blowing eighty miles an hour in the wind between a gas station and Chatham."[59] But in 1998 she was living two hundred kilometres north of Toronto, which isn't really *the* North, she confesses, but far enough outside the urban sprawl for her to live now with the wonder of the "short growing life of things, how huge maples and pines survive a drought of the sun and warmth so long," and with that peculiar melancholy that visits the soul of those who live through repeated visitations of winter when they catch their first whiff of nature's decay on the forest floor, even before the frosts have come: "I hate the fall. I can smell it coming." So she already has that Canadian nose, just by moving a degree of latitude north and into the airstream of the wild. She has even learned, she writes, to tell the difference, in some neighbour's "too-long, hot silence," to tell the difference between racism and cabin fever.[60]

Meanwhile, back in Toronto, the black artist Camille Turner was mulling over a project in which she will place "the black body in nature, because it is never seen, never shown." In all those television commercials, for instance, which depict Canada as polar bears, rivers, mountains, and campfires, "it's as if my identity is erased, because I think of myself as being Canadian, whatever that means," and so she was thinking of doing a series of photographs of Canadian women of colour "just sitting in snow."

Of such efforts to play deliberately with the vulnerable black body in threatening Canadian landscapes, critic Cameron Bailey summarized their statement: "It's too cold, it's too windy, it's too harsh, and to place these bodies, which clearly weren't 'grown' here, naked into that environment is an attempt to show that dissonance."

But it is not dissonance that the writer George Elliott Clarke is feeling as he imagines swinging his axe through the nose-pinching cold of Sudbury in January, say, chopping away at a spruce log for the stove. Winter is not a *problem*; his people have been in Canada since 1813 and have been toughened, and now Clarke claims its landscape as his own; it is watered by the sweat, blood, and tears of black ancestors who toiled on it and failed and rebounded and rooted themselves in it. Unlike Walcott in the art gallery, dissociated from the meanings attached to the Group of Seven canvases, Clarke, indelibly Canadian, feels implicated: "I confess that Tom Thomson and the Group of Seven – white boys all – speak to me. . . . I know sad woodsmoke and acrid harmonicas and chopped wood and slain horses and mouldered barns and hanged Black men. . . . The sound of bagpipes can make me cry. I, too, sing Canada. This land is my land."[61]

And who could dislodge him from such an imagined community with all our ghosts? None except those, like writer T. J. Bryan, who are haunted by history, not myth, the ones who don't belong here, they say, because they are invaded by memory of how they "slaved/worked, built, gave birth to generations, fought, cried out and died here. . . . I ain't no immigrant to this place, I'm a kidnapee turned nomad."[62] Or those, like Larissa Lai, who have found through futile journeys to the memory-place of the abandoned ancestors that "there is no perfect place of origin."[63] Or May Yee, for whom "here" is the only place she knows, but incompletely, awkward in her own skin: "When we are constantly made to feel like we don't belong here, the issue of 'home' becomes central."[64] Or for the First Nations peoples who have been evicted from the "essential" geography of Canada that non-Natives have imagined as tenantless, and so we do not even dream of them.

In talking with Ahasiw Maskegon-Iskwew about the "panicky, frenetic hysteria" of non-Native culture, as he had referred to it, I wanted to know how he could be *in* that culture, as a Web artist, and not *of* it. Did it not drive him panicky and hysterical? Apparently not. There is a certain calming focus in Native Indian culture, he said, "where people want to get together in community, whereas in non-Aboriginal culture there doesn't seem to be a history, a sense of continuity." This wasn't just cultural one-upmanship, this was a steady view of Euro-Canadians as immigrants who had disavowed themselves of personal and family history. "It's that loss that means no one feels rooted – white culture always worried about its Canadian identity – no one establishes a community but lives in little atomic bits and pieces that can be shuffled at will depending on whatever economic pressures are going on." I suggested that one of the benefits of the multicultural perspective among non-Native Canadians was to remind them they did belong to antecedent stories. Not good enough, said Ahasiw. The story they erased was the one of their own sufferings in the mother country. "They had to escape starvation, tortures, military attacks . . . but then, in order to prevail here, to make a space for themselves, they had to be able to push that memory aside to create a colonialism here." To have lost that historical memory means to have failed in human compassion for the desperation of the ancestors, and it means that into this void of forget-ting have vanished the knowledge of why they came here and "what the politics of pushing aside the Indian people was."

It's not so simple, I thought later. There are Canadians who have been here so long that their origins beyond Turtle Island have no resonance.

What lessons are to be learned by an Acadian or Quebecois or Red River Métis or Newfoundlander by a contemplation of the history of Scotland or France or Portugal? And what of the Euro-Canadians like the Ukrainians and Lithuanians, who lived as some kind of eastern borderland barbarians, excluded from "Europe" by all their neighbours? Or of those Canadians whose last glimpse of the motherland came just before entering the bowels of a slaving ship, and who were then pitched and tossed every which way about the colonies? If anything, such narratives of origin underscore that what is meaningful in them is that they have been disrupted by migration and resettlement. Surely there are many ways of being indigenous to a place?

I asked Catherine Crowston at the Edmonton Art Gallery what she thought of this challenge to all of us who are not native to the place we are in (I was quoting Jamaica Kincaid). Are we condemned always to be provisional dwellers, telling ourselves stories to make ourselves feel like we belong? No, no, no, she said: "You know what, and this is just a very personal response, and it's not a theorized one or educated or anything like that. It's just that, well, where else would I feel at home?"

> Sovereignty in practice. Or the transcendence of colonial mentality in order to restore "peace, power and righteousness as the bases of North American Indian community life and as the foundation of the relationship between nations in North America," according to Graduate Studies course 501: North American Indians and the Mythology of Colonialism. Instructor, Dr. Taiaiake Alfred.

Taiaiake Alfred and I spoke again when he invited me to join the participants at a colleague's Ph.D. seminar at the University of Victoria. He spoke at the seminar of linkages between Native and white "ways of knowing": "What are the key Native values? Mutualism, holism, respect, and inclusion. To say there is a Native way of knowing and a white way, and that they will never be reconciled, is a very un-Native statement." I was taken by surprise. Taiaiake had been markedly pessimistic earlier in his account of First Nations and Canadian relations; was it possible I had misunderstood the subtlety of his argument and that "reconciliation" was not only possible but desirable? "Dichotomizing and ghettoizing is not the way for Indian survival," he said now.

I didn't know he cared. Earlier, he had vehemently defined white society as "colonial" if it could not accept that the Natives were here first, that this is their land, and they have the right to their sovereignty over it. "What of the claims, historical, emotional, nostalgic, of the Euro-Canadians to these territories we too inhabit?" I had asked him. "If we could imagine the thirty thousand years of continuous human culture upon it," I went on, "if we reeled ourselves into the time before time of Aboriginal memory that remembers nothing before *this place*, then could we non-Aboriginal Canadians too finally have a home that is here?"

But Taiaiake seemed in fundamental disagreement with the notion that non-Natives "belong" to these territories too, at least as long as Euro-Canadians live by a colonial myth rather than embark on a new relationship with the indigenous peoples. His perspective was not ethnic but political, he assured me. "When I talk about respect for our rights and for our indigenous nations, accommodations of history, and so on, that applies to *everyone*. I think that Canada could be reconstructed as a society with fundamental principles that will serve everyone, not just Native people." We could all benefit as citizens from the elimination of racial prejudice and state coerciveness. "Canadian society isn't going to be denied access to Native people and Native lands, but you are going to have to negotiate in good faith." And now here he was, addressing white Canada: "We have to find the linkage."

The will to *share* the homeplace of Canada seems lodged within basic Native belief. Evoking the principle of "mutual recognition," the Royal Commission on Aboriginal Peoples called on their people "to accept that non-aboriginal people are also of this land now, by birth and by adoption, with strong ties of love and loyalty."[65] Theatre director Floyd Favel Starr had told me we whites needn't wander melancholically along the face of the land seeking our cultural identity as Canadians, thinking that our only way in is through the settler consciousness of colonists and explorers. "You *can* be of here. With *me*," he emphasized, "you get access to an ancient country. Go to a reserve. Look for it there."

He spoke of the revelation he had while taking Indian and white acting students through a series of exercises for body and voice he based on Indian vocal and physical traditions that are the building blocks of a new song and dance. Watching the non-Indians perform, he could see that it was no longer a question of their being only "pale Americans": they could see and feel what the Native does, and so they might now realize that here on Turtle Island very long and complex artistic and intellectual traditions do exist. "So what if you're Irish or Ukrainian? You live *here*."

This is a far cry from the cultural-appropriation wars of the last decade. In fact, it's the reverse: the invitation to read ourselves as non-Aboriginals into a profoundly indigenous mentality. This is *not* about fusion or synthesis in which the specificity of the colliding cultures gets transmuted into a generic blend.

At the conclusion of the arduous and exhaustive inquiry of the Royal Commission on Aboriginal Peoples, the authors of its report had become convinced that not only had distinctive Aboriginal world views and ways-of-being survived the purgatory of white colonization, they had a whole new value in meeting the demands of post-industrial society. And in this new relevance they spoke to non-Native people as well. "And we concluded," they wrote, "that this heritage must be made more accessible to all Canadians."[66] The philosopher Georges Sioui invites non-Aboriginals to become aware of their "Americity." "On this continent where they have just come ashore, they should see spirit, order, and thought. . . ."[67]

But political scientist Claude Denis, who has written meditatively, in *We Are Not You*, of the Aboriginal need for healing and justice and control over their lives outside Euro-Canadian notions of modernity and "civilization," is not sure there is an "Amerindian alternative" available to us in the claim of a "natural relationship" between humans and earth. "That's not how I understand things," he told me, "I understand nature as a cultural artifact rather than a 'thing' we live in. We can learn from their [Aboriginals'] construct but we can't live in it," and must be as creative as we can with exchanges and borrowings, resemblances and hybrids.

But I remain struck by the generosity of Starr's and Sioui's and the Royal Commission's vision. In spite of the deep cultural wounds, the shocking dispersal of historical materials, the failing languages and the traumatized body of the urbanized Indian, First Nations can still imagine the Euro-Canadians, among others, as collaborators in a kind of cultural "bilingualism" that, in a series of acts of translation back and forth between cultures, will be transformative of all our relationships to the homeplace.

For all of us who have rooted our memory and point of origin in offshore cultures or in fantasies of self-generated New World identity, the invitation to consider ourselves citizens of an ancient "island" is provocative. Especially when the message is being passed on to us by those who have lived here since time immemorial.

It is, in fact, the "sneak-up dance" of the ones for whom it is the only motherland.

Acts of Resistance   IV

THE DECLINE OF POLITICS

> Okay, *yes*, I think to myself, they *were* ugly times. But they were also the only times I'll ever get – genuine capital *H* history times, before *history* was turned into a press release, a marketing strategy, and a cynical campaign tool. And *hey* – it's not as if I got to see much real history either – I arrived to see a concert in history's arena just as the final set was finishing.
>   – Douglas Coupland, *Generation X*

For Douglas Coupland's narrator, Andy, the "ugly times" was the American era of the war in Vietnam, which he caught a fading glimpse of in black-and-white television images at the tail end of his childhood. And those images, he surmises, are the only History his generation will have lived through, a *representation* of violence and ideological struggle-to-the-death that is nevertheless a kind of collective past compared to the ephemeral history of the marketplace, which leaves him stranded without any markers to his own lived time.

If the present is so past-less, and so bereft of the kind of political engagement with the outcomes of American society that the Vietnam war and its foes represented, there seems also to be a common fear that the *future* likewise seems emptied out of any possibility for meaningful collective action. Gone are the "grand dreams peddling a brilliant future," writes Montreal architect and critic Alfredo de Romaña, of postmodernism's clean sweep of "hopes and aspirations" that once connected us to our past as well as to our future.[1] We seem condemned to a perpetual present of catastrophe – mutilation of our biosphere, fierce economic competition, vicious ethnic purges, unconscionable inequalities – which we are power-less to correct. The obscene powers of the global economic and political leviathans own the present; we earthlings toil within it.

When collective action in the name of a brilliant future can no longer be imagined, the implications for the idea of community are dire. *Globe and Mail* columnist Rick Salutin wrote of the decline of politics as the decline of "something responsive to ordinary people or even the majority,"[2] and I remember my conversation with the Toronto financial planner Paul Ghezzi, who felt so unrepresented by any political formation, so jaded, he may never bother to vote again. What's the point, he asks, when "society" and "history" have *always* meant that the "bigger and stronger person dom-inates the rest?" This is a social order not far removed from that of the animal kingdom: "What have we done to rise above it? Let's say your car breaks down in Toronto. How many people are going to stop and offer you a hand? We are so obsessed with our own struggles that we forget the strug-gles of others, but that's humanity." Jennifer Welsh, reading the entrails of her own generation from her perch at Toronto's d-Code, mourned the loss of people's sense of loyalty to the communities of their own neighbour-hoods and blamed it on globalized consumption. "My father is a small-business man in Regina who has supported the farmers there – everybody was in it together, bought their merchandise locally – but now he sees young farmers driving to Minot, North Dakota. That isn't exactly consis-tent with building a community *here*. Aren't we in circles of commitment any more?"

Circles of commitment. Gargantuan big-box outlets and parking lots the size of football fields spring up on the edge of town, leases on downtown retail property expire and are not renewed, local mom-and-pop businesses close – the dusty jumble of a hardware store, the small bookstore that was one woman's consuming passion, the late-night grocery that ran you a line of credit – because we are all consumers now, not neighbours, driven by the bottom line: *If it's cheaper, buy it.*[3] And it isn't just goods that are menaced by corporatization, homogenization, and the ubiquity of international franchises and chains; ideas also suffer. Historically, the dissenting and avant-garde have been most sympathetically circulated in the independent sector of publishing and media, but this too is massively threatened by global enterprise.

Canadian politics: Politics in Canada used to mean whining about the government, but since GATT, deregulation and the various corporate-inspired free trade mechanisms have dismantled most of the means of controlling our political and economic structures, Canada doesn't really have politics, just a lot of politicians explaining why we can't do anything except cut programs while platoons of wild-eyed economists and bond raters run around telling the people we elected what to do.

— Brian Fawcett, *The Disbeliever's Dictionary*

It was in October 1993 that philosopher Mark Kingwell experienced his "dark night of the Canadian soul" when the stunning collapse of the Progressive Conservative government and its detested prime minister Brian Mulroney left standing on the smoking landscape almost nothing other than hundreds of Liberals. The NDP, Kingwell's party, the social democratic party that had the Canadian Left all to itself after the retreat of international socialism in the late 1980s, went down in flames, even losing official party status. Kingwell remembers that when he was a teenaged socialist in Winnipeg, Mel Watkins, the unadulterated-Left political economist, was a "demigod" whom he "secretly idolized." Now, in 1993, the NDP no longer seemed either viable or particularly Left any more, having "let slide its cherished position as home of the social-movement groups," and stranding would-be socialist agitators like Kingwell without a place to stand with each other and act for social justice.[4]

In a 1997 round-table convened by the editors of *Inroads* magazine, Kingwell, Naomi Klein, and Irshad Manji, among others, all politically situated on the Left, hammered at the possibility of a new or revised Left in a post-nationalist Canada where progressive groups find themselves making the case for a "national sovereignty" that the state itself no longer seems willing to make. As the French sociologist Pierre Bourdieu has suggested, what is described as the crisis of politics is really despair "at the failure of the state as guardian of the public interest."[5] Some, like Klein, see that social justice issues will have to "transcend" nations and be fought within international movements, while Kingwell, who would still like to make the case for the regulation of rights protecting individuals "and not just toss them into a sea of market forces," nevertheless frets that all such rhetoric of state intervention makes one look foolish in the face of the "inevitable." But Manji understands the anxiety of millions of people as a globalizing culture trivializes their real and historic differences from each other, and wonders, then, what will have the greater pull on us as a survival tool: the rising international movements around ownership and control of economies or the withdrawal into circumscribed cultures of difference?[6]

Anton Krawchenko, a law student at the University of Victoria and the son of deeply politicized parents of the 1960s, finds compass in their left-wing political beliefs only to the extent that "to be a good citizen, you have to have a good liberal basis in the study of ideas, in history and philosophy and English literature." But he was otherwise casting about for direction, studying law after getting a degree in environmental studies in order to defer for another couple of years making a decision about what to do with his life, and pulled between working in public policy or for the private sector, where he would make more money and be able to buy lots of "stuff." "I've come to terms with these desires quite recently," he told me. "I used to be punk. Now I'm less ideological about life."

But the generation is not without its strategies for a time of the decline of politics. So-called techno-nerds, for example, the brainy youth immersed in Information Technology and its computer systems, "these productive, energetic brilliant people, who will command the heights of the 21st century," as so enthusiastically described by the editor of *Foreign Affairs* journal, are at the same time found to be apolitical and apparently unaware that the global free market, which is the source of their wealth and influence, is not a "naturally occurring phenomenon."[7] Their position is the shrug of the unengaged.

As for the *dis*engaged, there is disillusion and even bitterness, as I found in conversation with Craig Chandler in Calgary. A few scant years earlier he had been an impassioned crusader for the Reform Party, having abandoned liberal ideals as obsolete in the post-FTA world of global competition. When he came upon the ideas and philosophy of Reform in the early 1990s, he knew he had found a home: "Their ideas were exactly what the country should be like," he told me, meaning direct democracy, fiscal accountability, an elected Senate. He listened ecstatically to speeches by party leader Preston Manning. *No more politics as usual. We're here to represent you. We're* *your employee.* He went on: "No more Distinct Society. No more special recognition for any province. Tough on immigration. Tough on crime. Tough on this, tough on that. It's what everyone wanted to hear. I wonder if Manning remembers what he said in those beginnings, because he seems to be wimping out now." Having evolved into just another political party bent on power in Ottawa, courting liberal opinion and abandoning Christian values to focus on the Ontario vote, Reform has lost Chandler.

Although he threw himself into provincial politics as a (failed) Social Credit candidate ("Because Ralph Klein is morally bankrupt"), organized the *Roots of Change* conference from which to launch a national municipal party ("We purposely called it that to show we are the grassroots – check your ego at the door! – and not David Frum and the Snack Pack elitist-MPs in Ottawa with their 'Winds of Change' conference"), and formed and headed up the Progressive Group of Independent Business to lobby for small-business interests, I sensed in Chandler the melancholy of a young man who now calls himself a free agent but who really means he's a wolf without a pack to run with. His peak moment was in 1993 – that same election that cast Mark Kingwell into a funk – when he came a strong second to the Liberal candidate in Hamilton-Mountain in Ontario. "They" had called him too young and inexperienced and they were right: "I didn't have experience in screwing up this country and mortgaging the future, I didn't have experience in lying." But he had a campaign team of three hundred people, most in their twenties, and he had a slogan, *God bless the young for we shall inherit the debt*, and he came second in every poll in a riding everyone wanted. "The NDP brought out Bob White; Mel Hurtig was there and Chrétien and Kim Campbell, Audrey McLaughlan, the Greens, the Communists, the Natural Law Party. The Tories door-knocked for the Liberals – anybody but Chandler!" But Manning was a no-show. "Manning wanted Toronto, period." Chandler's campaign team was devastated. "This country was in a crisis. As young people, we were terrified of the debt. We were all fighting for our generation, for that new Canada, the next Canada."

> I stood aside and watched while my "true north strong and free" was weakened and shackled by socialists. I was ashamed. I

stood aside and watched, but I did not see. Until they began
stealing my country's future. I will stand aside no longer. Join
me. I am a Libertarian.

— From a text by Libertarian Party leader Hilliard Cox,
on a poster in Craig Chandler's office

This heart-on-the-sleeve avowal of Hilliard Cox is the kind of sentiment that reduces to giggles the practitioners of the fine art of Canadian
self-irony. It was an art history student in Winnipeg, Kevin Matthews, who,
over pints of ale in the city's arts district – we'd been trawling through the
galleries to see what his peers were up to, some of it clever, some of it, well,
snide – walked me through the problem. His generation had been educated
by people who had come to maturity in the 1950s and 1960s, periods of idealism and the possibility of social change that were, as Matthews conceded,
without irony. "That was the rhetoric. But for us living in the 1990s, it was
really hard to believe, looking back on the 1970s, that people really took
anything seriously. We ironize everything and it's hard to believe that
people in the 1970s weren't making fun of themselves in the first place . . ."
Indignant, I interrupted him: "Of course we took ourselves seriously. Those
were our lives. Why wouldn't we?" But for Matthews, for whom ideals have
been "pulled apart and deconstructed in so many ways," he can only
imagine being a hippie, say, from his own point of view, of someone who
knows that "ultimately, it wouldn't make any difference."

Irony, writes W. H. New in *Borderlands: How We Talk About Canada*,
"becomes a way of disempowering whatever appears to be a larger or more
dominant force." It is a way of seeming to be self-deprecating about values
and habits that are in fact shared collectively, which is why ironic statements about Canada raise a smile in all of us.[8] (For instance, B. W. Powe's
formulation of Canada as a "country that works well in practice, but just
doesn't work out in theory," is the sort of statement that Canadians "get"
but no one else is expected to.)[9] When I met Toronto artist Sally McKay to
talk about her recent installation at the Art Gallery of Ontario, which
wittily assembled multiples of popular made-in-the-U.S.A. toys, I observed
that there weren't any obvious critical Canadian markers among them. But
McKay felt that they had an "ironic stance" toward American mass culture
that an American viewer would not be capable of "reading" without first

being knocked on the head. For her, her assemblies of mass-market "stuff" which Canadians uncritically consume tell us that, in our love/hate relationship to American mass culture, "we don't have a lot of choice." McKay understands that she herself is implicated; for instance, she loves certain Hollywood movies. She believes that "we're screwed anyway, mass culture is all-pervasive, that's what our world is made of, and we might as well just jump in." But it's "tricky," because she also "believes in" all the culture that is being erased by the market and that there is still value in "the stuff that we can do as people together." She neatly illustrates the unresolved tension between Canadians' ironic preoccupation with American culture and our desire for it – a tension sustained by what W. H. New calls our "persistent need to choose" between American lifestyles and our own Canadian life.

That is a faint hope, according to McKay's own perspectives. "I think Canada is being erased. We're pretty much fading out. When I was a kid we were taught that Canada is different from the United States because we have health care. We were like a socialist people. That is being undermined now, and the factors that actually make it true are coming out like quicksand from under us. Health care is going to disappear, and we're not even going to notice. I'm very bleak about it. The ironic position is not a power position: we could be annexed to the States and still be ironic."

Increasingly, for those who have been adepts of the stance, the limitations of irony as a means of confronting power have become unavoidably obvious. Reviewing the zine *Stay As You Are*, editor Hal Niedzviecki announces that "irony for irony's sake is dead . . . when everything is ironic, even irony must be accepted as literal truth. . . . Humour has become a way of saying absolutely nothing."[10] To journalist Naomi Klein, veteran of the postmodern culture wars at the university of the 1980s, and of the notion that popular culture contains its own internal critique of mindless consumption, an "over-the-top" ironic stance no longer seems subversive, just "cowardly." "In the battle between pop and politics, it is clear that pop won. Political activism is positively retro these days. And irony is no longer the aesthetic of the avant-garde, but is instead a lifestyle choice for a generation of Alanis fans and serial-killer card collectors."[11] Even more ironic self-consciousness is not the solution; a good hard look at and engagement with un-ironic "reality" may be the only true subversive stance left. Something like this shift, from a complicit yet alienated observation of pop culture – which, some argue, is *the* defining cultural condition of Canada – to a non-cynical appreciation of human emotion, seems to have happened to the actor/writer/director Don McKellar in the course of making the film *Last Night*. It is a story that begins with his character's sarcastic detachment from the tumult of emotions around him as people face the last few hours of existence on earth, and ends with his self-abandonment to love in the final seconds of his life. McKellar had wanted to keep an ironic stance through the whole of the film, he told a journalist, to expose the "hypocrisy" of manipulated emotion, but when even television ads made use of such self-conscious knowingness, it was time to question the effectiveness of irony as cultural criticism.[12]

> Democracy . . . could very well die a natural death if politics, in its noble sense . . . doesn't regain its proper place, if it doesn't stop hiding behind borrowed languages. . . . Behind cultural and identity claims, the domination of economic argument, the withdrawal into individual morality, the power of judges, unarticulated political choices are being covered up. Politics has become mute. It has lost its tongue. . . . Does it still have a vision to put forward about the future of society, is it still able to inspire action, to speak of the future?
> – Roch Côté, in a review of Olivier Mongin's
> *L'après 1989* in *Le Devoir*, August 29-30, 1998

Even those who are political actors fret about the limitations of conventional party politics. Like Craig Chandler, the disillusioned right-winger, Reform MP Rahim Jaffer joined the party out of frustration with traditional parliamentary politics that marginalize non-caucus sitting members by channelling power from the leadership downwards, and out of an idealism that Reform meant "positive change" and truly representative democracy. From his base as co-owner, with his parents, of a popular café in Edmonton, he made links with a business and cultural community for whom he feels a great deal of direct responsibility that makes him feel not so much powerful as sensitive: "It seems that people really trust someone who pours their coffee." His constituents, he told me, "see a guy who is not a politician, hasn't been desensitized to community, because he's still involved with it every day and brought a lot of people onside with him." When we spoke in 1998, he was still very comfortable with this low-key populism in a party that prided itself on having attracted a media-savvy, French-speaking, urbane, visible-minority small entrepreneur. Jaffer admitted he had broken ethnic ranks by not being a Liberal – "I was the black sheep of the family for a time" – but in fact a party poll in 1998 revealed that the majority of 1,300 Canadians between fifteen and eighteen years old said Reform was their second political choice after Liberal. And 39 per cent called themselves "political independents."[13] These are the voters of the future, who just may be lured into Reform for keeps if the party can pitch itself convincingly as grassroots, bucking big, arrogant government on behalf of the underdog – an eerie echo of what had traditionally been the NDP's social democratic pitch for the "ordinary Canadian's" vote. But if those principles are betrayed, "if our base changes, if we move to more corporate support, bigger money support, we will fail our own people," Jaffer cautioned, and he will be politically homeless.

At the other end of the political spectrum, Jenny Kwan, NDP MLA for Vancouver–Mt. Pleasant and B.C. minister of municipal affairs in 1998, said her roots in community activism gave her both a "natural" political home in the NDP and a certain discomfort in being identified as a politician. "Nowadays, when people mention politicians, it's to say they are all liars, cheats, and crooks." But she accepted the challenge of winning back their confidence, demonstrating that she, at least, was not in politics for personal gain, not for just "talking the talk," but for inciting people themselves to engage politically, at however modest a level. "If you don't have the participation of people, you don't have democracy. So you've *got* to engage people and show them they have a legitimate role to play, absolutely, and that their role is *vitally* important. Like my mother, who is engaged simply by talking with the people she rides to work with on the buses. Or you can be involved in a particular issue in your community, like building a new community centre or petitioning government or sending a letter. At another level, you can join a party."

But when Kwan says that despite the public perception she is "proud" to be a politician, you have to wonder if it isn't still her old activist self speaking, the community legal advocate, the agitator around residential and tenants'-rights issues and human-rights campaigns, and not the politician-manager of party compromise and discipline. It was as that activist she would have best understood, I think, what CBC *Newsworld*'s Evan Solomon had in mind when he wrote of a yearning for political leaders "who can inspire us, leaders who give us reason to re-invent the social experiment that is Canada every time we exercise the right to vote."[14] It isn't politicians we yearn for, it is revolutionaries of our everyday lives.

When I met up with Irshad Manji to talk about the fallout from her 1997 book *Risking Utopia: On the Edge of a New Democracy*, I had in mind a discussion of her proposals for social transformation beyond the frame of Right and Left politics and centred more on the ethics of *empathy*, *agency*, and *accountability*, the basis of her plan for a new democracy. One of her reviewers at the time of the book's publication had found her views piquant but ultimately without much to say about what is arguably *the* political question concerning democracy: "How to convince those who have to share with those who have not." This is a political question about the redistribution of social power through economic equity, but when I spoke with her Manji was if anything even more disengaged from such a blatantly strategic issue. Our conversation opened with her disclosure that she had become a member of the Metropolitan Community Church of Toronto, the city's most open congregation for lesbians and gays, and she was higher than a kite about it. "I think that going to MCC is an act of the heart," she said. The weeping, the smiling every single week during the Eucharistic prayer. The rejuvenation. The message of unconditional love. I could understand the appeal, but was she, until recently at least a Muslim, now a Christian believer? Her response was ecumenical: "I realize how incredibly privileged I am to be 'out,' to be loved, to be employed meaningfully, to be in a country which, for all its warts, is to me still a slice of heaven on earth. To have a voice and public influence at a relatively young age, above all to have friends. I am so happy that I fear, in a good way, disappointing a loving and merciful God, whereas I used to fear angering a capricious and malicious one. To have my creative power reflect God's own as a creature of my Creator ... what I do, I do as a tribute to God's creative power."

She spoke with rapturous energy – it was impossible to doubt the authenticity of her belief – but what interested me was the connection, if any, between this new spirituality and her older political frustrations. "Do you sense there is an *opportunity* for the spirit in the retreat from or disappointment in politics?" I asked her. "Had you been able to sustain yourself on the Left, you may never have had this encounter with spirit." This was close to the truth of it. She acknowledged her disappointment in the "deficit of spirituality" on the Left, the people driven by ambition and success, the arrogance of people who think they have all the answers, the reliance on "orthodoxy" and group resentments and not on personal agency. But it was the revelation about her own being, about "how important the heart is in its own thought processes, what a reservoir of intuition lies there," that moved her most. Up to that moment she had been driven by reason, not emotion (by the same token she had gone to mosque out of "religion" not "faith"). It was from that braininess that she had written her book, in a kind of fury about the Left's refusal to be honest with the public about not having all the answers. "Why is it that, at the same time that so many members of the trade union movement rant and rail about the record profits of Bay Street, they invest their multimillion dollar pension funds in the very corporations, including banks, that lay off workers? I'm not asking for purity but for honesty about this!" Now that she is ruled by the intuition that "shines through" the mesh of heart and head, she can see that in the past she violated her personal integrity by not listening to her heart. I wondered if she feared the possibility that the more spiritual her world view became, the less tenable her political beliefs about citizenship, democracy, exploitation . . . but, no, she was "both afraid and excited by the possibility that my journey of faith could undermine some of my most basic precepts. Learn! Learn to learn! There's no shortage of things in this world to be agape at." In the meantime, as she would no doubt acknowledge, them what has still gets. . . .

Is happiness possible in the decline of politics? Mark Kingwell would say no, having made it very clear in his writing – notably in *Better Living: In Pursuit of Happiness from Plato to Prozac* – that happiness is a function of engagement in political and ethical action. In fact, he would go as far as to claim, as he did in conversation with me, that "there is no valid notion of happiness that isn't engaged in such action." Without necessarily issuing a party platform, Kingwell insists that all of his writing is political, whether in social philosophy or in cultural studies or in television criticism, because it is all about how to make the world a more just place, in or outside electoral politics or social movements. He calls himself a "theorist of justice" who nevertheless would agree, along with Irshad Manji, that a certain degree of self-interest is "allowed" in the construction of it. "You can be very comfortable, you can be very happy, and you can still feel you are doing your citizenly duty in some way. You don't have to be an asshole. This may be the best we can hope for."

As we talked, the ambiguous British example of Tony Blair's New Labour came up – the opportunity to pursue a marginally superior political program by capitulating to capitalism on all its main points – but at least, I added, to elect a Labour government after interminable seasons of Thatcherism meant that many people had responded to appeals to their best, not their basest, selves. Their citizenship and mutual responsibility had been evoked, and they had responded with wild relief: people *want* to live in full ethical consciousness, not as moral pygmies. Kingwell agreed, from a slightly different angle. "I think everybody is increasingly aware the privileges they enjoy are in some deep, moral sense insupportable. Genuinely insupportable. We're all trying to find morally viable places to stand." This may not be so much the decline of politics, then, as the necessary reflection in a time of profound dislocation before the re-engagement with the timeless struggle for justice.

RESISTANCE

> The young are citizens set aside from the society they inhabit. They are not "evolving." They are already mixed up in politics of the family, of housing, of economic development, of poverty, of exclusion. And not as "the young" but as the citizens they already are. Jointly and severally.
> – Anne-Marie Brunelle, "The Trap of the Youth Lobby,"
> *Recto Verso*, November-December 1998

Writer and columnist Naomi Klein, who cut her teeth on university journalism in the 1980s, remembers the very long time "when the coolest thing you could be doing was 'Madonna Studies'" and now welcomes with relief any sign of the end of cool or, its close cousin, the ironic stance. She argues that both have been the source of her generation's political paralysis, the acute self-consciousness, the smirk, for they make "real politics" impossible, politics being decidedly un-ironic. So she cheers every instance of a Madonna Studies graduate who now lobbies against sweatshop labour in Asia, or the anti-APEC activists who "quoted" *Sesame Street* when they set up Democracy Street in Vancouver, or the rave enthusiasts who now read and quote Abby Hoffman, the Yippie impresario of the 1960s New Left. "And that's not disgustingly 'retro'?" I asked, for we had also been talking about the constant recycling of imagery in ad campaigns that renders even the 1970s as a source of nostalgic desire for people who, unable to assimilate their own recent experience, can only consume its signs. "No," she retorted, "that's history."

Having a history allows you to do politics. You can see how things have formed, deformed, reformed over time, you can construct your own agency in the flux of social forms in your own time, you can imagine its trajectory into the future. "The socialists are back!" Klein exulted, for we had also been talking about the Reclaim the Streets events in downtown Toronto in the summer of 1998 and held simultaneously around the world, events that demonstrated the un-ironic determination of young people to reclaim public space for themselves and create their own culture at the same time, while waiting for some ultimate framing political discourse to emerge from the tormented self-examination of the Old Left.

These are pretty funny socialists, these demonstrators without placards or megaphones or slogans chanted relentlessly under the bullying direction of a parade marshal; these demonstrators invite you to "choose your own adventure" and turn the day into an anti-Harris or pro-bicycle or make-your-own-music celebration. There's no law that says politics can't be playful. *Huge puppets, hundreds of drums, street theatre, zine tables, guerrilla gardening, dancing, chalk drawing, costumes, food*: this is the repertoire of the global street party. Bloor Street in Toronto's Annex neighbourhood is declared a Public Boogie Zone, no cars allowed. A man with a shovel plants a garden on the pavement. Chalk-graffiti artists inscribe their texts. *Resistance is fertile. Fuck the rich. Clear air, ride a bicycle. Love your mother.* Balloons and crepe-paper streamers and soap bubbles.[15] A children's crusade to secure the holy places of their own pleasure in the time before the Blue Meanies of corporate capitalism got their hands on it and sold it back to them, with a logo.

> So we [the Black Panther Party] concluded that socialist revo-
> lution was the road to our freedom. I don't believe that means
> anything anymore, if a *global* economic arrangement has suc-
> ceeded in overwhelming capitalism. . . . The U.S. capitalists are
> threatened by a limitation of marketplaces. They not only *need*
> to sell the whole world a Coke, they're moving to do it. Consider
> Vietnam. . . . They need the marketplace! I think Vietnam is
> about developing a marketplace of forty million potential con-
> sumers. It's a play-or-pay proposition: they *will* buy a Coke.
> – Elaine Brown, *A Taste of Power: A Black Woman's Story*

Elaine Brown, editor of the Black Panther newspaper and sometime lover of the party's absolute leader, Huey P. Newton, was summoned in 1971 to Newton's Oakland penthouse to hear him out on his vision. We now call it the New World Order, and socialists believe it is the great undoing of our freedom. But Huey Newton was excited, even as the war in Vietnam still burned, by the implications of the burgeoning order of transnational capital: just as capitalism would overflow national boundaries, so would the revolution of the oppressed. Capital would think it was selling them a Coke, but the revolutionaries knew better. Capital's organization of world economies into a single system meant "there's only *one* machinery to seize, the toppling of which makes way for an egalitarian redistribution of the wealth of the whole world – true communism."[16]

Newton graced a thousand posters in the communes of his admirers during the 1960s and early 1970s, sweet-faced ghetto boy enthroned in a rattan armchair like a rajput of a reborn African kingdom, his authority exemplified in the long smart rifle he wielded. But the Black Panthers died, many in a storm of bullets or in exile or in moral collapse, and once the war was over Coke did go to Vietnam, at the invitation of the new order of revolutionaries in Ho Chi Minh City.

Coca-Cola is now a $150-billion colossus astride the planet, the best-known brand name on earth, rivalled only by PepsiCo. Pepsi's advertising creative director, Ted Sann, said in a television interview, referring to the slogans "Pepsi Generation" and "Generation Next," "The soft drink as a badge, something saying who you are, what you are, what social group you aspire to and hang with – that was the big leap. And put [Pepsi] into the icon category."[17] So, even with 50 per cent of the worldwide market,[18] Coca-Cola feels the heat of competition and the need, from its shareholders' point of view, for constantly expanding market share. Vietnam, China, Indonesia were already being serviced, as was the Russian national soccer team, who had chosen Coke as its official soft drink;[19] where to next?

In 1995 the University of British Columbia signed an agreement with Coca-Cola that guaranteed only Coke products would be sold on campus. By 1999 Coca-Cola had "snared" seven campuses, PepsiCo twenty-two, in what was known as the "cola wars" of that decade. The majority of the universities' intelligentsia – administration, faculty, students, and students' unions – remained remarkably cool under fire, shrugging their shoulders at it all. But others were infuriated and humiliated. "Whatever happened to the days when a college campus provided refuge for idealistic, young, cash-strapped students from the evils of capitalism, corporations and consumerism?" Andrew MacDonald wanted to know, in an article in *The Student Activist*,[20] and I mourned along with him, remembering hanging out with friends in murky corners of the rickety Hot Caf by the library at the University of Alberta or, off-campus, in the loud, jam-packed booths of the family-run Tuck Shop where everyone, revolutionaries included, congregated in the morning for the cook's fresh batch of cinnamon buns. Today's students are obliged to eat in food courts dominated by franchises like (Pepsi-owned) Pizza Hut and Taco Bell, their students' collective spaces thus transformed into strip malls by (this is the humiliation) agreement of their very own students' union executives and councils. Dalhousie University's vice-president, for instance, was mightily impressed by Pepsi's agreeing to pay for the uniform of the students' union employees. The uniforms, of course, bear the Pepsi logo. "Are deals being struck to sell Pepsi to students, or students to Pepsi?" MacDonald wanted to know.

2 + 2 = 5-ism: Caving in to a target marketing strategy aimed at oneself after holding out for a long period of time. "Oh all right, I'll buy your stupid cola. Now leave me alone."

– Douglas Coupland, *Generation X*

In the fall of 1997 I met Jeta Das at the opening session of the Alternative Growth Summit, a parallel conference to the government-initiated, by-invitation-only Alberta Growth Summit summoned by premier Ralph Klein to deliberate the province's economic future. At the alternative summit, grassroots Alberta would have a chance to put in its two bits' worth, including Das and his buddies from STORM (Student Organized Resistance Movement), of which Das was a founding member. (The University of Alberta's students' union had been invited to the *other* summit while uninvited students gathered to protest in the street outside.) When we got together for an interview, and I mulled over the issue of the university's corporatization, Das leapt in with the example of the cola wars, whether the University of Alberta was to become a Coke or a Pepsi university. Even he was shocked that it had come to this, that administrations, so strapped for cash after government cutbacks on education spending, were contemplating delivering public space to a soft-drink company. But more disturbing still was the fact that students' own representatives were collaborating beyond the call of duty. Clearly, many of them were fully persuaded either of the value of corporate charity or of its moral neutrality and had become instruments of its processes. "They say we're getting money for this or that," said Das, "and what difference does it make. But this is an ideological position. If we had a seriously left-wing administration in the students' union, they wouldn't be pursuing this right now." This was in fact the same union that gave STORM permission to promote the Alternative Growth Summit on campus on the condition that the group say nothing negative about the official summit. Patricia Foufas of STORM thought this was ridiculous: "The whole point of the Alternative Summit is to say that the Growth Summit is inadequate. I think it's no place of the Students' Union to be telling us what we can and can't say."[21]

> The Coke deal reached a new height of madness Wednesday as the University administration, in conjunction with the Students' Union, followed through on their threat to strictly enforce the single-source beverage agreement on campus. All students found with Pepsi in their possession yesterday were promptly executed . . . "We warned students again and again, and now they are paying for their refusal to submit to the highest power

in the world, the Coke corporation," said [University president
Rod] Fraser, watching custodial staff pile bodies in the Quad.
– "Coke, University kill dissidents," *The Getaway*
[satirical issue of University of Alberta
newspaper *The Gateway*], December 3, 1998

There were some student victories in the cola wars, however, aided by
the new style of global activism of the Information Age. As the direct result
of a six-year campaign against its business dealings in Myanmar (Burma),
in which Canadian students with modems were active, Pepsi announced in
early 1997 that it would no longer produce and sell its soft drinks in that
country, notorious for the military dictatorship's abuse of its own citizens.
The cola mogul had discovered that "Generation Next" cared very much
about the power of the corporate logo to sell the desirability of a soft drink
in a country where the democratically elected government has been condemned effectively to house arrest. In 1993, students at Carleton University
in Ottawa had issued "campus action kits" on the Internet that included
pamphlets, letters, petitions, and "Gotta Boycott" stickers, and called on
others to put pressure on their schools to cancel contracts signed with Pepsi
until it withdrew from Burma. Decisively for the shareholders of PepsiCo
stock, Harvard University cancelled its million-dollar deal over the Burma
issue, but not before students at University of Guelph, University of
Toronto, and McGill University joined the international boycott of Pepsi
products. Naomi Klein was thrilled: "Pepsi's debacle should serve as a cau-
tionary tale for all the corporations who see the world as their free-trading
playground."[22] A utopian media democracy had pulled it off, "hyper-
connected" students using technology as tools of passionate agitprop.[23]
    Naomi Klein tracked this kind of activism while researching her book
No Logo. The campaigns against Pepsi or Nike sometimes showed an
incomplete understanding of the issues, she told me, and the effort was on
occasion misdirected, but international boycott campaigns did get something right: by targeting a universally recognized brand name, they were
symbolically targeting globalization itself. "Globalization in miniature,"
Klein called it. If there once had been a moment of young activists' feelings
of helplessness before the facts of globalization and the "total inability to
deal with the shifts going on in the outside world," there was now a core of

young people who are mobilized, not paralyzed, by the plight of the young women workers burned to death in toy factories in Bangkok or the Thai children driven into the sex tourism trade or the Burmese students fleeing for their lives into exile.

These facts, and the 1998 ruinous collapse of the economies of the so-called Asian tigers that have housed these desperate workers, mean there are new opportunities for a critical politics. "Students Against Sweatshops" has chapters on three hundred campuses involved in the "Free Burma" campaigns, mainly in the United States. Some have moved on from Pepsi to a boycott of Ericsson Communications, a Swedish cell-phone manufacturer with plants in Burma, that included picketing a Céline Dion concert sponsored by Ericsson. By spring 1999, the campaigners had got every single brand-name manufacturer out of Burma.

"People are hungry for ideas," Klein asserted, "and increasingly feeling bullied by advertising." There had been a spontaneous backlash at Concordia University in Montreal, where students vandalized toilet cubicles plastered with advertising. "We are sick of seeing Nike, sick of being marketed to death; give us any reason to hate Nike and we'll seize on it."

Klein doesn't want to exaggerate the political potential of a protest movement that is completely decentralized without any obvious leadership (of which it is inherently suspicious anyway) and that depends on the hospitality of peers at the universities and in the media who have blank screens where their collective memory should be. Can they feel outrage when they've known nothing but the sensation of the present? But one can hope that the protesters in the thirteen Canadian cities who turned out in April 1998 to rally against Nike's labour practices on International Day of Action in Solidarity with Nike Production Workers felt their own power as they sashayed down the ramps of a dozen anti-sweatshop fashion shows and savoured the moment a month later when Nike's CEO Phil Knight announced six new initiatives in his pledge to hold its subcontractors to improved labour codes, including a "zero-tolerance stance" on child labour.[24]

Who will get the private sector off the back of civil society?
– Benjamin Barber, *Jihad vs. McWorld: How Globalization and Tribalism Are Reshaping the World*

I had no idea Carly Stasko was a mere twenty-year-old when I asked her for an interview in Toronto. No one that young, I had foolishly assumed, could be so politically busy, forgetting the evidence of my own generation's precociousness in ban-the-bomb, civil rights, and anti-war organizing. But even Stasko could speak of a still-younger generation than hers, the "kids" she'd meet in high school when she did media literacy workshops who would moan and groan about how they were victims of racism, all the while dressed head to toe in Nike gear. "Do you know what's happening to the people who are making those products?" she'd confront them, driven crazy by the dazzling visual literacy of a generation that seemed unable to make the connection between the "sign" (the Nike shoes) and the "signified" (the exploited Third World worker). You want to talk racism? Let's talk racism! "They are so media savvy, though, that this is a good place to begin with them. They grew up with it. So we talk about culture jamming."

Stasko would tell them of the time she and her comrades in the Media Collective (part of a loose network of groups that combined ad busting, zine publishing, pirate radio, and community activism) dressed up in phony workers' uniforms with a company logo – someone they knew had a small printing company – and in the middle of the day, brazen as could be, climbed up on billboards advertising Target cigarettes to hang banners, *The target is children*. "The trick was to also get the action on videotape and pass it on to the media, because then it lasts more than the day it takes for the billboard companies to come around and take our banner down. The taping made the action a documentary, for which we were interviewed by MuchMusic.

"I can't stress how influential the media is for us. It's the soup we grew up in," Stasko reflected. "Music, radio, television, magazines, advertising. Everything is sponsored, all your fun things are linked to products or take place in a designated fun area where you consume products. It used to be that your peers were the people sitting in the desks beside you; now it's equally the people you see on TV or the bodies you see in magazines. That's why we [culture jammers] emphasize making, not consuming, culture." It's insane, this seamless link of personal identity with consumer products, and to fight it some kids just get depressed and consume more, stuffing the interior void. But others start questioning what is going on. And then they act.

In 1996 Jubal Brown, an active member of the Toronto Media Collective, took a magic marker to Calvin Klein billboards, transforming models' heads to skulls. The first issue of *Guerrilla Shots: A Tiresome, Self-Serving, Money-Grubbing Newsletter from Guerrilla Media* in Vancouver reported in 1997 a billboard-altering action ("Don't Drive, Take a Bike"). Ten thousand phony B.C. Transit leaflets were distributed announcing new measures for bicycles on public transit. "Black Contaminated Ink" warnings were stencilled on plastic bags used to deliver the Conrad Black–owned newspapers *Vancouver Sun* and *Province*. And Montreal's Work in Progress Guerrilla Circus, a spin-off from the Media Collective, sent clowns, stiltwalkers, acrobats, jugglers and fire-eaters to demonstrations, rallies and sit-ins in 1998.

But in Summer 1998, the Toronto Media Collective announced – indeed, celebrated – its dissolution into its constituent groups after two years as a non-organization of seat-of-their-pants cultural activism. The trouble was, they felt, they were all tactics, no strategy, or as P. J. Lilley analyzed the problem: "After a while you have to have some kind of a point."[25]

Pranks didn't seem to go beyond inspiring spin-off groups to attempt their own hijinks in the marketplace. Granted, a lot of high-voltage energy came together in the jammings, but what do you do after the billboards get repapered, when Internet servers stop carrying your Web site but carry Yahoo!'s official culture-jamming site filed under "alternative,"[26] when culture-jamming *Adbusters* is named Magazine of the Year at the National Magazine Awards, and when the anti-commercial spoofs, so slick, so lovingly-rendered, are so appealing that lampooned companies like Diesel jeans buy extra copies to pass around? What can you do to really get up the nose of the corporate advertising peddlers when it's all the same to the kids whether they're wearing *Kraft* or *Krap* logos? Culture jammers writhe in self-loathing ("Today we are the 'North American pig,' bloated with excess, heavily in debt and out-pigging everyone else in sight,"[27] a sudden tone of high seriousness reminiscent of older, stricter countercultures) while everyone else goes shopping.

"We are the foot soldiers in an image battle that can't be won," writer and critic Hal Niedzviecki says of his generation, who think the issue of their time is not how to live life but how to perceive its representations. "Welcome to the culture wars, nineties style."

Now, the streets belong to the people: They have seized control of the city's elemental matter and made it their own. They have created life amidst urban decay et ils ont proclamé la rue ouverte.

— Elisa, "Sous les Paves, La Plage,"
The Student Activist, May 1998

Carly Stasko had talked about the Media Collective and its spin-off activities, in small events and happenings, zines, visits to alternative schools, as having been a training ground for the big event, the Reclaim the Streets festival in . . . Toronto! Birmingham! Melbourne! Sydney! Tokyo! Bogota! (and sixteen other sites) in the summer of 1998. We were sitting at an outdoor café right where the festival street party had taken place three weeks earlier, the corner of Bloor and Brunswick, and she was describing the context, giving Reclaim the Streets the dimensions it deserved, which was the reclamation of public space while faceless men with power determine our fate in private negotiation.

That same day of Reclaim the Streets, eight leaders of the eight leading industrial nations were meeting in Birmingham, England, to decide the fate of millions of lives, sucking power out of local and even national levels of government, and what were we going to do about it? Getting out of our car for a day was a start, breaking open the bubble in which we habitually move around our city to go *walking down the middle of the street* as though this is what it were for and not for private parking lots. Stasko doesn't believe that political change is going to come about by collecting a few people to yell at demonstrations, although there is a place for aggressive dissent; it has to go deeper than that, it has to reach the bedrock of what people most deeply want, "the commonality, the desire for a community itself," and there, where there is such lack, build something that hadn't been there, before you came with your spade and shovel and dug an urban garden in the middle of the street.

The summer before, Stasko had travelled in Europe, visiting activists in Berlin, Munich, Warsaw, and Prague, their bookstores and community centres, and returned to Canada with relief. Compared to the Europeans, with their Berlin anarchists in Reeboks and their Polish hipster artists cheering the brand new Coca-Cola billboard, Canadians, living cheek by jowl with American pop culture, know what's really going on. "Because we're little brother to the States, we recognize the importance of the *symbolic* environment. And the importance of communication, because not everybody has equal freedom to communicate and express themselves." And the European politicos! The most boring people she'd ever met. "At their events they stand and shout things like, 'Hey hey, ho ho, bad stuff has got to go!' . . . It was always based on anger and conflict. Really stuck in that groove." That groove. *Hey, hey, LBJ, how many kids did you kill today? Ho ho Ho Chi Minh, Viet Nam's gonna win! L'imagination prend le pouvoir!*

> Active Resistance is working towards an anarchist society . . . a world where people have power over their own lives, bodies and sexualities, where we cherish and live in balance with the earth . . . where we work together cooperatively to nourish community, autonomy and mutual aid. L'imagination au pouvoir!
> – *Active Resistance: A Radical Gathering* Web pages

Stasko said that, while the Reclaimers were dancing and chalking on the sidewalks and exchanging information and zines, "this milling about," there were others, arms crossed, standing on the periphery of events, just watching it happen. "I know who they are. They never come to our meetings because we aren't hardcore enough for them. There are rifts happening." She meant the anarchist group Active Resistance, who were organizing an event called Radical Gathering, which would take place in August 1998 in Toronto.

The draft schedule of the Radical Gathering listed a smorgasbord of activities for every political inclination imaginable: a radical history exhibit; an action with the Ontario Coalition Against Poverty; a performance art party; the freeskools; core group discussions about alternative economics, art, and revolution; a Propaganda Carnival featuring zines, posters, and books; neighbourhood walking tours; anarchist picnics – to name some. Please bring a mat and sleeping bag. There will be vegan and vegetarian meals. Childcare provided. Total cost for the week: US$25/CAN$35.

"The Active Resistance Toronto Organizing Core committee meets weekly under a consensus process with a 80% majority backup vote upon unresolvable blocks. . . . All meeting and workgroup facilitators will be trained before the conference in organized and focussed consensus decision-making and discussion techniques with gender parity." They had thought of everything, it seemed – based on bitter experience, if Carly Stasko's misgivings about "hardcore politics" could be trusted. "Active Resistance: A Radical Gathering (AR) is a revolutionary left, anti-capitalist gathering and convention uniting theory and practice."

There was a rather extraordinary amount of respectful media coverage of the Radical Gathering (where, I wondered, had the paranoia of the straight press, whipped up to a lather during the events of 1968–69, seeped away to?) as though the point was not to fear or loathe these young anarchists, with pink hair and tattooed shoulders, sleeping on rooftops, hanging in "freeskool" workshops on bike activism and sex workers' rights, but to understand them.

NOW magazine reporter Leah Rumack, once she had got over the chagrin of being handed a green (for corporate) media badge instead of the black one (for community-friendly), felt kindly about the goings-on. Perhaps the freeskool topic "Does the Revolutionary Left Have a Future?" was a bit earnest, and the street theatre of cops on stilts beating off squeegers washing the windows of cardboard cars wasn't very subtle, and organizers wouldn't let her stay in the scamming workshop, and, yes, outside this "mini-universe" of order with no bosses it seemed unlikely that the toiling masses would have "a glorious group consciousness-raising and go take over the means of production (nicely, of course) in the near future." But she was moved nevertheless by the palpable and vital sense of community that expressed itself naturally, from the commitment to transparent and participatory process to rotating bathroom detail. A thousand punks, hippies, anarchos, radical Christians, prostitutes, squeegers, taking care of each other.[28]

Hal Niedzviecki, writing for the *Globe and Mail* (green badge for sure), located the Radical Gathering in its historical context of anarchism, the "sophisticated anti-government, anti-corporate philosophy of voluntary co-operation" with roots at least as far back as the Paris Commune of 1871 and through to our era of George Woodcock, the Yippies, Diggers and Provos of the 1960s, and now to turn-of-the-century culture jammers and street performers and in-your-face anti-racists. Niedzviecki took them very seriously indeed as he made his way around sundry activities, nodding in sympathy with the sophistication of a generation that knows it will take more than love-ins on Yorkville Avenue and LSD in the Kool-Aid to effect radical social change.

Jim Munroe, reporting for *This Magazine* (black badge, surely), got high on what he saw of the Gathering's rhapsody of the impossible, the dream of living fully, humanly, *because* without power. "They came to build a magical, impossible machine. A perpetual-revolution machine." The perpetual revolution, of course, is the one that keeps dethroning itself, keeps reinventing itself not as successful revolutionaries bossing workers' councils around, but as these "crusty punks" clumped outside dingy halls, the "squatting queens" among the homeless, the freight-train hoppers, the Krishnas serving chickpea stew: "The dirty kids finally have something to dance to."[29] *Resistance looks like you*, says a graffito. *Soyez réalistes, demandez l'impossible*, wrote the Parisian of '68: Be realistic, demand the impossible.

> Number of people at "Non-Monogamy and Anarchist Relationships" and "How to Silkscreen," the two best-attended seminars: more than 70. Amount donated by anarcho-pop group Chumbawumba: $2500. Amount left at end of the week and then distributed to like-minded organizations: $7000.
> – "Build It and They Will Come,"
> *This Magazine*, November/December 1998

"In the freaks, in their fantasies of love and beauty, their eroticism, their mysticism, their playfulness, in their flexibility of lifestyle, adaptability to environmental changes, and in the quickness of their reflexes as danger closed in, a new human personality was taking shape, along with new definitions of family, community, productivity and responsibility. 'Open up your senses, shed your old skin, prepare yourself for an evolutionary leap out of sight.'" I wrote that (quoting Robert Hunter, a founder of Greenpeace) in 1980 about the hippies. We thought we were talking about something that would become manifest within the time of our own youth, and it did, for some people, for some communities, for a while. And for a long while after, too, long enough to encode itself in the DNA of the next generation, if the dirty kids and merry pranksters of the summer of 1998 are any evidence. But the point is the evolution, not the repetition.

Changes in individual consciousness, while necessary, are insufficient for revolution, some had believed, and dreamed of total transformations in violent catharses of bourgeois society. Only the scorched earth of their aftermath could be the seedbed of the new personality, implanted in what we imagined would be the post-scarcity, post-repression bliss of play. But that is not the future that materialized for the generation trapped in a metamorphosizing capitalism without end. And when they talk of what is possible for themselves, it is with a grounded patience for the long view and the long haul. Mark Kingwell spoke to me of the "invisible" resistance that takes the form of the thousand weekly decisions people make, from what they watch on television to how they spend their money. Being "political" in this culture is not just being out on the street in a demonstration. "Politics" can begin in the small, interior voice that says things are not okay, that people are being hurt by power and it feels terrible. He sees this in his philosophy students, that what they need first, before any act can be contemplated in full consciousness, are "techniques of decoding" the culture, "tools to understand the terrible things that are being done to them on a daily basis."

From there, it takes practice, practice in small events of commitment and self-determination, to get used to the idea of an authority and a desire held in common for the self-rule of community.

> The United States and New Zealand have both managed to lower their official unemployment rate in recent years, simply by changing the way they count their unemployed. The same ruse could work for poverty. . . . By any objective measure, poverty in Canada is rising, both in real numbers and as a proportion of the population. It will be no consolation to the millions of Canadians living in poverty to be told that, thanks to a new statistical device, they have suddenly become well-off.
> – Seth Klein, Jane Pulkingham,
> *CCPA Monitor*, vol. 4, no. 6, 1997

This is the idea of a left-wing resistance that I'm used to: gather a number of socialist brains together and put them on the case of the crises of capitalism. There is no end to the crises. Just this one issue of the *Monitor*, published by the Canadian Centre for Policy Alternatives (CCPA), a leftist think tank based in Ottawa, exposes: the real, as opposed to official, unemployment rates; the windfall profits to the rich from the stock-market boom; the right-wing agenda of the anti-nuclear group Energy Probe; and the biased media coverage of a Peruvian hostage-taking incident, to name but a very few. A steady diet of this kind of reading can be depressing and enervating, when it isn't enraging, for the conscientious citizen who is trying to be informed without concomitant suicidal feelings. Alternatively, one can join a group, such as the CCPA, and be comforted by the presence of like-minded humans. The bosses, of course, would prefer that dissidents feel their aloneness, not their collectivity. Many socialist brains are better than one, and if they all focussed together on the same weak bolts holding together the capitalist ideological structure, something just may give way.

Seth Klein thought so. As a researcher and writer at the B.C. branch of the CCPA in Vancouver, he had to think ceaselessly about not only the content of public policy issues but how to communicate them best to a public scared out of its wits by years of neo-liberal deficit delirium. Klein has been a socialist since forever: his grandparents were communists, his doctor father supports public health care, his mother has made feminist and anti-nuclear films, his sister is the critical journalist and writer Naomi Klein. It was a family legacy, this way of thinking, a kind of multi-generational solidarity with the ghosts of 1930s union organizers, anti-McCarthyites, civil rights marchers – so much so that, up to the age of eleven, Klein assumed that "all the good issues had been taken." But in 1980 he heard the anti-nuclear scientist Helen Caldicott speak in Montreal, and realized that there was still a struggle out there, the on-going issue of nuclear power and weapons, and by age fifteen he was active in the Montreal group Students Against Global Extermination. When he was eighteen, he spent a year travelling across Canada talking with high-school students about how to organize their own anti-nuclear groups. "Reagan was still the president of the U.S., the Cold War was still on, seventy per cent of surveyed Canadian teenagers thought a nuclear war was likely, and soon, and ninety per cent of those felt there was nothing they could do about it." By the end of his trip in 1987, Klein and his co-activists had spoken, he figures, to one in every twenty high-school students in Canada.

"Did *you* feel it was possible to 'do' something about the imminence of nuclear war?" I asked him. "Well," he answered, "the Cold War ended the next year!"

At university he was a student of the left-wing political economist Mel Watkins, and had a ringside seat for the last hurrah, during the anti–Free Trade Agreement fights of 1988, of the New Left nationalism of his parents' generation, which he viewed as "narrow," stuck in anti-Americanism. At the University of Toronto he was involved in an anti-racism movement that was a lot more exciting and challenging than the campus NDP. "It was the end of apartheid in South Africa," he remembered, "and we were trying to get more affirmative action happening at the university, more changed curriculums, and Jewish and black activists had a lot of hard thinking to do when the *Showboat* controversy erupted [around charges of anti-semitism in the black protest against the Jewish-authored musical]."

When the leadership of the federal NDP was contested by the openly gay, youngish and stylish Svend Robinson, Klein briefly revived his interest in the idea of radical party politics and made the nomination speech for what turned out to be a doomed campaign. But he doesn't think about party politics now. For one thing, the CCPA is politically non-partisan. For another, what draws him to his work there is the urgency of getting people to think differently about their situation: he says you actually can "reshift the culture," one of his favourite notions. The CCPA "means to engage directly with the public about what kind of society we want to live in and what economies are for. We have lost so much ground in the last twenty years, the challenge is to reshift our culture to remind people about *why* we have social programs, *why* we pay taxes – the price we pay for services we have decided to provide each other collectively."

> There was a time when the most fantastic thing in the world was not to be a rock star but a revolutionary. I put it to u – that time has cum again.
> – "Legionella's Manifesto," *Fuse*, Special Issue, 1998

The three of them sat sprawled across the fraying furniture in the rather dingy lounge area of the students' union building at the University of British Columbia, reliving the wars: Ayanis Ormond, who worked in a workers' co-op after finishing high school, then travelled in the Philippines on a work-exchange program before settling into university studies; Jaggi Singh, who quit university at one point to work with the East Timor Network and the Ogoni Solidarity Network, to do culture jamming, anti-poverty work with Food Not Bombs, and to set up an anarchist "discussion and action" group; Jonathan Oppenheim, who met Singh at a "billboard liberation" action. Their involvement in APEC Alert – the reason I was interviewing them – didn't come out of a vacuum. In fact Alert was a way of focussing into a coherent and amplified beam of energy the people already working in Vancouver in groups concerned with human rights, sexual assault, the corporatist university, free trade, East Timor's occupation by Indonesian troops, and the Days of Action sponsored by the Canadian Federation of Students against tuition hikes. But APEC (Asia Pacific Economic Cooperation) was the big one.

The APEC group of nations operates under the philosophy of open regionalism, to "service the needs of capital and promote its optimal expansion through unregulated markets, unrestrained foreign investment and unrestricted trade."[30] When it was announced that a summit of APEC leaders was to take place in Vancouver at the end of November 1997, on the campus of UBC no less, the trio was galvanized into action. And what had begun as a story buried in the back pages of the business section of news-papers, and then had "morphed" into a traffic story on the front pages when the RCMP announced that streets would be closed to local traffic during the summit for security reasons, finally became a human-rights story when RCMP officers doused protesting students with pepper spray. "It never did get covered as an APEC story," said Oppenheim.

I listened agog to their account of the extraordinary series of actions leading up to the confrontations during the summit, feeling I had been living on another planet the whole time, the planet of normal, not to say staid, party politics, the planet of organized and disciplined single-issue groups, the planet of CBC news broadcasts and *Globe and Mail* editorials.

In January 1997, marking the declaration of Canada's Year of Asia Pacific, thirty protesters in a group called Active Resistance tried to set up a tent city on the grounds of a downtown hotel to get the ball rolling on APEC. But, said Singh, "it never got off the ground, literally, because the city cops just ran their bikes over our tents. It was then we decided to form APEC Alert," to fight the summit's accommodation at UBC, and begin networking. It took a while to rev up. When Ormond joined, he said, APEC Alert consisted of eight or nine people meeting weekly. Still, they organized public forums on human rights in China and East Timor (both China and Indonesia were expected at the summit). Ten, twelve people would show up. Singh was not discouraged. "You learned more being in APEC Alert than in class. It was relevant, it was looking at issues that affected us, it was analyzing them." They appeared on panels, wrote and distributed leaflets, set up a Web page.

Things heated up in June. On the anniversary of the Tiananmen Square massacre in China, they held a "solidarity action," in which they crashed a farewell party for the outgoing president of UBC, bearing aloft a papier mâché penis they called the Corporate Dick Award, "not that we actually got to present it to him." By September they were conducting puppet-making workshops and rehearsing street theatre actions, which culminated in the arrest of two Alert members who were nabbed painting a circle on the pavement around a Goddess of Democracy statue – an intentional "citation" of the Goddess in the Tiananmen Square student demonstrations – and declaring it an "APEC-free zone." A month before the summit, a "big action" at Hallowe'en was designed to exorcise corporate demons on campus. In costume – Oppenheim wore a pair of Mickey Mouse ears, another a carved pumpkin on his head – they gathered in front of a Coca-Cola machine and burned some Coke cans inside a pentagram, a mystic symbol they had drawn on the floor, then traipsed over to the residence of the new university president, armed with washable marker pens and garlic. The protesters were scribbling graffiti on the glass walls of the building's atrium – "Say boo to APEC"[31] – when the RCMP turned up and arrested them on charges of mischief. Two of them spent five days in jail.

Before the notorious arrests at the time of the summit itself, there were to be seventy-eight others – "I call it routine intimidation," said Singh – with each arrest creating new momentum when arrestees returned to the scene of their crimes to repeat the offending action, this time with fifty supporters in attendance. Court hearings became a form of high theatre: "To hear the judge make statements like 'The man who can be identified as the man wearing the pumpkin on his head' . . . I mean, we were all laughing."

"After September, our meetings were weekly," Oppenheim explained. "Dynamics changed. We had a big [anti-Indonesian-president-Suharto] postering campaign and suddenly we had big meetings." It was at this time that foreign affairs minister Lloyd Axworthy apologized to the Indonesian foreign minister for the "outrageous and excessive" posters. In November, the East Timor Alert Network held a People's Court at UBC, tried General Suharto in absentia, and found him guilty of war crimes and crimes against humanity. The court "demanded" that Canada arrest Suharto on his entrance into the country. "And then when the tent city went up outside the student union building a week before the summit – students called it Demoville for 'democracy village' – we had a whole new bunch of people at the meetings, an insane number of people." As Oppenheim would later tell a *Maclean's* reporter, "We felt our campus was being taken over by the APEC leaders" – a three-metre security fence had been erected on university grounds – "so the tent city was a way of creating our own meeting place."[32]

They transformed the student union building, hanging up enormous banners, glass-chalking the windows, postering inside and out, as they hosted a Free University with "issue forums" that focussed on corporatization and the university, women, labour, Native sovereignty, all tied in with APEC's trade agenda. Speakers dropped in from the People's Summit on APEC, which was taking place elsewhere in Vancouver, as well as some university faculty, some high school students, and students from Washington State. Singh was thrilled. "You read about the Sorbonne occupations in '68, in Columbia and Berkeley, but when *you* actually do it and take over a building and turn it into a space that you want it to be . . . you realize the possibilities. We were doing our own research and making it accessible and expressing it in ways that were relevant to people. A teach-in and a speak-out. You don't need a grad education to figure out what's going on." It was popular education in a free space.

Then the pepper hit the pan. On the day of the teach-in, November 24, the day before APEC delegates were to arrive on campus, Singh was walking to the student union building, "really high emotionally and intellectually," when suddenly three plainclothes policemen surrounded him, threw him to the ground, handcuffed his arms behind his back, and told him he was under arrest. In an inquiry almost a year later, the staff sergeant responsible would explain he had pre-emptively ordered Singh's arrest on the grounds that he might incite a violent demonstration,[33] but at the time Singh was told he was being charged with common assault on the university's security manager for having blared too loudly over a megaphone and hurt his ears. (This caused much merriment among activists, who dubbed it "assault by megaphone.")

"An unmarked car with tinted windows screeched onto the scene and I was thrown into the back, head first. . . . I heard on the police radio that students at SUB [the student union building] were in an uproar about my nabbing."[34] He was brought before a judge and released on condition that he stay away from UBC until his trial date. Singh agreed, then promptly got himself smuggled on campus in a friend's car, publicly tore up his agreement, and was rearrested and held until the summit was over. (After the summit's conclusion, charges against all protesters were dropped save those against Singh, which would not be dropped until 1999.)

The following day, the most controversial of anti-APEC events, the "Crash the Summit" rally and march organized by APEC Alert, attracted almost five thousand people (according to *The Student Activist*, two thousand according to *Maclean's*), who, led by "jeerleaders," marched across campus to the security fence "protecting" the APEC leaders from unseemly protest. And there, confronted by several hundred police, SWAT team and riot cops, helicopters overhead and police sharpshooters on rooftops, some two hundred marchers attempted to get over the fence and were repulsed with several high-pressure blasts of pepper spray. "Cops then charged into the blinded, fleeing crowd, gave a second blast of spray, and physically assaulted several protesters."[35] Student Alejandra Medellin wrote to the *Georgia Straight*: "This is Vancouver. I am afraid. Not for my physical integrity but for my moral integrity. . . . We don't need to talk about human rights in China, Indonesia or Mexico . . . this is a nightmare. This is Canada."[36]

Almost a year later, as revelations about the extent of Canada's diplomatic grovelling emerged from the RCMP Public Complaints Commission into APEC – "I have directed my officials to spare no effort to ensure that appropriate security and other arrangements are made for your stay in Canada as our guest," prime minister Jean Chrétien had written to Suharto[37] – the broad Canadian public came to share young Medellin's shock. Nationally, only 38 per cent thought the RCMP had behaved "reasonably" towards the protesters.[38] Other opinion was stronger. "There's enough cowardice on the world stage as it is but the prostitution of

Canadian ideals and principles reaches grotesque levels when the political whoring takes place on our own soil," wrote Simon Kiss, a weekly columnist in Edmonton. "When foreign leaders visit our country, they had better be ready to hear what Canadians have to say."[39]

> Pepper spray is seen as a deterrent. But as people across the country express their outrage at police brutality and the crackdown on dissent, it's having the opposite effect. The November 25 Movement has begun and it's not just a stand against civil rights abuses, it's a stand against the varied crimes of neoliberal, corporate globalization. Watch for students and other protesters wearing chemistry lab goggles, defending public space, coming soon to a campus or city near you.
>
> – P. J. Lilley, "Assault and Pepper,"
> *This Magazine*, January/February 1998

If the Organization for Economic Co-operation and Development (OECD) hadn't dreamed up the Multilateral Agreement on Investment (MAI), with its intention to protect transnationals and their investments against national governments, Anna Paskal of Montreal may never have sorted her life out. In 1996 she had returned from studies in the United States to a community despondent in the aftermath of the sovereignty referendum, to a chilly employment climate, and to a feeling all around her of people overwhelmed and paralyzed by the number of things going wrong in society, this "huge hailstorm of problems that need to be addressed, steadily, one at a time, and by dedicated people," as she told it to me. "Many people look at all that has to be done and then think about how they need to make money for food because they're having a hard time too and can't deal with other people's problems. That's how everything is getting the better of us. There's no energy to go outside your own home. Working parents, kids in daycare, they come home, scramble together. . . ."

Luckily, she found work with a small film-production company, where, as a writer and director, she was able to pursue her passionate interest in development and human-rights issues. And this led her straight to a teach-in in Toronto on the MAI. "I think this is going to be the single biggest issue of the next ten years," she told me with excited conviction. "Corporations and their effects on our lives, as more people become aware of what corporations control in our education, our food." She threw herself into a frenzy of reading the background material to the MAI, discovered it really was as bad as the "radical activists" at the teach-in had said it was, even worse, then went looking for an anti-MAI group in Montreal. She couldn't find one in Quebec, so joined meetings of the Council of Canadians. These meetings became "People Against the MAI," who organized public forums and street theatre and the *de rigueur* puppets, and it was in the flurry of that activity that Paskal got wind of a francophone anti-MAI group, Salami (sâle ami), whose meetings she also attended. There she realized a new political generation had arrived among the Quebecois, one which believed passionately that the threat of the MAI superseded any local or national politics: "I've been to a million meetings with those guys and women, and the issue of sovereignty never comes up. They really feel the globalization issue is so important that anything that could divide people has to be avoided."

For all the excitement of the activity, however, the groups had received very little media attention, even while the MAI negotiations were going on. The time had come, they felt, for civil disobedience; many had been trained in it, and the opportunity presented itself with a plan to blockade the hotel to be used by OECD negotiators in Montreal and simultaneously hold a street demonstration with those who weren't willing to risk arrest. Paskal contacted all the "progressive" filmmakers she knew in Montreal and asked them to volunteer their time shooting the action, "and their response was, 'Yes, I'll be there, finally there's something I can put my energy and skills behind, I've been waiting for a project like this to come along!'" Paskal was there with her cameras, following around four people, French and non-French, who had never been involved in any such action, followed them kipping out in the community centre, marching in the demo, followed them to the blockade and filmed them getting arrested by the riot squad and going to jail. "The whole story is insane, but our film is really good." Paskal doesn't even think of herself as "radical," just someone who could see that the MAI was going to change the Canadian lives of ordinary people, and that you could fight globalization, or at least imagine yourself bringing down the MAI and stomping it into the ground.

Organizing Resistance. Prospects for Radical Student Activism at
the End of the Century
– Poster on the University of Alberta campus

The lime-green poster had caught my attention. A streaky photograph showed a scene from a protest against hiked tuition fees: a banner, a guy with a megaphone, two others banging on bongo drums. Well, every journey begins with the first step. It was two months after the anti-APEC actions in Vancouver, and the New Socialist Group meeting at the University of Alberta wanted to know what prospects there were for student activism and a student movement, "because you can't say there isn't one now," said Jeff, a philosophy sessional lecturer.

There were nineteen people in the classroom in the Humanities building, half of them women. Some were people of colour. They sat quietly, as for a lecture. The idea of a movement was key: "It's not just organizing around specific issues," said Greg, a visiting activist from York University, "it's a politicization on an on-going basis." When Jeff added, however, that "this isn't a good time to call oneself a radical," there was rueful chuckling, this being Alberta. Think of the failures: socialism, Marxism-Leninism, social democrats who in practice act like the neo-conservatives. "It seems the radical Left has run out of ideas," he claimed with impressive assurance. But in this sense it is a good time to be a radical, for the potential for resistance is high, given the "crushing" right-wing agenda. "It's easier to build links when all manner of groups are under attack. The university is not separate from the larger community and we have ideas about a better way to live."

The men were wearing hair long and thick, and earrings. No one seemed coupled up, no one seemed dominant. They all looked so sweet and fresh to me I couldn't imagine what sort of content "socialism" would have for them. Patricia, of STORM, dressed all in black, confessed that her father, who once lived on a kibbutz and was a socialist, now votes for Ralph Klein and lives in a big house in the west end. Contempt and bewilderment seemed comingled in her voice. There was much discussion about how not to be used by media that a movement is nevertheless dependent on to get its message out, how to sustain a national student newspaper – "a newspaper is a way of saying we are still here" – when quite a few activists on the

Edmonton campus hadn't seen any action for a while. Jeff cautioned them not to put too much faith in monster demonstrations; he'd been to some in Toronto that were "completely useless, quietist and full of moralizing." Much more critical is to first build a "political core." There were mentions of the cores that are already out there – Amnesty International, anti-MAI groups, Latin American solidarity networks, disgruntled NDPers – with whom it is vital to connect, for students are a cohort only for as long as they are on campus, and each graduating class yields place to yet another incoming wave of the unpoliticized. And I remembered the tempestuous debates of the New Left of the 1960s and 1970s about whether students really could be seen as revolutionary agents given that our status as "niggers" was short-term (there had been a famous essay from the U.S. Left, "The Student as Nigger").

Somebody said in conclusion that the only way to get students involved in activism was to give them a point; "otherwise, they think, 'Why bother?'" Well, yes, quite. "In fact, you *can* make a difference." There was a moment of silence as they all sat slumped in consideration of this possibility.

They seemed somehow unbelieving, their seriousness belied by the certain knowledge that they were so few, so very few, to make the deep connections between their malaise on the under-funded, tuition-hiked, Coca-Cola campus, and the larger quietism of society that absorbed the blows of policies aimed at its heart and then turned around and re-elected its tormentors. "It's very hard to organize in a vacuum," Jeta Das admitted in our interview, thinking of his time in STORM. I had read that a co-founder had already quit the movement, thoroughly disheartened by the forgetfulness of students who "look around" only for a minute, briefly register the iniquitous gap between their debt-ridden status and the ballooning surpluses of government, and then carry on as if it were all their own responsibility to make up the difference.[40] In a depoliticized period, Das said, the passive majority of student sympathizers are really only headed for their degree and private life. It simply wasn't true, he insisted, that people only fought back when they were really beaten down. In fact, they get demoralized and "go into survival mode." And I thought of that grey zone of repressive regimes in which citizens huddle, neither giving their consent to their governors nor willingly jeopardizing their own security but who contain the potential to do something *en masse* should they see their opportunity for kicking the SOBs out.

It's when youth are feeling more confident about their chances in life, when they start to win small victories, that they will see some point to a long-haul commitment. Das was encouraged by the fact that STORM seemed to be experiencing a bit of an upswing, my observations to the contrary, given that it had started with a handful of five students at meetings and could now count on thirty.

The key, as ever, was the link between their financial situation and issues of social justice. "It's hard to make these links on your own, but if you can see that your resistance is part of a broader counterculture, then, even if your group falls apart after a year, at least you will have gained experience organizing, and that will make it easier for the next group that comes along."

After all, Das had come along. For him, there had been punk music, and the *Brave New Waves* program of alternative music on late night CBC Radio, which "just totally converted me," and the new "cool" Canadian films. As with so many of his generation in their mid-twenties, he had only known a political culture deeply imprinted with the New Right rhetoric and agenda of Ronald Reagan and Brian Mulroney, none of it, however, inspiring the "distaste and hatred" he felt for the neo-liberal in Liberal clothing, prime minister Jean Chrétien. But U.S. president Reagan brought Das Nicaragua, in the sense of the U.S.–backed war of the counter-revolutionaries known as "contras" who had tried bludgeoning the young, leftist government into submission. This was Das's first big politicizing moment: the violence of American imperialism against a small country.

He had also read, like so many others I talked with, Noam Chomsky on "the culture of terrorism," and still remembered clearly opening to the page on which he read that, whatever were the political crimes of the revolutionary Sandinistas in Nicaragua, they paled in comparison to those of U.S.–backed neighbouring regimes who carried out brutal and sustained campaigns against their own citizens. "Right next door in El Salvador, government troops were murdering and beheading peasants, raping women, ripping the uteruses out of them, dragging children over barbed wire . . . and where was the outcry?"

He was speaking with considerable agitation, as though the electoral defeat of the Sandinistas a decade earlier, in that astonishing year of 1989, had never been fully assimilated. As though it were still too painful to accept that the beautiful revolutionaries had been turfed out of power by their own people, in whose name they had sacrificed themselves and each other, and not by familiar machinations of the CIA. Even though Das never accepted the collapse of the Sandinistas as a "moral defeat" of the Left, maybe this was his own version of that other deposition from power in 1989, the Communist regimes of Eastern Europe, which so many of my generation of socialists were loathe to accept as the triumph of "the people's will" (how could the people truly, authentically, choose the blandishments of Western PR over a traduced socialism?).

Das felt no "guilt" about the collapse of Communism, no "hang-up" with earlier generations' "obedience" to it. "We have as much guilt for the Soviet era as for the Nazi," he explained, putting things in perspective. *His* perspective had broadened with the Gulf War of the allied nations on Iraq in 1991, and a large teach-in at the university, followed by rallies and an "occupation" of the federal building, Canada Place, in downtown Edmonton. "We stayed the whole night after they locked the doors, and it was just incredible, there was so much energy, and we used one of the pay phones as a phone centre because no one had cell phones back then, and we contacted CBC and *Newsworld*, and they wanted pictures and interviews. It was so exciting."

In all my conversations with the "resistance," I was struck by the notable absence of a certain way of talking about political experience that had had so much currency a generation earlier: the language of Marxist economics, or the vocabulary of "international proletarian struggle," or the signifiers of revolt in the hammer and sickle or, at the very least, the red star (Das, for example, had dismissed it all as "basically Stalinism"). The new dissidents had fashioned their own memorabilia in stormy campaigns to save old growth forests, or in local rock band scenes, or occupations in bank buildings. But this wasn't the whole story. There was also a kind of feedback loop from earlier struggles: as when the anti-APEC protestors erected a replica of the Goddess of Liberty that had stood in Tiananmen Square – herself a Chinese "quotation" of the Statue of Liberty; or the persistent imagery of the lionized Che Guevara of the Cuban revolution; or the almost wistful evocations of styles of student radicalism from 1968. In an arid time of political apathy and self-doubt, when the master narratives of social change had been impugned by corporatism and irony alike, here was a brave effort of the young to insert themselves nevertheless in a story of political succession.

As Das put it to me, "Every generational politicization carries with it the accumulated victories of the past generation, so the issues of ecology and feminism and gay liberation, say, are almost second nature to our movement. They're givens, they're still being fought for, because we are trying to extend them, but the thing is they are a legacy." There was a "before" that produced them, there will come an "after" they in turn will have produced. In resistance, in their own time, they are not alone.

Eco-Activism

> Environmentalists . . . find comfort in opinion polls that identify environmental protection and conservation as "core values" or "enduring concerns" with most Canadians. Douglas Miller, president of Toronto-based Environics International Ltd., says his company's surveys show that throughout the 1990s, more than 90 per cent of Canadians have remained concerned about toxic chemicals, air pollution and water quality. "The public concern for the environment is deeper than many people think," says Miller.
>
> – D'Arcy Jenish, "Toxic Air, Tainted Land,"
> *Maclean's*, December 8, 1997

In 1998, a report commissioned by the Alberta government's department of the environment found that the "inexhaustible" boreal forest was under severe stress from industrial activity. This moved an editorial writer for the *Edmonton Journal* to observe that the simple *idea* that a pure boreal forest exists is "nearly" as important to our sense of well-being as the *actual* existence of wilderness. As pure idea, the boreal forest is a powerful signifier of our identity, and with its devastation, the editorialist advises us, we must get used to the reality that "Alberta is now not far different from anywhere else in North America, places where wilderness has been reduced to fragmentary tracts."[41] Identity crisis! Who are we if we do not have the blankness of wilderness seeping into our souls? Can we still be who we are with only a boreal forest of the mind?

Dr. Fiona Schmiegelow, conservation biologist at the University of Alberta, concedes we moderns are both in and outside the natural world. On the one hand, she explained in an interview with me, within a generation we will have to live with the reality that most natural areas are going to be "managed for some kind of extractive purpose." But on the other hand, like Schmiegelow herself, we will still want to replenish our spirits outside the cities, in the "*semi*-natural areas" that act as a kind of open-air museum of our Canadian identity. Like the Group of Seven canoeing amateurishly in Algonquin Park looking for things to paint, we haul out the family canoe (or skis or Ski-Doo or, God help us, the ATV) in a purely recreational gesture of intrepidity.

Or as Andrea Curtis, one-time tree-planter in northern Ontario, found, the "wilderness" is a human work scarred by clear-cuts. If it is empty, save for pestilential insect life and "blackened sticks, dark soil, and dried-out, half-burnt brush" at the end of bone-shaking logging roads, it is because the logging companies have been there before her, scything down the forest cover. Laboriously shovelling thousands of seedlings every two steps along twelve-foot corridors cleared by machine, Curtis discovers that "who she is" is a planter for a lumber company's tree farm.[42]

Tim Gray, executive director of the Toronto-based Wildlands League, was deep into the League's challenge to the Ontario government's Lands for Life consultations when we talked in Toronto in June 1998. Gray described the mentality of companies engaged in so-called industrial forestry: "Philosophically, most of the big companies are firmly committed to the view that the best thing to do with a forest is to cut it down. 'If you just let us get into that old growth forest, we'll make it better!' 'Sick' is a forest in which trees are getting old and falling over and rotting; in other words, natural. This is 'bad.' " But it can seem natural to Canadians, who think of a *farmed* landscape as part of nature. And it can seem natural to citizens of northern towns, where a "frontier mentality" is alive and well, who think, "Oh, we'll just go over the hill, there are more trees just over that hill." These myths co-exist with the urban romance of the wild, that there's nothing but bush from the city limits to the North Pole. The situation, Gray concluded laconically, "requires a bit of a change for Canadians in how they see land."

Clearcutting – the complete felling and removal of a stand of trees – is now the method used in Ontario to harvest 91% of the province's forest lands (up from 70% in the 1970s). . . . This increase in the rate and intensity of logging was not matched by an increase in employment in the forest industry. In fact, the opposite is true. . . . In 1965, there were 10,824 workers in the industry. By 1993 that number had been cut almost in half, falling by 5,550. . . . In the late 1970s, Koehring Canada estimated that two of its Short-Wood Harvesters, with an eight-person crew operating 24 hours a day, 6 days a week for 9 months, could deliver the same volume of wood to the road-side as – 30 years earlier – 300 bushworkers could produce in 7 months.

– "Where Have All the Loggers Gone?"
Fact Sheet Number One, Wildlands League

When Tim Gray was growing up in the Bruce Peninsula, the spectacular natural features of the semi-agricultural landscape formed a backdrop to his outdoor activity: "I had hiking trails, huge sand beaches in the other direction, rivers in my backyard." But by his early teens he could see the destruction wreaked by tourism and it drove him crazy. The stupidity of it. "Sauble Beach is sensitive wetland and sensitive dune vegetation; developers came and bulldozed most of the dunes to build parking lots, built storm sewers that drained right into the lake, got rid of narrow winding roads. [The authorities] allowed uncontrolled subdivisions to sprawl along the entire length of the beach, with no sewage or water provided. No planning, no thinking about ten thousand septic tanks polluting water that no one is going to want to swim in." The effort to think more creatively – for example, that tourism on Sauble Beach could have been developed without destroying its natural features – is what gets him out of bed every morning: "C'mon, guys, figure it out. It's not hard!"

That was a vision he kept in the back of his mind until he was at the University of Toronto doing applied terrestrial ecology research together with another lab doing aquatic research. The two labs, he says, were a kind of centre of political activism, which was quite unusual in science departments in the mid-1980s. It was considered unseemly for "pure" science to muck about in the world of human foibles, "but our supervisors were making sure their research was applied to something going on in the real world, and they encouraged their students to engage the media and political process. 'Don't just sit in the lab and publish quietly while someone else gets their hands dirty!' This wasn't party politics but social activism." Eventually, a number of people who graduated from the same program with Gray were to turn up on the Wildlands League board of directors; others found work as researchers at the World Wildlife Fund, or as staff for environment ministers.

In 1990 he started work with the Wildlands League, which in the 1980s had begun moving away from viewing the wilderness as a place to be protected for recreation and was starting to adopt a much more systematic, ecologically based approach, attempting to keep some of the pieces of a *natural* system in place. Inevitably, there was conflict with the League's founders, the new generation of activists arguing that the organization needed to move to a more technical model.

"I think the argument that we should protect wilderness area just because we should, that we don't have the right to destroy everything, is a very good one – I buy into it big time – but it's been marginalized as 'crazy tree huggers who wear sandals.' In order to engage, to be effective, we found in practice that bringing science to bear had a huge impact. Science and technology are the turf of the forestry industry, it's the language of the powerful, and to be able to take them on on their own turf and to show them they are wrong gives you leverage.

"The industry has become good at arguing, 'Well, it's very nice that you want to protect the wilderness but what about the jobs? What about the economics? This is the nineties, we don't have time for any of that hippie stuff.'"

Thanks to mergers and acquisitions in the forest industry, Gray has found himself working on the issue of the increasing control of public forests by increasingly large companies. In other words, working to defend the public interest. Corporate taxes are low. Stumpage fees don't even pay for the public cost of forestry infrastructure. And the logging companies continue to cut more timber and lay more people off and replace them with computers and machines. Gray argued this "benefits the guys who've invested in the machinery in a $150-million plant where a couple of workers bring in a log and shove it into the chipper and a board comes out the other end. But at what point do we see that [the public] is not benefitting at all?"

In Ontario, Partnership for Public Lands, a coalition of environmental groups, campaigned long and vigorously against the recommendations of a round-table that would allow intensive forestry and mining in protected areas, putting forward recommendations of its own that would secure 12 per cent more of the protected-areas system and protect biodiversity, promote a forest management that would sustain the total woodflow to mills and create at least six thousand jobs as a result. They developed a list server on the Internet with 2,500 participants, who in turn forwarded protest materials to thousands more. They launched television ads and a phone-banking campaign that swamped ministers' offices with calls.

Finally, Partnership for Public Lands was invited, along with government and industry representatives, to negotiate a new agreement for the protected areas. "There was a wary atmosphere," Tim Gray told me several months after the triumph of the negotiations, "but the costs of *not* coming up with a solution were huge. So . . . the Partnership now sits on the Ontario Forest Accord Advisory Board – inside the tent, as it were, not just communicating with industry through leaks and slogans – where we can set up projects. Where we are, in fact, the tactical arm of the public interest." So, even transnational corporations and their political allies have to take social forces into account. Activists express the community's concerns that justice and fairness be secured for people; where government has retreated from that commitment, corporations find themselves nose to nose with those who *will* battle for it.

As conservation biologist Fiona Schmiegelow explained the relationship, "Activists can take my research results and present them to the public and increase awareness. As a scientist it's dangerous for me to be too closely identified with any particular group and lose credibility. In fact, this was one of my major motivations in studying this stuff – to have more credibility when addressing the issues. If I lose that, I won't be much good to the movement anyway. There are more ways to be valuable than chaining myself to a tree."

She had earlier told me of her search for spiritual renewal within the "semi-natural" light and shadow, sough and twitter, of the beleaguered, great unknown boreal forest. She needs, she said, to separate her science from her feelings because some day science *may* find that the forest *can* sustain certain industrial practices but, as a human being, she would want to say: "There *is* intrinsic value in an intact [natural] system beyond anything you can really measure."

What is it about trees? About trees in great numbers (even spindly, punky, boreal ones), whose disappearance leaves us feeling somehow orphaned?

Velcrow Ripper, filmmaker and activist, grew up in Gibsons, British Columbia, where his father worked in a pulp mill, so he was, he told me, pretty used to the concept of a resource economy; and he and his partner, Heather Frise, had been tree-planters. But in 1988, he and Heather, then living in Montreal as artists, went kayaking for five weeks around Gwaii Haanas (Queen Charlotte Islands), eco-friendly tourists with a Super-8 camera. As they pulled into the islands near Queen Charlotte City, waiting to take a shot of the rising sun, they saw, with the increasing light, that the islands into which they had sailed were totally, grotesquely, bald. It was their introduction to clear-cutting, and it changed their lives.

In 1991, furnished with a grant, they bought a kayak and set out cross-country again, with cameras. Arrived on Vancouver Island, they drove right into an anti-logging protest blockade of the Walbran Valley. In three weeks, they "pumped out" a quick documentary about the blockade called *The Road Stops Here*, which, Ripper told me, has been seen all around the world and even bootlegged. And it gave them the subject for their remarkable award-winning 1995 documentary *Bones of the Forest*.

"The late eighties, early nineties, was a time of a real global rise in awareness of environmental issues. That's what we felt. We wanted to do something for the planet. As we worked on the film, we became more and more passionate and committed. We *lived* on the logging blockades. We were media activists, making our film at the same time as sending out our tapes to the news media, acting as video witnesses of the blockade."

With his camera, he became an environmentalist, part of the "biodiversity" of social activism, positioned somewhere between the radicals on the blockade and Greenpeace on the world stage. In search of clear-cuts to film, he walked into the forest.

"As we experienced the old forest first hand, we were stunned by what it's like to live in a place that's been untouched for a thousand years. Anyone who has walked through the Carmanah Valley [on the west coast of Vancouver Island], where the ecosystem has been untouched for ten thousand years, with trees that are literally three thousand years old, can't remain unmoved. And when you walk out of the forest into an ocean of clear-cuts after sleeping in the forest . . ." His voice trailed off in the chagrin of the memory.

Interested in root causes and grassroots groups, Ripper took his camera into people's homes ("our 'process' is to go out and talk to people, that's our research, we learn as we interview") including that of an old Native logger, Jim Gillespie, who enthralled them for hours. Gillespie, along with other Native elders, was living in a land that had been colonized for only a hundred years, almost within his own lifespan, and had a perspective all his own. Ripper was in awe of the elders who'd seen "a total shift of their world since pre-contact. Some hadn't seen a white person until they were seven." Gillespie had been an independent logger and was around when the big international loggers came in and "turfed the independents out and basically 'bought' B.C. Jim's been fighting them since the 1950s."

Though Ripper readily acknowledges the film's unity around an unwavering point of view – he is an activist, after all – it was a perspective that emerged from meeting "all those people" and distilling what they told him. He never uses voice-over narration; it's too close to the Voice of God–style in conventional documentary, where "you're being told something with such authority that you feel it must be fact." Instead, he interprets *visually* what has been said, often using experimental techniques including pixillation, slow motion, and colourization.

"One of the interesting things about these techniques is that we were concerned that they would alienate our interviewees, who were mostly old and maybe not used to them. . . . So, before we were finished, we sent the tape out to the elders in the rough-cut stage and asked them how they felt about the way they were being represented. And they all felt they had got their point across. It didn't matter what the technique was, it was understandable to them."

And if the elders had objected to their representation? I asked. They would probably have changed it, "because right through the whole process we were grappling with deep issues – appropriation, inclusion versus exclusion. We never used any stories that anyone told us were the property of their tribe or their people.

"We felt that making a film about the land was the most important thing we could be doing at that time, and how could you make a film about the land without talking about the people who were there first? How do you do that and not be telling *their* story?"

By the same token, he regrets not having spent time with loggers themselves, not having climbed over the blockades and gone into the loggers' communities and tried to deconstruct the Us vs. Them approach that Ripper sees as a shortcoming of environmentalism: the lack of strong class analysis or politics creates an opposition of "activists versus loggers, which the corporations encourage, whereas they should be on the same side."

This is indeed a notorious flashpoint for eco-activists. Greenpeace, for instance, has been there.

> When Greenpeace was born, there were about 12,000 grey whales making their annual migration from their calving grounds in Mexico to the krill-rich waters of the Bering Sea. These days there are almost twice as many grey whales making that same migration. But zooplankton – the stuff the whales eat – is vanishing from vast areas of the Pacific.
>
> When Greenpeace was born, there was no hole in the ozone layer. . . .
>
> When Greenpeace was born, the world's fishing fleets were taking about 50 million tonnes of fish out of the sea every year. Nowadays it's about 100 million tonnes, and most of the world's major fisheries are on the brink of collapse.
>
> – Terry Glavin, *Globe and Mail* column, October 9, 1998

In April 1997, Greenpeace Canada issued a withering report on the nature of logging practices in British Columbia, famously provoking premier Glen Clark to libel the organization as "enemies of British Columbia." In a counter-attack of their own, loggers blockaded two Greenpeace ships in Vancouver harbour for forty-eight hours. They were widely cheered. But Greenpeace is nothing if not indefatigable: the planet is on fire, and the firefighters are on their way to the scene of the disaster. This is an emergency.

When I visited Greenpeace's Vancouver offices in December 1997, there was little evidence of that summer's bruising events. Late in the afternoon of a dank and gloomy coastal winter's day, huddled in preoccupied groups on the floors of the warren of rooms that make up the organization's HQ, a bunch of teenagers were making placards for a protest against vinyl toys, a follow-up to a Toronto Greenpeace action in November when activists pulled soft PVC (polyvinyl chloride) toys from the shelves of a Toys R Us store. I had come to interview forest campaigner Tamara Stark.

Given that, according to Greenpeace's own research, only 5.8 per cent of British Columbia's lush temperate rainforest, which once blanketed the Pacific coast from northern California to southeast Alaska, is protected, a tree on the west coast can be considered an endangered species. This is always difficult for a prairie resident to appreciate, given the spectacular botany of the "coast," even in the middle of winter, and its apparently unceasing, almost creepy, growth and reproduction. Even Stark, who grew up with forests all around her, had to fight the easy notion they were "infinite." But she re-educated herself during the fight in 1993 – to preserve old-growth forest of Clayoquot Sound from clear-cutting – when some three hundred citizens struggled to preserve public property and were jailed for their efforts. Profoundly moved by people's willingness to fight for the last remnants of an inheritance from the wild, Stark was brought into Greenpeace's forestry campaign as media outreach. She knew that, by working for Greenpeace, she jeopardized her future employment possibilities in the mainstream media, that she would be seen as too much of an "advocate," but she decided she didn't care: "It was important to choose sides."

I asked Stark if she thought she was a different sort of activist than the founding generation of Greenpeace, which was twenty-five years old. She replied, with the sang-froid of one who has got used to thinking about this, that *half* of the timber that has been cut in Canada has been logged in the last twenty-five years. The issues, and therefore the strategies, she said, were different now. "Back then it was about nuclear testing and saving the whales. And the message to the public was: Just stop now! But for us it's in some ways more challenging. In order for all people to feel hope, the message has to go beyond 'Just stop.'" Stark was convinced there had been a "change in values, a growing public literacy, about the ozone layer, just for example." Fair enough – and I could see it myself, teenagers' familiar willingness to adopt "green" politics while maintaining steadfast cynicism about politics in general – but what, in Stark's opinion, could persuade the generation that something can indeed be done and that it is not necessary to disappear into hopelessness?

"When they see people banding together," she answered. "Ten thousand at Clayoquot Sound, one thousand arrested. First Nations are getting a decision-making voice, politicians do read your letters, the intact valleys haven't fallen to the chainsaw yet. An eighteen-year-old doesn't want to be nonchalant and cynical. Who would want to see it all 'go down' without a fight?"

They will certainly have a fight, or several, on their hands, if they join up. The "legitimacy" of civil disobedience as a strategy – the blockades, the chaining themselves to trees and machines, the ignoring of injunctions – was under attack by companies prepared more and more to sue activists and their organizations (Stark was named in three such suits) and, more subtly, launch "strategic lawsuits" in which the intention is not to win but to tie the activists up in court.

Stark had begun by speaking of the hope people need to feel, that all is not yet lost. She concluded by trying to cheer me up, reminding me that, compared to the Americans, who are fighting on their west coast for the "last five per cent of wilderness," Canadians have very few people per square mile and that, "even for those who grew up in large cities, there still is a sense of this vast land, quite wild, rugged and harsh." She is counting on it to wake us up in time, just as she had been moved and enlightened at the protests in Clayoquot Sound, by all those citizens making trouble in the rainforests of their homeland.

Eric Michaud, spokesperson and representative of environmental groups to a new, provincial energy board in Quebec when we spoke in 1998, dated his activism from the campaign, mainly fought in the courts, against a $13-billion mega-project known as Great Whale, planned by Hydro-Québec on Cree lands, that was shelved indefinitely in 1994. His sympathy with the Cree drew him in (though, in retrospect, it was "pretty romantic"; he'd never been outside Montreal and Quebec City), a reflection of his critical point of view of a Quebec nationalist politics "too wrapped up in itself." It was all very well being critical, but eventually he got tired of standing on the sidelines, and joined up with the Coalition for a Public Debate on Energy (Coalition pour un débat public sur l'énergie), which was very supportive of the Cree campaign against Great Whale, and then, after 1994, with the small Centre of Energy-Policy Analysis (Centre d'analyse de politique énergique) as their spokesperson at public consultations on Hydro-Québec's development plans.

Having abandoned Great Whale (temporarily, at least), the giant public utility took the high road of energy efficiency and energy conservation. But with the deregulation of energy markets in the United States, with the obvious interest of some states in finding cheaper energy than from their own nuclear-generated sources, and with Hydro-Québec's energy surplus, *presto!*, Hydro-Québec was once again dreaming big dams on the northern rivers. Of the 1998 scheme to dam the Churchill River in Labrador and sell electricity to energy-hungry northeastern American states, Hydro-Québec's vice-president of planning, Thierry Vandal, said, "How can we lose? We're the Wal-Mart of electric generation."[43] But this time, to Michaud's alarm, a new element was added to the ecological issues: the "denationalization" of energy, the progressive change of course since the 1980s of "our national Hydro" towards a logic of the market and profit-making, reshaping the public utility into a "clone of a multinational."

And suddenly Michaud found himself a reborn nationalist. "I'm not a true environmentalist," he emphasized in an interview with me in the summer of 1998, "for the reason that I have an *integrated* view – of the environment, economy, and society." And for the society of Quebec, the "nationalization" of electricity through the institution of Hydro-Québec had always represented "one of our big successes, a big part of our history," a collective achievement of modernization and development that was now endangered by the overriding dictates of business in the marketplace, shorn of commitment to serve ultimately the social good. Suddenly, Michaud wanted to *defend* Hydro-Québec, or at least the Hydro-Québec that had operated, since the so-called Quiet Revolution of the 1960s, according to "national rules by which the public space is constructed. And if you break those rules, there is no other law but the marketplace."

It is precisely this notion of the nation as public space – not as some private enclosure of commercial or ethnic interest – that has regalvanized Michaud's sovereignist imagination.

Independence for what? "For the public interest! To rebuild the public space. More and more people are becoming aware of the damage that neo-liberalism is doing, there is more poverty, more ecological crises. Under Premier Bouchard we have a new Duplessisme of the party, a closing-down of discussion and critique. There is no more 'Left' in the Parti Québécois that could make the connection between the old Marxist discourse of social justice and the environmental discourse which puts into question the ideology of unlimited growth. The Office of Public Hearings on the Environment [Bureau d'audiences publiques sur l'environnement] is increasingly marginalized. Already we have lost a lot at the level of commercial culture – all that American advertizing, so much American programming on television, forty cinema screens showing *Titanic*. . . . We won't be able to go on like this."

One way we may "go on," I suggested, according to an argument bruited about in some community-building circles, is to live more and more in the "local" as the nation-state disappears under pressure from globalizing institutions.

Michaud interrupted impatiently: "I don't agree with that. That argument is also a form of neo-liberalism – to displace power onto the local and away from the national because the local is easier to control. Like Hydro-Québec in its consultation process: they say they will only talk to the communities directly related to a project, as though no one else cares about it!" In fact, Hydro-Québec had bypassed public hearings and local municipal approval altogether in the Val Saint-François, where the utility was constructing eighteen-storey-tall high-voltage pylons.

> "Hydro-Québec is behaving like a foreign multinational that treats citizens like foreigners. We're going to stop them. This will be a 'first' in Quebec – but they shall not pass!"
> – Jacques Laval, Val Saint-François citizens' committee member, in Louis-Gilles Francoeur, "Débats publics,"
> *Le Devoir*, December 5-6, 1998

Tim Gray of the Wildlands League believes this estrangement of the "company" from the citizen, putting itself outside an ecological culture – "which a lot of people share to one degree or another" – is also about "the truncation of process, cutting off legislative avenues, depriving people of knowledge, getting rid of environmental laws." It's a rejection of the idea of the public good and the role of civil society in building it.

Yet most Canadians *identify* with the land as being somehow continuous with their sense of Canadian self and the space they share with each other as citizens, even while forest companies and their political supporters resent public control of natural resources and work to lubricate their transfer to the private sector. Citizens are offered up blandishments as "stakeholders" and "taxpayers," code language, said Gray, for "turning us into consumers, not people who live in a country. The language has changed so much – the whole idea that public policy is a worthy endeavour, that there is such a thing as the public good. You almost can't say that in Ontario any more. 'It's good for business': that's supposed to be our mantra. What about citizens being able to chart our own destiny, to have control? This is *our* country, not General Motors."

> We can talk. It is our only power. We can talk some more. Talk to each other. We can also get together. It isn't just the companies that have built Quebec. The community movements, the cooperatives, they too have always been here.
> – Richard Desjardins, "La Maison est ouverte,"
> *Le Devoir*, June 18, 1998

There were twenty-four of us in the gymnasium of the Digby Neck Consolidated School in Sandy Cove, Nova Scotia, seated in one voluminous circle and all staring with grave intent at Arthur Bull, mild-mannered ex-Torontonian who, this night, had convened a meeting of the Fundy Fixed Gear Council, which community-manages the inshore fishery resources in Digby. They were gathered to answer the question "Community-based management: Where to from here?" It was a mild spring evening, and Bull would not have been surprised if a mere handful of area residents had turned up, but there they were, mainly middle-aged and elderly fishermen, with a sprinkling of under-40s and fisherwomen and a couple of teachers and a vacationing potter from the States. And even the fatalistic ("the fishery is finished") lobster fisherman with whom I had spent an entire afternoon driving up and down the Neck on a variety of missions. Fred Horner had worked the boats since the age of fourteen, vaguely remembers the low-tech fishing of his father's and grandfather's time – two-man boats that fished within sight of land, using fixed gear such as longline, handline, and gillnet that caught just enough fish to keep a family working. But Fred worked on a dragger owned by investors, its nets a steel-framed wall of death scraping along the sea bed until there were no cod – "It's like smashing all the eggs in a hatchery and then wondering why you haven't got any chickens" – and now Fred fishes for lobster and scrounges for old-fashioned lobster traps ("antiques") in abandoned fishing boats that litter the coves of the Fundy shore.

Arthur Bull, managing editor of *Fundy Fisherman*, had e-mailed me about the council members who are putting up a fight against the depletion of their fishery, and, consequently, their communities. In their view, fish are a public resource, which it is a "public privilege" to harvest, but which are being exhausted by the big trawlers that dominate the fishing grounds. "Since the Magna Carta, fish are a commonly held resource, but now quotas, instead of being communally filled, are being privatized. It is the tragedy of the commons."

The Fundy Fixed Gear Council had a better idea: instead of treating the fishery like a smokestack industry until it's mined out, let's revisit the idea of the small-scale, home-based, environment-friendly fishing enterprises, community-managed, as the innovative fishery of the future. Ask the fishers: "If you had the power to create from scratch a system of fisheries management for the Bay of Fundy, how would you do it?"

And so the meeting in the school gymnasium. The federal department of fisheries and oceans had finally given the council the go-ahead for a three-year pilot project to manage their part of the fishery under a system of community quotas: "What should we be doing next in community-based management? How do we emphasize the *community* side and not just the fishermen?" asked Bull. The responses flew furiously around the circle, not always to the point, but impassioned.

Community-based management of the inshore fishery is one of those ideas beloved of Green parties and environmentalists who exhort us to "think globally, act locally." There are regional management societies in British Columbia, innovative clam research in a Maine community-based management plan, communally managed resources in Philippines coastal communities, an amalgamation of community-based fishing societies in Barbados, who all know about each other. The Fundy Fixed Gear Council had even been visited by a woman from Dhaka, Bangladesh, who worked with homeless children. Bull found no end of inspiration in this: "It will be increasingly important for us to make common cause on rebuilding the 'commons' in coalitions with environmental groups, social-justice groups, First Nations."

> Tom Thomson came paddling past
> I'm pretty sure it was him
> And he spoke so softly in accordance
> To the growing of the dim.
> He said, "Bring on the brand new renaissance
> Cause I think I'm ready
> I've been shaking all night long
> But my hands are steady."
> — "Three Pistols," The Tragically Hip

I'd asked Tim Gray if he thought our communal sense of Canadian-ness was bound to diminish as the land itself becomes more and more degraded. More to the point, what was environmental devastation doing to *his* patriotism?

"It makes it hard sometimes when I wake up and think, It's only me and the ten people I work with who see this place as more than just a source of raw materials." Is the Canadian identity really about the Group of Seven and wilderness landscapes and the north going on for ever? Or is it some "twisted American frontier mentality, sucking up natural resources until they run out? Sometimes I'm not sure." But, most of the time, Gray thinks people *do* believe deep down that Canada is about having something left that's wild.

But out on the Sunshine Coast of British Columbia, Salish Develop-ments, a tourism operation, has another view of the uses of the past: eco-tourism. Escorting excursions into the heart of the Sechelt First Nation's traditional territory and culture, the operators offer kayaking

instruction, hiking to historic village sites, oyster gathering, salmon barbe-
cues, and lodging in a luxurious hotel originally built by International
Forest Products for its executive retreats.

Is such a paradise any more "real" than the pine-spiked Georgian Bay
vistas brought to us by the Group of Seven just out of range of the sawyers
with machines? Or what about the cedar-clad chalets of a ski resort like
Whistler, which one critic has called an example of "West Coast cedar
fascism," spreading viruslike as the architectural style of choice among local
malls and housing developments; with it the transformation has been com-
pleted, of "wilderness as sportsground where 'leisure' ideology and 'nature'
ideology co-exist."[44] It is the suburbanized middle classes, the writer
argues, who demand their nature be contained and pretty, a respite from
the noise of the hoi polloi, and who are happy to pay their "eco-dues" by
shopping at Mountain Equipment Co-op. "Sure is pretty out there."

> Gates are in demand: gated communities with expansive views
> of snowy coastal peaks and the wind-whipped strait . . . pastel
> condos in the newly bulldozed clearing and the developments
> labeled with cheesy, cheery pastoral names: Mysty Woods, Oak
> Meadows, Mountain Mews, Ravensdale – places named after
> what they dynamited, pushed aside, trucked away, stripped,
> piled up and burnt with diesel. . . . To destroy first and then to
> draw attention to it as a sales pitch.
>
> – Mark Anthony Jarman, "New Orleans
> Is Sinking," *subTERRAIN*, Spring 1998

In remembering, almost dreamily, a beloved, haunted, immemorial
wilderness landscape in the raincoast forests of British Columbia, Lon
Cayeway wrote that now it is all gone, "now there is only the hard empty tilt
of the barren, burnt hills," and black ash in the high country wind, "a few
tattered fragments" of ecosystem clinging to the faces of raw rock cliffs.
Below, "clear-cut logging has obliterated the forest entirely," leaving ice and
rock and rain. "The global business economy swept the rest of it away."
Now, all that is left us of our "molecular interconnectedness" with the
forest is a fragmented bio-diversity with which we reconstruct our place
with "broken pieces and emptied realities."[45]

UNITS OF SURVIVAL

> Our [Canadian] core ethic is that everyone should be included
> fully in the community by the community itself, rather than
> being required . . . to hack out their own space in the jungle.
> . . . Our community is no longer simply our creation. We have
> become it, and we are perceived by others to embody it.
> – Richard Gwyn, *Nationalism Without Walls:*
> *The Unbearable Lightness of Being Canadian*

The attractive notion that the new technologies of communication facilitate the global interaction of social movements remains pie in the sky for a lot of grassroots activists. As feminist performance artists, who have a hard enough time occupying real space in a real world that still lacks legal and social safeguards for women, Shawna Dempsey and Lorri Millan find it terrifying that there are "people who think they are somehow having a community life by being on a chat group." Their own work they see as "performing ourselves into reality," reality being a public place, historical and communal, where the public good can be advanced; for example, the rights and freedoms of women, a public good we hold in common. Computer whiz Colleen Whelan agrees that this commonality is what's missing in the idea that you can "build community" by sitting at your computer and typing. Real building is done face-to-face in everyday life with the people around you, she insists, which is why, when she travels, she backpacks and uses local buses, spending a dollar a day, "and I walk around the marketplace and talk to people who have nothing, and it strikes me that they are some of the happiest people I've seen because of their sense of community and belonging." Yes, many are hungry or sick, but they live intimately with each other, a kind of bonding Whelan never knew growing up in the suburbs and only now has an inkling of in Toronto's gay and lesbian communities.

None of this would surprise researcher and writer Michael Adams, author of *Sex in the Snow: Canadian Social Values at the End of the Millennium*, who has taken a long look at the young Canadians who will live most of their lives in the next century. They have already moved, he writes, "beyond individualism to a sort of *post*-individualism, where experience-seeking connections are more important than the mere assertion of autonomy."[46] In this sense at least, they are the happy beneficiaries of a global perspective in which technological, ecological, and social *intercon-nectedness* is a palpable reality.

But a global view isn't required to see what's going on in the streets of your very own city. At Stop 103 in Toronto, where Nick Saul helps direct a food bank program for the neighbourhood's poor, the reality is that he has to tell a lot of people that he's sorry but they can't have another can of tuna. This drives him crazy, because "here we are on this tidal wave of poverty, and we are not going to solve it here, at Stop 103, if we just focus on giving out food to low-income pregnant women." Which is why he talks about focussing instead on the "macro stuff" of social development, making sure Stop 103 is represented at demonstrations in support of social housing or in the Metro Network for Social Justice or Food Action Now or Low Income Families Together. This is a monumental task, trying to mobilize low-income communities who have had the shit kicked out of them. He thinks furiously about how to do this: provide child care at meetings, provide food at meetings, get the poor to vote, create a new political party, rewrite *The Communist Manifesto* to incorporate all the new movements and get his head around the question of just who are the agents of social transformation . . . maybe it's not the working class, maybe it's everyone getting the short end of the stick in education, health, welfare.

The food bank is Stop 103's biggest program, but it also runs community gardening and cooking classes to show people how to stretch their food hamper. Those get-togethers in the community kitchen are not just a "social outlet," as important as that is, but moments in real community building, in helping people help themselves. On Wednesday nights, for the Healthy Beginnings program, the centre's small auditorium is action-packed with pregnant and post-natal women and a lot of rug rats running around, with visiting public-health nurses and a dietician, community workers and a social worker, and sometimes a speaker to offer information about nutrition, breast-feeding, domestic violence law. With sympathizers at Metro Parks and Recreation, Stop 103 and some local schools were collaborating on developing the community gardening project that would eventually, in Saul's vision, be tended communally and feed hundreds.

It was here that I began to appreciate Stop 103's determination to offer more than the charitable model of service. Saul had said several times that this was a "non-judgemental" agency, one that did not insist on proof of financial need – people were humiliated enough as it was, "they are here, they need help" – and did not, like some other food banks, insist that, after three consecutive visits, the client receive "financial counselling," or, like churches, according to Saul, "judge your situation." No, what excited him about the agency was that "because we recognize that the food bank can do very little to help people in terms of hunger, we need to advocate against cutbacks to housing, we need to make sure people on welfare get more income – the *community development* model, which is to get out there and fight the system."

Neither did John Schellenberg, outreach coordinator at Winnipeg's Village Clinic, have any illusions about how much he, and an underfunded program, could do. The project was an outreach to sex-trade workers on the "hill" on Broadway and Edmonton streets. It was centred at a restaurant in the neighbourhood where hustlers between their early teens and twenties rested between jobs. Schellenberg walked up and down Assiniboine Avenue, doling out condoms and lube, making sure people had the supplies they needed, handing out snacks and drinks. At Thanksgiving he brought out pumpkin pie and coffee to the hill, and everybody who wasn't working or sleeping or shooting up had a little picnic.

You can hand the hustler and junkie a condom, but whether they're going to use it is another issue: they have to *care* about not getting infected. "Not to make it seem more dramatic than it is," Schellenberg told me, "but for some people, getting HIV means you get more money from government, you get an identity, a community. Not everyone is clamouring to get HIV, they're not crazy, but the way things are set up is that you get all the attention *after* you've got HIV. A structure is in place once a positive diagnosis has been made: how to manage your health and bolster your immune system." Which is why, incidentally, people with HIV get more money on social assistance, because they need a protein allowance.

I interviewed Schellenberg among the paint fumes in the $18,000 house close to the city centre he and his partner were fixing up on a rather down-at-the-heels street of semi-boarded-up frame houses coming apart at the seams. The front door, wide open to the cooling evening, let in a feeble, alleviating draught. Furniture was makeshift.

I propped up the tape recorder on an upended box and asked

Schellenberg about the trends in HIV from what he could see on the street. He predicted that the upsurge of infection among non-gay populations – street people, junkies, prostitutes – is going to far outstrip the rate of infection in Winnipeg's gay community. To provide excellent, not just mediocre, health care to poor and Aboriginal people, who have the same right to it as gay middle-class men like himself, is going to be the challenge to society.

On the front lines, Schellenberg was impelled by urgency: affordable housing, hospice space, palliative needs all have to be addressed, and soon. "I don't want to predict doom and despair, but we have several populations that are vulnerable, and the issues have to be addressed *now* and not when the numbers finally 'justify' our concern." Among those populations are clients and dates of male sex-trade workers. "It's a pretty complicated scene. There's a prejudice against them – they're thought of as predators and the hustlers as victims, which is a little tiresome, I think. My focus is always health."

Several little cyclones, then, each with its own etiology, tearing up the human landscape. He thought we should be thinking about what it's going to mean for our *grandchildren* to be living with this.

Schellenberg, who is neither a social worker nor a doctor or nurse, had more or less learned on the job, he said. He had a clear service to deliver and had never found it any trouble to cross the cultural gap. "We're not seen as authority figures at all, we're not trying to get them off the street; our focus is health. There's always an expectation that an outreach worker or prevention worker is going to fix things. Well, fuck that noise, I'm not fixing anybody, and I'm not preventing HIV for anybody but myself. Here are some tools, some practical things, this is all I can do. If I have five conversations a day, that's my job. And I'm good at it."

The kids aren't from another planet. They're in the community, whether we turn from them or not, whether, for example, boards of agencies choose to open drop-in spaces and advocacy services for them or whether middle-aged white men refuse to sit in the same waiting room as sniffers, people with HIV, and hustlers and dates. The issues Schellenberg dealt with on the job are those of his everyday personal life, so there's an intimate link for him between what's public and what's private. "Not only am I trying to help people prevent HIV infection, I'm trying not to get it too. Prevention is just a bunch of baby steps, and there's not going to be any proof that it works until long after I'm dead." By then others will have stepped up and taken over. And some modest, local part of the commonweal will have been passed on.

> I believe we must build a new vision full of hope and opportunity. It must not be tied up in money. The focus must be on creating viable, vibrant communities. The community will be the unit of survival in the 21st century.
>
> – David Suzuki, in an interview in the
> *Edmonton Journal*, November 10, 1996

Nathalie Labonté, who writes for *Recto Verso*, added me to the magazine's mailing list after our interview in Montreal, and this is how I've learned that "social economy" enterprises have long been a staple of Quebec community life – ever since 1900, when Alphonse Desjardins founded the *caisses populaires*, which are still going strong – and that these enterprises are just as likely to be identified with the ideological concept of alternative social development as with alternative practices. Here is Josée Belleau, for instance, formidable militant of women's anti-poverty groups: "We want to show that the economy isn't just about the market." And community organizer Lorraine Guay: "The capitalist enterprise is ill-equipped to take care of human beings and culture." Under the rubric of the social economy – financial viability without a profit motive – you find home-care services, job creation for the handicapped, co-operative funeral homes, daycare centres, forest management, the renovation of abandoned factories into worker co-operatives. . . . Seventy-four per cent of the jobs created in this economy in Montreal were occupied by women, at an average salary of $21,245, all of whom had been living on the brink of poverty.[47]

The diversity of enterprise in this alternative economy is so impressive that some economists, examining the complex interaction between the non-profits, governments, donors and users, predict an important role for them in the creation of what Judith Maxwell, president of the Canadian Policy Research Networks, calls social capital: "the networks, norms and mutual trust that allow citizens to pursue common goals."[48]

Homeplace V

THE SHRINKING COMMONS

> In Canada, the new corporatism has reached the centre of national power via the Trojan horse of deficit finance. In the service of a corporate community that has become anti-government, the government of Canada obligingly has become anti-public.
>
> – Dalton Camp, "Consumers Are But Pigeons,"
> *Edmonton Journal,* July 29, 1997

Once upon a time, Canadian citizens owned an impressive portfolio of property: Air Canada, Petro-Canada, CNR, airports, air navigation systems, medical clinics, liquor boards. With every privatization, with each convocation of their new "stakeholders," however, we have shed a little bit more of a citizenship in institutions that glued us together with shared responsibilities and shared authority, not to mention a shared past. They were "ours," yet another plank in the construction of a collective identity.

As social programs were scaled back and underfunded at all levels of government, the Canadian "commons" – the public sphere in which we agreed together to care for the welfare of all Canadians – shrank with them. In 1997, an "index of social health" developed by Human Resources Development Canada was able to measure the growing gap between the overall health of the economy and the stagnant or declining well-being of much of the humanity dependent on it.[1] Where once we believed that social well-being was the particular obligation of the universal social programs, we were now persuaded that, through "trickle down," a recovering economy would bring the poor up with it. No such thing was happening.

Yet we prided ourselves on the annual top ranking given Canada by the United Nations' Human Development Index without asking why employment, unemployment benefits, or environmental protection laws were not among the UN's criteria of "quality of life" and only *per capita* income was calculated – the country's total wealth divided by the number of citizens, which produced $21,000 per person or almost $85,000 per family of four! Another figure, altogether more meaningful, was the some $40 billion in combined (Tory and Liberal) government cuts to social-welfare spending by 1997 and the reduction of access to Employment Insurance to 35 to 40 per cent of eligible unemployed persons, a truly massive transfer of taxpayers' money out of the public sector of social programming.[2]

The UN Index does not measure the distribution of wealth *within* Canada, and so misses the "subtleties" of proliferating homelessness, food banks, and underemployment, of user fees and deregulation. But Ed Broadbent, as president of the International Centre for Human Rights and Democratic Development in Montreal, was watching the inexorable undermining of the welfare state in Canada and vehemently rejected the glib reference to universal programs as a "social safety net." The programs were far more than a hammock in which the socially unfortunate were suspended mere inches from their destitution; the programs were a "commons," where we acted out our citizenship. Broadbent worried that a narrower commons not only increased the vulnerability and disenfranchisement of the poor but also the selfishness and political extremism of the lucky.[3]

As a civic community, we should be deeply ashamed when the top 8 per cent of our income earners are the most likely to support the abandonment of the very programs that have civilized us, to bawl instead for tax cuts.[4]

Canadian politicians regularly pay obeisance to the centrality and immutability of a Canada Health Act that commits our governments to the funding of a universal and accessible health-care system. *Public Health R Us.* But the price we pay is eternal vigilance, given the $7 billion the federal government cut from health transfers to the provinces after 1993.[5] There are those, scrutinizing the manoeuvres of governments and corporations, who warn of creeping privatization, whether in the Ontario government's moves to privatize home care or the opening of Canada's first for-profit hospital, the Health Resources Group, in Calgary in 1997, or the steadily increasing share of health expenditures by private insurance coverage so that it now represents 30.3 per cent of the country's total health bill,[6] or the desperation of one hundred hospitals and clinics in Ontario and Quebec who have rented out their walls – in corridors, cafeterias, waiting rooms, and washrooms – as advertising space to generate revenue for new equipment.[7]

You can see how it came to this: first, the widespread panic about Canada's debt and deficit crisis; then the stunning cutbacks on public spending for health care; then the much-reported crisis in the delivery of care in the public sector; then the piecemeal offering of "solutions" from the private sector; and, finally, the spectre of the two-tiered system in which those with the money to pay for privatized services opt out of medicare altogether. Those without private resources depend increasingly on an underfunded, understaffed public system. Or, as American consumer crusader Ralph Nader energetically put it to an Edmonton audience in 1998: "How do you bring down the [health care] system? Piecemeal, chip away at it, Trojan-horse it, starve its budget, squeeze out its services into the marketplace, generate more lack of confidence in it, create more delays because of budget restrictions, don't even keep up with inflation, don't even keep up with population growth, say it has to be done because of deficits created by your own party."[8]

Canadians are asked, Do we really want to live with American-style medical care for which citizens pay 13 per cent of GDP (compared to Canada's 9 per cent) that leaves 41 million people without coverage? *No!*

Attending a conference in Saskatoon in 1997 on public health care – in Saskatchewan, home of Canada's first medicare scheme introduced by Tommy Douglas's CCF government in 1962 – were the usual suspects, grizzled veterans of that monumental political struggle of the sixties, when the socialists went toe-to-toe with the doctors, and the doctors blinked. But also present – staffing the book and leaflet tables for myriad good causes – was the next generation of health-care activists, proving, I thought, that a society can reproduce ideas with some analogue to a genetic code. Hugh Armstrong, who has tracked the progress of privatization of health care, was a key speaker. He hit all the buttons: Private insurance expenditures were rising while public expenditure was under rigid control; Canada ranked below the OECD average of social spending; hospital boards were talking about business plans, contracting-out of services, the bottom line, the value-added, the stakeholders, the partnerships. We smiled ruefully at each other, remembering the time when stakeholders were known as patients. This was the language of property, he continued. Managers were added on while nurses were shed. Senior managers, management consultants, insurance companies, banks, and technology companies were all hanging around the scene of the crime waiting for the governments' final capitulation to private hospitals and the feeding frenzy of the huge American hospital corporations, let in by the NAFTA. Was this what we wanted? *No!*

We were already pretty riled up by the time Dr. Claudia Fegan, president of medical staff at the Michael Reese Hospital in Chicago, took the microphone and fired all barrels. She was a witness, she said, of corporatization of health care; her own hospital had been taken over by Humana Insurance Company, which in turn had been taken over by Columbia Health Care/HCA, the largest health services chain in the world with 390 hospitals and with annual revenues of US $25 billion. Yet, uninsured or underinsured patients delayed seeking hospital care, and did without Pap smears, mammograms, and glaucoma tests. When patients were insured, the HMO (Health Management Organization) could count on a profit of $520 per patient – the difference between the hospital's expenses and the amount collected from the insuree. Profits rose as services were curtailed: according to Dr. Fegan, HMOs gave bonuses to doctors who discharged patients early, made no emergency admissions, and offered no specialist referrals. In case we didn't get it, here it was again: "Physicians' incomes rise as care falls." For-profit care was enormously lucrative, and the HMOs spent $75 million annually lobbying in Washington to keep it that way. Yet American dialysis mortality rates – and 60 per cent of dialysis was performed at five thousand dollars' profit per patient – were twice those of Germany and almost triple those of Japan. Quality of life? "Don't you dare stop protecting what you have here!" She was almost shaking her fist at us. And we were on our feet, having fallen in love all over again with the Medical Care Act.

Still swooning, I put the question to my MP, Reformer Rahim Jaffer, who wasn't even born the year we celebrated the Act, in 1966. I suggested to him that his party, widely identified with a right-wing economic agenda of privatization of public services, might come "unstuck" from popular affection because of its Americanized rhetoric that says you are responsible only for yourself, you look after Number One, when in fact Canadians want to feel that we do have collectivist values and that there is something bigger than just our own private economic destinies. To my surprise, Jaffer did not disagree. He talked about government indeed having a role in providing services; he spoke of taking care of the "core social conscience" the country has evolved, and focussing on the "areas of compassion" and not moving to "American-style solutions." But there was a catch. Government has grown too large, "trying to be too many things to too many people," and the government, alas, can no longer meet its obligations . . .

Thus, on the same day that Alberta premier Ralph Klein wrote a memo to his treasurer in early 1994, asking for "an Alberta solution" to the financial woes of the owners of the West Edmonton Mall, the Edmonton Catholic School Board announced it was forced to charge user fees for full kindergarten because of the $25 million cut in provincial funding.[9]

Thus, when Macmillan Bloedel agreed to a $3.6-billion takeover by the multinational Weyerhaeuser Co. of Washington, there was scarcely a peep of dismay or chagrin from the politicians, not even from the NDP forest minister. "You may say that it's unfortunate that a B.C. company is being sold," he told *Maclean's*, "but that's the way the world is now."[10] Where once a Foreign Investment Review Agency had something to say to the public about foreign investments and takeovers of Canadian enterprise, now Canada's top stock-market companies, in the estimation of economics reporter Eric Reguly, were heading south under new ownership, whether Alberta's Nova Chemicals to Pittsburgh, the business divisions of Nortel Networks (once proudly called Northern Telecom) to Dallas, or 20 per cent of Bell Canada to Ameritech: companies with a collective market value of about $39 billion disappeared from the Toronto Stock Exchange from 1998 to 1999, taking with them head offices and career options for Canadians.[11] Post-FTA federal government, stripped "efficiently" lean, has done nothing to reverse the trend.

That fact is more than unfortunate. It is an ideological right-turn from the view that the country's possession of its own assets means the capacity to control our own future – and a turn therefore from the historic struggle for Canadian ownership of resources, private and public. More profoundly, it is the handing over of our symbolic heritage: we have much memory and sentiment invested in forests, railways, and broadcasting systems. Now our politicians puff up their chests with each new foreign investment in or purchase of Canadian enterprise and property, as though *we* had triumphed in the sale. There was a time when they would have been ashamed to have been so plainly trumped.

But that is the way the world is now. And it's been that way before. In 1965 George Grant wrote *Lament for a Nation* to warn us that the "power of the American government to control Canada does not lie primarily in its ability to exert direct pressure; the power lies in the fact that the dominant classes in Canada see themselves at one with the continent on all essential matters. Dominant classes get the kind of government they want."[12]

And that is how we lose the "commons" of the fishery – already prodigally stripped – to the device of the Individual Transferable Quota, which allows it to be leased or sold like private property. The fishery is in this way extinguished as a communal resource. About one-fifth of Nova Scotia's fishing vessels now operate under ITQs and take about half of all the fish.[13] And that is how our federal governments have signally failed to pass legislation prohibiting the export of bulk water, which would also keep lakes, rivers, and groundwater within the reach of governments and the rule of law. Either water is a public trust, says the Council of Canadians, or it is a commodity that will make some transnationals rich.

> Canadians are moving towards a philosophy of education and society which makes it virtually impossible to think *outside* of the market metaphor. . . . Students are "clients," parents are "customers," teachers are "front-line service providers." . . . There is something deeply troubling about equating virtually every human impulse with a consumer transaction, or with making consumerism *the defining* act of citizenry.
> – Erika Shaker, "Learning About the Commercialization of Education," *CCPA Education Monitor*, Summer 1997

As governments withdraw from the public squares, the corporate sector sees opportunity for business. It's a trade-off: the schools, libraries, city buses, stadiums, universities need money, the corporations need to advertise. In Edmonton, the downtown public library is now named for a private benefactor, the conference centre is renamed for a cable company, the new baseball park for a (privatized) telephone company, and the exteriors of Edmonton Transit buses have become mobile billboards for shopping centres. In Mississauga, Montreal-based Youth News Network, a private news and current-affairs network, has installed a satellite dish, television sets, and audiovisual equipment in a secondary school in exchange for a daily twelve-minute newscast that includes two and a half minutes of commercials. (Public broadcasters have provided current-affairs programming free for decades but stopped short of also providing VCRs, computers, and video cameras. That's what taxes were for.)

Wouldn't you like to expose your brand identity to over 1.5 million students in Ontario classrooms every 15 minutes of the school day? Well, you can! We are pleased to introduce this exciting new and innovative way to capture the minds of the dynamic student market in Ontario. The "we," here, is ScreenAd Digital Billboards Inc. of Brampton, Ontario, which creates computer screen savers bearing ads for Burger King, Pepsi, and Kellogg, and pays schools to put them on their classroom computers. That, at least, is the plan. "This is one of the most palatable ways that schools can create a partnership with corporate Canada that is controllable," said the company's CEO, John Robinson. "Certainly there's pockets of opposition. Some people don't want to hear anything about advertising in school. It's been a hard sell."[14] Some people don't think that public institutions should pimp for corporate enterprise looking to "imprint" their brand names on the young.

Maybe Robinson should try chocolate bars. In 1998, just in time for Easter, Cadbury Chocolate Canada mailed out free curriculum supplements – they were distributed to about six hundred thousand schoolchildren – that included *The Tale of the Great Bunny*, a story about how the Great Bunny created an enchanting underground world called the Land of Cadbury. "We're extremely happy with it," said Cadbury's senior brand manager, Dale Hooper. "Our goal was to make Easter more special and more memorable for kids and families . . ."[15] As if families were emotionally incapacitated. In an elementary school in Edmonton, also just before Easter, 1998, a sales agent for Mars Fundraising, an offshoot of the multinational corporation that makes Mars bars, Snicker bars, and M&Ms, raised a classroomful of whoops and shrieks among his new "sales team." For each box of his candy that the children sell, one dollar goes to the school and two dollars go back to Mars. The president of the school's parent advisory council agreed to the sales campaign because voluntary fundraisers, exhausted parents, had run out of steam.

> Text of a huge banner welcoming students to the University of Regina: *"Coca-Cola Welcomes You to the University of Regina; Partners in Education."*
> – "It Reigns, It Pours," *This Magazine*, March/April 1999

"Is nothing sacred?" *Maclean's* columnist Charles Gordon asked, referring to the decision of the Girl Guides of Canada to solicit advertising sponsors for their cookies, and remembering the contract between the Royal Canadian Mounted Police and Walt Disney corporation, and Disney's with Canada Post (which issued a series of stamps featuring Disney characters).[16]

It is questionable whether privately owned highways, utilities, provincial parks, and social-welfare agencies have the same capacity to assemble us in a common space. The writer Richard Gwyn, watching CBC television and then CTV, had the same question. "The CBC . . . is part of me and every reader. CTV is just there, available to be used or to be ignored, sort of the way each of us periodically decides to shop at Price Club rather than Home Depot."[17] CBC is public property, and our pleasure in watching *This Hour Has 22 Minutes* lies in the fact that it is a shared pleasure.

So, when the CBC/Radio-Canada is beat up on by parliamentarians and other *public* servants, cutting their pounds of flesh out of its "bloated" and "inefficient" carcass (from 1996 to 1999, federal money for public television dropped 28.8 per cent, while France, Germany, Japan and the United Kingdom all *increased* such funding), when Canadians accept market values as the best way to regulate media at a time when that market promises a five-hundred-channel universe dominated by a small number of gargantuan transnationals, when only 32 per cent of television programming that Canadians watched in 1998 was Canadian in origin, friends of public broadcasting have a right to be anxious about how much longer their pleasure will be shared and when they can expect to be evicted from the "public square" of their publicly owned media. That is political scientist David Taras's term for the electronic meeting place of national broadcasting

– coast-to-coast programming, Canadian news and dramas – which we watch as though we were all in the same movie house together, grumbling and exclaiming together. When a majority of viewers is no longer exposed to the same coverage of events, do we risk fracturing the shared "reality" that helped constitute the sense of civic community?

Historically, the response of Canadian policymakers to the temptations of the decentring television model has been the regulatory regime of Canadian Content: by hook or by crook, Canadian viewers would watch their own cultural production and thereby constitute themselves as a national community. But the new digital technologies, which are able to circumvent the infrastructures of regulation, have already rendered problematic the protection of CanCon in magazines and will have the same effect in broadcasting and telecasting when content becomes ubiquitously distributed by satellite TV, wireless cable, and the Internet. Whether this situation produces a rich diversity of "niche" and speciality programming or, market-driven, will simply spread over a trillion computer screens variations of the commercial drivel served up by McMedia Inc. remains to be seen – as does the vision that programs about golfing, French cooking, and toddlers' cartoons will each find a "deep and committed community"[18] rather than just clumps of couch potatoes who, like *Twitch City*'s Curtis, have no idea there is anybody else out there until someone comes crashing through the door and interrupts their communion with the screen.

The irony of our situation is that, having been evicted from our own public square in the name of the five-hundred-channel universe of "choices," we are reassembled in the global living room of Disney, Time-Warner, and Viacom, where "personal consumption" has privilege over "social understanding and activity," as U.S. journalism teacher Robert McChesney writes.[19]

You might think that if anyone could reimagine the "good" as a public exercise, it would be artists. But once they leave their studios, where are they welcome? Shawna Dempsey and Lorri Millan, performance artists in Winnipeg who love to take their work into the streets, have been baffled time and again by just how little "public space" there is out there. They could find no television station – even among those with room for public-service announcements, not even the CBC – who would take their pro-(sexual) choice public-service announcement, which was how they realized "broadcast space is private space." For performing a "safe sex" information piece in a mall, they were evicted, because the mall is private space and nobody there wants that kind of thing distracting the shoppers.

This had been the perspective of the leftist nationalists of my generation, that there should be a public culture, specifically Canadian, that "federates" people of different races, ethnicities, sexualities, occupations, who, in spite of their differences, recognize their commonality in the ideals of democracy, constitutionality, social justice. This commonality has become demoralized, its rage against what was happening to us as a body politic siphoned off by the "cultural wars" of representation. While the Right triumphed with its version of the most impressive commonality in history, globalization, the rest of us were being forced into smaller and smaller "spaces" of identity.

In the Quebec literary journal *Lettres québécoises*, for instance, Francine Bordeleau wrote a genuine *cri de coeur* about the long-lost clamorous time of the 1960s and early 1970s when all kinds of publishing houses and magazines and literary currents occupied the public spaces, whether labelled nationalist, formalist, urban, feminist, gay, or militant. It was the era of the "manifesto-poem," the "poster-poem," which "affirmed the will to occupy public and social space." But, Bordeleau goes on, ever since 1980, the year of the first referendum on sovereignty, the poets have been evicted from the public sphere. With 1980, a new era began, the era of triumphalist economism and neo-liberalism. The poets, uneasy with this ideology, have retreated to an intimate poetry of introspection.[20]

> Number of Internet users worldwide as of summer 1998: 147 million; estimated number of Web sites as of April 1998: 320 million; estimated number of email messages sent in 1997: 2.7 trillion; percentage of Net traffic that passes through the United States: 90.
>
> – "The Net," *Shift* magazine, October 1998

In 1998, researchers at Carnegie Mellon University in Pittsburgh determined that people who spend even a few hours a week on-line experience higher levels of depression and loneliness than those who don't, even though the research subjects had been using the most sociable of the Internet's features: chat rooms, e-mail, and discussion groups. The subjects reported that, as their time in front of the screen increased, they were spending less time with their families and had a shrinking circle of real-life friends.[21] Half of Canadians polled in 1998 for the Information Highway and Canadian Communication Household Wave I Survey said they thought the Internet was distracting, impersonal, and dehumanizing.

Asocial: Lacking the society of others. Or, shunning the society of people of our own gender, ethnicity, nationality, or religion for the "chosen" identity of the solitary ego in a relationship with images that change every 1.5 seconds, with a delete button and all of it "written in light." Social scientists point to the flattening of emotions that require reflection and call it "the profound narrowing of interiority."[22] Computer consultant Colleen Whelan had no conviction that "sitting and typing to someone" is an exercise in community-building, nor that much of her generation, schooled to be independent and self-reliant, would subscribe to an ethos of collectivity. "We didn't live through anything like hippie communes or a war. We grew up with the message, 'Go out there and prove yourself. You can do anything you want.' The focus was all on the individual." I asked her if she resented having grown up within such self-centred values. "Sure, every day."

It is the fear of *harm*, of the undoing of their lives, that animates so-called New Luddites, named purposely for their historical forbears in early-nineteenth-century England who, seeing they had a choice between the preservation of their labour and communities and the new mechanized work on "machinery hurtful to commonality," as they put it, in the holding-pens called factories, chose their communities. Digital software in the modern workplace has already transferred much of workers' control from hands-on labour to computer systems, and from workers' organizations to management. Adrian Randall of the University of Birmingham, interviewed on CBC Radio's *Ideas*, saw parallels with Luddism, in the sense that "community is being fractured, that ways of working which involve working with and collectively together with people are being destroyed by the fact that larger and larger numbers of us find ourselves chained to a desk and interacting simply with a screen."[23]

> These information technologies are so damn absorbing and
> forward-looking that the past recedes more and more quickly.
> – John Hannigan, consultant and researcher,
> from personal correspondence

Has the universe been unfolding as it should? "Today computers hold out the promise of a means of instant translation of any code or language into any other code or language. The computer, in short, promises by technology a Pentecostal condition of universal understanding and unity. The next logical step would seem to be, not to translate, but to by-pass languages in favor of a general cosmic consciousness . . . the condition of speechlessness that could confer a perpetuity of collective harmony and peace."[24] Saturated in Roman Catholicism, and dating from the 1960s, this "technomysticism" of Marshall McLuhan has nevertheless reproduced itself continuously in those who see in electricity's promise a new world order of post-literate, localized (because post-national), democratic communalization.

In 1991, World Wide Web computer communications protocol made it possible to link all the contents of any database anywhere in the world to any other computer on line. Within five years, there were 30 million users of the Web, and the number has grown exponentially since. But four-fifths of Web sites are in English,[25] and in 1997, North America already had 71 per cent of the world's databases; Africa, Eastern Europe and South America each had less than one per cent.[26] It is not the *world's* memory within which we are entangled in lubricious connectivity, it is North America's, which is of course the U.S.A.'s.

The anti-mystics see in the electronic monopolies a new world order of penetrated national borders, subordinated cultures, and diminished human freedom.[27] Within the next decade, three to five global telecom carriers will likely control the entire global communications system, estimates Jesse Hirsh of the telecommunications co-op Tao Communications, having read the writing on the wall in 1997 when a World Trade Organization agreement was signed that clears the way for international telecom deregulation, overriding national regulation and policy, and forcing all major telecom markets to open for competition.[28] Where it had taken radio thirty-eight years to build a 50-million-strong audience, and television fourteen, it had taken the Internet *four*. If there is a cosmic consciousness at work, it is one that finds its embodiment in the transnational corporations marketing high technology in the universalism of unregulated markets, borderless networks, and atomized workers deprived of civil society, not to mention social benefits. That this scenario neatly converges with the ideology of the New Right has been noticed. "Multinational, anarchically free, and laughably beyond the grasp of any government, cyberspace is an elegant metaphor," wrote journalist Clive Thompson, "for the new right's way of doing business."[29] He meant the almost iconic status of the anti-social, freewheeling geek at the screen, the technology and its content that cross national boundaries with impunity, the equalizing communication of virtual identities, "as if there were no black or white, no rich or poor." So there you have it: individualized, anti-government, market-driven: *Microsoft über Alles*.

This is not just an ideology having its way with us, it is a culture. It is an American culture, suffused with an aggressive winner-take-all ethic of heroic success. To assert that, in the era of transnational corporate transactions, this is not a specifically *American* culture, that we are all just postnational culture consumers gambolling in globalized cyberspace, that in any case a lot of Canadian culture is rooted in the North American, along with the American, is to ignore the overwhelming power and authority – hegemony – of American culture and entertainment industrial product around the world, against which the cultural expression of punier economies has almost no force, not even within its own national borders. All this applies equally to culture in Cyberia.

> Canadians must be the first people in history to define their nationalism in terms of "I have a social-security system, therefore I exist."
> – Marcel Masse, former culture minister, quoted in Ray Conlogue, "Spectator," *Globe and Mail*, February 18, 1995

Canadians are meant to chuckle along with Marcel Masse at this witty revelation of our homely self-consciousness. Yet, when Ralph Nader, the American folk hero, lawyer, and reformer, spoke in Edmonton in 1998 to a virtually sold-out audience about the staggering importance of defending the Canadian health care system, and Canadian democracy, on their "collision course" with multinational corporations, he made us feel we were doing it for all of humanity. The crowd was euphoric, and I was happy to see many younger activists amongst them. There was a genuine buzz in the air, people coming down off the high of that afternoon's Supreme Court ruling that Alberta's Bill of Rights was in violation of the Charter of Rights and Freedoms, followed by the justices' reading the missing parts, outlawing discrimination on the basis of sexual orientation, into the Bill.

We were caught in a conflict between an aggressive corporate culture and a civic culture, Nader told us. He spoke of what the Consumer Association's Alberta branch had already warned us, the creeping two-tier system in the "pushing of services out into the market." Be careful! Corporate greed knows no bounds, and even though for-profit institutions can't go head-to-head with the health care system – "it has too much public support" – they can chip away at it. But we were not going to let them get it. "The corporations have miscalculated the resolve and stamina of the citizens here." We were all enormously cheered by this vote of confidence from someone who had taken us more seriously than we had taken ourselves; we had become so used to the obloquys from our own politicians and business elite that we were whiners and freeloaders for wanting to be assured that our neighbours would not be beggared by the misfortune of being sick. "Canadians," Nader concluded, "are too modest about their achievements."

> Name the five most recent Canadian prime ministers. *Thirty per cent knew only two. Most mentioned [was] Jean Chrétien (spelled seven ways).* What is the date of Canada's founding? *Fifty-five per cent did not list 1867.* Name three Canadian novelists and the title of one of their books. *Sixty-two per cent could not name any author.*
> – Joanne Harris Burgess, "Low Marks in Canadian History," *Globe and Mail*, January 4, 1997

Joanne Burgess teaches a university course in Canadian Studies at Glendon College in Toronto. The responses she cites above are to a voluntary and anonymous questionnaire she handed out to first-year students, all of them graduates of Ontario high schools and its grade ten Canadian history course. Their average mark on her test was 32.5 per cent.

Adults fared worse, if anything, in a much-commented-on national survey in 1998 which found that just half those questioned knew the name and importance of the Underground Railroad, only 14 per cent named Lester Pearson as the Canadian who won the Nobel Peace Prize in 1957, and only 12 per cent identified both Emily Carr and Robert Service as the Canadians among a list of six artists or writers.[30]

Historian J. L. Granatstein, a polemicist on the state of affairs in Canadian classrooms where history is taught – or more likely not taught – informs us of the "hard truth" that in four provinces, Alberta, Saskatchewan, Nova Scotia, and Newfoundland, there is no requirement that history be studied in high school; in another four there is only one required Canadian history course. Two provinces require two courses. And it gets worse: "In some provinces Canadian history is interlarded with civics, current events, and pop sociology." The same situation prevails at the universities, where social history – gender studies, labour studies, women's history – are taught, crowding out "national history," which Granatstein defines as political, military, diplomatic, governmental, and policy history.[31] (I should say that I was a beneficiary of just that sort of history when it was still being taught in Alberta high schools in the early 1960s, and I still can't, for the life of me, remember the date, or even the century, of the Constitutional Act.)

Over a decade in Ontario, history was reduced from five compulsory courses in high school to one course on "Contemporary Canada." The Harris government in its first term decided to further decrease the study of Canadian history by eliminating a compulsory senior social science credit as part of a reform.[32]

There are consequences. If the teaching of history is essential to the inculcation of a common identity among citizens – so that we are all singing from the same songbook – the argument goes, then we are in danger of a shallow sense of Canadian self. This is particularly "calamitous" (Granatstein's word) in the case of immigrant Canadians who, not knowing the common story, the master narrative, of how we are who we are, cannot be expected to understand our "ways." Instead of a feeling of national pride, our ignorance and the thinness of our collective patriotism ensure our sense of shame or, at best, a modesty unbecoming to our accomplishments. These are eloquently summarized by Granatstein: "Canadians from all over the globe built a nation in some rough country with a miserable climate and made it the best place in the world to live. This is a great story. We have never fought an aggressive war, but only to protect our democratic ideals and help our friends and allies. This is a story of selfless sacrifice. . . . This is a history of freedom and tolerance."[33]

Bereft of this narrative, we are condemned to superficial and poorly thought-out positions on the great debates of our age (see, for instance, knee-jerk responses to Quebec's desire for distinct status) and to absorption willy-nilly by the forces of mindless, Americanizing, consumerism and entertainment. "Why learn about the 3rd Canadian Division in Normandy when *Saving Private Ryan* tells us all we need to know about how Americans won the war?" asks Granatstein, who is also director of the Canadian War Museum in Ottawa. To parents of school-age children, the question resonates of the need to pass on "community" to the next generation, which, to many, means belonging to a "memory, to a tradition – that [the child] is in fact related by history to all kinds of people she'll never know."[34]

As it is, we must trust their spontaneous interest in learning about themselves, as Prof. Burgess must do with the eager if ignorant students who present themselves to her strenuous course in Canadian Studies. It is not an internal failing in our youth that has put us on this dangerous road to communal eclipse. For they, like the rest of us, have been betrayed by the faint-of-national-heart who cannot or will not see that it is vital for the biodiversity of the human community that Canada survive as a distinct society.

RETHINKING VALUES

> Let us make no mistake about our situation: The Mulroney/ Chretien approach to governing has almost succeeded in creating a new Canada. That Canada is richer, greedier, more paranoid, more divided, less historically conscious, more ruthlessly eager to play a part in the global marketplace than the Canada of, say, 12 years ago.
>
> – B. W. Powe, "The Transnational Shadow,"
> *Globe and Mail*, January 17, 1998

Then, in 1997, came the so-called meltdown of Asian economies previously hailed as "tigers," miracles of the global marketplace and unregulated speculation, and the "mercy killing," in journalist Gwynne Dyer's phrase, of the MAI (Multilateral Agreement on Investment). Suddenly the media were in full cry about the menace to developed economies from the ruination of the more fragile. What had once seemed the iron-clad law of the sovereign market was now a scene of turbulent stock markets, collapsing commodity prices, and millions of destitute unemployed. "Hot money," the quick in-and-out of investment in speculative markets, and the circulation of capital hidden from public scrutiny (at one point the World Bank estimated that around $110 billion drained out of the four Asian countries most affected by the crisis)[35] now represented market *chaos*. Billionaire financier George Soros, speaking at 1998's World Economic Forum in Davos, Switzerland, claimed himself a "heretic" on the question of the market's rationality: "What *did* happen [in the meltdown] was incalculable." And German Chancellor Gerhard Schroeder, citing the anguish of the hundreds of thousands who had lost their livelihoods, called for the introduction of financial regulatory mechanisms to "ensure justice." In Indonesia, for example, rice prices had doubled, half the country's children were suddenly in danger of malnourishment, and the 250,000 rural health posts had all but collapsed.

The free market, it seemed, had come up short and myopic: "Clearly, markets aren't perfect," Canada's minister of finance, Paul Martin, offered. And so, in a fit of the heebie-jeebies, startled by their own citizens' organized protests, the governments of the OECD (Organization for Economic Co-operation and Development) backed down from signing the MAI. Linda McQuaig, economics writer and high priestess of market demystification, was elated: "It goes to show that all these policies [of the unfettered market] are far from being inevitable."[37] In fact, they have produced grotesque results. In 1999 the United Nations reported that the wealth of the world's *three* richest families is greater than all the assets of the 600 million people living in the world's least developed countries.[38] If there is a growing backlash to this obscenity, it is because millions of people have felt helpless and powerless in the light of the market's indifference to their deepening poverty, their children's blighted chances and their communities' wasted and toxic air, water, and soil.

Amplifying the call of economic nationalism for the panic-stricken Canadian workers and investors facing the prospect of a "downward spiral" of falling production and rising unemployment in the wake of the market meltdown, Bob White, president of the Canadian Labour Congress in 1998, said the international labour movement knew all along it would come to this. "We have been calling for controls on speculative international markets, recognition of the right of countries to regulate investment flows and to shape their own economic future."[39] It was the strangest of times: Mr. White found himself in bed – or at least in the lower bunk – with the president of the World Bank, James Wolfensohn, who wrote in the *Financial Times* that, just as there is a need to soothe markets, so there is an urgent need to address "human travail."[40]

Human travail. I began my interviews with the "next Canadians" back in 1997, when there seemed to be an unshakeable consensus in public opinion that the pain of deficit and debt reduction in our economies – the decimation of public sector payrolls, the closing of factories and hospitals, the squeezing of welfare programs, the savaging of cultural institutions – had to be borne for the benefit of future generations. They would come to thank us for reining in public spending we could no longer afford, for tightening our belts to get our house in order (the mixed metaphors are deliberate – they were repeated ad nauseam in the press), and for learning self-reliance after the "pig-outs" of the 1960s and 1970s. It was astonishing, then, to write about this next generation during 1998 and 1999, when, as my file folders stuffed with clippings attest, the consensus began to fracture, suppressed voices of disagreement and skepticism grew bolder, and a whole society, it seemed, began to reimagine its future in the light of the renewed debates about its situation. What was all that travail about? people wondered. Was it all worth it? And so, in the 1997 Speech from the Throne, the Liberal government of the day began to dissociate itself from the hackers and slashers of the neo-liberal Right and announced, in a text replete with references to "investing" and "building," that it was after all committed to a "publicly administered, comprehensive health-care system that provides universal access to high quality care for Canadians anywhere in the country." The public was happy to hear it, but the debate was hardly settled. Two months after the Throne Speech a national poll revealed that, although a majority agreed they would be "better off personally" once the deficit was eliminated, 55 per cent also believed that the federal government had caused "too much pain" in its dash to eliminate budget shortfalls.[41] In Alberta, an extraordinary ruckus was raised by the 1997 publication of Kevin Taft's *Shredding the Public Interest*. "Governments can tell the truth, or they can lie," wrote Taft, who had worked as a young research consultant inside Ralph Klein's government. His little book documented the thoroughness of the lies the Canadian public had been told by Klein and his ministers about the "out-of-control spending" on public services for which Albertans had been so harshly disciplined. In fact, during the decade preceding Klein's cuts to the health care budget there had been no significant change in per capita spending, yet in 1993 he began slashing away at the "unaffordable" monster. At the same time, Alberta's scale of *private sector* subsidy – $34 billion in twenty-five years, not counting inflation – is unprecedented.[42]

In the 1999 federal budget, Ottawa was running the largest government surplus in the Group of Seven leading industrial nations. Together with the United States, Canada was spending less money than it raised, and "no other G7 country came even close to imposing such deep cuts," according to the *Globe and Mail*'s Bruce Little. In response, he quoted the Royal Bank of Canada's chief economist, John McCallum: "Part of phase two [of the government's agenda] is going to be damage repair, particularly in health care."[43] As if on cue, finance minister Paul Martin announced an eventual $2.5 billion that would be put back into federal transfers to the provinces; back, that is, to the transfer levels of 1995.

As soon as governments declared the prospect of budget surpluses, not deficits, the public came back with a roar: Give us back our hospitals, schools, wages. A health summit convened by the Alberta government told the public paymasters that, unless there was an infusion of funds soon into the health-care system, Alberta could slip into a two-tier system, contrary to "Alberta cultural values." By 2005, Ottawa's annual surplus is expected to top $25 billion. The New Right offered tax cuts. The public said it wasn't interested. A pre-budget survey showed that over half of respondents felt the social net improves "quality of life" and that there had already been too many cuts to social programs.[44] When finance minister Paul Martin brought down the budget, his speech was a model of the rhetoric of Canadian decency. This is "a time to act upon a new national dream – a dream anchored in the good sense of Canadians and their sense of the common good."[45] He at least had the decency to give credit where credit was due: to the Canadians who had kept the faith throughout.

In the fall of 1999, it was reported that not nearly enough Canadian schools had lined up for the advertising programs offered by ScreenAd, a company that hoped to place commercials on students' computers, and that Youth News Network, a youth-oriented television news network with commercials that had targeted 2,300 schools, was scaling back to a six-month trial run in twenty schools. Five provincial education ministers had already rejected the network in their schools.[46]

On the heels of the provincial premiers' meeting in 1999 that submitted a long list of spending requests – agriculture, highways, child care – an ongoing national study called Rethinking Government found that 89 per cent of those polled felt the federal government should place a high priority on health care; only 19 per cent opted for "some" personal income-tax cuts in the next budget.[47] Since at least 1993 there had been economists in our midst to tell us that, contrary to what government and business had been arguing so strenuously, the real culprit in the alarming build-up of the debt was not social spending but the interest rates propped up by the Bank of Canada to fight inflation and protect the value of assets held by a financial elite, a debt exacerbated by the resulting recession and unemployment and, with them, the collapse of government revenues from an eroding tax base. Further, that tax base had been systematically bled by the corporate sector whose proportion of federal taxes had dropped, between 1961 and 1994, by 200 per cent.[48] By 1995 analysts and commentators like Linda McQuaig were wondering out loud just why it was that government spending, long understood as social *investment*, was suddenly a social burden? "It is hard not to draw the conclusion," McQuaig wrote, "that their [the voices against the deficit] real goal isn't deficit reduction – perhaps never was deficit reduction – but rather the reduction of the size and scope of our social-welfare system."[49]

And if that was the case, then their goal was the dismantling of the Canadian identity itself, so popularly described as the kinder and gentler identity that believed in public health care.

The Canadian Centre for Policy Alternatives congratulated the working class for having "moderated" the impact of the sustained downturn in living standards by defending what remained of social programs. "So let's be forward looking," wrote the political economist Mel Watkins, and accept that it's a remarkable tribute to the "resilience of the Canadian political culture" that we want public spending restored.[50]

It is precisely a cultural achievement. Given the premonitions of calamity from the Right, it was perhaps unexpected that Canadians *en masse*, even in their diversity of age, sex, and ethnicity, turned out to agree that they belong to a people who are "tolerant, generous, optimistic and committed to the same moral values," which include liberal social values (half of those surveyed in a 1997 national poll described themselves as having liberal values) and social tolerance. At the top of the list of what was important to them, 96 per cent put a "fulfilling job"; "making money" was at the bottom.[51] Six months later, an international poll testing national pride found that Canada ranked third of twenty-three nations on questions designed to test people's pride in national achievements in the economy, democracy, culture, the military, and sports. This was at a time when their national pride and forbearance had been sorely tried by exposés of Canadian military malfeasance and the "neverendum referendum." Significantly, even Quebecers were "almost" as likely to sing the praises of Canadian institutions as the rest of Canada.[52]

Prime Minister Chrétien himself began articulating the tax-versus-spending debate as a debate about "values." He and his cabinet had taken a hard look at statistical comparisons of Canadian and American society and concluded that Canadians should be impressed by our more evenly distributed wealth, our lower level of poverty "even if the statistics say they are much richer than us," and our comparative rates of crime, life expectancy, and infant mortality.[53] As he repeated before an audience at the Economic Club of New York, "No, we're not counting on the private sector. The medicare system . . . will remain a public one where everybody has the same access . . . it's free, it's portable and it's publicly administered, and it will remain like that. . . . Nobody in Canada is afraid to lose his or her home because somebody's sick in the family. . . . We have a good system of pensions . . . a good level of minimum wage. . . . I think that in a civilized country we need minimum wage; otherwise, there will always be people who will abuse some poor people who cannot defend themselves." John R. MacArthur, publisher of *Harper's* magazine, who was listening to all this, thought the audience might choke on their shrimp.[54]

It seemed, then, that the market, far from being beyond the claims of ordinary men and women and their governors, was after all a creation of society and its values, articulated through economic activity, which could be shaped and regulated, planned for the long-term, taxed, and whatever else governments deem necessary to ensure social well-being. As the politicians' declarations of social commitment show, far from being impotent in the face of market forces, governments, even the most neo-liberal, have never completely relinquished their power and authority to impose or organize property contracts and laws, environmental and labour regulations, health-care and pension regimes, and other measures that govern what French sociologist Pierre Bourdieu calls the "economics of happiness" that underlie people's social security and contentment. As the pathologies and ravages of the free-wheeling transnationals on the lives of millions so dramatically demonstrated in the last part of this just-ended century, security and contentment cannot be guaranteed in the private economic sector; they are satisfied in the public realm, most obviously by government.

Government, it seems, does have a crucial role to play in shaping a more human face of capitalism, all the more since citizens still have some measure of control over its workings, and none over those of investment banks. Besides, as we are reminded by Michael Adams, president of Environics Research Group, "the economy of Canada remains larger than those of the largest corporations in the world."[55]

One could even argue that an interventionist government is a specifically Canadian value, supported time and again by a majority of citizens while their elites hammered incessantly for free trade, decentralization of government through constitutional change, lower corporate taxes, and changes to pensions and social insurance. Not for nothing has the promise of the BNA Act for "peace, order, and good government" never been revoked in favour of pursuits of individual happiness: Canadians do not seem to believe that their contentment can be secured outside their attachment to the welfare state, however weakened, and especially when the only thing that stands between them and the sickening abuses of the transnationals is their government. It is "theirs" in the same way that other peoples have "tribes," as journalist Richard Gwyn argued in an interview with me. "Canadians have always needed a state, because we aren't a tribe.

Citizenship and commonality of citizenship is what you need, because there's so little else we have in common."

A younger generation that does not have to start from scratch in the construction of a commons, that has inherited the habits, however attenuated, of social responsibility, may already belong to each other in a practised and historical way. As the CCPA's director Seth Klein said to me, "What draws me to my work here is the challenge to reshift the culture to remind people how we have tried to make ideas around social solidarity and compassion concrete. . . . [Taxes] are how we discharge a moral obligation to look after each other."

CANCON

> Sometimes you're down in the States and if you close your eyes and squint you think: "I could live in the U.S." and then you open your eyes and think, "no way."
> – Douglas Coupland, interviewed in the *National Post*, August 28, 1999

"How do you know you're a Canadian?" I had asked Anton Krawchenko, a law student at the University of Victoria. He had claimed he was one. I was skeptical, thinking of all the American TV he must have watched in his twenty-four years and all the discharges from the continental media about the New World Order he must have absorbed like paper towelling on a cat's mess.

But he was also a graduate of Political Science and Environmental Studies and had an experience of what he called the "old Canada," meaning Canadian federalism in the 1970s and the Trudeau governments, of post-Expo Montreal as a potentially world-class city, of social programs that were solidly funded and, of course, much less cross-border cultural traffic. "Trudeau went to China, we never broke with Cuba. We had clean water and air, empty spaces. It all helped you identify yourself. My sister has no political consciousness of the eighties, but my generation remembers what it was like. We still have a residual memory of the old Canada, and that has a serious influence. I have a nostalgia for that kind of Canada." The new Canada within a new economy is governed by political compromise, he felt, self-interest is dominant and even personal liberal values have become compromised.

But not all memory is erased. "I'll give you a perfect example," he offered. "I have a good friend who asked me the other day – because there's so much happening in the States, so much money to be made there, lower taxes – 'Anton, would you ever consider working in the States? Could you do that?' I said I probably could if it was a job offer that took me there on a short-term basis. He said he'd do it but would feel like a traitor somehow. So for our generation there's still a residual feeling that we're supposed to be different, we're supposed to have a separate identity from the Americans."

Krawchenko tried to solidify his Canadian identity during six years of university, when he read the *Globe and Mail* every day and would set his alarm for seven o'clock each morning to catch the CBC news. While he sat writing his master's thesis, he listened to CBC's *Morningside* every single day. And when Peter Gzowski went off the air it was a crisis for him. "Totally. I had made him an important part of my Canadian identity. Part naturally and part purposefully he made his show distinct from American talk shows. I mean, the kinds of things he talked about, weaving in and out of talking with a foreign journalist, then over to a B.C. woodcutter, then over to some Cambodia activist, in a totally unpretentious and direct style. To so many Canadians, this was a link to other Canadians, this was how they did it, they listened to *Morningside* and got a spin on world politics, plus they heard other Canadians talk."

Just then the doorbell rang, and when Krawchenko returned he was excitedly waving a registered envelope. It came from Princess Mary's Scottish Canadian Regiment, in which Krawchenko had enroled to be commissioned as a reserve infantry officer. A confessed romantic about history and international affairs, he had a desire to be the *instrument* of history rather than some "old fellow sitting in an easy chair. I know that carrying that insignia on my sleeve is going to change the way I think about being Canadian: you swear an oath of allegiance to the Queen. The military has a very old-fashioned view of what Canada is. It happens to be a view of Canada I adhere to.

"I would really like to participate in a UN mission, the experience of being part of a regiment wearing the Canadian flag in some far-off land. It will reinforce my identity. Just being part of that mechanism, which happens to be very traditional and closely linked with national values and English history – this regiment wears kilts, for God's sake – I find very comforting."

He knew he might be fooling himself, holding on to this shrinking world of tradition, but it was the life he wanted for himself, not a life in some head office of some corporation in Calgary or Toronto. It was only Canada's relations with the *U.S.* that raised this question of values for him, he admitted. "Canadians have such a complex about this issue, and I have it too, because the U.S. is the richest, most powerful, arguably the freest and most creative society ever. And we have to struggle for an identity alongside that. But a core of our identity, which I think a lot of my generation share, completely subconsciously, is that we are much more willing to sacrifice some parts of our liberty for public values and social policy reasons. The difference in the way we see guns, for example, is going to take a lot longer than one or two generations to erode. To say Canadians are just another kind of North American is to underestimate these values."

After many hours of discussion with interviewees, and hours of reading about the economic agonies of our New World Order, it became clear that through them all ran a subtext of anguished self-enquiry: Who *are* we? Sooner or later, in the course of debate about social and cultural values brought into question by the radical turn in traditional Canadian economic culture, the question would be posed, as, for instance, Canadian Studies teacher Richard Nimijean in Montreal posed it. "Rather than asking what a Canadian is all about, ask yourself, What is citizenship really about? Think about it, What are countries for? We have a globalized economy and we can go to India in a flash or visit metaphorically on the Web, we've got e-mail. So on what basis do you define yourself? Not just, 'I'm Canadian because I'm not American.' But, What is this thing called Canada? And so it goes back to the social contract."

The contract in Canada has been between government and citizens, people seemed to be saying repeatedly. Government contracted with us to use its powers to guide the evolution of an equitable society. It collected revenue and redistributed it through social programs so that society's majority – "those unable or unwilling to indulge in the naked pursuit of wealth" – would be protected from the worst excesses of capitalism, to cite

Satya Das, senior writer for the *Edmonton Journal*. "If the compassionate state is no longer affordable, what is?"[56]

There hung over such questions the whiff of a betrayal, as though it were unCanadian for a government to desert the public in its time of need and leave us to the mercy of the tax-cutters, investment fund managers, and deficit hounds. There's more to life than taxes, people said. In Canada we can walk the streets at night, we have universal health care, we are not spending more money on prisons than universities . . .

No, we don't want to live like that. And we don't have to, unless of course the contract were broken under severe and irresistible pressure from the New Right in concert with what Mark Kingwell called "the double-agents in the service of the American Creed," such as "common sense revolutionaries," finance ministers, and certain newspaper and magazine columnists.[57] People can get very angry at the politicians who are wobbling on the contract. There is even an odour of collusion that attaches to the high tech workers and doctors we read about who leap at the chance to work in Texas and California and who do not miss our health-care system. (Why should they? Just by moving they have an extra $22,000 in their pockets – to pay for health insurance, presumably.) "I feel like [Canada] is a Third World country," said Rob Burgess, ex-Canadian now of San Francisco's Macromedia Inc.,[58] completely missing the point that average after-tax incomes in the U.S. are high and rising only because the *rich* are getting richer – while 40 per cent of the poor scrape together incomes that are still 50 per cent below the poverty line – in what a Harvard economist called "an apartheid economy."[59] Talk about your Third World!

Pete McMartin, who grew up in Windsor, "a branch-plant city if there ever was one," wrote in the *Vancouver Sun* that the hand-wringers had got it all wrong, there was no crisis of identity among Canadians, at least certainly not among the working-class toiling along the Detroit River with a real American city on offer not a mile away. "I did not once meet anyone who did not feel intensely different from the Americans. . . . We did not want to trade places with them and, if anything, felt vaguely superior."[60]

Our sense of superiority sometimes veils a quite remarkable hostility. I was struck by the tone of some commentary when the United States Olympic hockey team lost early to Canada in the 1998 games. "There's no question it was a hard trip for them," a university newspaper journalist gloated. "Claiming they would knock their northern neighbours on their asses, the U.S. club fell to Canada 4–1 and was eliminated before the medal rounds. . . . They did a full monty in front of the whole world, whipping out their arrogance and false pride for all to see. Wrap it up in the Stars and Stripes, boys. Your product doesn't interest anybody."[61] Volodymyr Boychuk, who needed three years in Canada to begin to feel like a Ukrainian-Canadian, recognizes the American superiority complex from his youth in Soviet Ukraine, the complex of the "bigger brother," older, stronger, smarter, and therefore entitled to more power. "I often compare the two machines," he said, "the old Soviet and the American, with their cultural domination, their ideology of superiority and economic control. When I was in Washington, D.C., I felt like I was in Moscow." When travelling in China, Lois Chiang knows that the Chinese will see her as apart from "loud and obnoxious" Americans. Barry Gordon has a lot of American friends and, "man, are they a pretty arrogant bunch!" which has led him to conclude that he could never live in the U.S.: "I consider most of the U.S. to be uninhabitable."

"America is sick!" So announced a book reviewer in the University of Alberta's *Gateway*. "Gangs are rampant, drugs are everywhere, unemployment is at record highs – at least according to the book jacket for *Prescription for Mayhem*. With a beginning like that, how could I, a patriotic Canadian, not enjoy this novel?"[62]

> Most of us think of our neighbors to the north as "America Lite,"
> but perky Canada (actually an entirely separate country!) has
> many distinguishing characteristics: nationalized health care,
> fewer guns and more snow.
>
> – Jason Zengerle, "Waits and Measures,"
> *Mother Jones*, January/February 1999

Writer Richard Gwyn argues in his book *Nationalism Without Walls* that Canadians should understand themselves not as anti-Americans or unAmericans but as the *other* North Americans, firmly planted in the same continental soil with those who broke away from the English empire to become modern Americans. "I have always believed that we Canadians have a different way of being North American," he told me, "and it was most strongly expressed by the Loyalists who were living in America all along, and who came to Canada, thinking of themselves as North American." The Loyalists could have returned to the "motherland" or gone elsewhere in the British colonies but they did not. They made a conscious decision to stay on the North American continent alongside the Americans but not *of* them. Two centuries later, Multi Health Systems Inc. of Toronto found from a "personality factor" questionnaire that the cultural differences between the two groups of North Americans have become profound: Canadians are more trusting and accepting than Americans; we are more open to change and experimentation, more apt to use abstract reasoning, more emotionally stable, livelier, and more animated. Of the sixteen personality factors measured, thirteen produced significant differences between Americans and Canadians.[63]

> We never heard of the War of 1812 in school. I had no idea we
> – well, the British – burned the White House down. I would have
> appreciated learning some of this instead of "conceptualizing"
> in Social Studies.
> – Paul Mather, humorist and improv comedian

While doing gigs in the U.S., Paul Mather, together with his collaborators, Wes Borg, Donovan Workun, and Joe Bird of Three Dead Trolls in a Baggie, went through an "anti-American kick." This was when Mather finally learned about the War of 1812, reading Pierre Berton on the subject, and then expanding the anti-Yankee repertoire by reading David Orchard's *The Fight for Canada* and everything he could find about the Avro Arrow. But it was the story of the war in 1812 that mattered most of all, if for no other reason than that "Americans completely don't mention that Canadians burned down the White House. I know. I have an 1812 Web page, and I get e-mail from American kids in total denial we kicked their ass."

The group produced *The War of 1812*, which I first saw at Edmonton's Fringe Festival and found so exhilarating that, when the Three Dead Trolls came to the University of Alberta as part of a CBC review in 1998, I went to see them again. The university theatre was sold out, to a mainly student crowd, who laughed with gusto at all the jokes told on the U.S. The program's climax featured the War of 1812, or, rather, a "rousing rendition of a beautifully anti-American song" from the play *The War of 1812*, as reviewed by the student newspaper, the *Gateway*. "Everyone seemed delighted to indulge in the blatantly patriotic lyrics: singing along, clapping, and sharing in the overall joy of reliving a proud moment in Canadian history – at the expense of the Americans, of course."[64]

> When the White House burned, burned, burned
> But the Americans won't admit it
> It burned burned burned
> It burned and burned and burned
> It burned burned burned
> and the Americans ran and cried like a
> bunch of little babies, wah wah wah!
> In the War of 1812!

> Big finish. Fine music. The audience goes nuts. Lights down.

The audience goes nuts, up on their feet, jumping up and down, hooting and hollering, punching the air, whistling . . . and I sit amazed. The reviewer would write of their "joy," and I suppose it was that, this deep pleasure of an emotion too often locked or seized up inside each one of us – pride in the dignity of our Canadianness – while we proceed defensively, with irony, with self-deprecation, with negotiation, in our relations with the Americans. But there was more here in this crowd of students than just the satisfaction of a displayed feeling. It seemed to me that in the almost feverish tone of their clamour *together* they were exorcising something that a brief and brilliant song-and-dance on the stage had given them permission to do: yank the American devils from their anchorage in their souls. If there had been a bonfire with a couple of Blue Coat effigies on fire, they would have danced around it. In the comedians on stage they had seen themselves represented as fighters who strike back against the curse of domination, against the Divine Right of the powerful to determine who they would be, what they would believe, and how they would live with each other. They were up on their feet to send us the message that, in spite of all the forces marshalled against their Canadian consciousness, they knew who they were and that they recognized themselves in each other.

THE NEXT QUEBEC

> The last ten years of constitutional debate has made it very painful to be a Quebecois outside of Quebec, because there is a significant level of intolerance and it's very hard to be heard. I've been invited to give the Quebecois point of view on any number of occasions, whether on radio or community TV or at the university or high schools, and it's very, very hard to be understood. And I can see why, because it's their very identity as Canadians that's being put into question. For people outside Quebec to accept what Quebec is about, their conception of Canada has to change; and for that to happen, their own personal and individual identity as a Canadian has to change. That's very hard, and it's a difficulty that is underestimated both by Quebecers and by English-Canadian intellectuals who say it's not so hard to agree with "distinct society." But it is hard, precisely because it's symbolic and has to do with who we are.
>
> – Claude Denis, associate professor,
> Faculté St-Jean, University of Alberta

I asked my non-Quebecois subjects a hundred times: "Does your Canada include Quebec?" And a hundred times they answered "Yes," insistent that the presence of Quebec within Canada was part of their identity as Canadians. In most cases, they had not travelled to or lived in Quebec, could not speak French, had meagre knowledge of Quebec's cultural and political debates, which, in any case, they would not have been able to follow given their inability to read francophone newspapers and magazines or listen to Radio-Canada. Confined to anglophone media, they live on their side of a cultural divide that effectively makes strangers of their Quebecois counterparts. As Mark Starowicz, director of CBC's Canadian History Project observed, "A teenager in Calgary will almost never see a teenager in Trois-Rivières in the televisual or cinematic universe. There will be no communality of experience."[65] How, then can there be any important meaning to their "inclusion" of Quebec in their sense of themselves?

In fact, the meaning can be full of internal contradiction. Here, verbatim, is how a young woman in Edmonton of mixed ethnic origin, neither

English nor French, expressed herself on this question: "I don't believe in a bi-cultural Canada but a multicultural one. I speak French because it was forced on us in school. I love it in Quebec, yet I can't understand how someone like Céline Dion who grew up in Canada didn't speak English until she was twenty! This country is a big place and they [Quebecois] are like a little whiny baby. Let them go? No, absolutely not! I don't have a problem with saying Quebec is unique. Great, go ahead. But I can't understand how they can even think of cutting out of Canada. Like, if you don't like it here, *go*! It's Canada's land. *Move*. There are other places in this world they can go to. . . . I wish they were able to see themselves as part of a multicultural Canada." The muddle is breathtaking. She appreciates Quebec's uniqueness but is bewildered by a *francophonie* that does not produce universal bilingualism. She "loves" Quebec but sputters with resentment about their "whiny" desires. She deeply resents Quebecois' ambivalence about remaining part of Canada, invites them to "move," yet "absolutely" cannot tolerate the possibility they may do just that. She claims the "land" for English-Canada, imagines that there is some solution to this mess in a mass emigration out of Quebec, and concludes with a wistful fantasy of the dissolution of *québécitude* in the ethnic soup of the Rest of Canada to rid us of the problem once and for all.

While not so spectacularly contorted, other arguments were nevertheless at cross purposes. Paul Ghezzi said "definitely" his Canada included Quebec and that he "loved" French culture and has "no problem" with bilingual signs, even in Ontario. But he abruptly retreated from this inclusive vision when he thought vengefully about the "separation thing": "If you want to separate, fine, we'll let you, but you get your portion of the national debt. You don't get any more transfer payments. You become a country; deal with that." Barry Gordon in Toronto identified himself as "firmly" in the Trudeau camp, by which he meant the certainty that Quebec "will be coming back to the trough over and over again, and if you give them what they want, they'll just come back for more, like a spoiled child. After a while you just have to put your foot down and say, No." On the other hand, Gordon is sure that a good part of his identity derives from being aware of Quebec's presence in Canada, although he wouldn't go so far as to say his identity *depends* on it. He would still think of himself as a Canadian were Quebec to separate, but "we're better with them than without them." This inclusiveness stops short of premier Lucien Bouchard, however, who drives him crazy. "And if you [separatists] think you're going to be successful on your own, then go give it a try, and, by the way, you will take your share of the national deficit and you will not use our currency, or if you do there will be a price to pay, and you will not use our passports and you won't take northern Quebec and probably not the South Shore either." Clearly, Gordon has given some thought to the prospect of Quebec's separation, and I am struck, as with Ghezzi, by the infantalizing language of their resentment ("we'll let you," "whiny," "like a spoiled child") and by the embittered tone of the pan-Canadian whose magnanimity about Quebec is wholly conditional on Quebec's acquiescence to our vision for it.

In Calgary, Mark Heard, who has only had a stopover in Montreal, hoped Quebec would not separate, as their presence was part of his "identity thing," even though there will eventually be no countries anyway as we join the "global village." However, a separate Quebec will be responsible for "breaking us up."

In his Canadian Studies classes, Quebecer Richard Nimijean deals with a generation of anglophone students shaped by the "discourse of rights," and their consequent anger about Quebec's claim to distinctiveness as a rights grab. "I ask them why they care whether Quebec has control over language and culture, and they say it's because 'Quebec is getting something that we don't get,' and I point out that that is part of federalism, marked by compromise and debate and negotiation. I grew up with the immediate legacy of Trudeau and the students like to listen to me as some sort of museum piece."

Others, while not spiteful about Quebec's restiveness in the federation, were deeply troubled by the implications of Quebec's secession for their own identity and political security. Volodymyr Boychuk in Edmonton includes Quebec in "his" Canada because, "without Quebec we are mono-culturally WASP." This is an interesting assertion, given the millions of non-WASP, non-francophone Canadians, but Boychuk meant the "protective umbrella" of the Quebec fact under which stand the "ethnics" who understand very well that, without the need to mollify Quebec with official bilingualism, the federal government could easily renege on multicultural-ism as the compensatory policy. "Unconsciously," he would not be unsym-pathetic with Quebec's desire for independence – he thinks of the independence struggles within the old U.S.S.R. – but "consciously" he believes their separation would be bad for the rest of us. "Multiculturalism is what distinguishes us from the U.S.'s melting pot."

Law student Anton Krawchenko in Victoria echoed the fear of Americanization in his attachment to the idea of Quebec as part of Canada, "because this is the last, greatest hope of Canada really being Canada and not a little part of America." I asked him, "So the Quebecois should stay in Canada so *we* can feel more Canadian? Don't you think your argument has to resonate in Quebec as well?" Krawchenko conceded his was more a sentiment than argument: " 'Please stay!' It's so pathetic but everything [in English Canada] revolves around the U.S., and Quebec is what distinguishes us. All my central-Canadian friends are rock solid about this. They all love Montreal. Quebec has got to stay." He admitted that he had "no idea" what his generation of francophones in Quebec thought about all this and that he and his friends didn't think about it either "in any detailed way." They don't spend much time discussing the "different institutional arrangements and compromises that might get us what we want. It's more emotional than that."

For those who have lived sympathetically in Quebec, ultimately it is the issue of language that divides them from the separatists. Pamela Edmonds, now in Halifax, grew up largely in Montreal and, as a student, lived in a francophone neighbourhood where eventually she "got tired of having to think before I spoke. Of having to be so sensitive about what I was going to say. I felt that it didn't matter that I spoke French, because, as a black woman, I wasn't French. It doesn't matter how articulate you are, it comes down to the fact you're not a Leblanc or a Dubois. Enough's enough, let me go back home to Halifax." Filmmaker and activist Anna Paskal, who was schooled in French from kindergarten on, who speaks the language fluently, and who once had an apparently untroubled friendship with francophones, left Montreal for five years to go to university. When she returned a year after the traumatic referendum of 1995, she discovered she could not put back together again her old circle of *copains*. Although not "viscerally" opposed to separation, she loves Canada and would like Quebec to stay in it with her. For the moment, that desire seems to put her outside the Quebec of francophone nationalists, even outside the francophone groups that were organizing against the MAI, just as she was organizing in the other "solitude," the anglophone Montrealers against the MAI.

When Linda Melnychuk arrived in Montreal she was in love with a "handsome, supremely articulate and intelligent separatist" and already predisposed, through romance, to his cause. She was thrilled by the seductions of Montreal, the city so easy to slip into. "You walk into a subway at eight a.m. in Toronto and already there's stress in the air. In the Montreal subway at eight a.m. people seem *expectant*. These differences are now mythologized, but I embraced that easiness. A city that is so gentle and unabusive, the pace of it. A city that gives you time, not money. It understands that people need to walk around in it, attend to it, breathe in the air, enjoy the vibe on the street."

But during the campaign for the 1995 referendum and working several jobs at once, she no longer had any time to "attend" and was now angered by the "constrained" feel of the street life she had found so seductive. "I had visited Toronto and was exhilarated by the fact there was a repartee, spontaneous conversation on the streets that I could understand. I felt that streetlife in Montreal was dying, that language on the street was a political act, an act of anti-communication; it was divisive. You'd open your mouth and people would shut down or open up, you took your chances."

As difficult as she found her situation, and as "cynical" as she found the politicians' debate around the referendum, she doesn't want to see Quebec "go." Like several others, she believed that the bi-nationality of a Canada inclusive of Quebec sets a "global example." She was thinking of older and more violent nationalisms around the world, "how bloody they are, how basic ideas of human decency have been sacrificed, but that doesn't happen here. I look at Quebec and Canada and think, My God, we are doing it!" For all her excitement about the experiment, however, Melnychuk was moving to Toronto.

"Although I've spent five years really struggling, learning to speak French, I know I will always be an outsider. That's so sad, because this is still Canada and I'm a Canadian. And yet I think a French-speaking immigrant would be at home here within a couple of years." "So," I concluded for her, "language is a country," and she agreed.

The most clear-headed of my interviewees were those with unambivalent positions whether optimistic or pessimistic. In St. John's, John Fitzgerald was resigned to the prospect of the people of Quebec having referenda "until they win it. Then they'll separate. And we'll be the poorer for it." John Curkan, on the other hand, contemplating the Canadian length and breadth from his high-rise perch in downtown Calgary, was sure that Quebecois remained "very attached" to the rest of Canada, that likewise there is no basis for separation of the western provinces, that Canada's economic and political infrastructure is strong enough to sustain us as a unity for another couple of generations at least. "I think at the end of the day we're all Canadians. Some of us have different religions, we speak differently, we have different languages, our heritages are vastly different, but I think Canada continues on forever as one country."

> What do Quebecers want? But it's quite simple: a free and independent Quebec in a strong and united Canada!
> – Yvon Deschamps, actor and writer, 1980

Deschamps was able to make a joke of it, in the bitter aftermath of the first failed Quebec referendum on sovereignty, but he was onto something. In spite of the defeat in 1990 of the Meech Lake Accord to constitutionalize Quebec's special status within Confederation, the rejection of a second effort in the Charlottetown Accord amendments submitted to country-wide referendum in 1992, and the heart-stoppingly close defeat of another sovereignty referendum in Quebec in 1995, a poll found in 1997 that two-thirds of Quebecers described themselves as "profoundly attached to Canada."[66] In 1998, in a more nuanced polling, 68 per cent of Quebec *francophones* felt they belonged both to Quebec and Canada, and, of those, 37 per cent felt they were Quebecers first but also Canadians.[67] This is evidence perhaps of what observers of the national unity debates call the "longing" for a solution that will include both "national" communities, Quebec and English Canada, in the same body politic.[68]

There was once a concept bruited about for this, Sovereignty Association, and it is this, or "sovereignty-partnership," that Quebec journalist Lysiane Gagnon says people "buy" when offered the option.[69] They feel they live in two homelands, Quebec and Canada, and do not want to have to choose between them. As Montreal environmentalist Eric Michaud put it to me, "My own wish is that Quebec would stay in Canada but within a real confederation. Not as a province like the others but with power over culture, education and immigration, one hundred per cent." ("Confederation: a group of countries, states, etc., joined together for a special purpose," *Gage Canadian Dictionary*.)

Eric Michaud voted Yes in the 1995 referendum, "but right now [summer of 1998] I would not vote for those people, the Péquistes. I wouldn't even vote Yes if they organized another one, because the nationalist thing is now beside the point. I'm still nationalist but my principal objective is not an independent Quebec but the *principles* behind it: justice and diversity. The agenda of the Parti Quebecois is the complete opposite."

Covering the Quebec election for *Le Monde Diplomatique*, Christophe Wargny described the rift between traditional supporters of the Parti Quebecois – who continue to see the state as *the* carrier of collective values, whether support of the social safety net and "social solidarity" or management of hydro power and "economic development" – and the new breed of Péquistes – who along with the federal Liberals share a philosophy of weakened government intervention, expanded free trade, privatization of public resources and the market-discipline of labour.

When 73 per cent of Quebecers – and an even higher percentage of the young – felt that there should be a "left-wing political party dedicated to the needs of workers and the underprivileged,"[70] then a PQ that looks more and more interchangeable with the so-called American model of the new right is not the party to lead Eric Michaud out of Canada. *His* sovereignty would fight, not join, the trend to what he calls the "global village," with its emphasis on market and money values, spoken in English. *His* Quebec would still have its identity linked with nationalized electricity, the French language, and a cultural diversity (pointedly not the bloody mess or *bordel* of multiculturalism) that would nurture "exchange" among autonomous cultures, or *transculturalisme*.

Historian Daniel Francis, in *National Dreams: Myth, Memory and Canadian History*, writes of the "myth of unity" indulged in by English-Canadians who have believed that "French and English were partners, co-operating in building the same Canada."[71] In a "counter-narrative" of their own, francophone Quebecers tell the long story of their humiliation inside Canada after the conquest of the English army over the French on the Plains of Abraham – a catastrophe that reverberates as the "fear of oblivion" of a colonized minority within an Anglo-Celtic dominion.

This myth of a traumatized people has produced an abiding sense of insecurity and multiple complexes that a "post-nationalist" generation is impatient to throw off, to judge from media-celebrity Richard Martineau's characteristic volley in conversation with the venerable elder Jacques Godbout: "I dream of the day when we will get rid of these ancestral complexes that keep us captive; when we will stop thinking of ourselves as a besieged and threatened people with no salvation outside the group, all of us together in the same sleeping bag to escape scurvy and the savages."[72] For good measure, he mocks the artists and intellectuals of the heroic Separatist generation, also known as the Lyric Generation, for whom it is enough that a government minister wave a flag around for "a horde of guitarists and poets to show up at his side. Our culture is desperately romantic, it strives for transcendence, dreams of History, of passion, lyric flights, ecstatic crowds, forests on fire,"[73] coming very close indeed to making fun of me too, who once memorized verses by the sainted backwoods *chansonnier* Félix Leclerc, read Pierre Vallière's *White Niggers of America* with conviction, and agreed that the Front de Libération de Québec was a national liberation struggle: *Create one, two, many Vietnams!*

In an essay that provoked a furore in 1996, novelist and literary scholar Monique LaRue wrote of a literary friend who, after the 1995 referendum, had complained to her that "our literary institutions are letting themselves be overrun by immigrant writers. . . . Whether from bad conscience or political correctness or the automatic reflex of a colonized minority, we were letting our literature be usurped."[74] As in English-Canada, with its gnashing of teeth about the failure to sustain a common public culture under pressure from minorities of all kinds to be written into it, this grievance in Quebec is, according to LaRue, completely beside the point of our times. "Imagine what Quebec literature could be if it were to become simply literature . . . truly a world, a place, from which all points of view spring forth and where the diversity of French expression in America is expressed?"[75]

Children of seventy different language groups attend the schools of Montreal, and more and more of them are speaking French as a second language, compensating for the falling number of students whose maternal language is French.[76] Among them, the "allophones," those whose mother tongue is neither English nor French, now outnumber anglophones in

Quebec. The vast majority have attended, or send their children to, French schools (as they are obliged to by Bill 101), with the result that 69 per cent of them now speak French, up from 47 per cent in 1971.[77]

Richard Nimijean, born in Quebec of a Romanian-Canadian father and British mother, raised wholly within a bilingual environment in St-Jean-sur-Richelieu on the way to the eastern townships, is happy to be living in French and to identify with the francophone communities. "I think I'm actually one of the few people who lives the Canadian ideal, the bilingual person comfortable in either language," he told me in an interview over an impossible number of plates of fried eggs and fries and beans in a café east of St. Denis in Montreal. "I certainly don't think of myself as Romanian! For an anglo, I'm told, I speak French really, really well. I call myself a *Québécois* because I'm integrated into Quebec society, and a Canadian, even though I was often the only 'English' guy on my hockey or baseball teams."

Or take the recent *succès fou* of the francophone rap/hip-hop trio Dubmatique, whose origins are in Algeria, Senegal, and Cameroon, and whose debut album, *La force de comprendre*, went platinum in Quebec in 1998. In an interview with the *Globe and Mail*, they emphasized that they "represent multiculturalism, unity and antiracism."[78] In an interview with *L'Actualité* they confessed to having practically no knowledge of Quebecois literature and film but could hold forth at length about rappers and alternative rockers of their generation around the world: "Hip-hop is the current youth movement, whatever your country or language."[79] The circulation of racial, linguistic, and cultural difference fascinates Richard Martineau, who has always preferred "individuals to nations. What interests me in a man or a woman is not their roots but their branches. . . . Cultures are mixing, identities melting down, economies interpenetrating. The world is becoming porous. . . . Our [Quebec] culture is only going to take off the day it opens itself body and soul to other cultures."[80]

Or what Richard Nimijean called a "consolidated place called Quebec," thinking of his students. "Quebec knows who it is now, and that's why young Quebecers today support teaching English earlier in school. They're not worried about speaking English, because they can go to Boston with it, to California, and still be a *Québécois*." So they don't worry about becoming American either? "No, because they have the French language." They don't worry about being swamped by the totalizing force of

American culture? "No, because they're self-confident. Old-school nationalism no longer appeals, because they've grown up linguistically secure in a modern Quebec."

In 1998 *Le Devoir* published the results of a poll about the "Americanité" of the Quebecois. This does not refer to their Americanness – as in United States of Americanness – but to their North Americanness. Asked if they felt that the "movement to a greater North American integration" should continue "at the same pace," 57 per cent replied yes. This dovetails with the 52 per cent who believe that the impact of NAFTA has been "mainly positive" on the economic development of Quebec and the 64 per cent who believe that the American market is going to be more important in the future than the Canadian.[81]

The irony is inescapable: the more modern Quebec has become, the more assimilable it is into the global (read: American) culture. From Vancouver to Quebec City, from Chicoutimi to New Orleans, people are lined up for the same blockbuster summer movies from Hollywood, the same bestsellers peddled on American talk shows, the same latte *du jour* in the franchised coffee houses owned by a guy in Seattle. The tourist strolling along a mere half-kilometre of rue Sainte-Catherine in Montreal could be anywhere in North America: Dunkin Donuts, Famous Players, Clearnet, Burger King, Sunglass Hut, Future Shop, Foot Locker, Guess, the Gap . . . They speak the language of the cash register and the credit card, wrote *L'Actualité*'s editor. "What planet did you say this was? The planet of the apes . . .?"[82]

Polled in 1998, 73 per cent of Quebecois said they "prefer" American movies to French or Quebec films. A majority do not think that culture should be excluded from NAFTA, do not agree that NAFTA constitutes a threat to social programs, nor that economic globalization threatens cultural diversity.[83]

Yet, as larger and larger trading blocs are being assembled, with nation-states sliding into economic integration with global systems, "a sovereign Quebec can no more influence the investment houses of Wall Street or London or Tokyo than a sovereign Canada seems able to do," observed Philip Resnick, a Simon Fraser University political scientist who broke with his comrades in the sovereignty movement when they heralded the FTA.[84] Yet Quebecers continue their massive support of free trade even as Quebec society "Americanizes," an attitude summarized by Guy Lachapelle, political scientist at Concordia University, as "a strong national feeling combined with a strong desire to open up to the continent."[85]

Don't they get it? Anyone watching with trepidation as Canada bobbed and weaved its way around the punch-drunk manoeuvres of the U.S. State Department in the "magazine wars" of 1999, or as the idea of a currency union with the Americans was floated shortly after, would have to wonder about Quebecois' blithe continentalism. How long could a sovereign or even sovereign-associated state of Quebec resist assimilation into an economic and political culture thirty times its size as it loses, not gains, the decision-making powers it enjoys inside the Canadian federation? Jacques Godbout understood: "The freedom of monetary exchange is replacing the solidarity of human exchange. 'A sovereign Quebec'? To do what?"[86] He presses on: "Why not admit it? The new communications networks, the disappearance of heavy industry to Mexico's advantage, the new global alliances, competition that favours free trade in goods and services, the bankruptcy of socialism – all have signed the death warrant of independence."[87] But you can't scare Richard Martineau: "Is not every man an island? Is not every individual a country? I'll wave my own flag, display my own colours. I'll speak in my own name."[88]

As we torture ourselves with this and that rearrangement of the federation – and with every devolution to provincial authority as Quebec's desire for its *national* control of policy and program is accommodated – we risk the debilitation of the Canadian project understood in English Canada as federal. With solutions forthcoming neither from the sovereignist imagination, as it has been constructed since the first "separatist" government was elected in Quebec in 1976, nor from the old English-Canadian dream of a uniform and unified territory from sea to sea to sea, it is more than time for new ideas. Perhaps we should look again at some sort of asymmetrical federalism, perhaps a House of Commons that would meet in separate sessions of "all-Canada" and "Canada-outside-Quebec" representatives,[89] the "associated state" of Quebec presumably continuing to function in Quebec City? Or recognize the "deep diversity" of the Aboriginal and Quebecois collectivities by enlarging our notion of multiculturalism?[90] Or separate nation-state status for each of them, including the English Canadians?[91]

It is the dance of our dialectic, and it will go on, for we have been fated to cleave to each other, Quebec and English Canada, as constituent parts of each other's imagination and desire. Our roots lie in entangled patterns two hundred years old; anglophones, francophones, we are laden with the same mythologies. I would call them the longing for a homeplace in which we can implant in the specific soil of our experience the universal hope for peace and communion with those peoples that history has brought together and mere politics does not seem able to rend asunder. "The mental landscapes of Canadians and Quebecois are made up of similarities and differences," writes the critic Louis Cornellier, thinking of our mythologies. "To get to know them and learn to respect them, is this not to hope for the victory of the centrifugal vision over the centripetal?"[92] We have been present together in the same fur trade, the rebellions against family compacts, the great campaigns of the indigenous peoples of the Northwest, the agony over languages and religions, the fury of the world wars, the *refus global* of the artists, the camaraderie of labour, the trauma of the War Measures Act . . . each time in our particular cultural skin but present nevertheless to each other. We have, in other words, made our way all along as the "Siamese twins," as John Ralston Saul would say, of the New World, and this furnishes us the substance of a shared community of aspiration.[93] However muddled or sentimental or resigned their expression may be, this vision seems to be the fate of yet another generation of Canadians.

RECLAIMING THE PUBLIC GOOD

> Lister Sinclair: The public good matters, is that right?
> Arthur Ripstein (University of Toronto philosopher): Well, it plainly matters, because it's the context within which whatever else is going to matter, is able to matter.
> – "The Public Good Matters," *Ideas*, CBC Radio, 1996

In his acceptance speech for the Governor General's non-fiction literary prize in 1996, John Ralston Saul summarized the argument of his winning book, *The Unconscious Civilization*: "[The book] is about the new face of power – corporatism – a system which simply replaces the public interest with self-interest." Of course it is not a simple event, this revision of what Saul called the "underlying ideas" of Canadian society, which were the architecture of public interest institutions, and the subsequent reduction of civilization to "the sum of its interest groups." We are headed back to the early nineteenth century, Saul feared, and the notion of the public good as "nothing more than a beggar at the tables of the kings and the rich."

The consequences for civil society bear on our moral lives, if we think about the loss of public space and its institutions as the loss of a place in which shared ideas of the "good" might be debated and have an effect. Lacking such a place, lacking what historian Tony Judt has called a "common community of destiny," society decomposes into interest groups and "communities of origin," usually ethnic and racial, he suggests.[94] But Edmonton schoolteacher Malcolm Azania told me that, to combat social injustice, it was never enough for him just to be a "black nationalist" with an agenda only to attack "white supremacy." No, social destiny was more comprehensive than that: "There has to be *real* justice for *real* people, with true social and civil rights, not just an attack on capitalism or racism . . . but a speaking to powerful evil and calling it that name." The venerable economist Robert Heilbroner of New York's New School for Social Research would say that historically it has been government that "spoke" a counterspeech to that of private economic speech, contained and redirected it to the public good where it has been hostile to that good. It is encouraging that young Canadians do not generally express paranoia about "government" and instinctively appreciate Heilbroner's assertion that "all things considered" the operations of government have enlarged not diminished social and political freedom throughout Western democracies.[95] When political economists talk of the "economics of happiness," they mean the contentment that originates in the public realm of policy to protect social, cultural, environmental, and labour goods that are always in danger of being eroded by private interests. This is the importance of all my subjects' testimonials to the commitment to a Canada of "social conscience."

For all that the world has changed since the heyday of cultural nationalism in the late 1960s and 1970s, it seems that we have produced yet another generation looking for its place in the "essential civilization." This is the conclusion that Bob Davis also comes to in his book about the teaching of history in Ontario high schools, *Whatever Happened to High School History?* Having taught history for more than thirty years, he surveyed the "fragments" of that great discipline in the 1990s and reluctantly agreed with the proponents of the sociological approach to the subject of our history, that, if topics like abortion, sexism, racism, sexual abuse, environment, law, and gun control have replaced the discussions of parliamentary and military history in the schools, it is because there was a need for them. They are "the current pulse of life" in schools, which remain, in their public obligation, to be open to society's arguments with itself, especially in an age of alarming economic forces and fragmenting national cultures. These are the conditions that shape this generation's environment, and they have no choice but to find purchase with them, hanging on all the while to the stability of "core values." So Davis will go on pressing for a sociology that sees the "larger picture" and the history of issues and hears about how the world can be changed. "A new and larger historical narrative may only return when voices from below feel they can speak clearly their own oppositional stories yet are able to link their struggles with others."[96]

"When voices from below feel they can speak clearly . . ." This is an exceedingly important condition, for the philosophers of our turn-of-the-century are cautioning us, in our enthusiasm for the feel-good comprehensive and inclusive and overarching "public space," that as long as conditions of social and economic inequality persist in democratic societies, even the public sphere will be dominated by the privileged and powerful. Davis tells us we must wait for the return of the large historical narrative of Canada until such time as the "voices from below" have spoken to us without fear of supervision and censure. The dream of inclusiveness, warns American theorist Nancy Fraser, is a way of "masking domination by absorbing the less powerful into a false 'we' that reflects the more powerful."[97] Political scientist Claude Denis, in his *We Are Not You: First Nations and Canadian Modernity*, writes flatly that "there is no such thing" as a general public, "all publics . . . are specialized," each with its own set of cultural "texts," the familiarity with which makes a person a member of that particular "public." "In this sense, a public is in fact an interpretive/ imagined community."[98]

The Vancouver artist Hadley Howes spent some time in London, England, studying "public art," and came away from the experience determined never to use the word "community" again, "because it means too much and too little." Students worked on the site of a mouldering housing estate which had been designed twenty-five years before as an ideal community and now was a bleak landscape of International-style apartment blocks marshalled in rows on scrub ground. "We struggled to define the community . . . that was supposedly defined by the border of the estate. I felt uncomfortable about making guesses about these people who saw each other through the light of each other's windows at night."[99] Community is not pre-determined but emerges from what Howes calls "lines of desire," those pathways beaten down by people and animals who repeatedly choose a route of their own, a short cut, across a demarcated space. They are by definition unplanned-for, undisciplined, and peculiar.

Can such community be "public"? Or, as some would ask it, can community be "the" public? Those of us who believed, or hoped, that there was some kind of ideal public into which all diversity and difference would dissolve are challenged by those whom "the public" never did include at one point or another: workers, disenfranchised minorities, women, the disabled, the gay and lesbian, children; and who may have experienced that public as coercive and dominating. In reaction, they formed their own counterpublics or alternative publics. The *lone lost public* never did exist, there is no single overarching public sphere. Get used to it. For the moment, perhaps the best we can do is live in a series of alternative but overlapping publics, linking up our struggles for a social destination we all want, down the road.

Simon Fraser philosopher Ian Angus calls it "a new, universalizing, civilizing compact," an "us-we relationship."[100] As John Ralston Saul noted in *Reflections of a Siamese Twin*, Canadians have understood that we live in several different communities at once that overlap and operate at several levels of intensity and commitment and that we see this as a positive achievement of our culture, not a problem that needs to be solved by erasing our differences in One Big Identity.[101] In the cases of my interviewees, no one embraced separatism and ghettoization; identity politics had become more nuanced, they said repeatedly, more complex and less narcissistic in the face of the need to *re*construct a social space ravaged by racism and discrimination. People preoccupied in the 1980s with the "politics of difference" spoke now of mobilizing on the basis of "shared understanding" rather than assuming a "blithe commonality." Now they spoke of the *public* importance of Ukrainian-Canadian culture, the Canadianness of blackness, the possibility of First Nations and Euro-Canadian cultural hybridity, the fact of interracial sexual desire, the creative potential of "dissonance," and spoke repeatedly of the urgency to revise the Canadian cultural narrative from one of centres and margins to one of intersected identities-in-process.

This allows Lisa McDonald, half-Ukrainian, half-Scottish, to call her own values "cross-cultural"; for John Montesano to believe multiculturalism "works" because it has "created an expanded sense of what a Canadian is" and that the "immigrant experience" is about what we have in common, not what separates us from each other; and for Colleen Whelan to be "very, very proud to say I'm Canadian when I travel," meaning she is proud of Canadian ideals of inclusiveness, including her lesbian identity. "I don't feel so certain of my identity," said Cameron Bailey, "that I can't engage with someone else's." This is Nancy Fraser's "plurality of public arenas" and Ian Angus's "unity articulated through rather than against diversity."[102]

This has made it possible for artist Gary Varro to wrap himself in the flag of Gaynada: a big red heart in place of the maple leaf. It allows the writer Tamas Dobozy to make a joke of it: "Canada isn't its people," a character in his short story "Motherland, Motherland" explains to his Hungarian-born mother. "Canada is a neutral space. This country lets you be whatever you like – Hungarian or Chinese or Italian. And that's the great thing about it: Canada doesn't oblige you to be anything in particular, not even Canadian!"[103]

With the "national project" under attack around the world, Zool Suleman isn't even convinced that being a *Canadian* in particular matters: "You don't have to be a Canadian nationalist to fear a world dominated by Disney culture. To me what matters on a day-to-day basis is spiritual or ethnic identity." For Newfoundlander Maura Hanrahan, there is a "living memory" of the country of Newfoundland that people may be willing to transcend *if* they lived in a true federation with Canada, "where you have a redistribution of resources and you have the idea of the common good, a commonwealth, and where our cultural integrity would be respected and allowed to thrive, and it would be a place where people had a choice about whether they could stay or go and people had a choice about doing the kind of work they wanted to do in the fishing industry and a place where we had control over our destiny." Cameron Bailey understands how

African-American culture is adopted as black Canadians' own, "because it's sold to us at such a high volume, in the first place," but also because it offers a comfort for blacks that simply does not exist in "white" Canada outside the biggest cities. "It's hard to feel at home," he said, in a country that has no "core narrative" of black Canadianness and hasn't made it easy for people of colour to "stitch themselves into the basic narrative," unlike in the U.S. where even a traumatized "blackness" is integral to the idea of the nation from its very origins. Ahasiw Maskegon-Iskwew feels he lives at a place of "rupture" between the failure of the Euro-Canadian ideal and the strengthening Aboriginal creative voice, which opens up the core self as an instance of the "very human, very deep common experience," not necessarily Canadian.

These pluralities were equally true of sexual identity, of "grrls" in the (sister)hood, of queer identities that opened up to all kinds of gender inter-ferences, and insisted on their public performance.

When in 1987 Gary Kinsman wrote his pioneering *The Regulation of Desire: Sexuality in Canada*, he located gay and lesbian liberation in the social movements of the late 1960s, notably women's liberation, with its focus on gender and sex. Homosexual men and women "may have affirmed the need for lesbians and gay men to come out and help build public com-munities," but the notion of "community," he warned presciently, had its limitations.[104] By agitating for "minority community" status within main-stream culture, gays and lesbians directed attention away from the *social deviance* of their sexual practice – all those "bad" queens and "bad" dykes – and onto their social respectability as what Kinsman called a socially acceptable "commercial ghetto."

Since his book was published, the "bad" boys and girls of queer culture have noisily stormed out of the ghetto, flying all over the social space of mainstream sexual culture as "gay women/wimmin/womyn, female homo-sexuals, lesbians, butches, femmes, bulldaggers, lipstick lesbians, tomboys, bisexuals, leather daddies, butch bottoms, femme tops, girljocks, baby dykes, F2M's, machas, two-spirited persons, transgendered warriors, earth mothers," to speak only of the women, as the *queering absinthe* editorial collective did in 1996.[105]

But the question of whether such diversity of sexual practice and gender identity leads to *public* community, not to mention social revolution, hung in the air after my conversations with the queers. Being outrageous was all very well, but did this constitute an act of citizenship, to borrow from Dan Gawthrop? If, within "queer," it didn't really matter any more who you slept with, "then by what criteria do we form community?" Rachel Giese wondered.[106] Like his cultural hero, Bruce LaBruce, Winnipeg film-maker Noam Gonick already refers to being "post-queer." Now that queer has been "co-opted by academia and become the topic of every fucking thesis out of OCA [Ontario College of Art] in the 1990s and made very boring, now that it's been taken out of the hands of the cutting-edge, front-line revolutionaries, the artists, the activists, the sex trade workers, the junkies, the people who make life worth living, and become something to be studied, it's time to jump ship." He's post-gay too, and like LaBruce hates the word gay, "*gay* in the sort of big puffy letters, 1970s-flashing-sign kind of bubble-gum gay." On the other hand, Gonick firmly believes that there is meaning out there in the world for those who celebrate their distinctiveness, their differences, from the society at large. He had done some thinking about this, about what gay men like LaBruce and himself, who are already post-queer, have to "offer." Given his left-wing world view, the offering is obvious: Gay men have something to contribute to *society*. "As shamans. Healers. I've got the books, it's documented, it's what we've always been. That's a lot more powerful then being a retail queen co-opted by capitalism."

The trap for people of my generation – of the 1960s and 1970s – is the nostalgia for the political *solidarity* that the earlier social movements stood for, but feminists after us, such as Lise Gotell, who teaches that history, don't present feminism as being *about* solidarity or even collectivity but as a "series of debates organized around a common goal that permits us to have political differences." Shawna Dempsey and Lorri Millan called the queer movement an "umbrella" under which all people "who want to change things" gather; they unambiguously put themselves within a history of social justice movements everywhere, a history that includes what they call "testifying," the individual who gets up in front of her sisters and brothers and tells her story. "We don't want to be viewed as lesbian specimens," Dempsey told *BorderCrossings'* Robert Enright. "We want an empathy with a larger community, with a movement in politics that includes all of us."[107]

> During these years, when tensions and failures are more likely
> to be the order of the day than resolutions and successes, it will
> help to have another social destination in our imagination.
> — Robert Heilbroner, *Twenty-First Century Capitalism*

My conversations and readings for this book have swirled repeatedly, in myriad variations, around what numerous writers and citizen-thinkers had zeroed in on, in the broadest of terms, as the fundamental conflict of our times: the preservation of community life versus the privatizing of social bonds by the market. But there was a recurrent motif to their anxiety, verging on the obsessive: the viability into the new century of the public health-care system in Canada. That system's importance, it seemed to me, was being forced to bear the burden of a deeply felt but implied meaning: that the social self that had been the work of generations was in serious danger of derangement.

> With glowing hearts, we see thee rise
> In the true north, health is free.
> — Christopher Levan, "A Cure for Canada's Cultural
> Amnesia," *Edmonton Journal*, June 28, 1998

Public health care is a treasure because – as Neil Brooks, public policy and tax lawyer put it to the participants at a 1997 Saskatoon conference on health – it is fair, it is compassionate, it balances power between business and workers, it is popular, it promotes social cohesion, and it gives citizens credit for having "civic desires and preferences" as well as "consumer choices." But this whole set of assumptions and experiences was imperilled by a counter-culture of "private greed" whose criticism that medicare wasn't affordable had been "misleading, without evidence and morally reprehensible and conceptually incoherent," Brooks asserted with impressive umbrage. The real agenda, he said, was a "redistribution of wealth and power upward," and we applauded in hearty agreement. And when he concluded with an impassioned reminder that "the worst legacy to our own children is not the debt but a society without a sense of itself and collective responsibility," the room resonated not just with people's memory of the great thing they had done in solidarity with each other all those years ago in Saskatchewan but also with the hope that its meaning would be translated into the new and very different lives of the young.

Two years later Tom Kent, who, as an adviser to prime minister Lester Pearson, had been one of the architects of the medicare system, railed against succeeding governments for their "political betrayal" of the system by destroying its financial basis.[108] It made me think of Jennifer Welsh of d-Code and how her research had shown her generation supported social programs in favour of tax cuts, which she took to be "incredibly good news," and her hope that the social commitment to have "every Canadian with a health card" would not be eroded. And I thought back to my interview with Kyle Shaw at Halifax's *Coast* newspaper and his diffidence about his own sentimentality about Canada, and how I pushed him to say why exactly he would "certainly love" to have Canada "stay together." What would be lost if it didn't? "I run this newspaper," he offered. "It's based in Canada. I must have some sort of connection with Canadian culture. Maybe it's just socialized medicine." But it was on its way out, unless we were all really careful, I pressed him. His generation could lose it if we didn't stop the politicians right away. There was a very long pause. "There will always be a Canada," he finally replied. "Here, there seems to be less of a competitive capitalist approach to things than in the U.S. There's a little bit of collectivism . . ." And I thought, If he can still see that, perhaps the "betrayal" has not been complete?

Over and over again, Canadians viewed from every which angle tell those who ask that their sense of themselves as distinctly Canadian is seamless with the viability of public health care. It is a "defining characteristic" of Canada and therefore of ourselves in communion with each other. In 1996, doctors and other health professionals left their positions at York University's student health facilities rather than sign a contract with the U.S.-based company that had leased the operation. "We felt somewhat offended that multi-billion-dollar corporations would be making money on the back of the Canadian health-care system," said the doctors' spokesman.[109] Interviewed in *L'Actualité*, Dr. Paul Lévesque of the severely stressed Maisonneuve-Rosemont Hospital in Montreal categorically rejected any degree of privatization as a solution to his hospital's woes: "We have a unique health-care system, it perfectly reflects our Canadian fibre. More than with any other thing, Canadians identify with our social programs. The political class has to understand that, if they want to save this country, they must give first priority to this problem."[110]

They do seem to have understood some of that urgency. In 1999, in Ottawa, echoing the sustained and vociferous arguments made by health activists and supporters over a decade of painful cuts, the finance minister Paul Martin conceded that more federal spending was required to help build a modern economy, including "reinvestments" in health. It was an acknowledgement, better late than never, of the Canadian way of doing things, including how public funds are spent.[111] Pressed to reassure us that Canada would not give in to American demands to open up health services to trade liberalization at World Trade Organization negotiations, trade minister Pierre Pettigrew grew eloquent: "I can tell you loud and clear that any suggestion that health and social services are in danger is preposterous. Canada's health-care and education systems are models for the rest of the world."[112] It was as though the political class, after what had seemed an interminable regimen of New Right nostrums about how to run a country, had woken up to the fact that the public would give a mandate to the federal government for only as long as that government was seen to be defending the "last of the great social programs," health.[113] For millions of Canadians the public health-care system *was* their country.

Somehow, in spite of the vulnerability of our arts and media to the clamour of the marketplace of American entertainment and infotainment, in spite of the dismal achievement of public schooling in reproducing the standard history, if any history at all, in spite of the solipsisms of identity reduced to the private self, there is nevertheless a broad consensus, according to the public and pundits alike, that Canada is worth defending not just as a country but as an *idea* of a country. It is the materialization of a *moral* idea, to use Richard Gwyn's phrase, that, through tolerance, civility, public order, and a genius for compromise we have created a society in which millions of diverse peoples cohere in a culture of fundamental fairness and decency. Philosopher Trudy Govier argues that our complex society can only function on a basis of "social trust," an ethical web of beliefs and expectations that implicate us in the transcendent hope of communal harmony.[114] In B.C., journalist Terry Glavin took his inspiration from the civility of the Supreme Court's finding in the Delgamuukw lands claim case that placed Aboriginal oral evidence on an equal footing with common-law tests of occupation and ownership. The decision reminds us, wrote Glavin, "that this is Canada, and we do things a certain way here."[115] We are a light unto the nations. Author Peter C. Newman argues we Canadians have been creating, as if "instinctively," a new kind of political culture and personality he thinks of as "sophisticated democracy," common to us all through citizenship. He borrows from writer Scott Symons the image of the "thinking heart" as the fused capacity for reflection and compassion we have been "groping" our way toward.[116]

Human beings, not just Canadians, are under unprecedented pressure from the expansion of free markets, the shrinking of their workplace with the off-loading of labour to other parts of the world, the aggressive domination of our consciousness by advertising. "So we are all struggling with making sense of this and what we should be as citizens," says Mark Kingwell. "The only way to make sense is to think clearly at the deepest level about what we think we are up to. Ask ourselves that question."

In their working lives, the young Canadians of my enquiry, even at the leading edge of technologies and innovations, even when self-employed with a vengeance, share with others in labour unions and labour advocacy a firm belief in the primary value of all labour. Paul Tartaglio, the Starbucks *barista* member of the Canadian Auto Workers, had called it stitching the "social fabric," whether this was in the struggle for the dignity of labour in a coffee shop, or in the pooling of community resources to save a fishery or the rearing of the First Nations young, or social activism in an industrial labour union. They hoped to work in collaborative workplaces, gathered together in what Jennifer Welsh called "communal space," at a job they saw as a vocation, in which the ethical means triumphed over the financial ends. They wanted to be socially responsible with technology, and class-conscious with profit-making. Peter van Stolk, for example, was acutely aware of the symbiotic relationship between his soft drink business and the "community" whose financial support he was dependent on. None was unaware of the extraordinary privilege of their lives compared with those of toilers in the developing world. Entrepreneurs of small business believed their local enterprises were a "return to community" at a time when global stationers and hardwares and computer companies are parking in megaplexes in the suburbs. There was not a single person among my interviewees who spoke for the "right" to enrich himself or herself at the expense of others. If anything, eschewing this "right" was what made them Canadian, they argued.

Right, left, or centre, they acknowledged the responsibility discharged throughout the Canadian collective for maintaining the social safety net and the core social conscience. That they would believe this, tenaciously, in a precarious economic context, was entirely unexpected.

For at the heart of the struggle between these two cultures of community and market is the issue of commitment to social spending: are we to be privately self-reliant or socially co-operative in having our needs met as Canadians? Loss or diminution of programs has devastated the capacity of community collectively to fulfill responsibility, as the young workers in the health clinic, the food bank, the street drop-in, have said, and yet they and their supporters hang in, even as the gap between the rich and the poor widens, for they hope, as Seth Klein hopes at the Canadian Centre for Policy Alternatives, to "reshift our culture" and make concrete in everyday lives the ideal of social solidarity. Activists of that solidarity talk of working in a "community of the poor," honouring the dignity and need to belong and the equal importance of the lives of poor people. Years after it had been declared too expensive to afford, they reinvent the Canadian social experiment, and extend it, with truly internationalist imagination, to passionate agitprop against the sweatshops and *maquiladoras* of Asia and Latin America. With an ecological consciousness bound with deep feelings of connection to the Canadian "wild," they assume on-going responsibility as a new generation to defend it from rapacious and ruinous development.

Active resistance to the manipulations of the New World Order takes place in the non-cynical need for post-ironic meaning and emotion. Think of the humour and pleasure of reclaiming the streets as public property, the glee of "jamming" the bullying culture of advertising, the exhilaration of throwing spanners into the works of APEC and MAI and WTO, whatever it takes to obstruct the logic of the market bent on deconstructing collectivities. In resistance's necessary collectivity comes the in-gathering of community and memory, the conservation of what Pierre Bourdieu calls the "heritage of words, traditions and representations"[117] that constitute what society remembers of what it has done in the past. "Let us not be reticent,"

John Kenneth Galbraith urged his audience at the University of Toronto. "We, the socially concerned, are the custodians of the political tradition and action that saved classical capitalism from itself."[118] Is this why so many of my subjects insisted on the primacy of public health care in the Canadian social system: because they saw their generation as trustees of tradition across the threshold of a new century?

> I think it's a result of globalization. As people see borders dis-
> appear, they look for neighbourhood and community where they
> *know* somebody. If you're in a room where the walls suddenly
> disappear, you want to find a corner.
>
> – Wes Borg

The editor-publishers of Calgary's *Spank!* e-zine, for all their cheerful openness to an international readership of computer-literates, told me they see *Spank!* as "avowedly Canadian, except for our spelling." Stephen Cassady sounded a little cheesed off about that, but Robin Thompson defended the decision to go with "color," not "colour," on the grounds that 68 per cent of their readers are American. "But, given the choice to cover an interesting American artist and an interesting Canadian one, we'll always choose the Canadian." Cassady added that, while it is not always important to say when a story is Canadian, it is definitely important to say when it's American, "because if it is American-specific, I don't want it to be thought of as Canadian. I don't want to start believing the American myth that, if it's *their* problem – for example, mass homelessness, or weapons or gangs – then it's ours too."

So Cassady did not agree there is a single continental culture or that the Internet erases national frontiers: "Internet is the channel *between* cultural differences. Unionism, for example, is a Canadian trait, and that's why Wal-Mart and Starbucks are facing union challenges in Canada. . . . By the way, did you know Americans eat four hundred calories a day more than Canadians?" On the other hand, *Spank!* didn't breathe a word about Canada's flag debates in the House of Commons but did ask readers what they thought of the American high school teacher who had a baby by her thirteen-year-old student.

> I think Canadians are cool. Anyone from Canada is all right by
> me. . . . Anyone from Ohio?
> – "It's Groovy Baby!" hotlink, *Spank!* e-zine, September 1997

Jeff Nachtigall had his heart set on going to art school in the U.S. when he had finished high school in Regina. He gave Illinois a year of his life and right away started painting pictures of moose. "I realized I was a Canadian, that I was someplace no one else was. The Americans asked me to say 'about'; they thought it was so cute. I knew there were differences between us, and that, once I was there, in America, I loved being a Canadian." It fell into place the day he went to see the blockbuster American movie *Clear and Present Danger*. Nachtigall and I were drinking slow beers in a Regina free house. For two hours I stared at the crown of his baseball cap, which he never took off, at the grubby little decal of the Canadian flag sewn there. "There's a line that James Earl Jones says to Harrison Ford," he continued, relishing this anecdote. "He says, 'Don't do this for me, do it for the Boss,' meaning the President. Ford says, 'No, no, we do it for the people of the United States!' Well, I giggled. I was in a theatre packed with people staring raptly at the screen, and I was giggling. And I thought: How come in Canada we'd never ever hear a character in a movie say, 'Do this for the people of Canada!'? I mean, it would sound silly."

But as soon as he was back in Saskatchewan, he started a painting called "Canadian Content" of four animals, crow, cow, moose, and alligator. The moose and cow were "obvious," he said, the crow was the prairie vulture, and the alligator represented "history." It was in East End, Saskatchewan, that the biggest-ever skeleton of Tyrannosaurus Rex was found. "The painting is about looking where I am." Later, he did a little tin-plated box on wheels, with a large caged door like a perambulating jailhouse, three moose imprisoned within, and the stylized blood-red flames of a campfire on the attic door, in a show called "Cannon Fodder." "Fire, flames, a moose within the cage: it's very Canadian," he said.

In his *Borderlands: How We Talk About Canada*, W. H. New talks about the idea of "boundary" not as a *cordon sanitaire* flung around a territory to keep infectious ideas at bay, nor as a passive medium of cultural exchanges, but as an "opportunity" to assert alternative expressions that give voice to Canadians' own thoughts, and hear and see and read those of their compatriots. Canadian art will persist, he claims, as long as we want to act out our own social alternatives. The true threat to our distinctiveness is not that we cease acting it out but that we substitute it for someone else's action, namely Americans'.[119]

More than once in the course of conversations with the next generation of Canadians I was told that, unlike my generation, the younger Canadians aren't "scared" of American culture. They've lived with it all their lives and still haven't been vaporized into the American ether. Others, post-nationals, seemed sanguine that "Canada" as a site of identity may disappear. It was the anti-APEC activist Jaggi Singh who told me that the protesters at UBC had burned a Canadian flag "to show our disgust" at the "ugly Canadian" syndrome, in which a trade delegation goes to China hoping to sell Candu nuclear reactors. "People talk now about Canada's loss of innocence [in the modern world] but it never was innocent. This country was founded on principles of greed, exploitation and genocide." But when he and his comrades burned the flag, he admitted that he got an "adrenalin rush" from it, as though the bit of scorched cloth actually did mean something.

The meaning rests in what we may call the "outer nation" of publicly constituted symbolic acts and institutions which we all recognize as elements of our "we-ness," and it is in this externalized self that so many Canadians, many of my interviewees included, feel their distinctiveness threatened and their attachment to the idea of a country weakening. There were numerous nods at the CBC as a "uniquely" Canadian institution with "top-notch" programming that would otherwise not see the light of day, but there was corresponding alarm about its future – its funding, its commitment to Canadian content, its proposal to the CRTC to name shows after corporations. This alarm about an endangered cultural "specie" was perhaps the source of the copious weeping even among twenty-somethings when Peter Gzowski's long-lived *Morningside* radio program finally went off the air. The show had enjoyed the reputation of being the "glue" that bound so many listeners to each other, strangers flung together across the air waves, but, "if only 15 per cent of the country's listening," Geoff Pevere wrote irritably in *Mondo Canuck*, "who is holding everybody else's country together?"[120]

"Most Canadians will remember that 25 years ago, a hockey player named Paul Henderson scored a goal for Team Canada in Moscow to win the Summit Series against the Soviet Union," wrote sports reporter James Christie in 1997, and I suppose they will, provided they had already been born or had immigrated by 1977. I remember catching the sound of the game off a book editor's transistor radio – apparently three out of four Canadians were similarly tuned in – although I did not understand the nature of the euphoria of fans whose self-doubt could be so deeply assuaged by a fluke of the puck. But I did understand the grieving disbelief of fans when Wayne Gretzky announced at a press conference in Edmonton in 1988 he had been traded to the Americans. When he pulled on a new L.A. Kings jersey with silver lettering and wiped tears from his eyes, our humiliation was total: Gretzky the artist was mere spoils in continental gladiatorial games. "If Gretzky hadn't gone to Los Angeles," wrote Stephen Brunt in the *Globe and Mail*, "they might still be playing in Winnipeg and Quebec City," not to mention how the kids might still be playing on the frozen ponds of a thousand flooded prairie gardens in the bracing cold of deep winter, all dreaming of one day taking their place in the genealogy of Maurice Richard, Bobby Orr, and Wayne Gretzky. "The Greeks want the Elgin marbles that were swiped from them, and the Scots got their Stone of Scone. We'll take Gretzky any time, just to help make us whole."[121] The lyricism of the mythology of the great game now seemed a virtue of an earlier, more earthy and communitarian time, impossible to resuscitate in a world of crass business deals – "Puck" Pocklington sells the Great One for a mess of pottage – except in the marketed nostalgia of beer ads, a world in which guys still know what to do with a crumpled can and stick as they walk, swinging briefcases, down Bay Street and into a game of shinny.

This shrinking of expressive alternatives undermines democracy, in the thinking of media analysts who define the cultural development of citizens as the process by which they acquire precisely the individual and collective resources necessary to participate in public life. The political will may slacken under pressure of economic agendas, but if democracy is to survive, "cultural development must be oriented towards the public interest," writes Marc Raboy.[122] I gloomily considered the prospects for the public interest in the parsimoniousness of arts funding agencies, in the retreat of citizens into the privacy and isolation of microcultures of television, and in the global epidemic of programming emanating from what Canadian writer Brian Fawcett has called the Akron Design Center, smack in the middle of America Inc. and beamed at miniaturized audiences with ever more tenuous relationship with their own historical and social experience.

Is cyberspace a public space? Critics argue for and against the sociability of the Net and whether relatedness and responsibility to immediate others can be recreated there. The optimists among my interviewees claim it as a new site of social integration and community-building and make use of it to communicate around the world with like-minded souls, overlapping their fractured selves with the hope of some kind of integration in the sharing of a project, or just a conversation. "Online tools are just that," said Erin Clarke at Web Networks, "and it's *people* who use them for communicating." The technologies and software of the new media are broadly available and spread democracy around, in the vision of Ana Serrano of MediaLinx. *Spank!*'s editors are enthusiastic about the electronic in-gathering of generational rather than geographical community.

But my interviewees were optimistic, even visionary. Some artists have not so much occupied public space – you need grants for that – as created a parallel or alternative notion of the public, as with interactive art on the Internet or DIY sound recording or free zines and e-zines produced on the fly or independent film production in "pools." Alternative newspapers "speak to community," I was told, alternative publishing creates "free zones," readers are citizens not consumers. Regions, languages, genders, and ancestors or elders all exist as communities of art as well. But they all seem to be working in a Canadian "headspace," in which Canadian content and Canadian skill are not only taken utterly for granted but actively desired. This was a space defiantly of their own action, nurturing a biodiversity of technical skills, a forum of the non-commercial and anti-corporate in which the public was invited to assemble and reflect. But this Canadian headspace was above all – it was said to me repeatedly – a communication among their own people, Canadians, for communicability was their first obligation, circulating the "stories" that bring communities together in an "inner nation" of shared desires.

Global penetration of local and national cultures is a real and present danger, but the creative intelligence of young Canadians remains transfixed by the possibility of retribalizing, of drawing into circles of relatedness, even at the computer interface, by the power of their own story-telling. They have not arrived at the page or screen or canvas alone, they do not sit in the blue-lit dark without company, the stories they circulate are not just phantasms of a private dreamtime. They listen, they imagine, they watch – as members of a commonwealth of memory.

The Next Canada   VI

> . . . I discovered I had a Canadian heart beating inside me.
>
> — Seth Klein

Although I have declared that this project of mapping the "next Canada" was completely open-ended as to the conclusions I would draw from it, I admit that I was always especially alert to evidence that the people I was talking with represented some continuity with the political culture that I grew up in – the post-war culture that preceded what I think of as the Great Rupture of 1988, the year of the federal election that decided Canada would sign the Free Trade Agreement. I did not *choose* my interviewees for that evidence, but I always noted it when it presented itself. And at the end of the interviewing process, with the hundreds of hours of conversation saturating my thoughts, I began to discern a theme of that continuity. If, by the old political culture, the *pre-revolutionary* culture, we mean the Canada in which the institutions and morality of the public interest dominated over the private, there is at least anecdotal evidence from my interviewees, as this book has laid out, that the public space in which that interest had agency has not been completely evacuated.

These are instances of the reiteration, after so many years of a grim morality of survival-of-the-fittest, of something like hope. There is the persistent identification with the idea of Canada as a shared "commons" of social consciousness. Although economic well-being is important, my interviewees were not prepared to give up everything for it. Given the ubiquity of globalizing American culture and values, they can be said to have *chosen*, not simply inherited, as was true of my generation, Canadian values, or what philosopher Ian Angus calls the "communitarian tradition – the virtue of putting community before the individual most of the time,"

rooted in the social history of Canada. (Erin Clarke spoke of her generation's "cultural hunger" for rootedness that American mass media claim
spuriously to satisfy.) I was told, over and over again, that the only authentic satisfaction lay in a Canadian heritage of compassion by which we have
collectively and repeatedly agreed to defer individual and sectoral
gratification to the public interest. But that act of deferral translates over
time as the projection into the future, translates, in other words, as hope. A
decade earlier, in Doug Coupland's novel *Generation X*, a character says of
his boomer parents that he envies "their upbringings that were so clean, so
free of *futurelessness*."[1] Well may he envy the sense of *futurefulness* of those
coming after him.

Canada is a "covenant between the generations," wrote Andrew Coyne.
"A country is not located only in space but in time."[2] In this he may find
agreement with his ideological adversaries on the postmodern Left, who
have come to view Canada as the provisional outcome of a series of debates
through time, in Jeremy Webber's formulation. "Members [of a democratic
community] come to care about public issues through the terms of that
debate."[3] The contents of the debate will be various according to the time
in which they are argued, but their framing, their range, and the historical
context against which arguments are judged are inherited from earlier generations and are the way in which the past reproduces itself in the present,
beyond any individual choice or creation.

In this sense, all those, left and right, who look backward into or project
forward into Canadian society for social patterns, for traditions, are conservatives compared to the revolutionaries of the Free Trade Agreement.
For the revolutionaries, the corporatist language of markets supersedes any
particular language of Canadianness, open borders and mobility are privileged over traditional settlement, and globalization and mass communication deliver the benefits of dissolving difference. "The ideology of the new
world order held that there are no different places," observed French journalist Serge Halimi.[4]

Along with the new order there has been an unstoppable retreat from
the hinterland from which we have drawn so much of our imaginative sus-
tenance, according to Richard Gwyn. He and I were talking of the pressure
on the idea of a territorial Canadian nationalism from Aboriginal land
claims and non-Native colonial guilt and ecological consciousness of

environmental degradation – all of it attenuating the sense of "belonging" to a specific physical and historical place – when Gwyn pointed out that Canadians are also literally leaving the land to settle in urban islands, immigrants and offshore fishers and ex-farmers all moving to the cities: "Canada is retreating from Canada."

As against placelessness, some scholars have located identity in the "rooted, limited, and specific"[5] – think Newfoundland, think Quebec, think Poundmaker Reserve. But this is not how the young postmoderns think about their national identity. They begin with a great discomfort, the ambiguity of "here." Whereas my generation accepted that "here" was a defined geohistorical place that needed only to be "named" in order to be appropriated, novelist Evan Solomon said, "We inhabit stories, not places."[6] In a conversation on CBC Radio's *Ideas* on the end of the nation-state, the French intellectual Jean-Marie Guehenno thought he detected in most people of the Western democracies a need to be reassured of a physical sense of solidarity – "of being part of the same crowd, of the same place" – that had historically been satisfied by living in "territorial community" known as the nation-state. Nowadays, "there's a great malaise when you realize that maybe you are there, but *there* isn't so relevant."[7] But my interviewees did not talk like that. "Nationalism, having your own state, is passé," declared Jennifer Welsh, echoing several others for whom the Canadian "project" was to make many nations and many cultures together work together. Waving little flags was beside the point when what is needed is a "vision" rather than a set of institutions.

The characters that novelist Russell Smith sends rushing about downtown Toronto's clubs and restaurants are in hot pursuit of the forever-receding realm of Americanized, hyper-urban "cool," not to be confused with the extravagantly embodied characters in the literature of the 1960s with their "return to the land," their cultivation of the organic and sensual in mystical union with the "sad cry of the loon," as Smith argued in a review of the anthology *Concrete Forest: The New Fiction of Urban Canada*, edited by Hal Niedzviecki. The twenty-somethings, he wrote, "were desperate for stories about hamburgers, subways, television, anything but bloody loons."

At home in the city, Russell goes on, his generation experiences a rootlessness and vague internationalism that, thanks to electronic media, is now a sensibility the entire country may embrace: "technological, international, media-soaked."[8] It wasn't just urban originality the hyper-urban Hal Niedzviecki was looking for in the new fiction, he wrote in his introduction, but also for "invoked landscapes recognizable to those of us whose lives are interlocked with the conflicts and crises we share as Canadians." He referred to the theme of "shared metaphorical landscape" that unifies many of the stories he has collected, the "constant communication," not solitude, among characters and their "camaraderie," albeit reluctant.[9] If this is rootlessness and denationalized urbanity, it has been assumed under protest. As though purposely to link his project to the cultural nationalism of the preceding generation, Niedzviecki epigrammatically cited Margaret Atwood's canonical *Survival,* and I note that, in a nice flourish of solidarity with all those urbanly challenged Canadian painters of actual landscape, he metaphorized the brave new urbanism lying just beyond the last suburban mall exit as a *forest.*

Some of my interviewees knew they were challenged in their feeling of being at home by the dislocation of immigration and migration, and by a certain degree of "disquiet" and "uncertainty" given their differing sense of history or lineage from those who have been generations rooted in Canada. Others felt themselves to be members of several "nations" – racial, gendered, linguistic – whose boundaries kept moving around in the flux of change and which sometimes overlapped with the older, fixed boundary of a historical Canada located in specific space and time. As migrants, not fully participating as Canadian "subjects" in a white-dominant society, people of colour were the original postmoderns, "because we had to be," Cameron Bailey proposed. "But you know what? I don't think that's a bad thing. I think it produces really interesting people, and I like the sort of dissonance and the unsettled quality that a lot of black Canadians have as compared to the certainty of a lot of African-American culture."

Others, considering the history of Quebec and English-Canada's relations, noting this is a history of negotiation and compromise and renegotiation since the day after the Conquest, conclude we should finally accept that the long co-existence, whether troubled or pacified, of the Aboriginal, francophone, and anglophone, is the foundational complexity of Canada, *is* the nation. Perhaps by this process of necessary and mostly civil mediation and improvisation, even of sometimes violent error and bewilderment, it has evolved precisely toward what so many have discerned as

Canadians' greater faith in the community over the heroic individual, what W. H. New calls the "coping community" that desires connectedness over difference.[10]

Where my generation experienced the Canadian "identity crisis" as a form of neurosis (internalized colonialism) or malaise (powerlessness) to be cured of by specific public policy decisions (public support of publishing, say, or creation of a Foreign Investment Review Agency), Ana Serrano talks of the identity crisis as part of "being" Canadian. She does not find the crisis regrettable but sees it as the opportunity for the development of a series of "morphed" identities: "Are we a techno-culture, an art, a social community, or a political space?" Our deepest resources, writes B. W. Powe, lie in "flux."[11]

In any event, several of my subjects argued, Canadian cultural nationalism misses the point that the power really to be contended with is not American chauvinism or cultural imperialism but "market capitalism." Acadian cultural activist Ronald Bourgeois in Nova Scotia feared that being Acadian or having a superior health-care system "means nothing when you're watching TV." For Cameron Bailey the problem lies not in American television shows as such but in their gross commodification through a relentless globalization of media. "It's about *selling* this stuff," and emotional or moral arguments about the "superiority" of Canadian cultural production are not going to win that battle.

Art historian Kevin Matthews is no anti-American – there is much about America that is "fun" and "exciting" and he loves to travel there – but he *hates* corporate America (the one my generation called Amerika), detests Disney at a visceral level, and feels enormously guilty about shopping at Wal-Mart. "The trouble with Canadian content," he confessed, "is that you run out of material." Intellectually, he accepted that Canada is culturally colonized, but he didn't *feel* oppressed. Besides, people who are oppressed always end up absorbing and exchanging ideas with the culture that's trying to assimilate them, and that's where really interesting art comes from: friction. Yet even he acknowledged that the border, a "permeable membrane," is still *there* and we can still resent the Americans. "I don't think anyone wants to let go of that, even though I've thought that the ultimate postmodern nation would not be based on geography but on a system of networks."

Read your McLuhan, your Harold Innis and Arthur Kroker and Derek de Kerckhove, all theorists of the "body electric," of Canada as a virtual community – "always has been," said Mark Kingwell, "a wired world, one of the most wired on the globe" – of Canada as a system of communications across distance; think fur trade routes and railways and telegraphs and now telecommunications. "Canada is this telegraphic string," Kingwell went on, warming to the theme, "beads on a wire . . . able to transcend this huge geographical distance and make it work."

There is irony in this vision. While we have typically thought our Canadianness was shaped by the fact of our vulnerability in unfathomable geophysical space, we have been shaping it by the relentless shrinking of that space to metaphor, the "electric city of the teleworld," wrote B. W. Powe, the "alchemical transformation of self."[12]

But is everything transformed in that alchemy, so that nothing remains of the original molecular structure of Canadian self-knowledge? Dissonance, for all its creativity, does not preclude an attachment to Canadian citizenship or identity. It's a matter of putting it into play with a number of other different elements of identity at the same time, like satellites whirling and transmuting around a core Canadian self. Others used the language of "discourses," "multiple selves," and "contingent connections or organizations of interest," but at the end of the day, in front of his philosophy students, Mark Kingwell too acknowledged that the way in which we "make things happen," hold ourselves and others to social responsibility, is with a "unified consciousness."

"It may be fractured," he said, "it may be fussy, it may be variable and contingent and all those things. And that may be great. But if I am not *me*, from day to day, then nothing is possible."

Kevin Matthews has tried his best to be Canadian. He was a proud fan of Peter Gzowski, so charismatic a presence on radio that "he could have been American and I would still have listened to him," and he visited the Expo 67 site in Montreal only to find there wasn't much there, not even other people. The amusement park was closed, so he walked to the top of a small hill to look around at the buildings he'd become familiar with from photographs, only to see spread before him grey polygons surrounded by gaudy amusement park structures, a casino, and the ruined hulk of the Canada Pavilion, poorly built on a wooden frame with stucco sheathing and now become ramshackle. He thought he saw some squatters in residence, a sign of some sort of life.

His friends at art school talked a lot about Expo 67, how it was supposed to have been this great moment of unity for all Canadians, to hear their parents tell of it, but he thought it was more likely that, what with the whole world arriving for a visit, Canadians just pretended to get along. "Company's coming, we can't be fighting." He knows that being Canadian now means "celebrating" doubt and inconclusiveness, that the great convictions of the past weren't inclusive enough, and that the "convinced and dedicated stance to one single cause" was born of ignorance, because, if he thinks about it, throughout the course of Canadian history we have always doubted ourselves. "Still, sometimes I feel wistful and wish I was clear about where I stood in the world." I knew he was feeling wistful about that older generation who in hindsight seemed to know exactly where they stood, when the world was still laid out on a fixed grid of nation, class, sex, culture, and who acted accordingly, as anti-war activists or feminists or eco-terrorists. Matthews might find consolation in Marshall McLuhan's dictum that Canada is the only country in the world that knows how to live without an identity. And it is in their ease with such a proposal that I see the place where my generation of Canadian patriots ends and the next begins.

> Last night there were no Nazis by my window. I lay awake with country radio and a picture of the Spice Girls by my side. In my land I am still allowed to exercise political choice! I want the CN Tower and Robert Kroetsch to reach an enlightened solution. Can we not love our stone cloaks *and* dry, brittle bones? . . .
> – "Psalm," Jonathan Garfinkel

"Are some countries more postmodern than others?" sociologist Marilyn Porter asked in 1995. The question had been provoked by her own self-confessed naive belief that there *is* a real world out there – of distressed fishing communities on coastal Newfoundland, for instance – whose problems really exist and whose hopes for emancipation rise above postmodernism's vision of the futility of politics that fragment in "endless plurality and fluidity."[13] What about the fish? we want to cry. We can see they have disappeared from the theoretical discourse, but the point for us is that they have *actually* disappeared. Whatever timely correctives post-modernism has offered to our unthinking liberalism and nationalism and ethnocentrism, what we need now is not more diffusion of "totalities" but a "completion of emancipation."

This is all the more urgent given the younger generations' capacity to feel at home in a virtual or representational, even symbolically Canadian, media universe while actual Canada – its shrunken social programs, its undefended cultural organs, its traumatized environment – disappears.

But Claude Denis, in conversation about postmodernism's effects, thought it a "caricature" to say they were apolitical. Postmodernism is properly skeptical about the "quasi-religious hope for human emancipation" in the grand old narratives of Marxism and Leninism: "Postmodernism draws some lessons from the century's history, that sometimes the highest hopes produce the worst results. There are limits to what politics can accomplish."

We can look back to the twentieth century's highest hopes of social revolution, all the "isms" that elaborated societies' desire for justice and equality and fellowship, and be instructed by the results; we can, that is, look deep into the spirit of our own age in which we invest that same desire, and find in the new century the same "excesses" of modernity, greed and cruelty of economic globalization and its moral vacuity. Yet Claude Denis goes on to assert that even though modernity has tried to remove spirituality from the centre of human life, the individual able to stand against the community "is not possible."

> How do we think about our relationship to ideas that are not quite true?
>
> – Interview with Ian Angus, Vancouver, 1998

Stephen Cassady's parents have always had two cars, he has always had colour TV, he's never not had access to public transportation, he's never not had medicare. Stephen Cassady, electronic magazine publisher in Calgary, is younger than medicare. "Do you think all that just dropped out of the sky?" I asked. "Yeah, it's very natural," he said.

By "natural" he seemed to mean that that was just how things are, in Canada. Assaults on social programs were part of a cycle, he figured, the political swings back and forth, the shifts, the modifications and changes, over the long haul of history. "But you can't permanently damage things. I think that in Canada there are some inalienable trends that have existed historically. Canada will always be a social-system-supporting country with health care and advances in education and in telecommunications. Without it we're toast." I didn't ask about the U.S., but he brought it up, with the accusation against its culture that it is loud and abusive and exploitive and doesn't support its own citizens. Cassady feels supported. "Canada has a magnificent support structure and it reflects in our youth. We don't see here the problems that our neighbours to the south have with mass unemployment and mass homelessness. We've got good health care, social assistance, great schooling. That's what still breeds each generation. And it gives each one the sense they are going somewhere."

This seemed very wise to me. I don't suppose Cassady has ever heard of the social philosopher Ian Angus, much less read him, so perhaps there is an intuitive kind of wisdom that one sucks up from the *Zeitgeist*, for it was Angus who said, in talking with me about health care, that it is because of social movements that "we don't live in the type of technological empire that George Grant talked about in *Technology and Empire*, when he argued that we would have to give up all our particularities to become abstracted nobody-in-particular" in the new age of technology. The social movements have kept Canadian society "livable" by the perennial visionary act of reimagining the future. And when people say "health care is, therefore I am," they're saying hopefully, Angus argued, that it makes us different from the U.S. and that we're going to have to protect it. "What is the health-care plan? It's symbolic of the larger statement: We take care of each other."

I had finished all my interviews but had one big question that had arisen from them to put to Ian Angus. He had recently written *A Border Within*, an enquiry into "national identity, cultural plurality, and wilderness," which, in spite of its theoretical up-to-dateness, he had written as a "left nationalist." How is it possible, I wanted to know, that my interviewees, who live in so many radically new circumstances that could not have been foreseen when the various elements of Canada's social safety net were being woven together, who seem to have assumed the burdens of the "new" consciousness of contingency and multiplicity, and the normalization of the transnational globe, who have no illusions about the long-term survivability of a specific Canadian identity, who have been handed the apparatus of theory that warns them social cohesion is a romance of the Old Narrative – how is it possible that, when I asked them not just whether they were Canadians but *how* they knew they were, they almost to a person answered some version of "I know I am a Canadian because I believe in social compassion."

I was thinking of what Paul Tartaglio said with such vehemence, remembering his negotiations with the Canadian management of Starbucks in B.C.: "They got their comeuppance for having sold out to the Americans. It was the vice-president who was the hard-liner, the one who decided the profits weren't big enough and to roll back the wages, the all-Canadian boy who came along and worked for this multinational American corporation and essentially sold us out. He betrayed something which I think is Canadian. I know that now it is more vague than ever, but I do think that what's different about us is that we have to work together to get things done. For him it was only about the almighty dollar. He'd forgotten what it means to be Canadian."

What does it mean, I asked Angus, when young Canadians say that social programs lie at the core of their identity, knowing all too well they are in jeopardy, if not being dismantled as we speak? How is it possible that they could still believe that a health-care plan could be a homeplace? It's possible, he replied, if you think about it as a statement that stands for more than it says. It's especially interesting that they say it – "health-care plan" – when everybody knows it's in real trouble. So, how do we think about our relationship to ideas that are not quite true?

"People say, 'We take care of each other.' And it's not exactly true, it's a *fictive* history. It's not that people are ignorant of the fact that there are homeless people living on the street. You've got to think about not whether what they say is true or not, but about what is it they *do* by saying it. And what they do is they put themselves in a position that says, 'We are not Americans, we have something in common here,' which then allows them to say, when they see the homeless person in the street, 'Something's wrong here.' Why? 'Because we take care of each other.'"

We take care of each other. Money isn't our bottom line. We are a compassionate society. You can take away the Crown corporations and lift all the regulations at the border and lie down like doormats in front of the CEOs, but we have more faith than you in why it is good to live a Canadian life.

It may not be true that it is so good, it may not even be so Canadian, but they say it is. They *assert* it. It's what they want.

Through the myriad conversations about everything under the sun ran a coherent narrative after all – a narrative of pure desire. Somehow, at the turn of the millennium, we have in our midst yet another generation of Canadians who have found a way to dig deep enough that they have struck their own roots. The next Canadians are right here, they are at home, and they call it Canada.

NOTES

Chapter I: New World Order

1. Greg Ip, "The Borderless World," *Globe and Mail*, July 6, 1996.
2. Murray Dobbin, *The Myth of the Good Corporate Citizen: Democracy Under the Rule of Big Business* (Toronto: Stoddart, 1998).
3. Noam Chomsky, "The Poor Always Pay Debts of the Rich," *Manchester Guardian Weekly*, May 24, 1998.
4. "Waking Up in a World Ruled by Corporations," *Canadian Perspectives* (Autumn 1998) [no author].
5. Erin Anderssen, "Canada's Squalid Secret: Life on Native Reserves," *Globe and Mail*, October 12, 1998.
6. David Korten, "Sustainability and the Global Economy: Beyond Bretton Woods," hyperlink http://www-trees.slu.se/newsl/29korten.htm.
7. Bob White, "Will Governments Intervene in the Global Crisis?" *Globe and Mail*, October 20, 1998.
8. Martin Woollacott, "Behind the Myth of the Self-Made Man," *Manchester Guardian Weekly*, May 25, 1997.
9. Jennifer Hunter, "The Deadly Streets," *Maclean's* (December 8, 1997).
10. Jane Gadd, "Canadians Got Poorer in 90s," *Globe and Mail*, May 13, 1998.
11. Mark Lisac, "Klein Tories Just Fishing for Work," *Edmonton Journal*, September 20, 1997.
12. Heather Menzies, *Whose Brave New World? The Information Highway and the New Economy* (Toronto: Between the Lines, 1996), p. 53.
13. Judy Rebick, Kiké Roach, *Politically Speaking* (Vancouver: Douglas and McIntyre, 1996), p. 55.
14. Mitch Cooper, "At Home Work Needs Work," *Edmonton Journal*, March 11, 1999.
15. "Forum File," *The Canadian Forum* (June 1999).
16. Dorothy Livopenko, "Part-timers Being Shut Out, Study Says," *Globe and Mail*, November 17, 1997.
17. Murray Campbell, "Part-time Work Stats Questioned," *Globe and Mail*, March 18, 1998.
18. Linda Goyette, *Second Opinion: The Best of Linda Goyette* (Edmonton: Rowan Books, 1998), p. 73.
19. Ijeoma Ross, "The New Temp Wears a Lab Coat," *Globe and Mail*, December 23, 1997.

20. Steven Theobald, "Making Temp Work a Career," *Toronto Star*, October 24, 1998.

21. Richard Bingham, "Rebels with a Business Plan," *Report on Business* (November 1998).

22. Mark Stevenson, "Free for the Hire," *Edmonton Journal*, n.d.

23. Barbara Moses, "The Challenge: How to Satisfy the New Worker's Agenda," *Globe and Mail*, November 10, 1998.

24. Christopher Caggiano, "Brand New," *INC Online* (April 1997).

25. Douglas Coupland, *Generation X: Tales for an Accelerated Culture* (New York: St. Martin's Press, 1991), p. 113.

26. Jeremy Rifkin, *The End of Work: The Decline of the Global Labor Force and the Dawn of the Post-Market Era* (New York: G.P. Putnam's Sons, 1996), p. 249.

27. Naomi Klein, "The Skinny on Starbucks," *This Magazine* (January/February 1998).

28. Betsy Trumpener, "Coffeetime," *This Magazine* (January/February 1998).

29. *Ibid.*

30. Klein, *op. cit.*

31. Julie Perreault, "Jeunes et Syndicats," *Vie Ouvrière* (November/December 1996).

32. Reginald W. Bibby, "Canadians and Unions: A National Survey of Current Attitudes," hyperlink http://www.interlog.com/~wrf/report.htm.

33. John Roberts, "Just Desserts," *The Coast*, August 10-September 7, 1995.

34. Clive Thompson, *Report on Business* (April 1998).

35. Kevin Wilson, "Killer Overtime," *NOW*, June 11-17, 1998.

36. Ezra Levant, *Youthquake* (Vancouver: The Fraser Institute, 1996), p. 14.

37. Nadene Rehnby, Stephen McBride, *Help Wanted: Economic Security for Youth* (Ottawa: Canadian Centre for Policy Alternatives, May 1997).

38. Stephen Clarkson, "Poor Prospects: 'The Rest of Canada' Under Continental Integration," in Kenneth McRoberts, ed., *Beyond Quebec: Taking Stock of Canada* (Montreal, Kingston: McGill-Queen's, 1995).

39. Stephen McBride, John Shields, *Dismantling a Nation: Canada and the New World Order* (Halifax: Fernwood, 1993), p. 166.

40. Stephen Clarkson, "Are Canadians Impotent Before the World Trade Organization?" *Globe and Mail*, July 19, 1999.

41. Kevin Carmichael, "Free Trade Is a Given, But at What Cost?" *Edmonton Journal*, December 31, 1998.

42. Mark MacKinnon, "Foreign Ownership Is on the Rise," *Globe and Mail*, February 1, 1999.

43. Barrie McKenna, "More Firms Flock to Mexico," *Globe and Mail*, July 8, 1998.

44. Mark MacKinnon, "U.S. Companies Keep Buying into Canada," *Globe and Mail*, February 1, 1999.

45. David Roberts, "UGG, Archer-Daniels Unite," *Globe and Mail*, July 18, 1997.

46. Lisa Birnie, "There Goes MacBlo," *Globe and Mail,* July 2, 1999.

47. Mark MacKinnon, Bruce Little, "Is Canada's Dollar Headed to the Altar?" *Globe and Mail,* June 24, 1999.

48. George Grant, *Lament for a Nation: The Defeat of Canadian Nationalism* (Toronto: McClelland & Stewart, 1965), p. 47.

49. Heather Scoffield, "Canadians Feel NAFTA Does More Harm Than Good," *Globe and Mail,* July 2, 1999.

50. Ken Georgetti, "It Would Be Folly to Adopt U.S. Dollar," *Globe and Mail,* July 2, 1999.

51. Grant, *op. cit.,* p. 41.

52. Richard Gwyn, "Leaders Neglect 'Work-Poor'," *Edmonton Journal,* July 9, 1996.

53. François Normand, "Vers un monde de travail précaire," *Le Devoir,* June 27-28, 1998.

54. Victor Keegan, "Steady Jobs in a Freefall," *Edmonton Journal,* August 18, 1996.

55. John Schofield, "On the Cutting Edge of Change," *Maclean's* (January 25, 1999).

56. Murray Campbell, "Changes to Work Do Not Compute," *Globe and Mail,* January 3, 1997.

57. Miro Cernetig, "U.S. Futurist Gives Clark Ideas for Creating B.C. Jobs," *Globe and Mail,* November 30, 1996.

58. Andrew Jackson, *The Future of Jobs* (Ottawa: Canadian Centre for Policy Alternatives, January, 1997).

59. Sally Lerner, "The Future of Work in North America: Good Jobs, Bad Jobs, Beyond Jobs," in Scott Bennett, ed., *Technology and Work in Canada* (Lewiston: The Edwin Mellen Press, 1990).

Chapter II: Culture

1. James Keast, "Twitch City: Curtis's Kingdom," *Exclaim* (February 1998).

2. Antonia Zerbesias, "Media's Generation Gap," *Toronto Star,* March 16, 1997.

3. Ray Conlogue, "Writer Decries Media Concentration," *Globe and Mail,* December 2, 1997.

4. Dave Caulfield, "Postoperative," *The Coast,* October 22-29, 1998.

5. *See* magazine promotion copy, 1996.

6. André Picard, "Street Culture Finds a Voice in Vice," *Globe and Mail,* March 19, 1998.

7. Thomas Wade and Hadley Howes, "Lines of Desire," *Fuse* (Special Issue 1998).

8. Michel Filion, "Radio," in Michael Dorland, ed., *The Cultural Industries in Canada: Problems, Policies and Prospects* (Toronto: Lorimer, 1996), p. 138.

9. Al Johnson et al., "Four Former CBC Presidents to Save the CBC," *Globe and Mail,* January 24, 1996.

15. "Animation in the Computer Age," *Take One* (Summer 1997) [author unknown].

16. *Ibid.*

17. Pierre Demers, "Extrêmes techniques," *Recto Verso* (March/April 1999).

18. *Ibid.*

19. Mark Slouka, *War of the Worlds: Cyberspace and the High-Tech Assault on Reality* (New York: Basic Books, 1995), p. 27.

20. Sherry Turkle, *Life on the Screen: Identity in the Age of the Internet* (New York: Touchstone, 1995), p. 10.

21. Sven Birkerts, *The Gutenberg Elegies: The Fate of Reading in an Electronic Age* (New York: Fawcett Columbine, 1994), p. 164.

22. Sherry Turkle, *op. cit.*, p. 257.

23. *Ibid.*, p. 235.

24. Don Tapscott, "Next Generation Shakes Windows and Walls," *Globe and Mail*, October 30, 1997.

25. "More About Utopia Cafe," hyperlink http://www.saskweb.com/~uc/mail.htm.

26. Ijeoma Ross, "Cyberpunks Know How to Operate," *Edmonton Journal*, February 6, 1998.

27. Pamela Klaffke, "Silicon Valley North?" *Avenue* (October 1998).

28. Michael Hoechsmann, "Revolution Goes Global: Zapatistas on the Net," *Border/Lines* (April 1996).

29. Sharon Airhart, "Will No Birds Sing in the Wired City?" *Globe and Mail*, January 3, 1998.

30. Russell Smith, *Noise* (Erin, Ontario: Porcupine's Quill, 1998), pp. 135-6.

31. *Ibid.*, p. 227.

32. Jeffrey Simpson, "Un-American Activities," *Globe and Mail*, December 23, 1998.

33. Chris Dafoe, "Is the Flag Only Flapping in the Wind?" *Globe and Mail*, October 31, 1998.

34. Dave Bidini, *On a Cold Road: Tales of Adventure in Canadian Rock* (Toronto: McClelland & Stewart, 1998), p. 31.

35. Sandra Sperounes, "Hip Notes," *Edmonton Journal*, March 1, 1999.

36. In "The End of the Nation State," prod. Max Allen, *Ideas*, CBC Radio, 1996.

37. Jane Taber, "Talking Tough about Trade," *Ottawa Citizen*, January 9, 1999.

38. Southam News, "Culture Worth Fighting U.S. On – Copps," *Edmonton Journal*, March 27, 1999.

39. John Geddes, "A Run for the Money," *Maclean's* (June 7, 1999).

40. William Thorsell, "Making Room for Non-Conformity," *Globe and Mail*, October 17, 1998.

41. Marta Gold, "Prof Warns Against Government Arts Cuts," *Edmonton Journal*, October 2, 1997.

42. Michel Theriault, "Lani Maestro," *Perspectives* (Art Gallery of Ontario, 1993).

43. Jowi Taylor, "The Tribal Beat," *Shift* (July 1997).

44. Robin Schlaht, "What Good Are Films?" *Splice* (n.d.).

45. John Meisel, "Canada and the Global Media Challenge," prepared for the Canadian Studies Centre, Duke University, 1995.

46. Robert Fones, "Toy Box Junkies," *C Magazine* (September/October 1998).

47. *Ibid.*

48. Michelle Jacques, "Sally McKay: Present Tense," *Perspectives* (Toronto: Art Gallery of Ontario, 1998).

49. Noel S. Baker, *Hard Core Road Show: A Screenwriter's Diary* (Toronto: Anansi, 1997), pp. 242-3.

50. Dave Bidini, *op. cit.*, p. 239.

51. Margaret Macpherson, "Maritime Watch on Lynn Coady," *Edmonton Journal*, September 30, 1998.

52. Myrna Kostash, "Is There a Future for Prairie Film?" *Prairie Dog* (March 1997).

53. Liz Nicholls, "Java Life," *Edmonton Journal*, April 10, 1998.

54. Pierre Salducci, "Les Journées de la culture exploitent les artistes et les créateurs québécois," *Le Devoir*, September 26-27, 1998.

55. John Bemrose, "Play Therapy," *Maclean's* (March 15, 1999).

56. John Geddes, "Canada's Culture Cash," *Maclean's* (July 13, 1998).

57. Anita Lahey, "Going Underground," *Quill and Quire* (July 1997).

58. Marie-Andrée Chouinard, "Comment échapper à la tyrannie des best-sellers," *Le Devoir*, November 21-22, 1998.

59. Pierre Filion, "Rapport d'activité secteurs des lettres et de l'édition," address to the Board of Governors, Canadian Conference of the Arts, June 1998.

60. Josh Glover, "Mee, Myself and I," *Mic Check* (June 1998).

61. Betsy Powell, "A Little Sheet Music," *Toronto Star*, October 25, 1998.

62. Nathalie Labonté, "Des barricades aux entreprises," *Recto Verso* (January/ February 1999).

63. David McIntosh, "Cyborgs in Denial," *Fuse* (Spring 1994).

64. Barrie McKenna, "Will U.S. Threats Scare Off Ottawa's Ban on Magazines?" *Globe and Mail*, January 25, 1999.

65. Nicola Simpson, "Canadian Actor Has Paid His Dues," *Vue*, March 4-10, 1999.

66. Richard Martineau, "Le mythe de l'ogre américain," *L'Actualité*, June 15, 1998.

67. Ted Magder, "Going Global," *Canadian Forum* (August 1999).

68. Myrna Kostash, "Free Trade," *Hungry Mind Review* (n.d., 1989).

69. Doug Saunders, "TV Stations Fear U.S. Trade Threat," *Globe and Mail*, August 19, 1999.

70. Jean Daniel, *Affirmation nationale et village planétaire* (Montreal: Editions Fides, 1998), p. 8.

Chapter III: Beyond Identity Politics

1. Louis Cornellier, "Le féminisme à la varlope," *Le Devoir*, November 28-29, 1998.
2. Isabelle Rivest, "Les nouveaux enjeux," *Le Devoir*, May 23-24, 1998.
3. Myrna Kostash, "Dissing Feminist Heterosexuality," *The Canadian Forum* (September 1996).
4. Boa d'Ruelle, "There Isn't a Truce Coming," in Zoë Newman and Kelly O'Brien, eds., *Revolution Girl Style* (Toronto: Fireweed 59/60, Fall/Winter, 1997), p. 91.
5. Jennifer Perrine, "Education," in *Revolution Girl Style, ibid.*
6. Sonja Mills, "Screaming for More," in Lynn Crosbie, ed., *Click: Becoming Feminists* (Toronto: Macfarlane Walter & Ross, 1997), p. 123.
7. Stephanie Nolen, "Girls Just Wanna Have Fun," *Globe and Mail*, February 13, 1999.
8. Shawna Dempsey, "On Becoming Fatale," *Prairie Fire* (Autumn 1994).
9. Sonja Mills, *op. cit.*, p. 124.
10. *Ibid.*
11. Jennifer Henderson, "My Friends Call Me a Mother Hag," *Border/Lines* (December 1996).
12. Naomi Klein, "Becoming Unclicked," in *Click: Becoming Feminists, op. cit.*, p. 114.
13. Jaime Kirzner-Roberts, "I'm Not a Feminist, But...", in *Revolution Girl Style, op. cit.*, p. 77.
14. *Ibid.*, p. 78.
15. Rachel Giese, "Sleeping with the Enemy," *This Magazine* (November 1994).
16. Gary Kinsman, *The Regulation of Desire: Sexuality in Canada* (Montreal: Black Rose Books, 1987).
17. Bert Archer, "Peeking Under Those Big Garden Stones," *Toronto Star*, May 2, 1998.
18. Perry Skye, "Glam I Am," *UTNE Reader* (September/October 1998).
19. Darrin Hagen, *The Edmonton Queen: Not a Riverboat Story* (Edmonton: Slipstream Books, 1997).
20. Brent Ledger, "Beyond Clones and Muscle Queens," *Xtra!*, August 27, 1998.
21. Ian Iqbal Rashid, "Naming Names," *Rungh* (Vol 3, No 3, 1995).
22. T.J. Bryan, "Of Chocolate Queens and Rice Queens," *Fuse* (Special Issue 1998).
23. Reginald W. Bibby, *The Bibby Report: Social Trends Canadian Style* (Toronto: Stoddart, 1995).
24. "Family: The Facts and Theories of Relativity," *Shift* (August 1998) [no author].
25. Nikki Gershbain, "Same-Sex Marriage," *Border/Lines* (Spring 1997).

26. Timothy Appleby, "In the Tolerant 1990s Attacks on Gays Persist," *Globe and Mail*, October 17, 1998.

27. Brian Bergman, "Garden of Paradise," *Maclean's* (October 6, 1997).

28. Reginald W. Bibby, *op. cit.*, p. 57.

29. See Ian Angus, *A Border Within: National Identity, Cultural Plurality and Wilderness* (Montreal and Kingston: McGill-Queen's, 1997), pp. 153-54.

30. Lavinia Lamenza, "On Language," *Eyetalian* (Spring 1998).

31. Heather Olivetz, "Living with the Language Tyrants," *Zdorov* (Spring 1998).

32. André Alexis, "Borrowed Blackness," *This Magazine* (May 1995).

33. Ayanna Black, "Introduction," in Ayanna Black, ed., *Fiery Spirits: Canadian Writers of African Descent* (Toronto: HarperPerennial, 1994), p. xvi.

34. George Elliott Clarke, "Introduction," in George Elliott Clarke, ed., *Eyeing the North Star: Directions in African-Canadian Literature* (Toronto: McClelland & Stewart, 1997), p. xii.

35. Ted Whittaker, "In-Between Language," *Books in Canada* (September 1998).

36. Andrew Moodie, *Riot* (Toronto: Scirocco Drama, 1997), p. 28.

37. George Elliott Clarke, *op. cit.*, p. xix.

38. Gamal Abdel-Shehid, "Raptor Mentality: Blacks, Basketball and National Identity," *Border/Lines* (n.d.).

39. Kristine Maitland, "Oh! Canada," *At the Crossroads* (January 1997).

40. Charles Taylor, "Globalization and the Future of Canada," *Queen's Quarterly* (Fall 1998).

41. Roger Burford Mason, "The Impassioned Exile of Barry Callaghan," *Books In Canada* (n.d.).

42. Andrew McIntosh, "Multiculturalism Critics Botched Research, Professor Says," *Edmonton Journal*, November 3, 1997.

43. Judy Rebick and Kiké Roach, *Politically Speaking* (Vancouver: Douglas and McIntyre, 1996), p. 74.

44. Jeffrey Simpson, "Of Cultural Politics," *Globe and Mail*, April 2, 1998.

45. Mary-Jo Nadeau and Renuka Sooknanan, "Representing Dissent: Talking About Politically Speaking," *Fuse* (Vol. 21, No. 2).

46. Sean Lokaisingh-Meighoo and Arif Noorani, "Some Keywords and Arguments in Cultural Politics," *Fuse* (Vol. 22, No. 2).

47. Heesok Chang, "Differently Together: An Exposition on Community," *Self Not Whole* catalogue (n.d.).

48. This point was made by writer Heather Menzies at the 1997 Writers' Union of Canada AGM, as reported in the Union's newsletter (Vol. 25, No. 3).

49. Irshad Manji, *Risking Utopia: On the Edge of a New Democracy* (Vancouver: Douglas and McIntyre, 1997), pp. 35-6.

50. This point was made by Peter Kulchyski, Department of Native Studies, Trent University, at a conference, "Canada without Quebec," Trent University, March 1996.

51. Danylo Hawaleshka, "Face of a Nation," *Maclean's* (November 17, 1997).
52. Marie Arana-Ward, "Divided We Stand," *Manchester Guardian Weekly*, October 4, 1998.
53. Cameron Bailey, "Virtual Skin: Articulating Race in Cyberspace," *Border/Lines* (n.d.).
54. In Derrick de Kerckhove, *The Skin of Culture* (Toronto: Sommerville House, 1995).
55. Samir Gandesha, "Safe European Home: Notes On and From Cesar Chavez Street," *Border/Lines* (July 1996).
56. Benedict Anderson, *Imagined Communities* (New York: Verso, 1991), p. 6.
57. Rinaldo Walcott, "Lament for a Nation," *Fuse* (Summer 1996).
58. Geoffrey Chan et al., "Fortress in the Wilderness," *Border/Lines* (No. 45, 1998).
59. Dionne Brand, "Out There," in Carol Morrell, ed., *Grammar of Dissent* (Fredericton: Goose Lane, 1994).
60. Dionne Brand, "Driving North, Driving Home," *Canadian Forum* (October 1998).
61. George Elliott Clarke, "Honouring African-Canadian Geography," *Border/Lines* (No. 44, 1997).
62. T.J. Bryan, "Of Chocolate Queens and Rice Queens," *Fuse* (Special Issue 1998).
63. This point was made on a panel at the "Wordfest" conference, Banff, October 19, 1996.
64. May Yee, "Finding the Way Home Through Issues of Gender, Race, and Class," in Himani Bannerji, ed., *Returning the Gaze: Essays on Racism, Feminism and Politics* (Toronto: Sister Vision Press, 1993), p. 14.
65. Mel Watkins, "Out of Commission," *This Magazine* (July/August, 1997).
66. *Ibid.*
67. Georges Sioui, *For an Amerindian Autohistory*, trans. Sheila Fishman (Montreal-Kingston: McGill-Queen's, 1992), p. xxiii.

Chapter IV: Acts of Resistance

1. Alfredo de Romaña, "Coming Unhinged: Modern Civilization in Crisis," *Confluences* (April/May, 1999).
2. Rick Salutin, "When Politics Doesn't Do Much for You, There Is Always Crime," *Globe and Mail*, August 8, 1997.
3. Charles Gordon, "When Bigger Is Not Necessarily Better," *Maclean's* (October 20, 1997).
4. Mark Kingwell, "Who's Left?" *Saturday Night* (April 1995).
5. Pierre Bourdieu, *Acts of Resistance: Against the Tyranny of the Market* (New York: The New Press, 1998), p. 2.

6. Mark Kingwell et al., "Is There a New (or Revised) Left?" *Inroads* (No. 6, 1997).
7. Richard Foot, "'Techno-Nerds' Are Bright, Wealthy, and Have No Sense of Duty," *Edmonton Journal*, April 27, 1998.
8. W.H. New, *Borderlands: How We Talk About Canada* (Vancouver: University of British Columbia Press, 1998), p. 47.
9. Bruce W. Powe, *A Canada of Light* (Toronto: Sommerville Press, 1997), p. 8.
10. Hal Niedzviecki, hyperlink http://www.interlog.com/~halpen
11. Naomi Klein, "Lou Reed and the Clash of Reality and Irony," *Toronto Star*, May 25, 1996.
12. John Lorinc, "Pokey's Progress," *Saturday Night* (November 1998).
13. Canadian Press, "Reform Wooing the First-Time Voters of the Future," *Edmonton Journal*, February 22, 1998.
14. Evan Soloman, "Where Is the Idealism in Our Politics?" *Globe and Mail*, June 3, 1997.
15. Sheila Gostick, "The Day Bloor Fell to the People," *NOW*, May 21-27, 1998.
16. Elaine Brown, *A Taste of Power: A Black Woman's Story* (New York: Doubleday, 1994), p. 281.
17. In Irene Angelico, dir., *The Cola Conquest*, 1998.
18. Guy Dixon, "Coca-Cola Reflects the World's Turns," *Globe and Mail*, November 6, 1998.
19. *Ibid.*
20. Andrew MacDonald, "Corporate Universities, Corporate Student Unions," *The Student Activist* (May 1998).
21. Chris Miller, "Speak Out Quietly," *Gateway*, September 25, 1997.
22. Naomi Klein, "Students Win the Pepsi Challenge," *Toronto Star*, February 3, 1997.
23. Eli Spiegelman, "Media Group Celebrates Split," *Adbusters* (Summer 1998).
24. In Patricia Zeedick, "Letter to the Editor," *Globe and Mail*, February 5, 1999.
25. In Eli Spiegelman, *op. cit.*
26. Naomi Klein, "Subvertising," *Village Voice*, May 6, 1997.
27. "Editorial," hyperlink http://www.adbusters.org/main2.html.
28. Leah Rumack, "Altered States," *NOW*, August 27-September 2, 1998.
29. Jim Munroe, "Playing Revolution," *This Magazine* (November/December 1998).
30. Jane Kelsey, "APEC Created Solely to Serve Business Interests," *CCPA Monitor* (July/August 1997).
31. Jennifer Hunter, "Autumn Days of Dissent," *Maclean's* (October 12, 1998).
32. *Ibid.*
33. Jane Armstrong, "Police Made Pre-emptive Arrest at Summit," *Globe and Mail*, September 24, 1998.
34. Jaggi Singh, "Well, It Worked in Other APEC Countries," *This Magazine* (January/February 1998).

35. Garth Mullins, "Anti APEC Resistance Sweeps Vancouver," *The Student Activist* (January/February 1998).

36. Alejandra Medellin, "Letter to the Editor," *Georgia Straight*, December 4-11, 1997.

37. Jane Armstrong and John Saunders, "The Day the PM Was Host to a Despot," *Globe and Mail*, October 5, 1998.

38. Jeff Lee, "No More Stunts, Protesters Warned," *Edmonton Journal*, October 22, 1998.

39. Simon Kiss, "We Stand on Guard for Whom?" *See*, October 8-14, 1998.

40. Kevin Young, "No Hope for Alberta," *Gateway*, October 2, 1997.

41. Editorial, "Alberta Denuded of Special Places," *Edmonton Journal*, June 28, 1998.

42. Andrea Curtis, "Excuse Me While I Screef the Duff," *Toronto Life* (May 1998).

43. In Judith Lachappelle, "Des trouble-fête sur la ligne," *Le Devoir*, June 18, 1998.

44. Clint Burnham, "Whistle(r) While You Work," *Border/Lines* (No. 44, 1997).

45. Lon Cayeway, "Sunrise Faces, Sunset Mists," *Canadas:Semiotext(e)* (No. 17, 1994).

46. Michael Adams, "The Millennium Is Already Here," *Globe and Mail*, June 6, 1997.

47. Jean Robitaille, Anne-Marie Brunelle, Nathalie Labonté, "Les entreprises qui veulent changer le monde," *Recto Verso* (November/December 1998).

48. "Canada's Nonprofit Sector: What Is It Worth To Us As a Nation?" hyperlink http://cprn.com/f_work/pressrel.htm.

Chapter V: Homeplace

1. Eric Beauchesne, "Nation's Richer But Its People Are Worse Off," *Edmonton Journal*, November 3, 1997.

2. Larry Brown, "After the Cuts," *CCPA Monitor* (January 1997).

3. Paul Knox, "Broadbent Fears Loss of Social Safety Net," *Globe and Mail*, June 15, 1996.

4. Angus Reid, *Shakedown: How the New Economy Is Changing Our Lives* (Toronto: Seal Books, 1997), p. 316.

5. Kevin Carmichael, "Private Spending on Health Care Passes 30 Per Cent Mark," *Edmonton Journal*, November 20, 1998.

6. Mark Kennedy, "Private Sector Health Spending Growing Steadily, Report Says," *Edmonton Journal*, November 19, 1998.

7. "Hospitals, Schools Begin Selling Ad Space," *Vue*, February 25-March 3, 1999 [no author].

8. Ralph Nader, "Why Canadians Must Defend Their Health-Care System," *Alberta Views* (Summer 1998).

9. Linda Goyette, "Amazing What Hindsight Can Tell Us," *Edmonton Journal*, December 4, 1998.

10. Jennifer Hunter, "The Giant Falls South," *Maclean's* (July 5, 1999).

11. Eric Reguly, "The Devouring of Corporate Canada," *Globe and Mail*, September 4, 1999.

12. George Grant, *Lament for a Nation: The Defeat of Canadian Nationalism* (Toronto: McClelland & Stewart, 1970), p. 41.

13. Silver Donald Cameron, "Privatizing the Ocean," *Globe and Mail*, December 21, 1998.

14. John Heinzl, "Are Ads OK on School Computers?" *Globe and Mail*, January 18, 1999.

15. Michael Grange, "Cadbury Causes Chocolate Controversy," *Globe and Mail*, March 23, 1998.

16. Charles Gordon, "Have We Forgotten the Trojan Horse?" *Maclean's* (March 1, 1999).

17. Richard Gwyn, "Public Institutions Bind Us Together," *Toronto Star*, December 8, 1996.

18. Matthew Fraser, "When Content Is King," *Globe and Mail*, November 15, 1997.

19. Robert McChesney, "Market Media Muscle," *Canadian Forum* (March 1998).

20. Francine Bordeleau, "Le souffle des poètes," *Lettres Québécoises* (Summer 1998).

21. Douglas Rushkoff, "Virtually Depressed? Welcome to Real Life," *Globe and Mail*, September 26, 1998.

22. Jenefer Curtis, "Social Distress, Teenage Unrest," *Globe and Mail*, April 24, 1999.

23. "Luddites and Friends," prod. Paul Kennedy, *Ideas*, CBC Radio, February 24, 1997.

24. Marshall McLuhan, "The Spoken Word: Flower of Evil?" *Understanding Media: The Extensions of Man* (Cambridge: MIT Press, 1996), p. 80.

25. Charlotte Denny, in *Manchester Guardian Weekly*, July 15-21, 1999.

26. Doug Saunders, "The People Who Slip Through the Net," *Globe and Mail*, August 22, 1997.

27. James W. Carey, *Communication as Culture: Essays on Media and Society* (Boston: Unwin Hyman, 1989), p. 135.

28. Jesse Hirsh, "Don't Call Us, We'll Call You," *This Magazine* (May/June 1998).

29. Clive Thompson, "In Space We Can Hear You Scream," *This Magazine* (August 1995).

30. Douglas Todd, "Children Taught To Be Ashamed of Canada," *Edmonton Journal*, June 28, 1998.

31. J.L. Granatstein, "Canada Needs Its Historical Memory Back," *National Post*, April 19, 1999.

32. Peter Lipman, "Letter to the Editor," *Books in Canada* (September 1998).

33. J. L. Granatstein, *op. cit.*

34. Anne Metikosh, "Links in a Chain or Learning Outcomes?" *Globe and Mail*, April 3, 1997.

35. François Chesnais, "Will the World Catch Asian Flu?" *Le Monde diplomatique* (September 1998).

36. Barrie McKenna, "IMF Eyes Tourniquet for Capital," *Globe and Mail*, October 15, 1998.

37. In Richard Langlois, "Du Viagra pour l'État," *Voir*, June 11-17, 1998.

38. John Barber, "Canada Again Tops Survey As Best Place to Live," *Globe and Mail*, July 12, 1999.

39. Bob White, "Will Governments Intervene in the Global Crisis?" *Globe and Mail*, October 20, 1998.

40. Larry Elliott, "Globalisation in Need of Repairs," *Manchester Guardian Weekly*, February 8, 1998.

41. Scott Feschuk, "Cutting Debt, Taxes Top Canadians' List," *Globe and Mail*, November 1, 1997.

42. Kevin Taft, *Shredding the Public Interest: Ralph Klein and 25 Years of One-Party Government* (Edmonton: University of Alberta Press and Parkland Institute, 1997), p. 45.

43. Bruce Little, "Paul Martin: The Turnaround Man," *Globe and Mail*, February 13, 1999.

44. Edward Greenspon, "Canadians Are Losing Interest in Tax Cuts," *Globe and Mail*, March 16, 1999.

45. In Bruce Wallace, "In Good Health," *Maclean's* (March 1, 1999).

46. Rachel Furey, "School TV, Computer Ads Not Paying Off for Boards," *Edmonton Journal*, August 16, 1999.

47. Hugh Winsor, "Canadians Prefer Social Programs over Tax Cut," *Globe and Mail*, August 21, 1999.

48. *A Question of Choices* (Ottawa: Action Canada Network, 1997).

49. Linda McQuaig, *Shooting the Hippo: Death by Deficit* (Toronto: Penguin, 1995), p. xii.

50. Mel Watkins, "Membership Has Its Privileges," *This Magazine* (May/June 1998).

51. "Defining a Canadian Easier, Poll," *Edmonton Journal*, December 22, 1997.

52. Julian Beltrame, "Canadians' National Pride Among Tops in the World," *Edmonton Journal*, August 28, 1998.

53. Joan Bryden, "Don't Expect U.S.-Style Tax Cuts, Chretien Says," *Edmonton Journal*, July 1, 1999.

54. John R. MacArthur, "When Chrétien Said His Piece in New York," *Globe and Mail*, March 20, 1998.

55. Michael Adams, "Measuring Canada's Economy," *Globe and Mail*, June 6, 1997.

56. Satya Das, "World Economy Being Shaped by Radical Right," *Edmonton Journal*, January 29, 1995.

57. Mark Kingwell, "Why America Is the Exception and Not the Rule," *Globe and Mail*, n.d.

58. In Patrick Brethour, "Canadian Lifestyle Not Enough to Keep Tech Types," *Globe and Mail*, June 10, 1998.

59. In Judith Maxwell, "Don't Be Seduced by the U.S. Boom, Averages Lie," *Globe and Mail*, August 30, 1999.

60. Pete McMartin, "We're Canadian, and That's Non-Negotiable," *Vancouver Sun*, December 9, 1997.

61. Barrie Tanner, "Hockey Players Forget Their Commitment," *Gateway*, February 26, 1998.

62. Jamie Friesen, "Prescription for Mayhem," *Gateway*, January 8, 1998.

63. "Canadians v. Americans: One of Us Is Livelier, Warmer, and More Stable. Guess Which?" *National Post*, April 12, 1999 [no author].

64. Iain Ilich, "Funny Edmonton Folk Raid National Radio," *Gateway*, March 19, 1998.

65. In Graham Fraser, "Canadians Described as Short on Long-term Memory," *Globe and Mail*, February 1, 1999.

66. Angus Reid poll, *Globe and Mail*, December 8, 1997.

67. Lysiane Gagnon, "Quebecers and Canada," *Globe and Mail*, April 18, 1998.

68. See, for example, Jeremy Webber, *Reimagining Canada: Language, Culture, Community and the Canadian Constitution* (Montreal, Kingston: McGill-Queen's University Press, 1994).

69. Lysiane Gagnon, "Bad News for Sovereigntists," *Globe and Mail*, April 10, 1999.

70. Christophe Wargny, "Quebec's PQ Worn Out by Power," *Le Monde diplomatique* (November 1998).

71. Daniel Francis, *National Dreams: Myth, Memory and Canadian History* (Vancouver: Arsenal Pulp Press, 1997), p. 96.

72. Jacques Godbout and Richard Martineau, *Le Buffet* (Montreal: Boréal, 1998), p. 46.

73. *Ibid.*, p. 61.

74. Monique LaRue, *L'arpenteur et le navigateur* (Montreal: Editions Fides, 1996), pp. 7-9.

75. *Ibid.*, p. 28.

76. Paule des Rivières, "Les allophones parlent de plus en plus français," *Le Devoir*, June 18, 1998.

77. Jeffrey Simpson, "For Most Francophones, Bilingualism Is Now More Myth Than Reality," *Globe and Mail*, December 9, 1997.

78. Martin Siberok, "Trio Creates Hip-Hop Groove in Quebec," *Globe and Mail*, March 3, 1998.

79. Carole Beaulieu, "Rappeurs de bonne famille," *L'Actualité*, May 1, 1998.

80. Jacques Godbout and Richard Martineau, *op. cit.*, p. 26.

81. Antoine Robitaille, "Les Québécois veulent s'ouvrir à l'Amérique," *Le Devoir*, May 10, 1998.

82. Jean Paré, "Rue Sainte-Catherine, Montréal (QC), 1998," *L'Actualité*, November 1, 1998.

83. Antoine Robitaille, *op. cit.*

84. Philip Resnick, "Quebec Secession May Not Mean Much in a Global Age," *Edmonton Journal*, October 8, 1995.

85. Guy Lachapelle, "Les Québécois sont-ils devenus des Nord-Américains?" *Le Devoir*, December 21-22, 1998.

86. Jacques Godbout and Richard Martineau, *op. cit.*, p. 19.

87. *Ibid.*, p. 35.

88. *Ibid.*, p. 31.

89. Gordon Laxer, "Distinct Status for Québec: A Benefit for English-Canada," *Constitutional Forum* (Winter 1992).

90. H.D. Forbes, review of Kenneth McRoberts' *Misconceiving Canada: The Struggle for National Unity*, *Books In Canada* (April 1998).

91. Philip Resnick, *Thinking English Canada, op. cit.*, p. 100.

92. Louis Cornellier, *op. cit.*

93. Jeremy Webber, *Reimagining Canada: Language, Culture, Community and the Canadian Constitution* (Montreal, Kingston: McGill-Queen's University Press, 1994), p. 33.

94. Tony Judt, *New York Review of Books*, October 31, 1996.

95. Robert Heilbroner, *Twenty-first Century Capitalism* (Toronto: Anansi, 1992), p. 42.

96. Bob Davis, *Whatever Happened to High School History? Burying the Political Memory of Youth* (Toronto: Lorimer, 1995), p. 210.

97. Nancy Fraser, "Rethinking the Public Sphere," in *The Phantom Public Sphere*, Bruce Robbins, ed., (Minneapolis: University of Minnesota Press, 1993), p. 112.

98. Claude Denis, *We Are Not You: First Nations and Canadian Modernity* (Peterborough: Broadview, 1997), p. 37.

99. Wade Thomas and Hadley Howes, "Lines of Desire," *Fuse* (Special Issue 1998).

100. Ian Angus, "Cultural Plurality and Political Reflexivity," unpublished paper, 1998.

101. John Ralston Saul, *Reflections of a Siamese Twin: Canada at the End of the Twentieth Century* (Toronto: Viking, 1997), p. 438.

102. Ian Angus, *A Border Within: National Identity, Cultural Plurality and Wilderness* (Montreal, Kingston: McGill-Queen's University Press, 1996), p. 144.

103. Tamas Dobozy, "Motherland, Motherland," *subTerrain* (Winter 1998).

104. Gary Kinsman, *The Regulation of Desire: Sexuality in Canada* (Montreal: Black Rose, 1987), pp. 179-80.

105. "Editorial," *Queering Absinthe* (Vol. 9, Issue 1, 1996).

106. Rachel Giese, "Sleeping with the Enemy," *This Magazine* (November 1994).

107. Robert Enright, "The Art of Shawna Dempsey and Lorri Millan," *Border Crossings* (Winter 1998).

108. In Richard Mackie, "Ottawa Slammed for Medicare Cuts," *Globe and Mail*, January 3, 1998.

109. Jane Coutts, "York University Doctors Protest U.S. Contract," *Globe and Mail*, July 20, 1996.

110. Michel Vastel, "La soviétisation de la médicine," *L'Actualité*, June 15, 1998.

111. Shawn McCarthy, "Martin Discusses Healthcare Reinvestment," *Globe and Mail*, February 2, 1999.

112. Heather Scoffield, "Canada's Social Programs Not on Table, Minister Says," *Globe and Mail*, October 7, 1999.

113. Edward Greenspon, "Canadians Defend Healthcare Spending," *Globe and Mail*, September 28, 1996.

114. In Michelle Weinroth, "Trust, That Precious Commodity," *Canadian Forum* (May 1998).

115. Terry Glavin, "A Ruling for Aboriginal Traditions," *Globe and Mail*, January 2, 1998.

116. Peter C. Newman, "English Canada's Wake-Up Call: Grow Up!" *Maclean's* (December 14, 1998).

117. Pierre Bourdieu, *Acts of Resistance: Against the Tyranny of the Market* (New York: The New Press, 1998).

118. J.K. Galbraith, "A Message for the Socially Concerned," *Globe and Mail*, January 17, 1997.

119. W.H. New, *Borderlands: How We Talk About Canada* (Vancouver: UBC Press, 1998).

120. Geoff Pevere and Greig Dymond, *Mondo Canuck: A Canadian Pop Culture Odyssey* (Scarborough: Prentice Hall, 1996), p. 76.

121. Stephen Brunt, "So Much Changed the Day of the Trade," *Globe and Mail*, April 17, 1999.

122. Marc Raboy et al., "Cultural Development and the Open Economy," *Canadian Journal of Communication* (Summer/Fall 1994).

Chapter VI: The Next Canada

1. Douglas Coupland, *Generation X: Tales for an Acceleration Culture* (New York: St. Martin's Press, 1991), p. 86.

2. Andrew Coyne, "Canadians Need a Sense of Rediscovered Nationhood," *Globe and Mail*, July 2, 1997.

3. Jeremy Webber, *Reimagining Canada: Language, Culture, Community and the Canadian Constitution* (Montreal, Kingston: McGill-Queen's University Press, 1994), p. 223.

4. Serge Halimi, "Liberal Dogma Shipwrecked," *Le Monde diplomatique* (October 1998).

5. David Bercuson and Barry Cooper, "Ottawa Hunts Our National Identity Again," *Globe and Mail*, May 9, 1998.

6. Hamish MacAuley, "Media Guru Makes Shift to Novelist," *FFWD*, May 13-19, 1999.

7. Jean-Marie Guehenno, "The End of the Nation State," prod. Max Allen, *Ideas*, CBC Radio, 1996.

8. Russell Smith, "CanLit Takes It to the Street," *Globe and Mail*, May 23, 1998.

9. In Hal Niedzviecki, ed., *Concrete Forest: The New Fiction of Urban Canada* (Toronto: McClelland & Stewart, 1998), p. xii.

10. W.H. New, *Borderlands: How We Talk About Canada* (Vancouver: UBC Press, 1998).

11. Bruce W. Powe, *A Canada of Light* (Toronto: Sommerville House, 1997), p. 24.

12. *Ibid.*, p. 45.

13. Marilyn Porter, "Are Some Countries More Postmodern Than Others?" *Journal of Canadian Studies* (Spring 1995).